KU-113-666

Creating *the* NATION

Creating *the* NATION

Identity and Aesthetics in

Early Nineteenth-century Russia

and Bohemia

David L. Cooper

NORTHERN ILLINOIS UNIVERSITY PRESS

DeKalb

© 2010 by Northern Illinois University Press

Published by the Northern Illinois University Press, DeKalb, Illinois   60115

Manufactured in the United States using postconsumer-recycled, acid-free paper.

All Rights Reserved

Design by Shaun Allshouse

Library of Congress Cataloging-in-Publication Data

Cooper, David L., 1970–

  Creating the nation: identity and aesthetics in early nineteenth-century Russia and Bohemia / David L. Cooper.

    p. cm.

  Includes bibliographical references and index.

  ISBN 978-0-87580-420-0 (clothbound : alk. paper)

1. National characteristics, Russian, in literature. 2. Russian literature—19th century—History and criticism. 3. Czech literature—19th century—History and criticism. 4. Nationalism and literature—Russia—History—19th century. 5. Nationalism and literature—Czech Republic—History—19th century. 6. National characteristics, Russian—History—19th century. 7. National characteristics, Czech—History—19thsp century. I. Title.

  PG3015.5.N34C66 2010

  891.709'3584707—dc22

                  2010001720

Contents

Acknowledgments   vii

Introduction   *3*

PART I—Shifting Terms: Literature, Language, Culture

1   A New Paradigm Emerges   *15*

2   Is There a Russian Literature? No…   *31*

3   The Roots of the Russian Language and Literature   *51*

4   The Culture of the Czech Language and Czech-Language Culture   *65*

PART II—Translation and the National Literature

5   Translating Folk Discourse
     Folk Song Echoes and Ballads   *89*

6   *Translatio Studii–Translatio Prosodiae* I
     Quantity as Quality in Czech Meter   *108*

7   *Translatio Studii–Translatio Prosodiae* II
     The Greco-Russian Meter   *135*

PART III—Terms in Conflict

8   *Narodnost'* Invented and Deployed   *165*

9   The Fate of Quantity, *Libozvučnost*, and *Klasičnost*
     (with a Sideways Glance at Romanticism)   *187*

10   Dissent over *Narodnost'* and Romanticism   *211*

11   Toward the Reform of Institutions
      Education and Narodnost'   *233*

Conclusion   *251*

Notes   *259*
Works Cited   *307*
Index   *321*

Acknowledgments

Humanities scholarship is, in relation to other university research, remarkably inexpensive. Very little money goes a long way. But without that minimal investment, there is no research possible. I would like to thank in the first place, therefore, those institutions whose small but critical investments I hope to have returned as a worthy piece of scholarship. Early research and writing was supported by a PepsiCo/Harriman Institute Summer Travel Fellowship to Prague in 2001, a dissertation fellowship in 2001–2 from Columbia University and the Department of Slavic Languages and Literatures along with a summer stipend from the department's Rose Raskin fund, and a summer stipend in 2003 from Columbia's Core Curriculum program. Support from the University of Illinois Campus Research Board in the form of travel funding and Humanities Released Time enabled additional research and a critical reformulation of the project. A semester leave from the Department of Slavic Languages and Literatures at the University of Illinois allowed completion of the manuscript. Support to present parts of the project at several conferences was provided by the Russian, East European, and Eurasian Center at the University of Illinois through a grant from the U. S. Department of Education.

Chapter 2 appeared in an earlier form as "*Narodnost'* avant la lettre? Andrei Turgenev, Aleksei Merzliakov, and the National Turn in Russian Criticism" in *Slavic and East European Journal* 52, no. 3 (Fall 2008): 351–69. Material from chapters 6 and 9 appeared in an earlier form as "Competing Languages of Czech Nation-Building: Jan Kollár and the Melodiousness of Czech" in *Slavic Review* 67, no. 2 (Summer 2008): 301–20. Thanks to those journals for permission to republish. Illustrations were provided by and appear courtesy of The National Library of the Czech Republic and

The State Literary Museum, Moscow, Russia. A special thank you is due to Tomáš Foltýn of the former institution and Pavel Fokin of the latter for their assistance in coordinating the fulfillment of my requests. Thanks also to Vera Kudelina and Aleksandr Bobosov of The State Literary Museum for their efforts in finding and digitizing images.

This project was conceived in and inspired by the late Robert Maguire's course on eighteenth- and nineteenth-century Russian criticism and Alfred Thomas' course on the literature of the Czech Revival. For their contributions to and assistance with my dissertation or the book, thanks to Bradley Abrams, Karin Beck, Mark Lauersdorf, Kateřína Pavlitová, Ilya Vinitsky, and an anonymous reader. My sponsor, Boris Gasparov, encouraged and inspired my work on this period; Irina Reyfman went far beyond the normal duties of a second reader in supporting and challenging me; and, in spite of a difficult illness, Robert Maguire agreed to be on my committee and edited my work closely. At the University of Illinois I have found a wonderfully supportive and encouraging group of colleagues and friends. They have read parts of my work in the Russian Kruzhok and East European Reading Group and made valuable suggestions or asked productive questions, as well as motivating me by their examples of fine scholarship. Eugene Avrutin, Michael Finke, Harriet Murav, and John Randolph in particular gave me the benefit of their assistance. Colleagues and friends from the Czech Workshop have critiqued and encouraged the parts of my work that I subjected them to. For asking the hard-to-answer questions that brought out my best work, thanks to Bradley Abrams, Irina Reyfman, and Ilya Vinitsky. A special thanks to Tomáš Hlobil, whose critical reading of my dissertation and productive suggestions for revision and further research constantly guided my work in the project's later stages, and to Jonathan Bolton, whose perceptive reading of the entire manuscript allowed me to clarify and highlight my major points. The manuscript found a nurturing home at the Northern Illinois University Press. Thanks to Amy Farranto, Susan Bean, Shaun Allshouse, Julia Fauci, and the other staff of the press for their work and contributions to the final product.

Last but not least, my best friend, colleague, and wife, Valeria Sobol, supported and assisted me throughout the entire project, read and reread drafts, checked translations from the Russian and the Czech, inspired me with her work ethic and excellent scholarship, gave me time and space to work, and encouraged me at every stage. Her love and support are essential. I completed my dissertation during the summer and autumn of Nika's first year, and the book in the summer and autumn of Lana's first year (thanks for letting me sleep at night, so I could work days!). Thanks, girls, for the play that keeps work in proper balance! This book is dedicated to all three.

Creating
the NATION

Introduction

Let's admit with humility, but also with hope: there is a Russian language, but there is not yet a literature, a worthy expression of a powerful and courageous nation!—Prince Petr Viazemsky, "On 'The Captive of the Caucasus,' a Tale, by A. Pushkin"

Prince Petr Viazemsky's nihilism regarding the whole of Russian literature in 1822 reflects a profound change that was taking place at the time in the perspective of leading Russian literary figures on their own literary patrimony. Just two decades earlier, Viazemsky's brother-in-law and guardian, Nikolai Karamzin, now the official historian of the Russian state, had surveyed the preceding century of Russian literary development and had outlined an entire pantheon of Russian authors, replete with Russian Pindars and Horaces—signaling that Russian literature had reached a respectable level of maturity. Now Viazemsky, firmly in the camp of Karamzin's students and followers, was implicitly consigning most of that century's literary development to the dustbin of history. Far from an outlier position, Viazemsky's rejection of the literary heritage of the Russian eighteenth century would be repeated endlessly in the decades to come.

What had changed? New was the expectation that literature be, in Viazemsky's words, the "expression of a . . . nation." Viazemsky's dismissal of the Russian literary patrimony derives from a revaluing of literary values that accompanies the emergence of a new literary paradigm in which the nation plays a central role. If Aleksandr Pushkin's new verse tale offered Viazemsky hope for a literature with the national qualities he sought, the extensive verse production of the eighteenth century and the first two decades of the nineteenth century were like old wineskins that burst when one sought to infuse them with the heady new wine of nationality. But why did Viazemsky and so many others like him suddenly develop the expectation that literature should express the nation? A host of studies over the past few decades have amply demonstrated how profoundly the nation needed literature to serve as a powerful symbolic tool. But why did literature need the nation? Why did the nation become the new ground of literary value?

In this book I will attempt to answer that question, and I will examine the emergence and development of the new paradigm of "national literature" in Czech and Russian criticism, literary history, historical theorizing and mythologizing, and theoretical and practical fabrications in the first three decades of the nineteenth century. I will pay particular analytical attention to the terms with which this new point of view is articulated, to new literary-critical and literary-historical vocabulary, as well as to the transformation of older terms as they are deployed in the delineation of entirely new systems of literary values. My attention to the transformation of metaliterary discourse is not, however, narrowly philological, but is rather an integral part of a broader analysis of the modernization of the institution of literature. Analysis of systematic developments in terminology is complemented by significant attention to the multiple roles that translation—construed both in the narrow sense to mean the translation of particular foreign texts and more broadly as a way of naming processes of cultural appropriation and assimilation—plays in efforts to modernize Russian and Czech literature. Once established, the paradigm of "national literature" emphasized originality and the development of one's own national resources, such as folklore. But for both the Czechs and Russians, folklore's place in the national literature came to be established through translation, a fact that appears paradoxical. As a culture- and identity-forming process, translation proved necessary even to the formation of an "independent" national literature. The engagement with alterity that constitutes translation was a critical part of the formation of the national "self."

The transformation of the institution of literature into a national form involved, in the first place, the reform of metaliterary discourse, the genre system, and the literary language (all of which receive attention in this study). But it also required the reorganization of journals, the book trade, and educational institutions, ultimately changing the entire relationship to the audience. What was the motivation for this massive labor? What drives the nationalization of literary culture? Insofar as this nationalization is a part of the broader nationalization of culture in Europe and the rise of nations and nationalism, we might look to the extensive literature on nations and nationalism for answers. While scholars have noted the prominent place of intellectuals in national movements and particularly of writers and philologists, the causes for this have not been adequately explored. That is to say, the motivations for literary actors to embrace the modern concept of the nation, to articulate new understandings of national identity, and to promote national awareness are not differentiated from the motivations of other types of intellectuals. The same broader social and political transformations of modernity that are given as the general causes of the rise of nations and nationalism are presumed to form the matrix of their motivation as well. At the level of general description on which this discourse works, such a view is no doubt true enough and sufficient. But when one examines the literary sphere more closely, it appears inadequate. Why is literature among the first cultural institutions to nationalize? Why do writers and literary historians occupy such prominent places in national movements and the formation of national ideologies? Might there not be some internal factor in the institution of literature, something specific to the literary sphere, that further motivates this transformation? In other words, once again, why did literature in particular need the nation?

Before trying to answer that question (in chapter 1), we should consider the ways in which some important students of nationalism have approached, however tangentially at times, the question of the motivation for literature's transformation. Ernest Gellner, in his prominent study *Nations and Nationalism*, offers a functionalist explanation for the formation of nations, which in his view tend to unite a single high culture in a single state. He thus generally avoids any question of the motivation of individual historical actors. When Gellner turns to the nations of the Habsburg Empire, however, as Peter Bugge has observed, his functionalist perspective wavers. The question of whether one of the state's folk cultures can become a rival high culture (and thus contend for its own state) seems to turn on the will and activities of "intellectuals-awakeners" (this would include our literary intellectuals). Gellner observes that "the resulting situation is of immediate and significant advantage to the said awakeners," but what that advantage and thus their motivation is, as Bugge notes, is not developed, probably because it remains outside the purview of his functionalist perspective.[1] Anthony D. Smith is much more centrally concerned with the role of culture and cultural figures in nationalism. For him, nationalism is "a form of historicist culture and civic education."[2] Intellectuals have an important role to play in the formation of this culture, particularly in the nationalism of subject *ethnies* that form their nationalism through the mobilization of the vernacular language. "There is a mass of evidence for the primary role of intellectuals both in generating cultural nationalism and in providing the ideology, if not the leadership, of political nationalism," Smith observes.[3] These intellectuals include "poets, musicians, painters, sculptors, novelists, historians and archaeologists, playwrights, philologists, anthropologists and folklorists."[4] Smith asks why these intellectuals were attracted to nationalism and answers that they were experiencing an identity crisis springing "from the challenges posed to traditional religion and society by the 'scientific state' and the Western 'revolutions.'"[5] To this identity crisis nationalism offers an identity solution. Broad social, cultural, and political developments prompt a cultural identity crisis, for which nationalism offers a historicist cultural solution. Smith places particular emphasis on the challenge that nascent historicism presented to the traditional worldview and its conception of time—this would seem to be of critical importance for explaining the involvement of the historians, archaeologists, and even philologists. But Smith offers no explanation for the prominence of intellectuals in aesthetic fields among the nationalists. Is there something about the historicist conception of time, we might ask, that is particularly relevant to the aesthetic sphere?

One's thoughts naturally turn here to Benedict Anderson and the attention he gave in *Imagined Communities* to the novel in connection with the modern conception of time that characterizes the national imagination. Anderson's example has led to a privileging of the genre of the novel in scholarship on literary nationalism, but also, in many cases, to a distortion of his argument and doubtful formulations of literature's role in the forming of nations. Jonathan Culler has noted the "slippage" from Anderson's point that the novel reflects "a condition of possibility for imagining the nation" to seeing "the novel as a force in shaping or legitimating the nation," and adds, "When there is slippage from an argument about conditions of possibility to one about the effects of certain novelistic representations, the argument may become richer and more specific in some respects but also considerably weaker, vastly more dubious. If, for instance, we ask what made

Britons 'Britons,' it is more plausible to answer 'war with France' than 'Jane Austen.'"[6] Anderson's point is that the novel is an aesthetic form capable of representing the modern conception of homogeneous, empty time that is the essential condition for imagining the nation as a community. But the novel does not create that modern conception of time, that condition of possibility.[7] Rather, as Anderson argues explicitly, the new conception of time became possible "when . . . three fundamental cultural conceptions . . . lost their axiomatic grip on men's minds." The first such conception is the belief in the truthfulness of a particular written language; the second, belief in the divine right of monarchs; and third, "a conception of temporality in which cosmology and history were indistinguishable, the origins of the world and of men essentially identical."[8] Anderson thus cites the broadest of sociocultural factors. And for Anderson, print-capitalism plays a key role in creating the new meaningful linking of "fraternity, power, and time."[9] Literature may be a part of that, but ultimately it is the economics of print that drives the new ideology for Anderson. The truth is that, in the end, Anderson gives scholars interested in the central issues of literary scholarship—in questions, for example, of aesthetics and literary form—no way to engage the larger questions of nationalism studies. In his analysis, as in so many others, literature can be read as a complex sign that passively reflects the changes of modernity and nationalization, but nothing in the literary sphere itself particularly contributes to the advance of the modern nation.

Joep Leerssen's recent *National Thought in Europe: A Cultural History* will, I think, prove to be a much better starting point for literary scholars wanting to intervene in discussions of the rise of nationalism and nations. Like Anderson and Smith, Leerssen is interested in the cultural side of nationalism, but not so much in the broad cultural transformations that underlie the national "social imaginary" as in the specific cultural history of national types and stereotypes—of ways of imagining the collective self and other—and their role in imagining national identity. Philology and literary criticism play pivotal roles for Leerssen in developing modern national thought.[10] In particular, Leerssen notes the leading role of literary criticism in working out a systematic typology of "national temperaments" or "national characters" in the seventeenth and eighteenth centuries, work that played a role in systematizing character types in treatises on poetics based on Aristotle's model. He observes, "It is not for nothing that literary criticism should have been in the vanguard of this development: for it was in these poetics that people thought most specifically about how to bring all the world together on a stage, and on the link between what people *were* and what they *did.*"[11] It is noteworthy that for this particular development, Leerssen finds a literary need—for a systematization of character types—that fosters the development of national thought by literary figures. In the larger picture of the development of national thought in Leerssen's narrative, however, political and social developments—such as the seventeenth-century consolidation of state/monarchical territories, the fall of the Holy Roman Empire, or the Napoleonic Wars—remain the primary motivators.[12] The particular needs within the various cultural spheres themselves for the nationalization of culture are not further explored.

I will show in this work that the national transformation of the institution of literature was motivated by a modern crisis in the constitution of literary values. This crisis drove the programmatic efforts of Czech and Russian cultural figures to reform their literatures and articulate a new system of literary values, with the nation in the center. Here, too, literary criticism and literary history were in the vanguard of the development of national thought.[13] These cultural figures offered some of the first elaborations of what constitutes Czech or Russian national identity. This suggests that the crisis in literary aesthetics motivated the development of modern national identities as much as any other social, political, or religious crisis that has been examined in the field of nationalism studies.

Among historians of Central Europe there is an active, ongoing engagement with the problems and history of nation-building. The best of the works of these historians exhibit a healthy skepticism toward the categories of nationalist thought and develop new perspectives on the empirical data that suggest discontinuities and resistances in what had been presumed to be the smooth, gradual progression of national movements.[14] In moving away from intellectual history toward social history, however, the historians have largely abandoned the earliest stages of national movements in order to examine the transition from national agitation to mass movement and the final consolidation (or the lack thereof) of national identity within new nation states, pushing the boundaries of the discussion forward into the twentieth century. There have been, however, a few notable exceptions. Derek Sayer's rich cultural history, *The Coasts of Bohemia: A Czech History* (2000), delves into the medieval and early modern sources that were later developed by Czech national thought. But Sayer is weakest precisely on the theory of nationalism, and with his primordialist perspective, continually reads that early history through an anachronistic nationalist lens, missing the fundamental transformation of Czech culture into a national form in the early nineteenth century. Hugh LeCaine Agnew's *Origins of the*

Czech National Renascence (1993) remains a valuable source on cultural developments in the earliest stage of the Czech national movement. Agnew's narrative ends precisely where mine will begin. Finally, among historians with an interest in Czech nation-building in the latter nineteenth century, only Peter Bugge, in his 1994 dissertation, *Czech Nation-Building, National Self-Perception, and Politics, 1780–1914,* begins with the cultural and ideological developments of the early nineteenth century.

Historians of Russia have of late made the Russian Empire the primary context for any discussions of nationalism and nation-building, and have also emphasized the later stages of nation-building over the earlier history.[15] To be sure, one should not lose sight of the fact that the paradigm of "national literature" develops, for both Russians and Czechs, within their own individual imperial contexts, and each different program for the national literature or conception of the essence of the national literature forms a particular relation to that imperial context. As Thomas Wallnig has observed in relation to the Habsburg Empire, "'State,' 'People,' 'Nation,' 'Government': all of these words, and the ideas they denote, underwent considerable development in our period of study, which had a marked impact on the political history of the age: to . . . inter-group conflicts . . . we must add the nature of a continually renewed negotiation of power that found its expression in a struggle for the necessary materials, but also for the necessary vocabulary. 'Nation,' 'people' and so on were not descriptive labels in this process, but paradigms for whose establishment the struggles took place."[16] In my analysis of the development of the vocabulary of discourse about literature that is a part of the struggle for the establishment of the paradigm of "national literature," I will have occasion to comment on the relation of particular authors and their conceptions to their imperial contexts. In particular, I will argue that some ideas about literary appropriation and assimilation have been too easily assigned to the side of negative cultural imperialism and that translation theory and close analyses of translation practices offer ways to distinguish between appropriations that play a part in the kinds of cultural dialogues that form all cultures and more aggressively imperialist appropriations.

In fact, the development of Russian national culture, from a position of hegemony, has far more in common with the development of Czech national culture, from a position of subordination, than one might expect. But comparative analysis across these borders has been lacking, both among historians and literature specialists. Certainly the choice is not obvious. The two literary cultures are about as different as they can be at this point in their histories. Russian literature had more than a half century of modern history behind it in 1800, and literary activity was seen as prestigious among the noble class, who remained its primary cultivators. Czech literature was being developed by a mere handful of educated middle-class intellectuals and had seen only a few small anthologies of new poetry in the last few years of the eighteenth century. There was almost no contact between the main figures either, though some new contacts were being established on the basis of the development of Slavic linguistics. And yet, the process of national modernization for both literatures occurred at approximately the same historical moment, so that Czech and Russian writers were often responding to the same developments in current literary ideas, with the result that there were a number of surprising correspondences between Czech and Russian literary ideas, terms, and debates during this period. Comparing them to each other, rather than to the English, German, or French literatures that are the usual object of comparative attention, helps to avoid two false conclusions that such comparisons have frequently been subject to: (1) the idea that Czech or Russian developments are derivative and inferior because delayed; and (2) the idea that Czech or Russian developments are unique because different. But ultimately the justification of the comparison is in the insights it brings into the history of literary and national developments, both within and beyond these particular national traditions.

A pair of recent studies of Nikolai Gogol has been greatly enriched by bold comparative perspectives: Anne Lounsbery's *Thin Culture, High Art: Gogol, Hawthorne, and Authorship in Nineteenth-Century Russia and America* (2007); and Edyta Bojanowska's *Nikolai Gogol: Between Ukrainian and Russian Nationalism* (2007). Lounsbery examines how Gogol and Hawthorne each contended with the problem of creating a "national literature" ex nihilo. Bojanowska dares to probe the problem of Gogol's own conflicted national identification. This study offers another comparative perspective on developments in a period that in many ways is essential if one is to really understand the issues explored in these two works. Both the difficulties surrounding Gogol's national identification and the problem Gogol faced as a writer having to deal with Russia's lack of a national literature are products of the nationalization of Russian literary culture and literary cultures across Europe and the Americas. The establishment of the paradigm of "national literature" is a process that fundamentally changes the literary and cultural landscape. My study will explore the impetus for and specific history of that transformation in Russian and Czech literatures, as well as the implications the transformation has for literary and national studies.

In part I of this work, "Shifting Terms: Literature, Language, Culture," I will examine the first articulations of national literary programs in Russia and the Czech-language realm in the first decade of the nineteenth century and the terms, new and old, with which they operated. Because translation was deeply implicated in these programs, and in the second decade of the nineteenth century, translations and debates over translations helped to establish fundamental values in the emerging national literary discourses, the chapters of part II, "Translation and the National Literature," analyze the many roles played by "translation." Part III, "Terms in Conflict," returns to the terminology of the national metaliterary discourse, the attempts to define terms and the disputes over terms that dominated the third decade of the nineteenth century, when contemporary European discussions of "romanticism" provoked Czech and Russian debates.

To begin, let us return to the moment when Russian literature still had its Pindars and Horaces. . . .

Part I

SHIFTING TERMS
Literature, Language, Culture

1

A New Paradigm Emerges

In 1802, Nikolai Karamzin (1766–1826), the future historian of the Russian state, published his *Panteon rossiiskikh avtorov* (*Pantheon of Russian Authors*), in which he made use, on several occasions, of a time-honored rhetorical technique for canonizing and praising authors. The Russian author was compared with classical and French authors who worked in the same genre in a formula that can be distilled to "*X* is our *Y*," where *X* is the name of a Russian author and *Y* the name of a canonical writer. Thus, Prince Kantemir is "our Juvenal," since Kantemir is particularly known for his poetical satires; and Mikhailo Lomonosov "has inscribed his name in the book of immortality, where shine the name of Pindars, Horaces, [Jean-Baptiste] Rousseau"—praise that would suggest without doubt, even if we knew nothing more of Lomonosov, his success in cultivating the ode.[1] This rhetoric of praise is the product of a particular understanding of literature, in which a timeless, universal model defines a system of genres and styles that can be embodied and reembodied in different times and places. Karamzin's use of the plural, "Pindars, Horaces," is suggestive of the kind of repetition implied by this conception. The writer is defined by a relationship to the universal system of genre norms and to the model authors of that system, not by the more local and specific relationships to other writers who worked in the same country or the same language.

Such critical judgments are particularly common in eighteenth-century Russian classicism. A typical example can be taken from Aleksandr Sumarokov's second epistle on poetry (1747), an epistle that also treated Lomonosov as a writer of odes: "He is the Malherbe of our lands, akin to Pindar."[2] Nicolas Boileau-Despréaux's *Art poétique* (1674), which Sumarokov is adapting here, was particularly influential in establishing a normative, universalist poetics in Russia.[3] But this conception of literature has its roots in antiquity itself, in the Hellenistic critics' formulation of the model value of the literature of the fourth and fifth century B.C.E., and in late antiquity's educational uses of literature. The European Renaissance adopted the value system embodied by the Roman-Greek literary canon, which embraced the implicit possibility of cultural unity across ethnic and temporal differences, especially as the ancient world was now distant and unfamiliar and could be viewed as a largely undifferentiated whole.[4] Boileau was himself updating Horace's *Ars Poetica* for a rationalist age and canonizing his contemporaries in Louis XIV's France alongside the Roman poets of the Augustan Age and their models before them, the Attic Greeks.

The timelessness of this model would soon, with the advent of a modern historical point of view, come to look absurdly anachronistic. Jean Paul Richter, in his *School for Aesthetics* (1804), underlines the impossibility of the repetition across time and across cultures implied by the model:

> It is an old mistake of men witnessing the eternal spectacle of time to call for repetitions of the beautiful (ancora), as if anything in superabundant nature could return. Not even the worst can. The duplication of a whole people would be a greater wonder than a fantastic sky of clouds completely matching some former sky. Not even in Greece could antiquity be resurrected. Indeed it is idle for one people to call another to account about intellectual riches, as when the French ask us, "Where are your Voltaires, Rousseaus, Diderots, Buffons?" "We have none," we say "but where are your Lessings, Winckelmanns, Herders, Goethes, et al.?" Not even wretched authors have matching apes abroad. In all England and France, among all novelists, the famous ——— (in ———) has no twin; and of course, these countries are lucky.[5]

For Richter, writers occupy positions in the history of their particular peoples that are fundamentally unique. Indeed, in parts of Europe a paradigm shift had occurred in discourse about literature, one that accounted for temporal and geographical specificity in grounding literary values. In Russian and

Czech letters as well, a fundamental reconceptualization of literature, in which the nation came to be a defining subject of literary-historical and literary-critical discourse, was getting underway in the first decade of the nineteenth century. Though Karamzin was far from the last among Russian critics to make use of the rhetoric of the universalist system, his *Panteon* can be read as marking the twilight of the form.

Both Czech and Russian critics would come to parody this type of comparison in a fashion similar to Richter. In an 1827 article that redefined the sense of the word "classic" in relation to the *national* literature (discussed below in chapter 9), the Czech writer Josef Jungmann treated such evaluations with irony: "Some already see perfect classics amongst us, and in their opinion, we have no lack of Ciceros, Livys and Horaces."[6] By that time such evaluations had largely disappeared from better Czech criticism.[7] In Russia such evaluations, rather than disappearing, were adapted in the 1810s and 1820s to a new canon that envisaged Russian Homers, Shakespeares, and Goethes—the emphasis being on a new type of culture hero who initiates a national form and discourse (Shakespeare's drama was key to the critique of classicist drama rules and was interpreted as particularly English in form) or who synthesizes inherited forms in creating new ones (Goethe). Such an evaluation in its new form emphasized originality and national particularity rather than imitation, and the norms of genre that stood behind Karamzin's comparisons are replaced by a more fluid conception of artistic form. But even such evaluations could still be critiqued on the basis of national identity. In 1832, Nikolai Gnedich encouraged Aleksandr Pushkin to be himself and ignore the comparisons made by his critics, even as he himself made yet another new comparison: "Byron's genius, or Goethe's or Shakespeare's/ Is the genius of their climate, their mores, their lands./ But you, who have learned the secret of the Russian soul and world,/ Sing to us in your own way, Russian Boian."[8] Boian was the ancient bard referred to reverently by the author of the twelfth-century *Slovo o polku Igoreve* (*Song of Igor's Campaign*, first published with a modern Russian translation in 1800), and thus represented the mythological first poet of the native Russian tradition. The changed form of the given critical statement in Russia and its disappearance in Czech criticism are but two symptoms of the advance of the new paradigm of national literature.

THE DEVELOPMENT OF A NEW SYSTEM of literary values seems to gain its first momentum in Europe in the "Quarrel between the Ancients and Moderns" in late seventeenth-century France, with added impulses from France's technical advances and cultural confidence during

Louis XIV's reign. Discussions of the value of the old versus the new had begun in antiquity itself,[9] but this time the discussion aired a wide range of issues quite thoroughly, and in the process introduced new ideas while giving impetus to methods that would have profound consequences for the value ascribed to the classical literary canon. A short examination of this Quarrel and its consequences will do much to situate and illuminate aspects of the Czech and Russian debates in the early nineteenth century. (I will suggest a few of the many possible connections parenthetically.) The larger Quarrel has been conceived as having had three phases: first, the Quarrel proper in France, with debates that culminated in the works of Charles Perrault and Bernard le Bovier de Fontenelle; second, the English "Battle of the Books," ignited by Sir William Temple and with important contributions by William Wotton and Jonathan Swift; and third, the French "Querelle d'Homère" in the early eighteenth century. Douglas Lane Patey, in an article that brings together a broad range of recent research into and around the Quarrel, suggests that "nearly all recent studies of the Quarrel have found its importance in fostering and diffusing a new understanding of history: one that contributed to an understanding of all human works as historical products (cultural constructions) and consequently to a relativization of taste, increased interest in nonclassical cultures both past and present, and ultimately to the late eighteenth-century body of thinking that has come to be called 'historicism.'"[10] As already noted, a modern historical point of view was fundamentally incompatible with the ahistorical and culturally undifferentiated literary values that the classics had first represented to the early modern world. This new historicism, then, created a crisis in literary values and the need for a new theoretical paradigm in which to ground literary values.

It was Boileau's defense of the standard of the ancients, and his personal attacks on certain of his contemporaries, that provoked the innovative replies of the moderns. Perrault led the charge with four volumes of *Parallèle des anciens et des modernes* (1688–1696) in which he compared in parallel the achievements of the ancients and the moderns in all fields of learning, finding progress in nearly all. But it was Fontenelle's *Digression sur les anciens et les modernes* (1688) that introduced a new division of knowledge. Fontenelle was not convinced of the possibility of progress in poetry, though he was sure of it in other fields. He therefore distinguished between those fields of learning that depended primarily upon the imagination, like eloquence and poetry, and those that are forced to progress by the slow amassing of knowledge, like physics and mathematics. This division of the arts and sciences was taken up by writers on both sides of the Quarrel and fundamentally changed the terms of the discussion.[11] Among other things, the field covered by the term "literature" narrowed considerably, and a new category, the "aesthetic," emerged alongside more modern conceptions of the sciences.[12]

A fully modern division of the arts and sciences would not finally emerge until the nineteenth century—it was the task of the eighteenth century to work out the division. The intense interrogation of the category of the aesthetic was a part of this task. Alexander Gottlieb Baumgarten introduced the neologism "aesthetica" into his master's thesis at the University of Halle in 1735, defining it as the "science of perception," as opposed to logic, the science of what is known. Later, in his monumental *Aesthetica* (2 vols., 1751 and 1758), he came to define it more broadly to encompass the theory of the liberal arts. Because the arts were not yet narrowed down to the fine arts, "the science of aesthetics, as Baumgarten conceives it, covers the entire field of human skills insofar as they are rooted in our sensuous faculties and shape and articulate perception."[13] The elevation of the fine arts and a consequent narrowing of the realm of the aesthetic occurred toward the end of the century. The old category of "literature" was also redefined as a part of the same process. It no longer encompassed all written learning, but came to refer only to imaginative literature, subsumed under the broader category of the aesthetic.[14] (In the first decade of the nineteenth century in Russia, Admiral Aleksandr Shishkov would suggest that the narrowing of Russian literature along these lines, which he conceived of as another imitation of French models, was akin to throwing out the bulk of the Russian national literary tradition. See chapter 3.)

The larger Quarrel's second and third phases, the English "Battle of the Books" and the French "Querelle d'Homère," deployed new methodologies and articulated new problems with similarly far-reaching consequences. In his *Reflections upon Ancient and Modern Learning* (1694), where the parallels between ancient and modern learning recall Perrault and others, going back as far as the Renaissance, William Wotton introduced a new field into the discussion in which modern achievements outstripped the accomplishments of the ancients: he put forward the science of philology, or criticism.[15] Wotton argued that as a result of careful philological study, the late seventeenth century knew ancient history better than the ancients themselves. By allying philology with historical study, Wotton was proposing a new methodological foundation for history, one that moved it closer to the sciences and away from the realm of literature, of classical rhetoric and narrative.[16] (Philology was particularly important for the early Czech national revival in the late eighteenth century, when leading figures like Josef Dobrovský helped to ground the national programs of the early nineteenth century. See chapter 4.)[17] Joseph M. Levine calls English moderns like Wotton, armed with the tools of classical philology, "the most avowed (and the most dangerous) of the moderns," because in the end, deeper knowledge of the classical period was the biggest threat to the ancients' position.[18] "The real addition to the understanding of classical authors that resulted . . . began to threaten the confidence in imitation and in the ancient wisdom on which the whole revival was based. To know Homer or Pythagoras too well was to open a gulf that divided them from modern life, rather than identifying them with it."[19] In the position of the ancients, a divide was opening up between two possible approaches, one that used philology and sought deeper knowledge of the ancient past and its historical difference but that potentially weakened its contemporary relevance, and another that elided the difference in order to maintain the model status of ancient works and the practice of assimilative imitation. In England one sees something more like the latter: the ancients opposed their gentlemanly wit to the pedantry of classical scholars who aligned themselves with the moderns and won the battle with lasting literary monuments (Swift's *A Tale of a Tub* and Alexander Pope's adaptive translation of the *Iliad*), though in the end the war was lost to the moderns.[20]

In France, the former approach predominated. Classical scholarship was deployed by the ancients, who apparently did not yet feel the potential contradiction such an approach revealed in their position. In fact, Anne Lefèvre, Madame Dacier, took a rather new step by defending Homer from the attacks of Perrault and Fontenelle on the basis of his historical difference, while at the same time still claiming the ground of universal taste. Her defense accompanied her new *prose* translation of Homer's *Iliad* (1711), a product of fifteen years' labor, that strove to present "the 'simple,' 'direct,' and 'original' manner of Homer's 'heroic age' (a concept she did much to consolidate)" and thereby challenge the falsely refined taste of her contemporaries.[21] Opposing her translation was that of Antoine Houdar de La Motte, which adapted Homer "without scruple" to the modern taste, producing in the end a pared-down *Iliad* of only twelve books in heroic couplets (1714).[22] For La Motte, the value of Homer was not in his historical character but only in those meanings that reason could rescue from the historically inferior age for contemporary edification. He was not so much a modern, then, as an ancient of an altogether different stripe.[23] But the French Quarrel broke out with renewed vigor in the following years.

In fact, the quarrel over Homer initiated an intense period of research into Homer and his age that spanned the next hundred years.[24] Many of the larger Quarrel's consequences were worked out primarily in critical discussions of Homer. Kirsti Simonsuuri reminds readers that "both England and France in the eighteenth century derived much of their critical vocabulary and theory from antiquity and in the Greco-Roman world Homer stood as the first and best of poets, the basis of education and a model for later writers. Any attempt to analyse and evaluate him was bound to implicate a great many fundamental assumptions about literature and culture."[25] This is no doubt true, but one should not underestimate the important role played by *the problem of translation* in opening up the Homer question to far-reaching new analyses. (In the second decade of the nineteenth century in Czech and Russian literature, the translation of Homer as a part of a broader project for the assimilation of Greek metrical forms, and Homer's hexameter in particular, becomes a key site for debating the new national conception of literature. See chapters 6 and 7.) It was, after all, in the context of defining the problems faced in translating Homer that Madame Dacier formulated a fundamental difficulty: the hermeneutic problem posed by cultural difference and historical distance.[26] Her principle, that the interpreter should strive to inhabit the historical context of the original work, was quickly made a commonplace by the new generation of French ancients.[27]

The quarrel over Homer thus articulated the fundamental problem, historical and cultural alterity, upon which any rigorous analytic of translation is based. But it also would become a central problem of historiography. Giambattista Vico, often credited with being the first to articulate a modern historical point of view, worked out some of the conceptions for his *Scienza nuova* (1725; 2nd edition 1730), which combined philology and philosophy in a new science of history, in response to Italian reverberations of the Quarrel. The quarrel over Homer in particular was an important inspiration for Vico, and Homer became a central proof of his new science.[28] Independent of Vico's achievement, German Aufklärers and British literary historians, among others, developed the problem of the historian's point of view and the necessity of thinking back into the spirit of the past, helping to prepare the ground for the general historicism of the late eighteenth century.[29] The myth of the universal poet was also transformed by this problem of alterity, as German critics formulated the role of the Protean poet, whose gift it was precisely to live into and transmit other times and cultures—in other words, to differentiate Goethe's genius from that of Shakespeare.[30]

Ultimately it would take a history of eighteenth-century literature and criticism to trace out all of the changes in literary values that seem to follow from these few fundamental new insights and problems first articulated in the Quarrel between the Ancients and Moderns. Here, briefly, is an outline of some of the changes that will be of particular importance for this study of Czech and Russian literature in the early nineteenth century. The French moderns initiated a critique of the doctrine of imitation that, in the context of the developing awareness of the difference between ancient and modern cultures, gained more and more momentum. English critics in particular were interested in the *opposition of originality to imitation*, where originality is defined as a freedom from artistic rules.[31] This new opposition had a critical role to play in the revaluing of the ancient literary heritage but did not lead to its rejection. Instead, as the picture of the ancient world became more differentiated, *Greek literature was elevated* for its originating role over Latin literature, which came to be seen as derivative.[32]

The new knowledge that humanistic philology produced also required *a new conception of historical periodization*. Renaissance scholars recognized a broad division of the past into antiquity, the Dark or Middle Ages, and modern times, which began with the revival of ancient learning.[33] The parallel between the ancient and modern periods this implied became untenable. It has already been noted how Madame Dacier based her new argument for Homer on the necessity of understanding the fundamentally different heroic age to which he belonged. The division of history into new, distinct periods often took individual human growth and development as its model, so that the oldest, primitive period corresponded to human childhood. Vico defended Homer from the rationalist modern charge that he had an inferior philosophy by denying that Homer neeeded a developed philosophy in the first place. As a representative of a primitive age, Homer had what he was supposed to have: an imagination that produced superior poetry. The age of philosophy would only come later, and the age of great poetry would pass.[34] While this argument critiques a certain kind of parallel of ancient and modern learning, like that of Perrault, it also opens up a new kind of parallelism: the medieval period is recast as the primitive age of European civilization.[35] Research into the heroic age of Homer thus also stimulated research into a wide variety of nonclassical ancient civilizations and early European culture.[36] The English ballad revival is born out of this stimulus as is the interest in all kinds of alternative European literary and folkloric traditions.[37] Simonsuuri goes so far as to suggest that "the discovery of Ossian's poems and the Ossianic movement can be seen as an inevitable outcome of the interest in the origins and nature of poetry and the epic in Scotland in the middle of the eighteenth century. It is not entirely cynical to say that if the poems of Ossian had not existed, it would have been necessary to invent them."[38] The necessity of such inventions was not lost upon the Czechs and Russians intent on defining and defending their own independent literary traditions.

These developments transformed literary history. Genre had been the primary organizing element, and literary histories examined how successive artists had developed new means to achieve the ends defined by the genres' founders. Such histories defined continuous traditions that crossed political and linguistic boundaries without difficulty.[39] But with the relativization of literary values came the tendency to associate literary phenomena with particular times or periods and places. Voltaire, in his "Essay on Epick Poetry" (1727), became one of the first to treat classical literature as a separate national literary tradition, arguing that there was no sense in forming rules for the European epic based on the epic of a nation with different customs, language, religion, and worldview.[40] *Literary history then came to be assimilated to larger histories of civilization, of cultures or nations.* Literature also became source material for these larger histories, and national historical identity could be read out of medieval literary monuments: the English found that their medieval texts expressed the love of "liberty," while the Germans found in theirs a sense of the Germanic "people."[41]

These changes in literary values, then, were an intimate part of the history of the development of modern national identities. The emerging modern concept of the nation, as an entity bounded by language or citizenship or historical continuity, became a new, more local and culturally specific center in which to explore or ground ideas of literary value. Literature, in turn, became primary evidence for the historical existence of a separate national identity. Thus literature and the nation came together in a new constellation of values. This new axiological system was in some ways the result of a whole host of changes of language—as "literature" itself came to name a narrower field in the eighteenth century. And the sense of the term "nation" had undergone a profound transformation as well.[42] The "primitive" had emerged as a positive value, and new terms, like "aesthetic," appeared as a part of the reorganization of knowledge. "Culture" was becoming something historically specific, rather than simply the result of cultivation.[43] The consolidation of the new national literary paradigm would continue to transform language and necessitate the creation of new terms to carry new values.

One innovator in terminology was Johann Gottfried Herder. Herder has perhaps at times been given too much credit for the innovations in literary values that emerged in the late eighteenth century—he clearly stands at the end of a long line of developments. But, as René Wellek has argued, these developments coalesced to form a new system in Herder's writings (which were, at times, far from systematic), and the new system required new terminology.[44] Klaus Weimar has suggested that Herder was arguably the first to use the term "*Nationalliteratur,*" citing a manuscript from around 1768.[45] Herder also found it necessary to invent the terms "*Volkspoesie,*" its equivalent "*Volksdichtung,*" and "*Volkslied*" (they appear for the first time in his writing) to play essential roles in his national-historical metaliterary discourse.[46] And Herder was not alone among Germans in introducing new terms to the discussion. Later, Friedrich Schiller would recast the entire ancients and moderns debate in terms of naive and sentimental poetry, and the Schlegel brothers, Friedrich and August, would reformulate this again to oppose the "classic" and the "romantic."[47] All of these new terms and their local equivalents played essential roles in the attempts of Czech and Russian writers to reinvent their literatures as national literatures.

Czech and Russian literatures did not, indeed could not, proceed step by step in the course of the eighteenth century with German, English, and French literature in developing the new ideas and perspectives introduced by the larger Quarrel. Rather, many of the gradual shifts outlined above only entered into Czech and Russian debates about literary values in the early nineteenth century, most often in connection with conscious programs to reform literary practice along national lines. The concept of a national literature, which had emerged as a new paradigm from the larger Quarrel, thus carried into Czech and Russian literatures a new system of potential new values that were debated, adapted, integrated, or rejected.

CZECH LITERATURE, ANCIENT AND MODERN. The Czechs had early contact with the Italian Renaissance, particularly under the reign of Charles IV in the latter part of the fourteenth century, but early Czech humanism was overwhelmed by the swelling church reform movement that came to dominate cultural life. The real flowering of Czech humanism would wait until after the Hussite wars and really until the sixteenth century. But then, too, practical literature and scholarly humanism dominated, with ties in particular to German humanist circles and the group around Erasmus of Rotterdam, and a full-fledged renaissance of the literary arts, particularly in the Czech vernacular, did not result.[48] The vernacular was not entirely neglected, however. Translation, of the Bible in the first place but also of ancient texts, played a particularly important role in transforming the language culture. In the late fifteenth century, Viktorin Kornel z Všehrd advocated translation from the classical languages into Czech for the cultivation of the Czech language and perfection of its literature. But even the few translations made from the ancient classics were of Latin prose works—the translation of poetry presented special problems and was rare.[49] The first to work out rules for a quantitative Czech prosody, following ancient verse theory, was Jan Blahoslav in his *Muzika* (1558), and the theory was further developed by Vavřinec Benedikti z Nedožer in the early seventeenth century. But this quantitative verse was used most often in songs and psalm translations, with only a few experiments in the translation of ancient classics. The reception of classical literature thus remained unsystematic.[50]

The Czech defeat at the Battle of White Mountain (1620) brought even this modest relationship of the vernacular to classical literature to a temporary end. The Counter Reformation brought with it a baroque aesthetics that was at best unsystematic in its relationship to the ancient classics and often anticlassical in its artistic means. Even the widespread education in Latin secondary schools that had been a continuous tradition throughout the Hussite period took on a much more limited, Jesuit-dominated, form. There was no quarter in which the French seventeenth-century classicism could be cultivated, and with literary ties to foreign lands circumscribed, the Quarrel found no echoes in Czech literary life.[51] German Protestant universities led the way in historical and literary research in the eighteenth century and Catholic universities followed at a safe distance. But with the advent of enlightened absolutism, careful reforms gradually gave new ground for the cultivation of Czech literature. Maria Theresa instituted instruction in Czech alongside instruction in German in her elite gymnazium and officer's academy around 1750, and following the dissolution of the Jesuit order in 1773 and the university reform of 1774, instruction in Czech language and literature began at the university in Vienna.[52] The university in Prague also became first among Catholic universities to appoint a professor of aesthetics in 1763.[53]

With the revival of a more multifaceted literary life in the last third of the eighteenth century, then, multiple models for the relationship to the literature of antiquity became simultaneously available to Czech writers. Immediate ties were established back to the Czech renaissance humanism of the sixteenth century, with a flood of republications of the work of Czech humanists, and Josef Dobrovský made late sixteenth-century Czech the standard for new works in Czech.[54] French classicism was also available through the German mediation of Johann Christoph Gottsched, though German classicism had been significantly altered and Czechs met with purer forms in contemporary Polish and Russian literature. Enlightenment classicism offered a variety of new genres and values without fundamentally changing the underlying conception of literature, but the so-called Weimar classicism—Goethe and Schiller were extremely popular among Czech intellectuals—already offered a new relationship to the ancient classics.[55]

The first new experiments in Czech poetry, then, brought multiple translations of classical works alongside new poems in Czech. Václav Thám's almanac (1785) included translations of Anacreontic verse, a fragment from Sappho, and two from Catullus, along with reprints of humanist translations. But the versification problem remained, with syllabic and quantitative systems competing. In the first almanac from Antonín Jaroslav Puchmajer's group (1795), Josef Dobrovský offered a modernizing reform in a syllabotonic versification system. Puchmajer published two more almanacs before the turn of the century (1797, 1798). Much of the classical aura of this new Czech verse was woven purely out of poetic commonplaces and ornaments from Latin schooling, however, and a poetically productive relationship to classical antiquity had not been worked out by the turn of the century. Josef Jungmann would take the lead in the early nineteenth century in developing this new relationship.[56]

ANCIENTS AND MODERNS IN RUSSIA. That Karamzin could still in 1802 make multiple critical statements of the sort analyzed earlier is indicative of how little change the genre-centered and universal approach to literature had undergone in the Russian eighteenth century. When the modern Russian literary tradition was consciously (re)constituted in the middle third of the eighteenth century, an essential part of the task was still to establish such a literary model, and Boileau became an iconic representative of this tradition as a highly visible recent proponent. The poetic aphorisms of Boileau and the tenets of his model (Horace), along with the genre hierarchy of Aristotle, became the shared background against which new literary work was conceived and judged.[57] But for the Russian tradition, Boileau had a fundamentally different aspect than for the French tradition. In France, Boileau championed what he saw as the best practices of his predecessors and contemporaries within the long-established literary tradition that mandated imitation of the ancients in the genres they had established. His was a reform of an established tradition. In Russia, Boileau became an ally to those who rejected outright the entirety of the previous Russian literary tradition and sought to establish something radically new. Boileau's statements had the power of not only elevating certain practices above others, but of founding entirely new practices.[58]

Sumarokov's adaptation of Boileau in his epistle "O stikhotvorstve" ("On Poetry," 1747), then, has a very different sense from Boileau's adaptation of Horace. It can be seen as a part of the larger struggle between Sumarokov, Trediakovsky, and Lomonosov over the right to be recognized as the founder of a proper poetry in Russia.[59] This polemics is inscribed in Sumarokov's adaptation. He mentions four Russian poets in his epistle on poetry. As A. M. Peskov has suggested, they occupy places analogous to those outlined by Boileau. Feofan Prokopovich and Kantemir take the place of the poetic founders, who are succeeded in Boileau's scheme by the arrival of true poetry with Malherbe (the Russian Malherbe being, of course, Lomonosov). Trediakovsky takes the place of the poets subjected to ridicule. But the place of the model poets, of Corneille, Racine, Molière, and implicitly of Boileau himself, is left open, presumably because Sumarokov sees himself in that place.[60] But while Sumarokov would be honored as the Russian Racine for his tragedies, he was not named the Russian Boileau, perhaps because there could be no Russian Boileau—Boileau himself occupied that place too firmly and his precepts were known well enough without Sumarokov's adaptation or Trediakovsky's later translation.[61]

The iconic status and authority of Boileau in Russia does not, however, imply a one-sided reception of the Quarrel. Viktor M. Zhivov has argued that Trediakovsky in particular made a conscious effort to synthesize the European debates. The authority of ancients like Boileau on the one hand was balanced on the other by the fact that in Russia a new, modern literary tradition was being founded, which implied a narrative of progress and a modern outlook.[62] But the more radical insights of the moderns and their transforming consequences gained little ground in a Russia whose writers were looking for firm guidance in constituting a literary tradition. The implicit norms of Boileau and the ancients were the basis of literary critique and practice, and the role of imitation in literary creation was not fundamentally challenged—though in the Russian practice, seventeenth-century French writers often took their place alongside classical, mostly Latin, authors. Even in their deviations in practice from the ancient norms, Russian writers often took their inspiration from the French ancients and from Boileau in particular. Trediakovsky modeled the Russian panegyric ode on an experiment in the Pindaric tradition by Boileau that challenged the classicist norms of moderation. And the principle of poetic *"vostorg"* [rapture] by which Russian writers justified their deviations from the language norms of classicism owed much to Boileau's mediation of Longinus's tract on the sublime.[63]

In the later eighteenth century, Russian writers continued to follow European developments and new genres and trends appeared, including meditative poetry, a sentimentalist movement, and some attention to folklore. But the underlying conception of literature was not seriously challenged. Karamzin's *Panteon* testifies to the accommodation of sentimentalist practice within a broader classicist model of literature.[64] Peskov located the "revaluing of values" in relation to Boileau and the normative aesthetics associated with his name in Russia withinthe second and third decades of the nineteenth century. Characteristically, Admiral Aleksandr Shishkov was one of the first (in 1811) to declare that the poetic rules of Boileau, Aristotle, and Horace could notbe used to measure the older Russian national literary tradition, though writers of his "archaist" camp appealed to such norms as often as did writers in the opposing Karamzinian or "innovator" camp in judging contemporary works.[65] And Orest Somov (in 1823) figured the "codex for poets" of Boileau as a strict boundary that circumscribed the activity of genius.[66]

NOT JUST LITERATURE, but a national literature. The conscious programs to reform native literatures emerging in the nineteenth-century Russian and Czech-language realms became a driving force for reconsidering their relationships to the ancient world and other modern literatures.This implicated a whole system of literary values and opened wide-ranging discussions in both literatures. The problem of why the nation in particular became the new locus of literary identity and value needs more attention. What promptedCzech and Russian intellectuals to reconceive their literatures in terms of the nation, and what problems did such a reconception solve for them? In some sense, this is a parallel question to that posed by Miroslav Hroch in his analysis of why national movements experience a transition from phase *A*, scholarly and linguistic inquiry into the national past, to phase *B*, when a group of intellectual activists begins to agitate for the creation of a nation.[67] In fact, in the Czech case (and arguably in the Russian case as well) programs to nationalize the literature are a primary expression of this new agitation. See inchapter 4 howJosef Jungmann mobilizes Josef Dobrovský's history of Czech literature (scholarly antiquarianism) for his program for a Czech national literature and culture. Hroch cites certain broad social factors that contribute: "(1) a social and/or political crisis of the old order, accompanied by new tensions and horizons; (2) the emergence of discontent among significant elements of the population; (3) loss of faith in traditional moral systems, above all a decline in religious legitimacy, even if this only affected small numbers of intellectuals."[68] The nation offered a new form of integration and a new system of values.

It seems not at all unimportant to add the crisis in the "old order" of literary values to the list of factors. Without it, the prominent place of literary intellectuals and literary activities in the Czech, Russian, and other national movements at similar junctures cannot be adequately explained. The need within literature itself for a new grounding of aesthetic values and the place that the developing modern concept of the nation took in new conceptions put literature into the vanguard of national thought. *The crisis in literary value might even be among the most important factors that drove the national movement at this point.* As noted earlier, the modern idea of the nation, as a bounded entity, offered a new site for exploring literary values in a more historically and culturally grounded form. Certainly the decision to reform literary practice around the nation waslargely overdetermined for Czech and Russian writers, as it wasthe only viable new model and value system. This modeling in no way suggests that their (literary) nationalisms weresomehow "borrowed" or "derivative" of German or other European nationalisms—the relative delay in the Czech and Russian crisis of (literary) values hadits concrete causes (explored above), but the crisis wasno less a real product of modernity for its having been slightly delayed.[69] The model of a national literature gave Czech and Russian intellectuals a new paradigm for understanding themselves and their place in their own society and the world, a potential new system of values, and concrete new goals and broader missions for their literary work.

If the national literature paradigm solved certain problems, it also created a number of new problems. Divisions between popular and educated or aristocratic literary practices were not a problem for the classicist model of literature, but for a national literature, the projected unity of the national body mandated that literary practice should also occupy a unified, if diverse, field. This problem beganto concern Czech and Russian writers in the later 1820s. The new paradigm also set up boundaries for what would be included in the national literature and what would not. Enshrined as the

Czech national poet posthumously in the later nineteenth century, Karel Hynek Mácha faced critical disapproval during his lifetime for his literary practice, which was felt to be insufficiently engaged in the national project. And the originality of Vasily Zhukovsky's contribution to Russian literature, in which translation took a prominent place, needed special justification by Nikolai Gogol. If the emphasis in this study falls more on the side of the advantages of the national literature paradigm, on its productivity and fecundity in forming new literary practices and ideas, that is not due to a lack of awareness of or interest in the problems this new perspective created. Rather, it derives from the attempt to explain the attractiveness of the new paradigm and thus the motivation for its development as well as the historical reality that many of the contradictions and blind spots in the national perspective were discovered or became manifest only later.

Is There a Russian Literature? No . . .

Some will be surprised to learn that both the question and the iconoclastic answer that form the title of this chapter were voiced already in 1801. Such denials became a commonplace in Russian literary criticism in the nineteenth century, where denying the existence of a cultural tradition was itself a cultural tradition. They are an integral part of the literary and cultural programs of such well-known figures as Vissarion Belinsky, Petr Chaadaev, and Dmitry Venevitinov that developed out of the intense discussions of the problem of the Russian national literature in the 1820s (see part III). What is the context of this denial, then, that precedes such discussions by at least twenty years? The man who so early articulated the need for Russian literature to become more national—to reflect the Russian national character—was enamored of the young Schiller and of Goethe's *Werther,* and was steeped in the poetics of the German *Sturm und Drang*—a period when the problem of a German national literature was certainly being debated.[1] Andrei Ivanovich Turgenev (1781–1803) began translating from the German and practicing his hand at his own poetic compositions as a youth under the guidance of a tutor from Geneva.[2] As a young man who avidly translated German drama, he inspired an interest in German literature in his friends in the Druzheskoe literaturnoe obshchestvo (Friendly Literary

Society), of which he was a founding member and the spiritual leader.[3] His iconoclastic denial was pronounced in a speech in that society, but was it part of a coherent literary and cultural program? If so, whose program was it? And did the speech or program have any influence on the development of Russian criticism concerned with the problem of the national literature— did it help to produce the series of denials that followed?

The Friendly Literary Society has taken a prominent place in the study of Russian literary developments in the first decade of the nineteenth century. The society was founded in January 1801 by Turgenev and Aleksei Fedorovich Merzliakov (1778–1830) as a formal association of a small group of young men who were already joined by ties of family and friendship. Except for the two founders, the remaining initial members were all students at the secondary school for nobles, the *Blagorodnyi pansion*, associated with Moscow University (of which Turgenev's father, Ivan Petrovich, was the director) and included Turgenev's younger brother Aleksandr, his close friend Vasily Zhukovsky, Aleksandr Voeikov, and the Kaisarov brothers, Andrei, Mikhail, and Paisy.[4] Turgenev's aims for the society involved developing the character of its participants according to the sentimental ideal of the *schöne Seele* (beautiful soul) through a deepening of their spiritual bond of friendship, and shared literary activity was the means.[5] Though the official activities of the society lasted for only five months (mid-January to June 1, 1801), the intense atmosphere of mutual criticism and literary exploration made a deep impression on many of the participants. Among them, Vasily Andreevich Zhukovsky (1783–1852) stands out both for the important role he was to play in Russian literary life of the early nineteenth century and for the significant role that the Friendly Literary Society played in his formation. Aleksandr Veselovsky first drew attention to the society and particularly to Andrei Turgenev and his influence in his 1904 literary biography of Zhukovsky.[6] Later studies have shown Andrei Turgenev to be a key figure for understanding the reception of German literature in Russia as well as the Russian melancholy tradition, the formation of the Russian intelligentsia and its many circles, and the development of psychological prose.[7] Furthermore, in a series of studies from the middle of the last century, Yuri Lotman wrote Turgenev and the society into the history of the formation of the Decembrist literary and revolutionary program, especially in relation to the prominent civic function of poetry and the concern with *narodnost'*.[8]

This last point is of particular importance here, in an examination of the articulation of new literary-critical language around the modern concept of the nation. *Narodnost'* was, after all, a new term that belonged not only to Decembrist critical discourse in the 1820s, but also to romantic criticism more broadly (e.g., Viazemsky) and even to various forms of late classicist-influenced criticism (see part III). What specific role, then, did Andrei Turgenev and the society play in the creation of new literary-critical language that began to articulate the role of the national subject (as a locus of identity) in literature? Lotman wrote, "the 'Society' is interesting for the fact that in it, in the moment of its formation, the three leading tendencies of literature in the pre-Pushkin period collided: the trend of dreamy romanticism, linked to the name of Zhukovsky; the trend represented by Merzliakov, alien to noble culture and developing eighteenth-century traditions of democratic literature; and, finally, the trend of Andrei Turgenev and Andrei Kaisarov . . . in the activities of whom there distinctly show through characteristics that prepared [otchetlivo prostupaiut cherty, podgotavlivaiushchie] the literary program of Decembrism."[9] The careful, almost tortured formulation of this last phrase provides thin cover for a difficult problem in Lotman's genealogy. While Lotman readily shows the characteristics of the work of Turgenev and Kaisarov that are analogous to Decembrist discourse, it is far more difficult to demonstrate that the work of Turgenev had any impact on what followed.[10] Andrei Turgenev died tragically of fever at just 21 years of age in 1803, and key texts remained among family papers, unpublished and unexplored until at least the early twentieth century. Andrei Kaisarov also died young, in 1813, in battle with the retreating armies of Napoleon, but he had by then completed not only a dissertation (in Latin) at the University of Göttingen on the need to end serfdom in Russia, but also a study of Slavic mythology, and in addition had served for a few years as professor of Russian language and history at Dorpat University (later Tartu).[11]

The problem for the scholarly study of the literary program of Andrei Turgenev and its place in the development of Russian critical discourse is one of mediation. Aside from speeches, conversations, and letters among friends, how did his ideas and critical formulations circulate more publicly, and in what forms? Certainly, he was not known to the Decembrists themselves as a precursor. In exile after the Decembrist uprising, Wilhelm K. Küchelbecker noted in his diary that the memory of Andrei Turgenev, whom he had never known but whose brothers were his friends, was always particularly dear to him. "I do not know why," he wrote, though he recalled his youthful enthusiasm for Turgenev's 1802 "Elegy."[12] Küchelbecker seems not to have known that his own devastating critique of the elegiac genre in

Portrait of Aleksei F. Merzliakov, by K. Ia. Afanas'ev. An engraving for the volume *Imitations and Translations from Greek and Latin Poets* by A. F. Merzliakov, 2 vols., Moscow, 1825–26. Courtesy of The State Literary Museum, Moscow, Russia.

1824 owed a debt to Turgenev as well. Marc Raeff offers a skeptical view of the scholarly reconstruction of the connections: "The public impact of [the society's] activities at the time was practically nil. . . . Scholars have tried in recent years to situate the group with reference to the literary factions of the time and to draw ideological implications for its role in the pre-history of the Decembrist movement. But it seems to us that this is stretching the evidence."[13]

While the public impact at the moment of the society's activities may indeed have been nil, one can argue that through the mediation of Andrei Turgenev's friends, many of his ideas did in subsequent years play a role in the formation of the 1820s critical discourse on *narodnost'* and the national literature. However, a reexamination of key society documents and their relationship to society figures, both at the time and later, reveals the critical, if sometimes ambiguous, role of Aleksei Merzliakov in mediating Turgenev's literary program to the broader Russian public, and even Merzliakov's more genuine ownership of some of the central ideas of what usually has been taken to be Turgenev's program. This troubles Lotman's careful clarification of lines of development in the attempt to show the "step by step, stage by stage development of Decembrist thought."[14] In fact, in the progress of the cluster of ideas that would coalesce around the term *narodnost'* in the 1820s, one step forward in the first two decades of the century often meant two steps back, as innovative literary-political ideas were advocated by figures who represented conservative politics (Admiral Aleksandr Shishkov) or outdated aesthetic systems (Merzliakov). And Decembrist literary thought owes its debt as much to these figures as to those whose political inclinations more closely resembled their own.[15]

THE "MOST INTERESTING" AMONG the speeches given at the Friendly Literary Society, in the evaluation of its first student, was that of Andrei Turgenev, presented on March 22 or 29, 1801, and entitled "O russkoi literature" ("On Russian Literature").[16] It was published in full in 1912 by A. A. Fomin, who suggested that the speech "could elicit only rapture before the young critic, urgently making of Russian artistic literature a categorical demand—the necessity of *genuine realism and unembellished narodnost'* [narodnosti nichiem ne podkrashennoi]. And this demand was set forth in 1801, when the rule of pseudoclassicism had not yet passed, when sentimentalism reigned and when romanticism was being born and gaining strength!"[17] Lotman had a more sober and rigorous conception of where Turgenev's speech fit into the developing literary trends of the time, but it still represented to him an auger of what was to come. In his treatment, the speech is the key text of Andrei Turgenev's literary program, which distinguishes Turgenev as a precursor to the Decembrists, in contrast to Merzliakov: "The literary program of Andrei Turgenev, in that form in which it appears before us in his speeches at the meetings of the 'Friendly Literary Society,' carries the imprint of Merzliakov's influence; however, it is not equivalent to the perspective of the latter, as it approaches in a whole series of fundamental principles the later statements of the Decembrists."[18] Indeed, it is hard not to read the speech through the lens of the criticism of the 1820s, with its debates over the meaning of romanticism and *narodnost'* and its more familiar rhetoric, which seemed to be precociously prefigured in this isolated document from twenty years earlier. Would such a reading reflect ignorance of the criticism of the two preceding decades, or rather the difficulty of reading the genealogy of the criticism of the 1820s out of the transitional and decidedly mixed critical activity of the preceding decades? A revaluing of values in the early 1820s brought new clarity to the critical landscape—new constellations of values had the modern concept of the nation at their center.[19] If this speech prefigured that clarity, the delicate task of determining how it may have prepared such a revaluing of values is all the more urgent. On the other hand, a necessary step in this analysis will be to return the speech to its own time and context, to a period of hybridization and/or syncretism in literary ideas.[20] One important aspect of this is to remember that the term *narodnost'* was not at all a part of the discussion until the 1820s. Until 1800 the heterogeneous ideas that would coalesce around this abstract term could be thought about together or separately but had not yet entered into a stable relationship around it. Indeed, the introduction of the term *narodnost'* into the discussion played a significant role in the revaluation of values in the 1820s.[21]

Turgenev's speech can be divided into two parts, the first of which treats the question of the existence of Russian literature, while the second considers the future development of Russian literature. Turgenev opens his speech with an ironic questioning of his title: "On Russian literature! Can we use that word? Is it not just an empty title when the thing itself in fact does not exist? French, German, and English literatures exist, but is there a Russian one?"[22] The answer, he implies in what follows, is no, there is no contemporary Russian literature in the sense of a literature that reflects the character of the Russian nation: "Read the English poets and you will see the spirit of the English; the same with the French and Germans, by their works you can judge of the character of their nations [*natsii*], but what can you learn of the Russian nation [*narod*]: reading Lomonosov, Sumarokov, Derzhavin, Kheraskov, and Karamzin, only in Derzhavin will you find tiny shades of the Russian, and in the beautiful tale of Karamzin 'Ilya Muromets' you can also see a Russian title, Russian metrical feet, and nothing more."[23] This opening is, as already noted, the most strikingly prescient moment of Turgenev's speech, anticipating the repeated denials of the Russian national literary tradition in the 1820s and after by such diverse figures as Chaadaev,

Venevitinov, Prince Petr Viazemsky, Aleksandr Bestuzhev, Aleksandr Pushkin, Nikolai Nadezhdin, Nikolai Polevoi, Ivan Kireevsky, and most famously, Belinsky, in 1834. At the same time, it also recalls, explicitly at the end of the speech, the reforms of Peter the Great and the poetic reforms of V. K. Trediakovsky and M. V. Lomonosov in the early eighteenth century. The denial of the Russian cultural tradition was already an old cultural tradition by Turgenev's day. Trediakovsky's and Lomonosov's negations of the previous tradition concerned primarily the lack of a secular poetic tradition, the lack of belles-lettres. Turgenev seems to be the first to make a denial of tradition that refers primarily to the absence of national character, a relatively new concept. The fact that during the next twenty years no one is as explicitly negative does suggest one way in which Turgenev and his fellows in the Friendly Literary Society were out of step with their times: participants long remembered the spirit of frank criticism that ruled in the society (and quickly led to heated disagreements), which contrasts sharply with the spirit of supportive sentimentalist criticism advocated by Karamzin.[24]

Turgenev blames the lack of a national spirit on the imitation of French literature:

> Our theater writers, instead of penetrating the character of the Russian nation, the spirit of Russian antiquity, and finally the individual characters of our ancient heroes, instead of showing us in the theater at least something grand, weighty, and at the same time truly Russian, found that it was much easier, having depicted Moscow and the Kremlin on the scenery, to have some kind of delicate, eloquent Frenchmen carry the action, calling them Truvors and even Minins and Pozharskiis and so forth . . . . We imitate the French; but the French are so original in their tragedies that they turned even the Greeks and Romans into Frenchmen, while we on the other hand lost all the originality [*original'nost'*], all the energy of the Russian spirit.[25]

Turgenev here opposes originality to imitation, or at least to the Russian form of imitation, which embodies the spirit of the nation that is imitated. At the same time, he assigns a kind of originality in imitation to the French, noting that French classicist tragedy is far more French in spirit than Greek or Roman. While Turgenev is interrogating classicist imitation theory here, he does not strictly oppose originality and imitation like writers in the 1820s, who allowed no originality to the French in their form of imitation. But he does at least relativize the value of imitation. He continues, "If we absolutely had to imitate, it seems it would be much more congenial to the spirit of our nation to imitate the English theater rather than the French."[26] Here again, Turgenev anticipates later changes in the dominant models, but this follows naturally from his own immersion in the German theater and particularly his interest in the *Sturm und Drang* and Schiller.[27]

Turgenev concludes the first half of the speech with a pessimistic assessment of the state of Russian literature:

> Now only in tales and songs do we find remnants of Russian literature; in these precious remains, and especially in the songs, we find and still feel the character of our people [*narod*]. They are so strong, so expressive in either their gay or doleful forms that they must have their effect on anyone. In the majority of them, especially the doleful ones, one meets such a captivating melancholy, such beauties of feeling, that we would seek for in vain among our new imitative works. But it is difficult to alter that which, it seems, no one seems even to suspect. At least at the current time there is no hope that someday a true Russian literature would blossom here. For that to happen, we would need to return to Russian originality, from which we grow more distant every day, in our customs, our way of life, and our character.[28]

This passage in particular brings together ideas that would later coalesce around the term *narodnost'*. Caution here is imperative. Like his theater interests, Turgenev's attention to folk song proceeds naturally from his *Sturm und Drang* enthusiasms, from the Herderian concept of *Volkspoesie*, and from the special attention to the melancholy aspect of the songs that was not uncommon in late eighteenth-century Russian criticism, including that of Aleksandr Radishchev. Turgenev was not promoting a simple folklorism, though. Notably, he does not suggest, here or elsewhere, that the imitation of these songs would bring contemporary literature closer to an embodiment of Russianness (pace Mark Azadovsky and Lotman).[29] The final sentence suggests a much more fundamental program for the national literature, anticipating the program of Venevitinov (see chapter 11) or the Slavophiles. But Turgenev does not follow up on this suggestion in what follows—the second half of the speech treats the future of Russian literature from an entirely different angle—so the program of returning to the original Russian way of life and character, along with the nod to folklore, remains nothing but a hint, a mirage that seems to suggest important future Russian ideas but that really has no programmatic content in Turgenev's text.

The nature of the new Russian literature is Turgenev's topic in the second half of his speech, both as it exists and as it ought to be. The discussion centers on Karamzin. Turgenev poses the question of whether the new century will be more abundant with writers than the last and replies, "Perhaps it will, but judging from the direction of our literature, might one not think that we will have more excellent writers of trifles and that Karamzin is to blame for this? . . . Karamzin has initiated a new era in our literature in spite of the Russian character and climate."[30] Turgenev grants the role of literary revolutionary to Karamzin, but argues that his revolution is counter to the natural one that should have taken place. Turgenev's organic conception of literary development requires that the literary tree grow with weighty and serious genres before the decoration of lighter genres appears: "He [Karamzin] inclined us too much toward softness and delicacy. He should have appeared a century later, when we would already have more compositions in more serious genres; then let him weave his flowers in the fatherland's oaks and laurels."[31] One should note the fact that Turgenev's scheme of development requires the orderly embodiment of a proper Enlightenment hierarchy of genres and styles.[32] He critiques some of the same features of Karamzin's poetry as Admiral Shishkov and his allies would, though not from the same basis. He does not deny any place in Russian culture to features of French salon culture and its related literary phenomena, literary nothings and the refined language of high society. In fact, he would welcome it, at the proper time. But the problem is that Karamzin's excellent example has led budding writers away from the weightier work of the higher genres. Karamzin's untimeliness relegates him to a lower place in literary history than his talent deserves: "Considering the general development of enlightenment and especially of literature as a whole, one has to admit that Kheraskov has done more for us than Karamzin," for Kheraskov, while "not deserving special reverence and fame," as a writer of epics "contributed to the successes of our Literature in a good direction, having prepared the way."[33]

Turgenev's requirements of high, serious genres and manly, patriotic expression in literature also seem to align him with the aesthetic program of Shishkov and his allies that would very soon follow. As Boris Gasparov has observed, the grandiose and heroic had also been enjoying a revival in Republican France since the 1790s, with a revived neo-classical aesthetic, different from the earlier classicism in its archaic tendencies and its suffusion with Roman republican and imperial imagery, that also included a critique of the affectedness of the previous period.[34] In Russia, archaist allies of Shishkov like Semen Bobrov made use of intense metaphorical language, often with irrational imagery, allegory, and eschatological ideas in an aesthetic that had as much in common with pre-romanticism as with the classical genre system they espoused.[35] But Turgenev's own poetic practice was free from this type of archaism and the influence of Lomonosov's grandiose odic style. Even in Turgenev's "K otechestvu" ("To the Fatherland"), which was published in *Vestnik Evropy* (*Herald of Europe*) in 1802 and became one of the most popular patriotic poems of the first decade of the nineteenth century,[36] the patriotic-declamatory genre is expressed smoothly, in clear metaphors and in Russian free from any Church Slavonic "archaic" admixtures. In this speech, too, Turgenev recommends a less elegant style only as a temporary means to an end: "Let Russian writers continue to write worse [than Karamzin] and not so interestingly, but only let them undertake more important subjects, write more originally, more seriously, and not only conforming to trivial genres, let them mix the ugly, Gigantic, and extraordinary with the great; one can assume that it would be purified little by little."[37]

Having raised the specter of Admiral Shishkov and his long-running critique of Karamzin and his followers, which was to begin just two years later with the publication of Shiskov's *Rassuzhdenie o starom i novom sloge rossiiskogo iazyka* (*Discourse on the Old and New Style in the Russian Language*), one might speculate on a possible link between this critique (the subject of chapter 3) and Turgenev's. Shishkov's critique was provoked by, among other things, Karamzin's article in *Vestnik Evropy* in 1802 entitled "Otchego v Rossii malo avtorskikh talantov?" ("Why Are There So Few Talented Authors in Russia?") in which Karamzin outlined his program for Russia's language and literature, openly modeled on French literature and the culture of the salon. Perhaps there are reasons to consider the possibility that Karamzin's programmatic article might have been prompted, in its turn, by Turgenev's speech. This is necessarily speculative, because unambiguous documentary evidence of any contact on this point is lacking. But Karamzin was an acquaintance of the Turgenev family, if no longer an intimate of Ivan Petrovich Turgenev's Masonic circle in the late 1790s, and was always interested in the views of the younger generation. Andrei Ivanovich recorded only one instance in his diary of a visit by Karamzin to the Turgenev home after the family's return to Moscow in 1796, in a note made on November 22, 1799.[38] Still, in a letter to his father on December 15, 1801 (this now nine months *after* his speech in the society), Turgenev asked his father to "tell [him], when you see Nik[olai] Mikh[ailovich] Karamz[in], that there are few people who could love him as much as I. As an author I love him no less than others; but I also love him just as much because I have known him and loved him since childhood; and when I think of those years, I always remember him as well, how he used to visit us for example, and how I always loved to listen to him; with what indescribable impatience I used to await each new issue of his journal, to which you yourself were witness; in a word, my heart belonged to him [k nemu lezhalo]; . . . and I will always, always respect and love him, as an author and a person."[39] This could be just another in a series of ecstatic texts addressed to Karamzin that alternated with doubts about his more recent work, but it could also be damage control if Andrei Ivanovich had reason to believe that his criticism of Karamzin's role in Russian literature had somehow reached the author. Unlike the other exalted expressions of admiration, Turgenev in this instance actually asked his father to pass his sentiments along to Karamzin.[40]

Karamzin's article, moreover, could be taken as a kind of general response to Turgenev's doubts. Turgenev asked whether the next century would be as abundant with writers as the last and answered that if it were, those writers might be writers of mere trifles and that Karamzin was to blame for that, for having led Russian literature against the Russian character and climate. Karamzin's article addresses a closely related question—why there are so few authorial talents in Russia—and answers that it is not the climate or the government but the fact that French rather than Russian is spoken in Russian salons.[41] Still, Karamzin does not respond directly to Turgenev's critique, to the role of light genres in the general scheme of development of Russian literature, but notes the obstacles to the formation of just such genres. Admiral Shishkov would direct attention publicly to the modeling of Russian literature on French salon literature and how doubtful a method this was of creating a truly national literature, and the debate between Shishkov's archaists and Karamzin's innovators would dominate the Russian literary landscape for the first decade and a half of the century. There is some reason to believe that Turgenev's speech might have played a small role in initiating this prominent development, which began to draw the modern concept of the nation into Russian metaliterary discourse, transforming that discourse.

Such speculation aside, though, there are demonstrable ways in which Turgenev's speech, through the mediation of his society cohorts, contributed to the development of a discourse on the national literature in Russia. Raeff notes that "the 'canonization' of Andrei Turgenev started immediately upon his unexpected death" and that "his brother Alexander Turgenev and his close friends A. Kaisarov and V. Zhukovskii were most active in creating the 'myth' of his life and role." Even more importantly, Raeff cogently observes that "Andrei . . . was far from perfect and far from truly having found his identity at the time of his death. His friends turned his expectation of identification into actuality, and thus the promise of his existence became the myth of his life."[42] His brother and friends each remain true to and reify an Andrei of their own imagination and literary inclinations. It can be argued that the one who takes the most from the program of the speech "On Russian Literature" and mediates it to the larger public is not among those named by Raeff, but is Turgenev's close friend and co-founder of the Friendly Literary Society, Aleksei Merzliakov.

This argument requires one to return the speech to its most immediate context, the literary quarrels of the Friendly Literary Society. In fact, the germ of Turgenev's speech was planted in a discussion that preceded the formal activities of the society, toward the end of a period when Turgenev, Merzliakov, and Zhukovsky undertook a number of literary projects together, including a deliberate exchange of correspondence and plans to publish a collection of works under the pseudonym M. Zh. T.[43] In a diary entry on December 20, 1800, Andrei Turgenev recorded the following: "This evening we three: M[erzliakov], Zh[ukovsky], and I, had a most interesting conversation: It began by M[erzliakov] or Zh[ukovsky] asking whether the next century would be just as abundant or more abundant with writers. We gave our opinions: I thought that their number would be greater, but noted that, perhaps, there would be more excellent writers of trifles and that Karamzin is at fault. Merzliakov and I: He should have appeared a century or two later. . . ."[44] What follows in the diary entry is nearly the entire text of the second half of Turgenev's later speech.[45] Clearly, then, the opinions expressed in Turgenev's speech are not his alone, but his and Merzliakov's as developed in dialogue with Zhukovsky. The speech remains Turgenev's, but one needs to relativize the conception of the degree to which it represents his program in particular.

For Lotman, this is a defining speech for Turgenev's program, and while he allows that it "carries the imprint of Merzliakov's influence"—he notes the diary entry—he also wants to distinguish between Turgenev and Merzliakov in relation to the future Decembrist literary program.[46] In particular, Lotman wants to assign to Turgenev the critique of Karamzin, because it prefigures the Decembrist critique of the elegy as practiced by Karamzin's followers, with Zhukovsky in the lead. To this end, Lotman consistently exaggerates Turgenev's hostility to Karamzin. But the diary entry and speech are witness to a different dynamic. The two most significant textual additions made by Turgenev from the diary to the speech represent additional qualification of the argument in relation to Karamzin. The first characterizes his critique as "doubts and guesses," advanced only "to elicit your opinions," while the second, in addition to suggesting that the harm caused by Karamzin may exist only in his imagination, actually places the explicit blame on Karamzin's blind followers rather than on Karamzin himself.[47] If anything, Turgenev seems to be further moderating here between Merzliakov's more strident criticism of Karamzin and the sensibilities of his listeners, including Zhukovsky, an intermediary role that he seemed to play more generally for his two closest friends, who themselves were never close without him.[48] Turgenev certainly had his doubts about Karamzin and especially his more recent poetic work, but these doubts were expressed alongside deep respect for his early poetry, fascination with each new volume of his *Pis'ma russkogo puteshestvennika* (*Letters of a Russian Traveler*), and hardly suppressed anxiety over how Karamzin would receive his own poetry.[49] As Mariia Virolainen has suggested, "the literary activity of An. Turgenev can be seen as a peculiar Karamzinism: not as an epigonic following of Karamzin, but rather as a striving to overcome his tradition and lead Russian literature to other shores. In that striving to overcome, the work of Karamzin always remained for him that unavoidable milestone by which, in constantly looking back upon it, one could determine what distance had been covered, what new spiritual space gained."[50] In this, Turgenev resembles Zhukovsky; in his mediation between Merzliakov and Zhukovsky in general he often appears to be closer to the latter. In a letter to Zhukovsky on December 15, 1801, he exclaimed, "We were born for each other. I love Merzliakov a lot . . . but it's not the same as you and me! So many correspondences in our characters!"[51]

Even the opinions in the first half of Turgenev's speech cannot be assigned to him alone. The one section of the diary entry that does not form part of the second half of the speech is the following, which comes after the decidedly mixed praise for Kheraskov's work in the epic genre: "The same with the theater! Sumarokov spoiled it, making Olegs and Sviatopolks and other Russian heroes speak the delicate language of Racine's Gallo-Greek heroes. To plunge into the imitation of German theater would not correct that. It's the same evil, just from the other direction. These are two crooked roads: the middle one—straight and true—has not been cleared."[52] Is this not the kernel of the first half of the speech, where to Sumarokov's name there have been added four others (including Karamzin) who failed to reflect the Russian character as well? And where the Russian theater comes up for particular criticism? This, too, derives ultimately from the shared position of Turgenev and Merzliakov, though Turgenev gets credit for elaborating it and clothing it in a most appealing rhetorical formulation. And this is the root of the "demand for *narodnost'*" (*avant la lettre*) that makes Turgenev (but not

Merzliakov) a precursor to the Decembrists for Lotman.

But for whom is such a point of view really programmatic? One expects central, programmatic ideas to be repeated, but if one looks through Turgenev's diaries and letters and other speeches and society documents, one does not really find additional statements that notably contribute to defining the constellation of problems that would later be discussed through the term *narodnost'* or activities that respond to that aspect of the supposed program of his speech. In arguing elsewhere that the idea of an independent national literature was one of the leading principles of the Friendly Literary Society, but that each member had his own approach, the only evidence Lotman can muster for Turgenev aside from this speech is Turgenev's later interest in Shakespeare and a comment he made in a letter to Zhukovsky about an anachronism he found in one of Merzliakov's folk song imitations, to which he exclaimed, "Shakespeare all over!" (*tochnyi Shekspir!*).[53] No doubt Turgenev expresses his own opinion, as well as that of Merzliakov, in his speech—his formulation speaks to his own work of analysis, particularly regarding the lack of a Russian spirit in the literary heritage.[54] But one wonders how deeply he held the opinion that follows, also key to any reading that would connect this to later discussions of *narodnost'*, an opinion that makes of folk songs and tales the only true Russian literature and recommends a return to a more genuine Russian character. The additional evidence outside this speech is so slim as to be ambiguous. And yet the *potential* program of this speech is consistently assigned to him and to him alone in the critical tradition.

For Merzliakov, on the other hand, the evidence is clear. One of his own speeches in the society, given in early May 1801 (perhaps on the 4th), entitled "O trudnostiakh ucheniia" ("On the Difficulties of Education"), reiterates the problem of the national spirit in literature, which he sees as derived from the forms of Russian education. Educated in foreign languages, the Russian "loses his own spirit, the spirit of his language; he writes in French or German, and in Russian he is forever deprived of the true part of an original [lishaetsia navsegda istinnoi chasti originala]." This is particularly true in relation to Russian nobles. "They will tell me that a prudent attention to the beauties of foreigners can avoid such vices—I don't know. Let's imagine a Russian [*predstavim russkogo*]—we do not yet have our own models in all genres of composition; all of our writers are born, so to speak, in a French library; when we are not yet capable of judging either our own or foreign works they place foreign books into our hands; foreigners bring us up; from the catechism to the calendar, everything is in a foreign language. Tell me, what will remain in them of the Russian?"[55] Moreover, Merzliakov's poetic activity demonstrates his interest in folkloric models. Between 1803 and 1806 he actively worked on composing songs that were based on models from the folk collections of the serf composer D. N. Kashin, and in 1808 in a work entitled "O dukhe, otlichitel'nikh svoistvakh poezii pervobytnoi i o vliianii, kotoroe imela ona na nravy, na blagodenstvie narodov" ("On the Spirit and Distinguishing Characteristics of Primitive Poetry and on the Influence It Had on the Mores and Prosperity of Nations"), he called others to their use as models: "Oh, what treasures we deprive ourselves of! In Russian songs we would see Russian customs [*nravy*] and feelings, Russian justice, Russian valor—in them we would love ourselves again and not be ashamed of our so-called primitive barbarism. But from time to time our songs are being lost, corrupted, spoiled, and finally they entirely give way to the brilliant trifles of foreign troubadours. Will we really never see again anything similar to the incomparable song of Igor?"[56]

Again, elsewhere Lotman allows that, in the question of *narodnost'*, Merzliakov was Turgenev's mentor.[57] So why not give Merzliakov his due as a precursor to the Decembrist literary program? Why assign him to the "trend, alien to noble culture and developing eighteenth-century traditions of democratic literature"?[58] Because the myth of Andrei Turgenev by the 1820s was the romantic one of a young author who represented a promising future for Russian poetry, but whose life was cut off too soon, while the reputation of Merzliakov was that of an author and critic who could not keep up with the rapidly changing times. Turgenev represents the progressive romantic trend; Merzliakov stands for stagnation, the eighteenth century, classicism.[59] These myths are built on the public work of Merzliakov in the decades following the breakup of the Friendly Literary Society and the unfortunate lack of such work from Turgenev, whose service responsibilities hindered his literary activity in the last two years of his life. But it should be noted that one of Turgenev's major publications in that period, the "Elegy" he published in *Vestnik Evropy* in 1802, helped to found (with Zhukovsky) the next stage in the poetry of Karamzin's followers, work that the Decembrist critics found necessary to reject in the name of national literature and *narodnost'*—in this way, it completely failed to further the presumed program of his speech. Whereas if one examines the work of Merzliakov one will find both foundation for the myth of his stagnant classicism as well as clear evidence that he continued the program of Turgenev's speech—a program that belongs as fully to him as to Turgenev—so that whatever effect that speech had on the formation of a Russian critical discourse on the national literature (a discourse that was developed by romantic and classicist-influenced criticism as well as Decembrist criticism) is attributable in significant measure to Merzliakov's mediation.

Students of Merzliakov's criticism agree that Merzliakov advanced critical ideas but that the impact of his advances is muted by his strict adherence to classicist critical terminology and by his failure to treat in his criticism the most recent trends in Russian poetry, including the work of Zhukovsky and later Pushkin.[60] They also agree that the major features of his critical program were formed in the Friendly Literary Society.[61] In fact, there is a kind of will to repeat that is manifested in Merzliakov's criticism. In a letter to Andrei Turgenev in Petersburg, Andrei Kaisarov complained that for a speech for his new literary society, Merzliakov had simply copied a speech he had made in the Friendly Literary Society.[62] Merzliakov himself explicitly connected his criticism to the society—his series of seven articles in 1815 dedicated to a critique of Kheraskov's epic *Rossiada* is cast as a letter addressed to a friend recalling "our thoughts on the *Rossiada* from those days . . . in memory of our priceless discussions."[63] This seems sure to refer to discussions that were behind Andrei Turgenev's speech, with its acknowledgment of the importance of Kheraskov's work in cultivating the epic combined with a real ambivalence regarding its poetic value. Filipp Dziadko has suggested that if Zhukovsky remained true to the memory of his friend Andrei Turgenev, the elegiac poet, Merzliakov commemorated his friend by propagating his legacy as the author of the speech "On Russian literature"—each thus recalling the place in which their own programs touched most closely on that of their deceased friend.[64] The articles on the *Rossiada* are not the place to look for echoes of the literary program suggested by Turgenev's speech, though. Merzliakov's criticisms are not directed toward a more national treatment of the epic but toward "rules" regarding formal characteristics such as the treatment of heroic characters and mythological elements.[65]

One place where the literary program of the speech does, surprisingly, appear is in Merzliakov's sustained engagement with the classicist theory of imitation—recall Turgenev's comparison of the Russian form of imitation in the theater, which brought with it a French spirit, to that of the more original French form of imitation, which made Frenchmen out of Greek and Roman characters. Merzliakov returned to the topic of imitation already in his early May speech in the society: "To the ancients the model was nature; for the moderns the ancients replace nature. Follow them! as the proud critics say, looking down from safe balconies on the boiling sea of thinking worms. But a question: in what exactly to imitate the ancients, who are distant from us in customs, life, mores, and government? Where are its limits? The rules for the imitation of the ancients are particularly difficult to write, and even more difficult to follow."[66] These reflections are followed by the problem of the Russian form of education, cited earlier. What links these thoughts is the problem of national authenticity.

After completing his doctorate in 1805, Merzliakov stayed on at the university—as professor of Russian eloquence and poetry (Rossiiskoe krasnorechie i poeziia)—where he became the first to make Russian literature a separate subject at the university.[67] In addition to his published literary criticism, he also gave a series of public lectures on the theory of aesthetics, which are notable for their engagement with theories of imitation. Merzliakov continued the difficult task of trying to write the rules of imitation. In his 1812 lecture "Ob iziashchnom, ili o vybore v podrazhanii" ("On the Beautiful, or on Selection in Imitation"), Merzliakov defined poetry as "an imitation in harmonious style . . . of everything that nature can have that is delightful or touching."[68] Nature is defined broadly as being made up of four worlds: "the existing or real world, that is physical, moral [*nravstvennyi*], and civic [*grazhdanskii*] . . . the historical world . . . next the mythological world . . . and finally, the ideal or possible world."[69] Limiting the artist to imitating such a broadly defined nature imposes few constraints: "[G]enius has no other limits in its riches aside from the limits of the universe," and artists therefore have at their disposal "countless treasures."[70]

The treasures of nature can be studied not only directly, though, but also through the work of other artists. Merzliakov used the same language of "treasures," as already seen, in promoting Russian songs (folk songs in a broad sense similar to Herder's concept of *Volkspoesie*—Merzliakov refers explicitly to the twelfth-century Igor tale) in 1808: "Oh, what treasures we deprive ourselves of!" And he would use it in an article on the current state of Russian literature in 1812 to suggest other models as well: "French literature no doubt has been raised to the highest degree of perfection, but the French themselves imitated; at the same time, in their imitations they adapted to their own time, to their own taste, so inconstant, and to their circumstances, so various! Why should not we, for the preservation of our own character and honor, not draw upon pure, unchanging treasures from that same hoard from which they drew? Why should we not make direct use of the precepts of their teachers, the Greeks and Romans?"[71] Both here and in the recommendation to draw upon the treasure of Russian songs, Merzliakov clearly echoes the program of Turgenev's speech in its concern for an authentic national character in Russian literature.

Such concerns are muted by the general tendency toward defining rules in Merzliakov's public lecture, where he also considers the question of literary models:

> The physical descriptions of Homer are just as delightful today as they were three thousand years ago; his depiction of character, the art with which he created them . . . arouses our admiration to this day: nothing has become dated, nothing changed. But the details related to opinions and decorum, the delights of fashion and propriety must, naturally, seem good or bad according to time and place, for there is not one century, not one land that has not considered its own mores as holy rules. . . . One who imitates only the ancients in everything is sure to offend the taste of his own age in many things. One who takes direction only from the tastes of his own age often binds himself to light, superficial beauties [*krasoty*], specters of beauty. He neglects refined beauty [*krasota iziashchnogo*]. From the combination of these two teachings, that is ancient and modern taste, derives a solid and true taste and all success in art.[72]

The concern with the historical relativism of taste here is not connected to national individuality and a desire to embody it, as it was elsewhere. Ultimately, Merzliakov's public concern with aesthetic rules—of imitation, of genre—made him a natural target for opponents of classicist aesthetics in the 1820s, opponents such as his own Moscow University students, V. F. Odoevsky and Venevitinov.[73] Still, Merzliakov continued to pursue his version of the program of Turgenev's speech well into the second decade of the century—another instance will be examined in chapter 7.

Andrei Turgenev's speech "On Russian Literature," given in the Friendly Literary Society in March 1801, is a remarkable document that indeed influenced the direction of Russian criticism toward a more nationally oriented paradigm. Andrei Ivanovich himself was a tragic, romantic figure who was long remembered by his friends as a literary leader with progressive literary ideas. One can understand the tendency to credit him for whatever seems most advanced of the Friendly Literary Society's activities and programs. Aleksei Merzliakov is a more ambiguous figure. In the 1820s, he had clearly fallen behind the times as a critic and was attacked as a representative of classicist aesthetics. But in 1830, in the year of his death, an edition of his *Songs and Romances* was printed, and his imitations of folk songs, which had been written over two decades earlier, were finally recognized by such prominent critics as Nadezhdin and Belinsky as a significant contribution to Russian poetry, and particularly to its *narodnost'*.[74] Belinsky later also recognized Merzliakov's contribution as a critic, allowing that "with Merzliakov a new period in Russian criticism began." He wrote, "as an aesthetician and critic Merzliakov deserves particular attention and respect. . . . His times are to blame for his errors; his virtues belong to him alone. That is why his theoretical and critical essays are still pleasant to read."[75]

One should join Belinsky in recognizing Merzliakov's merits. In many ways, Turgenev's speech belongs most fully to Merzliakov as a literary program. Merzliakov had pursued, if in a sometimes muted fashion, the program of that speech—in his work as a professor of Russian literature at Moscow University, in his public lectures, and in his published literary criticism—and had given it to Russian critical discourse in a way that prepared the debates of the 1820s. Objectively, Merzliakov did far more than Andrei Turgenev himself or Andrei Kaisarov, and perhaps not so much less than Zhukovsky, to prepare the "revaluing of values" that occurred in Russian criticism in the 1820s, for the influence of Turgenev's speech on Russian critical discourse is mediated in multiple ways by Merzliakov.[76] This conclusion muddles the clear lines of development outlined by Yuri Lotman in an attempt to clarify the often contradictory, transitional, and mixed literary groupings, political allegiances, and literary critical stances of the first two decades of the nineteenth century. The analysis presented in the present work relies in many ways on Lotman's clarifications, but demonstrates once again that literary developments in such a period often proceed in a nonlinear fashion, through back doors and unexpected genealogical lines. Yuri Tynianov had already taught that lesson using the example of the alliance of "younger archaists" like Küchelbecker (a Decembrist revolutionary) with the circle around Admiral Shishkov. One can argue that Merzliakov's positive contribution to the development of a literary critical discourse on the national literature presents itself as a similar and related paradox, only comprehensible in the context of a transitional period of literary and political alliances.

When one looks again at Andrei Turgenev's speech in its context, one sees that the literary program of that speech is as unfinished and unperfected as Andrei himself. While certain moments of the speech seem to prefigure important critical ideas that would appear decades later, in reality, those moments are rather vague and unformed. The fact that Andrei Kaisarov, Zhukovsky, Merzliakov, and Andrei's brother Aleksandr all pursed rather different directions, yet all considered themselves to be true to Andrei, suggests how open his supposed program was to different realizations. It is hard to answer such fundamental questions as, how does Turgenev conceive of the Russian nation, or, what constitutes a national literature for him and how can Russian writers pursue a more national literature. The iconoclastic question in his speech is really only an opening to the formation of a discourse on the national literature that would take decades to develop, but that would restate that iconoclastic doubt in more fully formed, programmatic terms. His speech, through the activities of his friends, did indeed give impetus to the formation of critical ideas on the national literature. But to read it through the lens of the later critical term *narodnost'* is to give it a coherence and sense that it did not have. There is no *narodnost' avant la lettre*.

3 The Roots of the Russian Language and Literature

The center of literary development in the first decade of the nineteenth century in Russia was a divided realm, split between two warring noble camps. Admiral Aleksandr S. Shishkov (1754–1841) initiated the polemics with his 1803 *Rassuzhdenie o starom i novom sloge rossiiskogo iazyka*, an attack on the style of the "new" school, understood by all at the time to refer to the followers of Nikolai M. Karamzin.[1] Shishkov had been provoked by Karamzin's article in 1802, "Otchego v Rossii malo avtorskikh talantov?" ("Why Are There So Few Talented Authors in Russia?"), to compose a lengthy reply and rebuttal that initiated a long and all-encompassing debate on the Russian literary language.[2] Karamzin himself slowly made his exit from the literary stage during the first decade of the new century, and the leadership of the "new" school fell to the rising talent Zhukovsky, Andrei Turgenev's friend, whose own poetry and translations marked him as the most original of the adherents of Karamzinian aesthetics. The change of leadership was marked most concretely by Zhukovsky's inheritance of the editorship of Karamzin's leading journal, *Vestnik Evropy*, in 1808.

Debates over the Russian literary language were not new to the nineteenth century. The question of what principle the literary language should follow—

whether it should be based on the most contemporary usage of educated Russian circles or whether it should continue to maintain some kind of relationship to the medieval Church Slavonic literary language—had been vigorously debated in the mid-eighteenth century. But by the beginning of the nineteenth century, the question had still not been entirely resolved and practices varied widely, while the perceived need for a more unified literary language began to be more pressing. In Shishkov's tract and the debates that followed it, the polemical arsenal of the mid-eighteenth century was frequently redeployed, giving a clichéd aspect to the polemics as each side— Shishkov and his archaist allies versus Zhukovsky and the innovators—took up the banner of particular word-signs from the older debates in order to mark off its position from the other side.[3] On the other hand, what was at stake in the new debates went far beyond which principle should guide literary linguistic practice, and included questions of new genres and the genre system, approaches to criticism, and the professional aspect of literary practice.[4] One of the more important new aspects was the question of national tradition. This chapter explores how Shishkov connected the problem of language and style to national identity and national literature.

Karamzin published his article, outlining his program for Russian literature, in *Vestnik Evropy.* Karamzin is open in modeling his program on French literature, and in particular, the elite, salon-centered literary language and forms from the pre-revolutionary period. Authorial taste and elegance of expression are the primary goals, goals which could be met only through the refining work of the literary salon: "All French authors that serve as models of refinement and pleasantness of style *revised,* so to speak, their school rhetoric in the beau monde, observing what pleases it and why."[5] Russian authors should do the same: "A Russian *candidate for authorship,* dissatisfied with books, should close them and listen to the conversations around him in order to perfect his knowledge of the language. But here is a new misfortune: in the best homes here they speak mostly in French! The charming women to whom one should only have to listen in order to embellish a novel or comedy with courteous, felicitous expressions, captivate us with non-Russian phrases."[6] This is a major obstacle to the development of an author's talent. The social structure on which the culture of refinement and taste was to be built is absent in reality. Karamzin proposes overcoming the problem with words, creating the illusion of this reality by producing the same effect in language through authorial work: "What remains for the author to do? Invent, compose expressions; divine the best selection of words; give some new meaning to the old, present them in new combinations, but so artfully as to fool the readers and hide from them the unusualness of the expressions!"[7] Perhaps, then, the social reality will follow its simulacrum and the beau monde will take up the newly refined Russian language in their daily life: "The French write as they speak, but Russians, on many topics, still ought to speak as a man of talent writes."[8] Karamzin had no illusions about the difficulty of performing such a task, but he recommended it as the way for Russian writers to begin to produce a literature and a Russian culture that could compare with that of France—in fact, this programmatic article in many ways describes a program he had already put into place years before, and it had already accomplished many of his goals.

For Shishkov, the orientation toward French literature and culture was anathema, especially since pre-revolutionary culture had led ultimately to the revolution, which repulsed him entirely. The pathos of his later attempts to politically, morally, and religiously discredit and even denounce his opponents is barely hidden under the surface of his first treatise. The enthusiasm for French culture and French books is repeatedly described as an infection (*zaraza*) and those who have it as infected.[9] On the second page he emphasizes the influence of the Greek language and especially of the church fathers on the Church Slavonic language, the abandonment of which (the church along with the language) he sees being advocated by the French school. He warns, by way of not warning, of the moral dangers presented by French literature: "I refrain from saying that a young person, like a helmsman guiding a boat, ought to enter into the reading of French books with great care in order not to strike the purity of his morals upon a stone in that sea full of danger; I simply say, considering literature: what benefit will reading foreign books bring them when they do not read their own?"[10] He observes, and lets the reader draw the implications, that his ideal model Lomonosov "wrote for people who love their language and not for those who do not read anything Russian and who favor neither their language, their customs, nor their fatherland."[11] And, perhaps most tellingly, in one place he already employs the apocalyptic language that he and his allies would develop so decisively in the years of war with France: "When Lomonosov wrote that [something concerning infelicitous calques from other languages], that infection did not have such strength, and thus he could say: *they sneak in imperceptibly;* but now one would have to say: they have broken in forcibly and flood our language like the biblical flood (*potop zemliu*)."[12] At this point, however, such an ideological apparatus is secondary to the linguistic and literary argument. Only in later repetitions of his argument does he spell out the ideological implications the matter had always had for him.

Shishkov's language argument has two pillars, one of which was a throwback soon shown to be false (and felt by most to be false at the time), while the other was quite innovative. Shishkov held that the Church Slavonic language and the Russian language were one and the same language or, at most, differed as dialects within the same language. While this may have been functionally true in medieval Russia, when the two languages served as a single language system—a situation of diglossia—in the modern Russian linguistic consciousness the Russian and Slavonic languages had long been perceived as distinct.[13] Even Shishkov's primary authority in questions of language and style, Lomonosov, though he also refers to the two as dialects, emphasized the appropriation by the Russian language of elements of the Slavonic language rather than the simultaneous use of both dialects as a single language system.[14] Developments in Slavic linguistics by the middle of the second decade of the century would demonstrate the falsity of Shishkov's thesis.[15] However, the other pillar of Shishkov's argument was strikingly innovative: an exploration of the national specificity of language as a cultural organism through a comparative analysis of word semantics. Shishkov used Russian and French to demonstrate the non-correspondence of word semantics between the two languages (and, by implication, any two languages), especially in derived and abstracted meanings. These semantic differences mark organic cultural differences (with Shishkov making great use of the organic metaphor of a tree growing up out of word roots) that are related to the culture's historical development and particular characteristics. He asks, "Can two nations in the formation of their language have identical thoughts and rules?" and his answer is definitive: "Each nation has its own speech structure and its own articulation of concepts, and therefore must express them in its own words and not foreign ones or those borrowed from foreign ones."[16] This is a theory of national language that goes beyond Herder's generalizations and anticipates, in primitive but identifiable ways, later romantic linguistic theories like those of Wilhelm von Humboldt.[17]

In his analysis of word semantics, Shishkov represents a word with its multiple meanings as a series of concentric circles. In the center is the basic word meaning—in his example, "*svet*," the basic meaning is rays coming from a light source. Metaphorical and abstract extensions of the basic meaning are represented by the additional concentric rings around the small circle in the center—here, the additional meanings of "*svet*" as "world" and "high society" as well as, in the phrase "*svet khristov*," the sense of "precepts proceeding from Christ's wisdom."[18] In Shishkov's other metaphor for word semantics, the basic word becomes the root of a word tree: "The lineage of a word is similar to a tree; for just as a young tree, arising from a root, extends from itself various branches . . . so too an original word [*pervonachal'noe slovo*] at first denotes some single main notion, and then many others spring forth and become established from it."[19] When one compares two words from two different national languages, then, what can be said about their circles of meaning? Shishkov observes that they never coincide and, moreover, insists that they are never concentric. He does not appeal to the organic metaphor at this point, but it is clear that words in different languages spring from different roots, and thus the centering points of words in different languages have to be different. Similar words from two different languages always present themselves as intersecting circles, with the shared meanings in the overlapping section and the meanings unique to each language in the part of the circles that do not overlap. Shishkov's example is the French verb "toucher" and the Russian "trogat'." They overlap in the literal sense of touching, "*toucher avec les mains, trogat' rukami*," but each verb has additional senses that are not found in the counterpart. In French one can "*toucher le clavicin*" but in Russian one must use the verb *igrat'*. Likewise, in Russian one can "*tronut'sia s mesta*" while in French one must use the verb *partir*.[20]

The conclusions to be drawn from this non-correspondence of languages are far-reaching and involve matters of style as well as the natural sources of a national literature. In general, Shishkov views the language practice of what he calls the "new style" as an attempt to recreate the Russian language on the model of the French: "But to desire to arrange the Russian language in the French manner, or to explain oneself with the same words or expressions in Russian as the French explain themselves in their language, is that not the same as to desire that each circle of meaning of a Russian word be equal to the circle of meaning of the corresponding French word?" Such a desire is vain and counter to the nature of languages according to Shishkov, and as such, is simply laughable. "But isn't that exactly what we do when, instead of a pitiful sight [*zhalkoe zrelishche*], we say touching scene [*trogatel'naia stsena*], instead of a change of government [*peremena pravleniia*], revolution [*perevorot*]; instead of approach the center [*sblizhit' k sredine*], concentrate [*sosredotochit'*] and so on?"[21] The formation of new words and phrases on French models is an improper means of extending a word's meaning for Shishkov. And this impropriety goes not only against the nature of language, but also against the nature of proper government. Shishkov's ideological argument shimmers beneath the surface in all such examples. The Russian verb *trogat'* was the example on which Shishkov made the argument about circles of meaning, but it was never a neutral example as it was also a key term in Karamzinian poetics. Shishkov here links it implicitly to "*perevorot*," or revolution.

This example of Shishkov's is an excellent one on which to reiterate the fact that the stylistic debates he initiated redeployed the polemical arsenal of the mid-eighteenth-century debates on the literary language in order to discuss new questions. The verb "trogat'" was first used in the sense in which Shishkov critiques it here by Sumarokov, and both Trediakovsky and Lomonosov critiqued and parodied this usage.[22] But Shishkov has a new national ideology of language. For him, a word's meaning is a part of its cultural history, and for the Russian language, the key source is the Slavonic language: "The ancient Slavonic language, father of many dialects, is the root and origin of the Russian language."[23] The expansion of a word's meaning is a process that must be an organic growth from these roots. Shishkov is trying to control semiotic processes that he clearly does not trust. The idea that an author can and should create new meaning in a willful way runs counter to Shishkov's conception of true language processes. In his running commentary on Karamzin's article (beginning on page 119), he naturally is baffled by Karamzin's recommendations:

> I do not understand at all what this art of deceiving readers consists of, and what need there is to present expressions in new combinations? Great writers invent, embellish, enrich the language with new concepts; but "to present expressions in new combinations," it seems to me, cannot mean anything but to arrange our phrases according to the character and mould of a foreign language, thinking that newness, pleasantness, and enrichment consists in that. If we are going to think in that way, then why do we complain that French is spoken everywhere in Russia? It's better to speak French than to write in French with the Russian language.[24]

For Shishkov, great authors invent *concepts,* not phrases. Invention of phrases is mere playing with words, which is dangerous in that it severs the language from its grounding. Phrases are given in the literary tradition, in books. Shishkov wants the literary tradition as well as common sense to govern the processes of language enrichment, as he explains most clearly in his commentary on the word *vkus* (taste):

> In the same manner, the word *vkus* is used sometimes in its original meaning, that is, it indicates a feeling differentiating ingested things; and sometimes in meanings derived from similarity to this, that is, it indicates selectivity or a

calling to distinguish the elegance of things. *In the latter meaning we do not find the word anywhere in our ancient books.* Our ancestors said, instead of *imet' vkus* (to have taste), *tolk vedat'* (to ken sense), *silu znat'* (to know the sense). Then, from the German *Geschmack* the word *smak* came to us; and finally, reading French books, we began to use the word *vkus* more in keeping with the meaning of their word *goût* than according to our own concept. From this appropriation of words from foreign languages is born that awkwardness of style in ours and that foreign and strange form of phrases. If, having expanded the meaning of the word *vkus,* we used it only where the phrase formed from it was not counter to the character of our language, as for example in the following: *u vsiakogo svoi vkus* (everyone has his own taste), or *eto plat'e ne po moemu vkusu* (that dress is not to my taste), then of course this would be an enrichment of the language. *For in both of these phrases there is nothing counter to common sense* [*zdravyi razsudok*]. The word *vkus* in them indicates with equal clarity both concepts, that is, the original one and the one derived from it. But we say: *on imeet vkus v muzyke* (he has taste in music). Although habit causes this phrase not to seem absurd, in fact it is composed of empty words that do not contain any sense at all. For in what way can we imagine *vkus,* that is the sense of our tongue or mouth, to reside in music, or in a dress, or in any other thing?[25]

For Shishkov, words borrowed in this manner are essentially empty, devoid of meaning, because their meaning is not a natural development from the word roots and system of the language. He thus tries to differentiate between this type of semantic expansion and a more natural one, controlled by common sense and some internal language logic, and initiated by great writers. He does not trust the meaning that comes from habit or usage to be real or true in a certain sense, because it does not proceed from a true origin, and thus he exhibits characteristic features of logocentrism.[26] Also, as already noted, *vkus* in the aesthetic sense not admitted by Shishkov is an essential category to Karamzin. Implicitly Shishkov is arguing that Karamzin's entire aesthetic program is alien to the Russian language and culture. Shishkov's linguistic arguments thus continually find broader ramifications in style, aesthetics, and culture as a whole.

Karamzin's focus on the spoken language and his description of the literary tradition as insufficient is taken as a rejection of the national culture by Shishkov, for whom the literary language is defined by books, not by speech. The proper high literary language in the Russian tradition was Church Slavonic: under the old conditions of diglossia when the two languages functioned as a unitary system, literature was defined by being written in OCS, (Old) Church Slavonic. Lomonosov defined its proper use in his doctrine of three styles for a period when the two languages were no longer a unitary system, and Church Slavonic elements remained the distinguishing feature of high literary style. But the evolution beyond diglossia also allowed the literary language to be defined in a new way, no longer on the separate code of OCS, but on the spoken usage of good society, for example, or, if that was not available, on some literary simulacrum of that spoken usage. Karamzin thus makes a new distinction between bookish language and the literary language. Lotman and Uspensky note that this change is accompanied by a change in the definition of literature, a narrowing from a sense that included all writing as well as learning in general to belles-lettres.[27] Karamzin's program was thus very much a program of modernization for the Russian literary language. Shishkov, as will be seen, fights change on all these fronts.

Shishkov disagrees with Karamzin on both the sources and the nature of the literary language, and he makes his case in terms of a natural and appropriate Russian style versus a borrowed model. In the opening of his treatise he quotes Karamzin's periodization of Russian style (as always, without naming Karamzin) and interprets it in his own way:

> Not long ago I happened to read the following: "dividing our style into epochs, the first should begin with Kantemir, the second with Lomonosov, the third with the *Slaviano-Russian* translations of Mr. Elagin and his multitude of followers, and the fourth with our time in which a pleasantness of style, called by the French *élégance,* is being formed." I thought for a long time whether the composer of these lines was speaking with a pure heart or whether he was teasing and joking: what? he calls the current ridiculousness of style pleasantness! the complete ugliness and ruination of it, its formation! He calls the earlier translations *Slaviano-Russian:* what does he mean by that word? Perhaps disparagement of the source of our eloquence [*krasnorechie*], the Slavonic language? It's no surprise: to hate your own and love what's foreign is now considered a virtue. But how would he call the current translations and even compositions? undoubtedly *Frantsusko-Russian:* and he prefers these translations to the *Slaviano-Russian?* True, if we translate the French word *élégance* into Russian as nonsense [*chepukha*], then we could say that, in fact, and in a short time, we have brought our style to the point where we have loaded it with the full power and sense of that word.[28]

Karamzin was certainly not joking, but neither was he saying what Shishkov put into his mouth. Karamzin's style highly limited the scope of Slavonic elements in the literary language, but this is not equivalent to disparagement and certainly does not imply, as Shishkov would argue, that he and his followers also neglected the entire literary heritage in the Church Slavonic tongue. In fact, the year before Karamzin had advocated the use of Russian chronicles and the material of Russian history as subject matter for writers with the goal of strengthening patriotic feelings.[29] It should also be noted that Karamzin differentiated the "Slaviano-Russian" style of Ivan P. Elagin from the style of Lomonosov, who represented the normative stylistic model for Shishkov. Ilya Vinitsky has shown that both Karamzin *and* Shishkov were working against the stylistic model of Elagin, which mixed Church Slavonic and highly colloquial elements in all stylistic registers. Vinitsky also demonstrated that most of Shishkov's examples of the style of the new school actually came from Aleksandr P. Orlov's *Utekhi melankholii, Rossiiskoe sochinenie* (*The Pleasures of Melancholy, a Russian Work*, 1802), which provided him with many humorous examples of Gallicisms mixed with Slavonic elements, examples that were also humorous to Karamzin's followers.[30]

Shishkov's tendentious and perhaps intentionally misleading interpretation of Karamzin's words still reflects the essence of their broader differences. Shiskov opposes his model of the literary language, based in the Slavonic tongue, to Karamzin's, which follows the model of the French literary language. In some sense, for Shishkov there are two forms of the Russian language, a Slaviano-Russian form and a Frantsusko-Russian form. The former is based on the true root of the Russian language—the Church Slavonic language. The latter is a contamination of the Russian language and amounts to writing in French with the Russian language, which leads to nonsense if not revolution. This opposition becomes embodied in the stylistic distinction between true Russian eloquence (*krasnorechie*), with its source in the Slavonic tongue, and Karamzin's Frenchified *élégance*, and Shishkov's treatise makes great use of this stylistic opposition. Karamzin would, in his 1820 collected works, remove the phrase referring to French *élégance*, perhaps as a result of Shishkov's attack,[31] and Shishkov, in a note added to the text for his collected works (in 1824), observes that he may have overreacted to the word. He offers, in that same note, some possible Russian translations of the word: "*blagoiazychie, chistorechie, krasnoslovie,*" but the focus of his *Discourse* is on Russian *krasnorechie*.[32]

The source of elegance, as seen from Karamzin's 1802 article, is the high society salon. Salon discourse is a discourse intended for a small audience of intimates, a light discourse, full of wit and allusions to common knowledge. In their epistles and elegies, Karamzin's followers in the 1810s would develop a literary discourse with these features.[33] But the literary practice of Shishkov and his allies, who gathered in the Beseda liubitelei russkogo slova (Colloquium of Lovers of the Russian Word, 1811–16) was centered on the ode as the highest genre, one which was marked in the Russian practice by its public, declamatory character.[34] Shishkov's *krasnorechie* is also marked by its declamatory nature. Although he recommends books as the source of *krasnorechie,* one of the effects of studying these books is a better sense of oral style: "While our reason is enriched by these concepts, our hearing gets accustomed to clear enunciation of words, to their pleasant pronunciation, to sensing the euphonious or non-euphonious confluence of letters, or, in a word, to all the charms of eloquence (*sladkorechie*)."[35]

Shishkov's authority on style is Lomonosov, whose "Predislovie o pol'ze knig tserkovnykh v rossiiskom iazyke" ("Foreword on the Utility of Ecclesiastical Books in the Russian Language," 1757) defined the system of "three styles" based on the use of various lexical elements from the Slavonic and Russian language, and recommended the literary heritage of church books as a source for Russian-language culture. Shishkov's advocacy of this system led, in fact, more to a revival of the baroque Lomonosovian odic style (with its bold metaphors, its *"vysokoe kosnoiazych'e"*—grand tongue-twisting[36]), and a genre system well in keeping with the latest French Republican trends of heroic Roman discourse (Boris Gasparov notes the sharp opposition between the ideological views of Shishkov and the forms of discourse and Republican aesthetics of his school).[37] Karamzin, in turn, advocated the pre-revolutionary French salon style, and this was labeled the "new" style by Shishkov. Both of these stylistic innovations were proposed against the background of the late eighteenth-century stylistic trend of Elagin and his followers, which mixed Slavonicisms into all stylistic registers. Shishkov wants to return Slavonicisms to their hierarchical place in the high style and avoid awkward mixing of Slavonicisms with colloquialisms: "It is reprehensible, of course, and not good to disfigure one's style by mixing high Slavonic phrases with folk and low expressions, but to insert a significant word in a proper manner and in its place is quite deserving of praise, even if it is not the usual word."[38] Parallel to the expansion of Slavonicisms in the written language, the late eighteenth century witnessed an expansion of the use of Gallicisms and Europeanisms in general in spoken, and sometimes written, Russian. As Uspensky and Lotman observe, the function of these calques and borrowed words was often the same as that of the Slavonicisms: a general raising of the language for high style, the development of an aesthetically demarcated language.[39] Karamzin's orientation toward the spoken language led him to adapt the means developed in aesthetically marked spoken language for his own literary language. It is worth noting that neither side in this debate was entirely free of the opposite trend—Shishkov used Gallicisms, as his opponents loved to point out, and Karamzin's language was not free of Slavonicisms, which were often used to trace European words.[40] But whereas Karamzin made use of developing language trends and tried to push that development further, Shishkov resisted the trends and tried desperately to submit language development to rational control, though the effect was sometimes to engender new developments.

The Russian language is different from the French: as a consequence, Russian style should be different from the French, and further, for Shishkov, *Russian literature* should have a different nature from the French. In some sense, the difference is a difference between *slovesnost'* and *literatura,* and these terms get linked to the difference between *krasnorechie* and *élégance,* between Slaviano-Russian and Frantsusko-Russian. In complaining about calque translations from French, Shishkov says, "They accept them [words] spontaneously in the same meaning from French literature [*literatura*] into Russian literature [*Rossiiskaia slovesnost'*]."[41] Instead, he suggests, "we ought to take them [the French] for an example in working, like them, to create our own *krasnorechie* and *slovesnost',* and not in dragging over into our language the beauties found by them in theirs, which are not in the least appropriate to us."[42] Shishkov does not maintain the distinction between *slovesnost'* and *literatura* rigorously, but it is implied throughout in his continual insistence that the church books advocated by Lomonosov remain the source of Russian *krasnorechie* and thus a central part of the Russian literary heritage. Karamzin indicated that the literary heritage lacked certain genres and the type of richness and refinement that he sought. Shishkov responds: "First-rate writers in various genres, of course, were few in Russia, but the secular sort, not the spiritual, and there were few of the former due to the fact that they do not read the latter. I am not saying that we can glean all genres of secular writing from spiritual books; but whoever, with a sharp mind and natural gifts, will be strong in his language and *krasnorechie* will, in whatever route he chooses, get along famously."[43] Rather than focusing on the lack in secular genres, Shishkov emphasizes the resource available in the literary heritage of spiritual books. Later, in his speech at the opening of the colloquium (1811), he would formulate this in a way that more emphatically highlighted the narrowing involved in moving from the concept of *slovesnost'* to that of *literatura:*

> Our *slovesnost'* can be divided into three types. One of them has long blossomed, and as much by its ancientness as by its grace and stature outshines the rhetoric of any newer languages. But it was dedicated exclusively to spiritual cogitation and thought. From this our current dialect or style received a stature and firmness unreachable by other languages, and can receive yet more. The second *slovesnost'* of ours consists in the popular (*narodnyi*) language, not so elevated as the sacred tongue, but quite pleasant, and which in its simplicity conceals the sweetest *krasnorechie* for the heart and feelings. . . . The third *slovesnost'* of ours, consisting of those genres of composition that we did not have, has been blooming less than one century. We took it from other nations, but in appropriating something good from them, we may have imitated too slavishly and, in chasing after their forms of thought and the characteristics of their languages, turned ourselves quite away from our own concepts.[44]

In his conception, Russia has three literatures: the sacred literature of the church books, the literature of the popular or folk language, and belles-lettres. An exclusive focus on the latter ignores the riches of the first two. The narrow modern conception of literature represented to Shishkov a loss of heritage for Russia. Folklore (here in the form of the popular language) was a new element for Shishkov in this speech that was not a part of his 1803 *Discourse,* where the heritage of sacred books is the primary marker of the difference between Russian and French literature. But already in his published commentary to *Slovo o polku Igoreve* (*Song of Igor's Campaign,* 1805) he suggested that old songs, proverbs, and tales—along with *Slovo* and the ancient church books—gave evidence of the blossoming of the Russian language before Christianity.[45] In his "Razgovory o slovesnosti" ("Dialogues on Slovesnost'," 1811), he would make the folk genres a model alongside the church books.[46]

One final aspect of Shishkov's *Discourse* is worthy of note. In defining the nature of the national language and the implications of that definition for the national literature, Shishkov continued to use French literature as a measure for the successes of Russian literature. However, he was not satisfied with merely matching the French—after all, his basic point was the non-correspondence of the French and Russian languages, and the related non-correspondence of their cultures. There could be no equivalence. Rather, he proposed that it was possible to outdo the French, and thus he introduced a competitive tone to the comparison of cultures: "We constantly comment on the quantity of books and excellent compositions of different types published by the French and complain that we have few of them in our own language; but are we using the proper means to catch up to them or surpass them?"[47] Spiritual books were a critical means for winning this competition: "The French couldn't borrow as much from their spiritual books as we can from ours."[48] Shishkov would later add Russia's folkloric literature, which surpassed France's in quality and abundance, to its literary resources.[49] In this competition, translation and imitation were not ruled out, but the result could not be the abandonment of one's own superiority: "It is quite good to follow in the footsteps of great writers, but one must express their strength and spirit in one's own language and not chase after their words, which do not have the same strength for us. Without knowledge of our own language, we will imitate them in just the same way as parrots imitate a person, or in other words, we will be similar to a peacock, who not knowing or disregarding the beauty of his own feathers, wants for his own beautification to borrow them from birds that are far less beautiful than he."[50]

The polemics over the "old" and "new" styles would polarize the Russian aristocratic literary world over the course of the decade and a half following Shishkov's publication. If the war years around 1812 marked a victory for the patriotic genres and heavy archaic style of Shishkov's school, in consonance with the anti-French feelings predominant in Russian culture as a whole, such victory was short-lived. The leading literary figures, beginning in 1815, began again to poke fun at Shishkov and his allies and, within the "Arzamas" circle, to develop at a high level the salon language and light genres advocated by Karamzin, though with added elements of irony, satire, and fragmentariness that moved beyond Karamzin's model. Major debates of the 1810s, like those over the ballad genre and the use of Russian hexameter, demonstrate the continued influence of Shishkov's critique, as they linked the form and style of certain translations to the larger question of a Russian national literature (see chapters 5 and 7). Shishkov had divided the Russian language from within into native and foreign elements, opposing the true Russian language—formed on the roots of the Church Slavonic language (a false bottom as soon became clear) and giving rise to *krasnorechie* and a Russian *slovesnost'*—to the Frantsusko-Russian tongue—a foreign tongue in Russian guise giving rise to a foreign *élégance* and a literature formed on the French model. In the very passage in which he opposes the Slaviano-Russian language to the Frantsusko-Russian one, both are described as languages of translation—the translations of the Elagin school and those of Karamzin's followers. Shishkov raises a serious question concerning translation—is it an appropriation of something foreign into one's native culture or is it a transformation of one's native culture into something foreign? For him, the latter is something to be avoided as detrimental to cultural identity. The style of translations thus becomes a site at which one can observe processes of cultural appropriation or assimilation and thus a place to analyze the Russianness of one's literary practices.

In this way, Shishkov effectively began public discussion of the question of a national literature. Having examined his discourse and the terminology in which it is articulated, we might now find it useful to conclude with an observation about our own scholarly terminology for discussing the period. Yuri Tynianov introduced the terms *arkhaisty* and *novatory* (archaists and innovators) to describe the two sides of the divided Russian literary world as an improvement over attempts to define them as classicists and romantics.[51] What these terms miss is the innovative aspects of Shishkov's appeal to the "old" style. As Lotman and Uspensky have observed, in many ways Shishkov was more of a utopian thinker than a real traditionalist, and many of his linguistic archaisms were in fact neologisms.[52] While he revived older debates over the Russian literary language, he gave them a new content through his romantic ideology of the national language. The "innovators," by contrast, were very slow themselves to take up the question of the national qualities of literature.[53] This is a common paradox of the process of modernization, for modernizers often appeal to old values even as they present them in entirely new combinations. Joseph M. Levine's observation concerning the battle of the ancients and moderns applies equally here: "The ancients were not simply defenders of the tradition against the new, they had in fact come onto the European scene in England and elsewhere as innovators, humanists, in revolt against the culture of their own (late medieval) times. Thus, paradoxically, an ancient could in certain circumstances appear to be a modern, as we shall see the moderns, more closely examined, could sometimes turn out to be ancients."[54] In fact, one is dealing with a related and parallel phenomenon here. In many ways this is a Russian version of the Quarrel between the Ancients and Moderns (or a small part of the Russian version, which has other manifestations as well). But if one had to choose, which side would be named as ancients and which as moderns?

The Culture of the Czech Language and Czech-Language Culture

Admiral Shishkov's tract helped to put the Russian language—
different lexically and stylistically oriented versions of it—into the center of
debates over the expression of Russian national identity in Russian literature.
Students of both Russian and Czech cultures in this period have often noted
the centrality of questions of language in public discourse and the cultural
process. In many cases, they have noted, discussions of language stood in for
discussions of literature, of culture in general, of politics, and of philosophy.[1]
In both cultures, this hyper-significance of language has deep roots. Boris
Uspensky and Yuri Lotman explain the Russian "linguocentrism" in terms of
the particularity of the given language situation (with two competing codes,
Russian and Church Slavonic) and the role that language and its naming
function play in the medieval Russian eschatological historical model,
wherein the remaking of the world is equivalent to its renaming. In this
context, political and cultural reform are linked to language reform.[2] They
note that this centrality of language is a constant in post-Petrine Russian
culture while linking it to the medieval historical model. Even aside from the
eschatological historical model, though, Russian medieval culture is marked

by the fact that language, in the Orthodox tradition, often stood in the place of philosophy, theology, and even aesthetics. Theological, philosophical, and aesthetic differences manifested themselves in the proposal of or resistance to linguistic or semiotic innovations: witness the early sixteenth-century resistance to proposed scriptural revisions (to correct mistakes and errors of textual transmission) and the seventeenth-century schism, which divided the church over the revision of church ritual and books (including the central symbolic question of how many fingers to use in crossing oneself).

Czech "linguocentrism" has, not surprisingly, entirely different roots. Late medieval and Reformation Czech culture is marked by its explicit theological disputes, and questions of language do not replace theological discourse; however, language is implicated in those disputes. The Hussite practice of preaching to the laity in Czech was one of a series of church reforms put into practice by Czech reformers and included in their demands. The Hussite wars further emphasized the identification of the Czech language with the reformers, as primarily German-speaking invaders tried to crush the movement.[3] Czech became the language of the reformist Utraquists and Czech Brethren, and Czech renaissance humanists in the following centuries selected their literary language in a way that conformed to their religious beliefs: Brethren and Utraquists wrote in Czech while Catholics wrote in Latin. During the Counter Reformation, the Czech language was marked as the language of heresy, and older Czech books were banned or even burned without discrimination. Only in 1781 with Joseph II's Tolerance Patent and the abolishment of church censorship were many of these older books able to be republished, giving them and their implicit language politics a newfound currency in a period becoming preoccupied with nationhood.

It is possible, moreover, that the currency of the implicit language politics of older Czech and Russian texts grew significantly in value as Czech and Russian writers responded to the challenges of modernity— that modernization further intensified any prior tendencies to ascribe heightened significance to language. Scholars have sometimes suggested that the centrality of language in Czech and Russian cultures in this period represents a kind of instrumentalization of language to discuss political and philosophical questions that were not admissible in the tightly controlled public discourse. In comparative perspective, however, the fundamental operator appears to be not the local facts of censorship but the general trend of modernity across Europe to ascribe greater and greater significance to facts of language in all kinds of discourse, from philosophy to politics to aesthetics. Language was not instrumentalized locally by Czechs and Russians to discuss philosophy and politics, but instead, it naturally became more and more implicated in philosophical and political discourses as these discourses modernized. This general trend may have been somewhat intensified by local conditions of censorship, but the centrality of language was not only a local condition. In the particular case of the modernization of literary discourse being explored here, language became a fundamental link between literary values and national cultural identity, so that discussions of language had both literary and national-political implications. Moreover, as literature and the nation came together in a new constellation of values—embodied by the national literature—discussions of literary values became directly, not indirectly, political. The reader has just seen in the previous chapter how Admiral Shishkov reignited older debates about the relationship of the Russian and Church Slavonic languages (the situation of diglossia having been, according to Uspensky and Lotman, the root of medieval Russian "linguocentrism") for their newfound valence in articulating a distinct Russian cultural identity, thus placing language at the center of the debates over new literary values. In this chapter the reader will see how an account of the history of the Czech language modeled a value system for the programmatic attempt to resurrect Czech literature and culture.

The author of the language history was Josef Dobrovský (1753–1829), who began as a textual critic of biblical texts and a specialist in Hebrew and oriental languages, finishing study in the theological faculty in Prague in 1776. His biblical criticism soon led him to realize the importance of old Slavic translations and their variants for establishing the textual history of the Greek New Testament. His interest in the Slavic literary heritage grew, and with some encouragement from Fortunát Durych, so did his interest in the domestic Czech tradition.[4] In 1779 he began a literary magazine, *Böhmische Litteratur auf das Jahr 1779* (*Bohemian Literature in the Year 1779*), which became, the following year and for the third issue in 1784, *Böhmische und Mährische Litteratur auf das Jahr 1780* (*Bohemian and Moravian Literature in the Year 1780*), in which his goal was to create a picture of the current state of Bohemian literature. Or perhaps his goal was even broader—a picture of the state of learning in Bohemia—for in addition to giving notice of new publications, he included news on the holdings of libraries, the state of the Prague university, and activities in other institutions of learning.

Dobrovský's concept of "literature" for his magazines was quite broad— he included scientific and scholarly writings and church publications in addition to belles-lettres. The narrowing of the concept that accompanied modernization had no place here. His concept was broad in terms of language as well: Dobrovský included any publication produced in Czech territory, including those in Latin and German as well as Czech. His initial definition of Bohemian (and Moravian) literature, then, was not based primarily on language, but on territory. For books in Czech, however, he also included foreign editions, such as those published in Vienna.[5] The inclusion of foreign editions only for publications in Czech points to a possible new, and narrower, conception. So does his decision to review certain books, in spite of his promise not to judge: "I did make it a rule not to judge any book; however books of this type [a book by Josef Rosenthaler on Czech orthography] that in the strictest sense concern Czech [*böhmische*] literature, are an exception."[6] Bohemian literature in the strictest sense is, for him, literature written in Czech or concerned with the Czech language (Rosenthaler's book was in Latin, but it concerned the Czech language and writing and printing in Czech). This narrower conception of Czech literature is embodied in his monumental *Geschichte der Böhmischen Sprache und Litteratur* (*History of the Czech Language and Literature*, 1792), which concerns the Czech language exclusively. While the adjective *böhmische* in combination with such nouns as "Litteratur" or "Nation" could refer to the historical Bohemian kingdom and its territory and peoples, in combination with "Sprache" it signaled the Czech language in particular, and the literature discussed narrowed accordingly.[7]

Dobrovský's 1792 *Geschichte* is in many ways the foundation of modern Czech literary history and is even an important work in the historiography of the Czech nation, but it was conceived as a history of the Czech language, and language is clearly its central concern. The history was first published in 1791 in an abbreviated form as "Geschichte der Böhmische Sprache" in the journal *Abhandlungen der böhmischen Gesellschaft der Wissenschaften zu Prag,* and as Josef Hanuš has shown, there is no real change in conception from the first to the second edition.[8] The addition of "und Litteratur" to the title signals the addition of a large amount of bibliographical material that gives evidence of the history of the language and attention to the history of book printing. Such additions break no new ground—the established tradition of Czech literary historiography at the time was largely bibliographical and had addressed book printing as well.[9] And yet, Dobrovský's recounting of language history does move literary and national history forward. It has already been observed how Dobrovský's concept of literature narrowed in terms of language.[10] In conjunction with the narrowing of the phrase "böhmische Litteratur" to mean literature in the Czech language, the phrase "böhmische Nation" or simply "Nation" in Dobrovský's narrative also narrows to invoke a community defined by language rather than territory.[11] In this, Dobrovský clearly moves beyond the ambiguity of usage that was typical of the local tradition of Enlightenment historiography, which vacillated between a collective defined by territory and one defined by language.[12]

In addition to such conceptual developments, Dobrovský also offered improvements in methodology. Of particular importance is Dobrovský's application of critical philological methodology to historical sources and questions (one should recall here the importance of philology to the development of modern historicism and the challenge it posed to the classicist literary paradigm).[13] The *Geschichte* summarizes years of his scholarly work on such important historical questions as the establishment of writing among the Czechs, the beginning of printing in Bohemia, St. Cyril's relationship to the glagolitic and Cyrillic alphabets, and the fate of the Slavonic liturgy in Bohemia. Dobrovský also offered the first synthetic periodization of the language's history, which was at the same time applicable to literary and national history.[14] The importance and originality of his contribution is in no way diminished by the observation that Dobrovský closely followed his model, Johann Christoph Adelung, in constructing his periodization.[15] While Adelung's short history of the German language that accompanied his German grammar offered Dobrovský a model and language for analysis, in the end Dobrovský's history succeeds on the strength of his own analysis of the Czech language's historical context in its particulars. A closer look at the ways in which Dobrovský does and does not follow his model will allow further definition of the innovative and conservative aspects of his language history. The structure of Adelung's history is a template for Dobrovský's: both begin with prehistory and the division of the language into dialects, treat the important influence of the acceptance of Christianity on the language, and go on to divide the language history into six periods.[16] Walter Schamschula observes that the causes for the rise and fall of the culture of the language in both narratives are the same—primarily the rise and fall (particularly in wartime) of the population—and both Hanuš and Schamschula note close parallels in the wording of particular arguments. As Schamschula notes, however, this perspective on language history and its terminology is entirely within the realm of the classicist paradigm that was common patrimony at that point.[17] In some sense, then, what Dobrovský takes from Adelung is only a particular manifestation of a generally available perspective and terminology that is not particularly innovative.

In fact, though, in some ways Dobrovský's use of key analytical concepts is even more conservative than Adelung's. Hanuš has suggested that Dobrovský's history is in many ways another in the series of defenses of the Czech language made by Czech patriots, because he wrote the history of a language that "even our intelligentsia considered . . . to be uncultivated, uncultured, barbarous [nevzdělaní, nekulturní, babarský]."[18] And indeed, at major points in his historical argumentation, Dobrovský refers positively to "die Kultur der Böhmischen Sprache"—even his periodization is not of the language history as such but of the cultivation of the language: "Perioden der Kultur der Böhmischen Sprache." Schamschula has noted that Adelung's terms "Ausbildung" (cultivation, education, culture), "Verfeinerung" (refinement), and "Bereicherung" (enrichment) were of particular use to Dobrovský, to which one should add the term "Kultur" as a part of the same complex of ideas.[19] And this is a term that deserves particular attention, because it was a relatively new term in German, borrowed from French/ Latin, and it was changing in its application. In their history of the term, A. L. Kroeber and Clyde Kluckhohn cite Adelung in particular as one among eighteenth-century authors who adopted the term and moved it closer to its modern meaning. Adelung first included the term in his dictionary (spelled as "Cultur") not in the 1774 edition, but only in 1793.[20] He also penned one of the general histories of human culture that began to appear in the latter part of the century, entitled *Versuch einer Geschichte der Cultur des Menschlichen Geschlechts* (*Essay on the History of the Culture of the Human Species*, Leipzig 1782).[21]

Comparing Adelung's use of the term in the short sketch of the history of the Czech language that he wrote as a foreword to Karl Tham's German-Czech dictionary (1788) to Dobrovský's in his 1792 *Geschichte* reveals a limitation in Dobrovský's adoption of Adelung's terminology.[22] In frequency and type of usage, Adelung is far more free with the term "Kultur" (spelled thus in this text) than Dobrovský. Where Dobrovský uses the term just ten times in 219 pages of text, Adelung finds need for it seventeen times in just twelve pages (and not at all in the first three).[23] The difference is not as significant as it first appears, however, for Dobrovský has no need of the term in the pages and pages of bibliographical exposition that constitute well over half of his work. The term appears exclusively in the sections of historical argumentation. While these add up to far more than twelve pages, one might still explain the difference in frequency (Adelung needs it nearly twice as often to narrate the entirety of the language's history) by Dobrovský's greater reliance on native terms, like "Ausbildung." But there is a qualitative difference as well. Kroeber and Kluckhohn observe that Adelung at times uses the word in a manner that approaches the modern sense, when he treats culture as a *product* of cultivation as opposed to a process of cultivation.[24] This is a more abstract use of the term, and one can find examples of it in his "Foreword" in such phrases as, for example, "die einzige wirkende Ursache der Kultur" (the only effective cause of enculturation), "ein Überbleibsel der römischen Kultur" (a remnant of Roman culture), and "keine Blumen der schönern Kultur" (no blossoms of better culture).[25] "Culture" rather than "cultivation" seems indeed to work better as a translation in such phrases. By contrast, in the majority of Dobrovský's uses of the term (8 of 10), "Kultur" is followed by another noun phrase in the genitive case, denoting a process of cultivation as in the older sense of the term, and most often it is the language that is the object of this cultivation.[26] Even here Dobrovský is more narrowly focused on the language than Adelung, who freely discusses the cultivation of the spirit or of the spirit and taste, but never merely of the language.[27]

Dobrovský's history of the culture (that is, the cultivation) of the Czech language is a product of an Enlightenment classicist point of view that would nonetheless prove inspiring for the next generation of romantic nationalists. While Dobrovský did not yet conceive of Czech culture as a distinct and independent phenomenon—he did not begin to think of culture at all in its modern sense—his treatment of "böhmische" literature and the "böhmische" nation as defined by the Czech language marked an important step in that direction. His history of Czech literature, insofar as it is a literary history at all, is not yet a history of the national literature. One never gets the sense that the literature *should* reflect the nation's history or some imagined essence of the national character. As he emphasized in his first magazine, his concern was not with how things ought to be, but simply with how they were: "[Some] people want simply to know: what genuinely is the current state of learning. Not how it could be or how it should be. In order to accommodate them, I've taken as my goal to concisely and clearly describe the current state of literature in Bohemia in general, *just as it is.*"[28] But Dobrovský's historical imagination and analytical language produce a convincing narrative that links language, literature, and nation. His 1792 *Geschichte* can thus serve as a significant example of how the new paradigm of national literature is generated out of developing historical perspectives on literary traditions.

To open his description of the fourth period of the Czech language (from Jan Hus to the development of book printing), Dobrovský states: "With the Czech reformer Hus begins a new epoch in the history of the Czech nation and its culture [der böhmische Nation und ihrer Kultur], thus also its language."[29] For Dobrovský this relationship between the nation and its language and literature is complex. In tracing the history of the language, he continues to apply the broad cultural perspective that characterized his magazines' treatment of literature, noting institutional and technological developments as well as political and social changes that had their effect, positive or negative, on the culture of the Czech language, that is, rising or falling literacy and the use of Czech for various social functions and by various social groups. He notes, for example, that a woman wrote in Czech in the Hussite period (to the consternation of an abbot) and that even noble men and women composed songs in Czech in Emperor Rudolf's time; he observes the revolution brought about by book printing and laments the great loss from the Counter Reformation's book burnings.[30]

Dobrovský's complex conception of the factors involved in the history of the Czech language enabled his history of the language to serve also as the first modern synthetic history of the Czech nation and of Czech literature. His portrait of the rising culture of the Czech language and its subsequent fall invokes major moments in Czech national and literary history. Dobrovský also provided a nuanced definition of a cultured literary language at a time when systematic attempts to rejuvenate Czech as a literary language had only just begun, and it guided the efforts of those to follow. In his discussion in the *Geschichte* of what he called the "golden age" (*goldene Zeitalter*) of the Czech language, the sixteenth century, he provided a model of the situation and status of a language culture at its height: language serves all social functions for all classes of society, most of which are literate; the language itself is rich and subtle in vocabulary, stable in orthography and grammar, developed in numerous original works and put to use in even more numerous translations of literature, ancient and modern. He further described the dissolution of this language culture in the seventeenth and eighteenth centuries, as well as the steps being taken to combat it, including the republication of material from the golden age. He himself contributed to attempts to normalize and stabilize Czech orthography and grammar in his reviews of works in Czech as well as with his *Ausführliches Lehrgebäude der böhmischen Sprache* (*Detailed Grammar of the Czech Language*, 1809). He also elaborated a syllabotonic prosody for Czech in 1795, to replace the competing and not-well-defined quantitative and syllabic systems then current. Dobrovský thus worked to create order where order was missing, in the spirit of rationalist classicism. But the results of such efforts remained unforeseeable for him: "Now whether through all these new encouragements, efforts, undertakings and sympathies of a few patriotic-minded Czechs the Czech language will rise, sooner or later, to a noticeably higher degree than the perfection that it achieved in its golden age under Maximilian and Rudolph II, I will leave to the future to decide, because this is dependent on so many external circumstances that are beyond our control."[31]

BEGINNING IN 1806, Josef Jungmann (1773–1847) outlined a program that would take control of any circumstances it was possible to control and encourage change in circumstances in the control of others. In a pair of dialogues under the common title "O jazyku českém" ("On the Czech Language"), published in 1806 in the new literary journal *Hlasatel český* (*Czech Herald*), Jungmann gave a vivid picture of the debased state of current Czech language culture and recommended actions that would lead to its improvement. Vladimír Macura has suggested that in the first half of the nineteenth century, the phrase "česká kultura" represented a kind of *contradictio in adiecto*—culture was something foreign, French or German.[32] Insofar as the phrase uses the term "culture" in its modern sense, it is also a bit of an anachronism, for Jungmann's use of the term is in its own way at least as conservative as Dobrovský's. And yet, in the context of Jungmann's program the cultivation of the Czech language becomes synonymous with the resurrection of a distinct Czech culture in the modern sense.

In the first dialogue, which takes place in the Elysian fields between Adam Daniel z Veleslavína—Dobrovský's model for golden-age Czech—and a contemporary Czech, Jungmann illustrates the fall of the Czech language in the radical difference between Veleslavín's Czech and that of the contemporary, which is marked by solecisms, typical German consonant devoicing, and macaronic combinations of Czech and German.[33] In the dialogue's opening, Because his interlocutor speaks such poor Czech, Veleslavín is unable to accept that he really *is* a Czech and presumes him to be, in turn, a German who had a Czech nanny, an expatriate Czech, and the son of a German tradesman in Prague. The Czech defends himself as a cultured Praguer: "Der is no kafehaus in Prag ver I vas not at home, no hall ver I haf not tanzed, theatr and church ver I haf not entertaint myself. I haf der smokt gut tabak, played gut billiard, ceched (drank) and feched (fenced) and done everyting der dat vas chic vor a man of kultur [od kultůr], better dan many a kavalier." When Veleslavín inquires as to the cause of his tortured Czech, he replies, "I tolt you dat my language ist German; and who has honor in his body and a gut coat on his body, he is shame to

Portrait of Josef Jungmann, by Jan Vilímek, 189?. The original is held by the National Library of the Czech Republic.

speak Czech."[34] While Jungmann exaggerates the nature of contemporary Czech speech, the lack of a place for Czech in cultural undertakings is not exaggerated. For Jungmann, "culture" as a concept is very much in question here: can one as a Czech speak an uncultured Czech and still claim to be a cultured person? Is culture indifferent to its linguistic means? The modern character has no Czech language culture, in spite of his trappings of higher culture. Although this is the only time in either dialogue that Jungmann uses any form of the word "kultura" (here "kultůr" in a Czech representation of the German word, with vowel length indicating the German stress), the concept is a central one to his program.

Instead of the French-Latin-German term *kultura,* Jungmann makes frequent use of forms of the Czech equivalent, *vzdělání.*[35] Although he thus avoids what would likely appear in that context to be a borrowing from German, he is very aware of the important example of German culture for the Czechs. At the end of the first dialogue a German enters to reassure Veleslavín that there is hope still for the Czech nation:

> [The Germans] ought to be an example to your people. It has been about sixty years since our people began to sincerely cultivate [*vzdělávati*] their language, polishing, refining, and smoothing until it could compare with any language in the world in riches and perfection. Soon the golden age blossomed for the Germans, the sweet fragrance of which gave delight to your people as well, especially since their own fruit tree, which was capable of bringing forth similar flowers, they frivolously tore from all its buds. Because for two centuries already they have been shirking everything that is Czech; having burned the old books of their ancestors, they wrote no new ones; they have changed their mores, their dress, and nearly even their fathers' tongue, or at least they are trying to change; in short, coming among them, one would say that the nation is not Czech but made up of Franks and Germans; the great from the Franks, the simple from the Germans, and that includes everyone, if not in fact, then in desire.[36]

Two significant points can be made about this representative passage. First, the object of the process of cultivation for Jungmann is, as it was for Dobrovský, the language itself. For Dobrovský that perspective was, in some respect, a product of genre: he was writing a history of the Czech language, so he analyzed all cultural-historical developments for their effect on the language. Jungmann generalizes that perspective and makes it foundational for a new cultural value system. It is striking that the German work is described as "cultivating their language." The many developments in German literature, history, philosophy, and culture in the eighteenth century are seen as having not merely the result of benefiting the language, but the *goal* of benefiting the language.[37] This is one of the more notable aspects of Czech "linguocentrism," in which work in culture, science, and literature are all seen as ultimately leading to a more refined language.[38] The language focus of the Czech revival becomes so dominant that language subsumes all other cultural values (in this sense, it is more extreme than the Russian variety). In writing a history of the Czech language that was also in many ways the first history of Czech culture and learning, Dobrovský had modeled this value structure, but it took on a life of its own in the nineteenth century. The German speaker in the dialogue notes the markers of Czech specificity that have been changed: mores, clothing, "and nearly even their fathers' tongue"—the betrayal of the language is the ultimate betrayal. Second, in avoiding the foreign term *kultura* and using the Czech equivalent, Jungmann actualizes the agricultural metaphor that underlies the term. Dobrovský used the foreignism, albeit in a more limited and more conservative manner than his model Adelung. For Dobrovský, *Kultur* was always a cultivation of something. For Jungmann, this process of cultivation is represented by an organic metaphor for culture, with the human labor of cultivation always at its root. This organic metaphor would become characteristic of the Czech revival discourse and would develop into a multifaceted gardening metaphor for cultural work.[39]

Paradoxically, in taking the concept of culture back to the agricultural metaphor at its root, Jungmann contributed to the modernization of the concept. As already seen with Admiral Shishkov, organic metaphors take on a new significance in modern thought about the specificity of cultural phenomena to particular places and peoples. And the central, national significance that Jungmann ascribed to language also had its effect on the concept of culture. If there is a metaphorical garden where the Czech language is cultivated, that would be a specifically Czech garden, a site of Czech national culture.

For Jungmann and his contemporaries the relationship between language and nation became a matter of explicit discussion. It has already been observed that one of the significant conceptual advances of Dobrovský's *Geschichte* was that it defined the "böhmische Nation" in terms of the "böhmische Sprache." In that case, however, the narrowed definition appears almost as a side-effect of the analytical focus on the history of the Czech language, rather than as a principled and conscious change in thinking. Dobrovský did not define his terms explicitly and he vacillated in his usage between broader and narrower conceptions in a manner that was typical of Czech Enlightenment historiography more generally. Explicit discussion would soon follow. In the same initial issue of *Hlasatel český* in which Jungmann's first dialogue appeared, there was an article by the journal's editor, Jan Nejedlý, entitled "O lásce k vlasti" ("On Love of the Homeland"), in which Nejedlý defined the notion of *vlast* in terms of language and mores, the dividing markers of a nation in his conception: "Every nation is divided from every other by its mother tongue and its mores, and by those two alone is known from other nations."[40] To give those up would be to betray one's *vlast*, to become a renegade son, and to fail in every way to be a patriot.[41] Jungmann's second dialogue appeared in the third issue of that year, and it begins with the question of the relationship between love of one's *vlast* and love of the Czech language. This dialogue is conducted between Slavomil (Slav-lover) and Protiva (Opponent), who represents a far more educated Czech opponent than the Czech in the first dialogue. Protiva asks Slavomil to defend the transition from love of *vlast* to love of language, which Protiva says he has overheard in an argument the night before. Slavomil argues the inadequacy of any territorial notion of *vlast* and the essentialness of language to a nation, and therefore to its *vlast*, for there is no *vlast* without a nation.[42] If Nejedlý had required language and mores to define national identity, Jungmann finds language itself to be sufficient—as will be seen, mores become subsumed in language.

Protiva doubts the equivalence of language and national identity and suggests that one language is as good as another, that the Czechs could take up the German tongue without detriment to their particularity. Slavomil responds with a striking argument for the centrality of language to national identity:

> And what if the idea that one language is just like another sounds nicer than it sounds true? Doesn't every nation have its own experience and its own upbringing, so to speak? And isn't a language like a great warehouse of all the arts and all human knowledge, which are transferred through it from father to son like the riches of every family? And what's more, language is the most superb philosophy, adapted to the particular geographic latitude, mores, ways of thinking, inclinations, and the thousands of distinctions of each nation, and therefore, just as every effect is related to its cause, it represents with its constitution, sound, and character the surest and most faithful image of the origin, communal formation, development, character, and habits of the nation itself; so, it is as if the whole nation lives in just the language and presents it as a sign of and reason for its personality; through its study, the nation itself is studied infallibly, and by it alone differs from other nations, just as one person differs from another by his education and upbringing.[43]

Jungmann here equates language with a national philosophy and makes it the carrier of all national cultural values. The nation itself lives primarily through its language. Throughout the dialogue, Slavomil equates the loss of language with the death of the nation. The survival of the Czech nation is what is at stake in the argument for the revival of the language culture. Moreover, Jungmann nearly argues explicitly here that Czech culture is a distinct, national phenomenon. If one were to replace the word "upbringing" (*vychování*) with its near-equivalent "education/culture" (*vzdělání*) in the second sentence, one would in essence arrive at a very modern conception of culture. Though Jungmann avoids the term *kultura,* by making language the carrier of all cultural values and the sole sign of national identity, he in fact articulates a very modern idea of a distinct Czech (-language) culture.

To the implicit question of the first dialogue—can one as a Czech speak an uncultured Czech and still claim to be a cultured person?—Jungmann has responded with a resounding no. Culture is not indifferent to its linguistic means, and a foreign language is not an appropriate means if one values one's national identity. The force of Jungmann's argument is to make it imperative upon any speaker of Czech to pursue the cultivation of the Czech language through every means and pursue his own cultivation in the Czech language. And one has the testimony of some of the most prominent members of the next generation of Czech awakeners, like Pavel Josef Šafařík and František Palacký, that Jungmann's dialogues played the role of conversion text for them. They recalled their encounter with the dialogues as a significant moment in their decision to dedicate their lives to the Czech national cause.[44]

Jungmann outlines a programmatic approach to the cultivation of the Czech language. The program, in its main thrust, is a literary one, for it is in literature that language reaches its fullest development. The influence of Dobrovský's history, with its nuanced picture of the Czech literary language and Czech language culture at its height, is manifest here. Like Dobrovský, Jungmann conceives of literature broadly. At the same time, literature in the narrow sense of artistic literature has a special place for Jungmann that it did not have in Dobrovský's history. In the second dialogue, Protiva is willing to admit only a limited necessity for certain kinds of Czech literature:

> I see, of course, and cannot contest the fact that, whatever the future may bring, at least for now it is necessary for everyone among us who occupies some kind of office to know Czech; yes, and I'll admit that, if not those types of people who ally themselves with the Germans, which includes all the bureaucrats, at least the remaining people feel the need for Czech literature

at least somewhat, I would say; but then, and I say this without reservation, the same cannot be said for the narrow tome of Czech literature of all the arts [*všech umění*]. It would have to be so perfected that even one who was familiar with German literature could fall in love with it, otherwise it would always be contemptible to him, just like the Czech language.[45]

He here allows that he has been convinced by Slavomil's earlier arguments on the necessity for educational and informational literature in Czech, but he attempts to draw the line at any literature with higher aspirations—the reference here to literature "of all the arts" includes not just artistic literature but also philosophy and other kinds of learned discourse.[46] He does not see how Czech literature in such fields could compete with the German. He thus implicitly designates the project of Czech literature, should it be taken up, as one of competition with German literature. This is embraced by Slavomil. Where Protiva doubts the ability of the Czech language to raise a worthy literature, Slavomil does not: "That this language is sufficiently polished and capable of the cultivation [*vzdělání*] of all types of arts, the old writings leave clear evidence, and also not only our people, but Germans (excluding those of ours blinded by hatred) have impartially demonstrated this. Of course of words desired by a philosopher or artist [*mudřec a umělec*] there are few; but please, has German had more for long? And who feels this lack the most strongly? Those who know the language least of all! . . . Finally I do not understand what would prevent a Czech from taking words from other Slavic dialects—sprung from the same mother—where any genuine lack would appear."[47] Jungmann here indicates two of the projects that would be central to his program for the Czech revival—developing terminology for work in various fields of learning and developing a marked poetic language—and one of the primary means to their fulfillment: borrowing from other Slavic tongues. The project of developing poetic language led away from the accessible poetics directed toward less-educated readers and toward a more exclusive poetics with the highest artistic ambitions. Belles-lettres thus had an important place in Jungmann's program.

The proposal to use other Slavic languages as a means for enriching the Czech tongue deserves further comment. Unlike the use of German, this is not a violation of linguistic and national identity because Jungmann conceives of the Czech language and nation as parts of the broader Slavic language and nation. Protiva insists that the various Slavs in the Austrian empire are of different nations and therefore do not constitute one nation that would be the most numerous. Slavomil responds, "But they are all

Slavs, only divided in dialect, though perhaps no more than the Germans of Tachov and Kamenice in our land. Literature and politics would quickly join them all. I, at least, can easily imagine a certain central dialect that could join the brotherly Slavs, provided it is like the high German among the Germans or like the poetic language, or at least Plutarch's, among the Greeks."[48] The German example of uniting the literary language and nascent pan-Germanism allows Jungmann to conceive of a similar and competing literary and political program among the Slavs. If the Czech language should not be given up for German, Slavomil imagines perhaps giving it up for a centralized Slavic literary language. The contribution of Dobrovský to this conception must again be noted. A certain Slavic consciousness among the Czechs was maintained even during the Counter Reformation, but it was strengthened considerably by Dobrovský's Slavic philology work.[49] It is also important to recall here that the conception of the Czech nation then was not what it is now, but included the Slovaks, so that even the narrower concept of the Czech nation crossed certain linguistic and political borders.[50]

The particular emphasis on literature in the narrow sense is not especially prominent in Jungmann's dialogues. But in the context of their place of publication and of Jungmann's own activities in the first decade of the nineteenth century, the emphasis is clear. The *Hlasatel český* (published 1806–08, 1818) made high Czech literary art its goal, and Jungmann's articles can be taken as programmatic. On the need to cultivate Czech literary works of the highest ambitions, Jungmann was entirely in agreement with the journal's editor, Nejedlý, though when it came to the means for achieving it, the two differed. Nejedlý stuck rigidly to the literary norm of Dobrovský, the sixteenth-century Czech of Veleslavín, which gave his work archaicizing overtones. Jungmann, in contrast, was intent on the language's renewal, and he actively pursued neologisms and a re-Slavicization of the language.[51] While Jungmann's original poetry of the first decade of the nineteenth century gives little evidence of a new program to enrich the poetic language, his translations, and especially his translations of Milton's *Paradise Lost* (1800–1804, published 1811) and Chateaubriand's *Atala* (translated and published, 1805), give evidence of a concerted effort to create not only lexical, but also syntactic and metrical means of differentiating poetic language from everyday language.[52] Both of these translations are marked by their extensive borrowings from Russian and Polish of lexical items to fill perceived lacunae in the Czech vocabulary, a strategy that, as already seen, Jungmann defended in his dialogues. But far from all of Jungmann's neologisms are motivated by lack. There is also a marked tendency to create lexical doublets for existing Czech words, a tendency, in other words, to create poetisms, words with no more precise or specific meanings than existing words that are marked instead as belonging exclusively to poetic discourse. Thus the overall tendency of Jungmann's translations is to increase the aesthetic markedness of the texts' language. This practice leads, however, to a loss of other nuances: Vodička notes that Chateaubriand's development of romantic individuality in characters' expression is mitigated by the more general and abstract tendency in Jungmann's translation toward grandiloquent expression.[53]

In translating Milton, Jungmann also developed a dissatisfaction with the syllabotonic prosodic system outlined by Dobrovský just five years earlier, in 1795, finding it too inflexible.[54] And indeed, because in Czech word stress is fixed on the first syllable of the word, in the eleven-syllable unrhymed trochaic line Jungmann used to translate Milton's blank verse, for every filled ictus the foot boundary coincides with the word boundary.[55] The effect could be a rather plodding line, not the sublime poetic line he felt that the Czech language was capable of achieving. His dissatisfaction led him to reconsider the quantitative verse system, based on long and short Czech vowels, a system that had been in some minor use in the late sixteenth and seventeenth centuries. In 1804 he wrote an essay, "Nepředsudné mínění o české prozódii" ("An Unprejudiced Opinion on Czech Prosody"), which he sent to a number of leading writers, arguing for quantitative verse. The essay has not survived and evoked almost no response at the time.[56] However, Jungmann continued to quietly promote the idea, and a few scattered poems were published in quantitative verse in the following years. Among the factors that recommended quantitative verse was the fact that Greek and Latin versification were based on quantity, and if Czech could make use of the same principle it would mean a major coup in the competition with German literature, which had already developed a vision of itself as the closest to Greek literature. Jungmann expresses this idea, if somewhat elliptically, in his poem in quantitative hexameter welcoming the Slovak Samuel Rožnay's translation of Anacreon, "Slavěnka Slavínovi" (1813, Slavěnka to a Slav—Slavěnka being the female embodiment of Slavdom): "You have earned my thanks with a bouquet from Enna and Tempe./ I know that dear Greek bloom by its pleasant odor;/ Plucked by delicate hand, and fresh in its beauty./ Oh if only you had also wanted to bind them with a simple and graceful bow,/ Like beautiful Helenka herself wore them in her bosom,/ Or like the excellent Herder bound them for Teutona:/ Then the Nymphs of the whole land would envy your Slavěnka."[57] Jungmann's wish, expressed through his persona, is that Rožnay would bind his verses (*vázati*) in meter in the same manner as the Greeks (*"vázaná řeč"*—bound speech, was one way of indicating verse). His own poem stands as an example of the possibility of using Greek metrical form and its quantitative principle.[58] For Jungmann, such a change would have greatly increased the aesthetic worth of the translations.

Jungmann's dissatisfaction with Czech prosody may have also led him to Chateaubriand's prose, which embodied certain poetic features, such as the elevation and ordering of sound and isosyllabic sentence structures.[59] This allowed Jungmann to experiment with a looser structure in attempting to create rhythm and suggested further means to the aesthetic marking of the literary language and the unification of poetic discourse, whether in prose or verse. Clearly Jungmann's conception of the literary language included an impetus toward a marked separation of poetic discourse from other discourse from the start, though he would only theorize this later.[60] The rich signification of poetic language he hoped to create, however, was realized in his translations primarily in the highly limited signification of the discourse's own poeticalness, whether in verse or in prose.

The new program to create Czech literature of high artistic aspirations and the use of translations as a means to further this aim met with no understanding on the part of Dobrovský, though it was founded on his own analysis of the history of the Czech language. He did not review any of Jungmann's translations, but he did review Nejedlý's translation of Florian's *Numa Pompilius,* published in 1808. Above all, Dobrovský fails to understand the purpose of such a translation: "The reviewer can hardly guess for which class of reader Mr. Nejedlý has intended his translation. He would nearly believe that he did it just for his students in order to present them a model of a linguistically correct translation, and perhaps also for the very few readers of the middle class, for whom there can still be a need for a Czech translation of this book. More educated readers certainly reach instead for the original or a German translation, for such readers in Bohemia already generally read German. If the Czech Numa were to mix among the oft-read folk novels, it would occupy a leading place among them."[61] For Dobrovský social reality was always the final measure, and language and literature reflected reality not, certainly, in the sense of literary realism, but in that literature and language served social functions and needs within a given context and changed in response to changes in that social reality. But the social reality of the Czech readership had not changed from the early revival, and the only real audience for books in Czech was largely uneducated. Jungmann and

Nejedlý in their striving for high literary art had severed themselves from their only possible readership, and in this sense, Nejedlý's sixteenth-century archaizing was no better than Jungmann's neologizing. What Dobrovský could not understand was the tendency toward unreality, toward the creation of a linguistic simulacrum: a literary language and literary works that responded to the needs of a cultured class of Czech speakers that *did not yet exist*.

Jungmann had turned Dobrovský's analysis of the literary language upside down. If Dobrovský had analyzed the effects of historical social reality on the culture of the Czech language, Jungmann would try to manipulate the Czech language in order to mimic a desired social reality. This was not mere willfulness, however, for the ultimate goal was the creation of the missing social reality, and the creation of the linguistic reality was only a step in that direction. In the given social reality, in which German, French, and Latin fulfilled the functions of cultured languages for the educated class, an uncultured Czech language could never compete and would never gain the educated writers and readers it needed to develop. Rather than wait for outside institutional changes to return Czech to its place, Jungmann, much like Karamzin, proposed the bold and somewhat paradoxical step of beginning to cultivate the language, so that it could win educated Czechs away from German. And in the second decade of the century, his work began gradually to find a response as younger writers, such as Václav Hanka, Josef Linda, Antonín Marek, František Palacký, Milota Zdirad Polák, and Pavel Josef Šafařík embraced the Czech language and Jungmann's aesthetic and cultural program.

Though Jungmann did not yet use the phrase "*národní literatura*" (national literature) in these dialogues, he had defined for the Czechs essential elements of a national ideology and a program for their national literature. He clearly conceived of Czech culture as a distinct phenomenon, defined by the Czech language, though again, he did not yet use the phrase "česká kultura." His conception of Czech national identity as being rooted exclusively in the Czech language was thoroughly modern, and if he continued to work with a broader conception of literature, his approach to and emphasis on artistic literature were modernizing. Both his choice of writers to translate and his approach to Czech prosody suggest a thoughtful reconsideration of the ancient classical tradition and the relationship of modern Czech literature to it. If Milton and Chateaubriand offered Jungmann the newer values of the European literary tradition, the fact that the Czech language was capable of the same prosody as the Greek language suggests an essential relationship between the Czech and Greek nations that could be expressed in modern Czech literature.

A RUSSIAN PARALLEL. A text with striking parallels to Jungmann's first dialogue, with its depiction of the contamination of the modern Czech language, was also produced in Russia soon after the turn of the century. Its author was Semen Bobrov (1763–1810), a representative author in Shishkov's camp, and the work, "Proizshestvie v tsarstve tenei" ("An Incident in the Kingdom of Shades," 1805), was published and analyzed extensively by Lotman and Uspensky.[62] There, Boian (the mythical ancient Russian epic poet) greets the arrival of Galloruss on the other side of the river Styx:

> Welcome, dear guest! I thank you for your greeting. May I ask from whence you hail? Your dress, gait, and foreign dialect prove you to be of another tribe. Not perhaps from Dalmatia? Or from Istria or Vandalia?
>
> *Galloruss*:
>
> What do you mean of another tribe? What do you mean from Dalmatia? [aside] Ach! Doesn't it all *reek of antiquity* [*pakhnet starinoi*]? —it's unbearable; —as though my language were foreign to him! [to him] Do you really not see in me a Russian [*rossianin*]? Do you know that now at home *everything has changed* [*vse peremienivshis'*]? —Let me tell you: —in place of your awkward dress, your zhupans, they wear jackets of the latest fashion, as you see on me; —a glorious hairstyle *a la Tite,* —they shave their beards; —the customs of old obstinates have been tossed aside; . . . now everything is younger, everything is *fresher* [*osviezhenniee*]; everything smiles; —feelings are *more refined* [*utoncheniee*]; the Russian language more polished [*ochishchenniee*]; . . . and now, —you can see and judge by me, —everywhere *it has blossomed* [*razsvietavshi*]; —in a word, everything is in its place [*v svoei tarelkie*].[63]

Like Jungmann's modern Czech, Galloruss responds to questions of his foreignness by a defense of his (modern) culture. Bobrov marks all of Galloruss's "unnatural" language with italics—unlike in the Czech text, most of these are not obviously humorous foreignisms or solecisms but new and fashionable Russian words, phrases, and syntactical formations. Bobrov needs to remind his readers of their French origin because usage has naturalized them.

This difference is quite representative of the difference between the Czech and Russian language and literary situations at the beginning of the century. While both Jungmann and Shishkov made language the carrier of national values, with consequences for literary practice, the perceived threat to the national language was entirely different. The German language threatened the Czech language with extinction, as illustrated by Jungmann's modern Czech, for whom using the Czech language for cultivated discourse is unthinkable. For him, German is the language of culture and his macaronic Czech represents not a debased new literary norm but the lack of any literary cultivation of the Czech language. In response, Jungmann does not appeal to an older and stable norm of literary Czech, like Dobrovský or Nejedlý. He needs a modern Czech language that can compete with modern German in all fields of contemporary culture. So he encourages innovation in the Czech literary language by borrowing from other Slavic languages. For Jungmann, the threat to Czech comes from the exterior, from the foreign German language, and its defense can be aided by borrowings from the interior, from the related Slavic "dialects." The threat to the Russian language, in contrast, is perceived as coming from the inside, from an established literary practice that has altered the Russian language by changing its vocabulary, phraseology, and syntax to conform to a foreign model. There is no threat of the extinction of the Russian language or its loss of status as a language of culture. Quite the opposite: it has been so altered precisely by the most cultivated members of Russian society. The threat is rather to the natural identity of the Russian language. Because there is an established literary practice that uses this new Franco-Russian language, Bobrov, like Shishkov, is able to treat the language question as a question of style. In the continuation of the dialogue, Galloruss has Lomonosov summoned to judge his language dispute with Boian. As Galloruss himself notes, "He will be the judge, standing [as he does] on the middle point between ancientness and modernity in Russian enlightenment."[64] Lomonosov appears and Galloruss gives him his notebook with passages from his favorite contemporary authors, upon the style of which Lomonosov pronounces his stern judgments. Lomonosov, as an eighteenth-century modernizer of the Russian literary language, is the authority for Bobrov on a proper manner of modernization that preserves Russian literary and linguistic identity.

Part II

TRANSLATION AND THE NATIONAL LITERATURE

Translating Folk Discourse
Folk Song Echoes and Ballads

Translation plays an important role in literary modernization. The role of translation in the development of the paradigm of national literatures in particular is perhaps surprising today, when society has internalized the emphasis on originality and native sources that became characteristic of the established paradigm. But already in the "Querelle d'Homère," the third phase of the larger Quarrel between the Ancients and Moderns, translation became a site for an exploration of historical and cultural alterity that ultimately challenged the model status of the ancient classics and led to modern historicist perspectives. Homer and his Greek language came to be seen as distant and different from modern European authors and their languages. The problem of translation became fundamentally a problem of difference and of possible ways of overcoming temporal and cultural distance. In the later eighteenth century, translation and its engagement with difference became integral to a new conception of German culture.

Antoine Berman has explored this relationship between translation and culture in German thought, which is inscribed in the concept of *Bildung*:

Bildung is one of the central concepts of German culture at the end of the eighteenth century. It can be found everywhere: in Herder, in Goethe and Schiller, in the romantics, in Hegel, in Fichte, etc. *Bildung* generally means "culture," and it may be considered the German counterpart of *Kultur,* which is of Latin stock. But because of the lexical family to which it belongs,[1] it means much more and it is applied to many more registers: thus it is possible to speak of the *Bildung* of an artwork, the degree of its "formation." Likewise, *Bildung* has a very strong pedagogical and educational connotation: the process of formation. It is no exaggeration to state that the concept summarizes the conception which the German culture of the time formed of itself, *the way in which the culture interprets its mode of unfolding.*[2]

In fact, as described in chapter 4, the borrowed term *Kultur* was developing similarly to indicate not only the process of cultivation but also its result. But the lexical family to which *Bildung* belongs is indeed relevant to its difference, because instead of agriculture *Bildung* invokes form. "What then is *Bildung?* It is a process, as well as its result. Through *Bildung* an individual, a people, a nation, but also a language, a literature, a work of art in general are formed and thus acquire a form, a *Bild. Bildung* is always a movement toward form, *one's own form.*"[3]

Berman argues that, whatever differences there are among authors on the particulars of the process of *Bildung,* the fundamental paradigm is the same: the self-in-formation must depart from itself, must have an experience of the foreign, of radical alterity, in order to return to the self as a reunited unity.[4] This is the essential culture-forming process, and as Berman notes, "*it is closely connected with the movement of translation—*for translation, indeed, starts from what is one's own, the same (the known, the quotidian, the familiar), in order to go towards the foreign, the other (the unknown, the miraculous, the *Unheimliche*), and, starting from this experience, *to return to its point of departure. . . . This circular, cyclical, and alternating nature of* Bildung *implies in itself something like trans-lation,* Über-Setzung, *a positioning of oneself beyond oneself.*"[5] That cultural formation is a kind of translation was not lost on the German writers of the period: they saw translation as an essential cultural task and viewed the German drive to translate and its manifold receptivity to other cultures as the glory of German culture.[6] In Germany, translation was integral to the creation of national culture.

For the Czechs and Russians, as already noted, translation had a similarly central role in the early programs for the national literature. The Karamzinian reform of the Russian literary language amounts to a translation of the refined language of the French salon culture into Russian, altering the Russian language in the process. And Jungmann sought a similar refinement of the Czech language, though in a rather more indirect manner: in translations from English and French he borrowed vocabulary from related Slavic languages to enrich Czech. But Shishkov opposed the alteration of the Russian language on the French model and posed the problem, at least in part, as one of translation—he suggested that translations that transformed the Russian language and literature were a detriment to cultural identity. In fact, the assimilation of the paradigm of "national literature" at this point created two conflicting drives in Russian and Czech culture. There was a critical need for new forms of language and literature that encouraged translation as a practice of formal enrichment. But the emerging drive to develop native sources and original literature heightened the resistance to translation. Berman formulates this problem as a cultural universal of sorts: "Every culture resists translation, even if it has an essential need for it. The very aim of translation—to open up in writing a certain relation to the Other, to fertilize what is one's Own through the mediation of what is Foreign—is diametrically opposed to the ethnocentric structure of every culture, that species of narcissism by which every society wants to be a pure and unadulterated Whole. There is a tinge of the violence of cross-breeding in translation."[7] While both poles may indeed be ever present, one could suggest that at this particular moment in Czech and Russian culture when programs for creating a national literature emerge, both the need for translation and resistance to it grow quickly and simultaneously, though eventually the resistance to cultural cross-breeding would come to dominate, making translation a suspect activity. The resistance to French culture in Russia grows steadily, having a spike particularly in 1812 with the burning of Moscow, but translation as such does not become particularly suspect until the 1820s (see chapter 10). The Czech resistance to German culture is as constant as the continuing dialogue with German culture. Translation more generally comes into question in the 1830s. Until then, translation would continue to play a central role in the national literature programs.[8]

VOLKSPOESIE IN TRANSLATION. The introduction of folkloric discourse into literature is a transformative process that changes language and literature by contributing new forms. In that sense, Berman notes, "the revival, from Herder to Grimm, of folk tales and folk poetry, of medieval songs and epics . . . is an intratranslation of sorts, through which German literature acquires a vast treasury of *forms,* even more than a repository of themes and contents."[9] There is a translation here from nonliterature into literature, from oral forms to written forms, or from older, already foreign forms of literature to forms that answered to the needs of a modernizing literature. To this implicit or internal translation, the Czech and Russian figures to be examined in this chapter added the explicit translation of foreign texts in their attempts to give their literatures the values carried by the folk forms.

The potential values of folk discourse included naturalness and authenticity, perhaps even the newly positive value of the primitive, and a connection to ancient national traditions that was undisputed at the time. The concept of *Volkspoesie* articulated by Herder and Gottfried August Bürger carried with it values with great potential for national literature programs, in part because it encompassed poetic works that *already* represented an artistic translation of oral traditions. Hermann Bausinger notes that the terms *Volkspoesie, Volksdichtung, Volkslied,* and *Volkssage* all appear for the first time between 1760 and 1780: "Not always can word history be directly interpreted as factual history; but this massive appearance of new terms supports the assumption that not only was something old discovered but something new was created, that not only was a name given to the nameless variety of the oral tradition but that it was transposed on another level and thus transformed." He insists on speaking of the *invention* of *Volkspoesie* because it "was not a fact of oral tradition but a creative fiction that brought together the *Volk* and art."[10] As Herder used the term *Volkspoesie,* and the term appears first in his writings along with its equivalent *Volksdichtung* and the related *Volkslied,* it is not at all equivalent to the current concept of folk poetry, but is vaguer and more fertile.[11] René Wellek noted that it "is a highly inclusive concept: it includes Genesis, the Song of Songs, the Book of Job, the Psalms, in fact nearly all of the Old Testament. It includes Homer, Hesiod, Aeschylus and Sophocles, Sappho and the *Greek Anthology,* Chaucer, Spenser, Shakespeare, and the contents of Percy's *Reliques* (not only English and Scottish ballads but Elizabethan songs). It includes medieval romances, the German *Heldenbuch,* the troubadours, the *Minnesang,* Bürger's ballads, and Klopstock, whom Herder admired beyond any of the German poets. It even includes Dante and of course Ossian."[12] And yet it excludes the rabble and any unnatural poetic productions, be they rule-bound imitations or artificial creations driven by aesthetic considerations. What today would be called folk songs, Herder took as scraps or remnants from a nearly lost authentic tradition and he recommended collecting them almost as a last-ditch effort to salvage the tradition.[13]

In his own publication of songs, Herder included not only songs from the oral tradition that could be taken as fragments of an ancient tradition but also modern productions that shared with the other songs a certain natural spirit, including a recent poem by Goethe. *Volkspoesie,* then, encompassed works from all periods, including the contemporary one, which had or reflected high poetic value and were marked in some way as natural. It is a category created to oppose a classicism of prescriptive poetics, to free poetic creativity from the bonds of rules. As Bausinger observes, for Herder *Volkspoesie* "was a timeless agent that penetrates all true poetry."[14] In that sense, although Herder needed the term for his historical analyses of various national literary traditions, *Volkspoesie* transcends the particularities of place and time, and thus of national traditions—his publication of folk songs characteristically includes not only songs from all times, but also from a variety of places.

A more national emphasis is apparent in the work of Herder's fellow *Stürmer,* Gottfried August Bürger. The truth is that Bürger's concept of *Volkspoesie* differed very little from Herder's. He, too, included the works of Homer, Ariosto, Ossian, Shakespeare, and Spenser.[15] But, his development of the ballad genre with marked folkloric elements, his emphatic theoretical opposition of artless, natural poetry to artificial high poetry, his pursuit of the popular, and his somewhat more forward nationalism have led to his relegation to the realm of lower poetry.[16] If for Herder *Volkspoesie* was a concept explored primarily in historical analysis, for Bürger the implications of the concept for contemporary German poetry received the primary emphasis. *Volkspoesie* became Bürger's program for creating a more national German literature. He asks, in his "Herzenausguß über Volkspoesie" ("Outpourings from the Heart on *Volkspoesie,*" 1776), "Where is it written in the natural catechism of the Germans that the German muse should procure foreign fantasies and feelings, or wrap its own in foreign costumes? Where is it written that she should stammer a divine language, as it were, rather than the human tongue of the Germans? Divine language? Dear God have mercy! This divine language, which many of our muse's infants claim to babble, is often nothing but the coarse roaring of lions and bulls, the neighing of stallions, howling of wolves, barking of dogs, and cackling of geese."[17] He suggests, rather, that "We are Germans! Germans who should not make Greek, Roman, cosmopolitan poems in the German tongue, but German poems in the German tongue, digestible and nourishing for the whole people. You poets who have not done anything like this, and therefore are read little or not at all, don't blame the 'cold and slothful' audience, blame yourselves! Give us a great national poem of the kind described, and we'll make it our vade mecum. Come down from the peaks of your cloudy learning, and don't demand that we, the many who live on earth, should climb up to you few."[18] Bürger demanded *Volkspoesie* in the present day as the remedy for a literature that no longer spoke to the nation as a whole in a comprehensible language.

In the translation of Herder's terminology into Czech and Russian, facts of language as well as the advance of the national literature paradigm strengthened the conceptual ties between folk songs and the national literary tradition. For the German *Volk* and *Nation,* Czech and Russian at the time both employed primarily a single term: *národ* and *narod,* respectively. Thus, while one can draw important distinctions between *Volkspoesie* and *Nationalliteratur* in Herder's discourse, in the equivalent Czech and Russian terms of the time, *národní poezie–národní literatura* and *narodnaia poeziia–narodnaia literatura,* the lexical similarity allows for easy conflation. Distinctions would develop later: in contemporary Czech folk songs are *lidové písně* while in Russian *natsional'naia literatura* would be more common for the second term. But at the time, the multivalence of the root term *národ/narod* proved productive and suggestive. Both languages had forms of an adjective that would denote folk traditions less ambiguously, *prostonárodní* and *prostonarodnyi,* but these were not generally used in appeals to incorporate folk traditions into literature, probably because the conflation of folk and nation better served the economy of such arguments.

ECHOES OF THE PAST. Václav Hanka (1791–1861) belongs to that Czech generation whose work should be seen within the context of Jungmann's program, and yet, because he brought to it something entirely new—the influence of folklore—his work has often been seen as opposed to that of Jungmann.[19] Jungmann certainly had no love of folklore,[20] and his national literary program, with its striving for high literary art and the dominance of the aesthetic aspect of the work, at best neglected the lower end of the literary spectrum, to which it definitely relegated folklore. Felix Vodička has explained the structural logic of this emphasis: the Czech revival in its initial situation had a continuous tradition of literary productions for less-educated readers, but the needs of more demanding readers were fulfilled by German and French literature. Any effort to create a full national literary culture, then, had to work first to fill the gap in the upper register, "so that the polarity of high and folk literature was not realized externally to the Czech language, but within it."[21] But the lower end of the spectrum also had a potential attraction. As Macura has observed, the lack of any developed high Czech culture could be interpreted positively: "The Czech world stood here in direct antithesis to culture, not just to German culture, but to culture in general. Rather it represented in the consciousness of the period the world of nature; with the growing cult of nature, interest in it also grew."[22] Hanka's contribution is to provide a means of incorporating this "natural" stratum into Jungmann's linguistic and literary program, to place folklore into relation with the development of the national language and culture using many of the same means Jungmann chose for his incorporation of the highest aesthetic models and values.

Both of Hanka's parents were active singers of folk songs, and Hanka's father gathered an extensive collection of songs, preserved by Hanka and included among his papers in the National Museum.[23] Hanka's father also owned an inn, and in his youth, Hanka learned some of the languages of the Austrian Slavs from visitors; later in life he was able to use them actively.[24] But his initial poetic efforts were very much in line with the Puchmajer school, to which Jungmann also initially belonged, and included Anacreontic lyrics, idylls, odes, epigrams, and fables. There was some tendency toward incorporation of folkloric elements in love lyrics and idylls within the Puchmajer school, enabled by the fact that both the Anacreontic and folk lyric worked within stable, though different, lexical and topical systems, and Hanka's own practice moved spontaneously in this direction.[25] Beginning with his stay in Vienna as a law student in 1813, however, Hanka's embrace of the folk lyric became conscious and moved to the center of his poetic activity.

Hanka came to Vienna with a letter from Josef Dobrovský for Jernej Kopitar,[26] a Slovene who served as a scribe in the Imperial Court Library and censor for Slavic and Modern Greek publications and was also becoming a leading Slavic philologist. Kopitar had also come to Vienna as a law student in 1809, just one year after he had initiated a correspondence on matters Slavic with Dobrovský. Kopitar's enthusiasm for *Volkspoesie* derived from his own rural childhood, his work before coming to Vienna in a Slovene circle that was reviving the literary language, and, most importantly, his discovery of a jewel of South Slavic Moslem oral epic in Herder's *Volkslieder:* the "Hasanaginica" in Goethe's translation. He referred to the latter frequently in correspondence and publications in which he called for the collection of Serbian and Croatian songs.[27] He found his collector in 1813 in Vuk Karadžić, who produced, with Kopitar's encouragement, not only a classic collection of folk songs that inspired romantic Europe, but also a grammar and dictionary of Serbian. Kopitar was likely encouraged in his interests as well by a query from his esteemed Dobrovský in 1809 about the existence of South Slavic folk materials.²⁸

Because Hanka had been briefly Dobrovský's student in 1813 in his private seminar on Slavistics before coming to Vienna, later becoming his favorite student, one needs to consider whether Hanka's interest in folk songs may have been encouraged by Dobrovský as well as Kopitar. Around 1810 in particular Dobrovský inquired after folkloric materials not only from Kopitar, but also from his other correspondents as well. As with the query to Kopitar, he asked for not only songs, but also fables, riddles, and especially proverbs.²⁹ As William Harkins has argued, this interest in folklore seems to respond primarily to philological concerns—the interest in proverbs in particular reflects concerns with antiquated language forms as well as an interest in the forms of folk wisdom that responds to Enlightenment rationality.³⁰ The national significance of the material is not pursued by Dobrovský. The particular formulation of his query to Kopitar about folk songs is telling in this regard. "Are there," he asks, "any demonstrably old [*erweislich alte*] Volkslieder? Are they 4- or 9-syllable?"³¹ His immediate interest is not just the formal features of the verse: in asking for *demonstrably old* songs, he reveals a deep skepticism toward the widely accepted thesis that the folk songs then in circulation reflected, however imperfectly, ancient national traditions. On the other hand, the medieval Russian *Slovo o polku Igoreve* may have been responsible for the awakening of Dobrovský's interest in the possibility that *Volkslieder* may indeed have existed among the Slavs in an early period.³² One definitely should not underestimate, then, the possible influence of Dobrovský's search for demonstrably old songs on his student Hanka. But Dobrovský probably could have introduced Hanka to the thesis of the national significance of the songs only in rejecting it.

Kopitar likely thought that he had found in Hanka, whose childhood familiarity with Czech songs has already been noted, a Czech collector to compete with Karadžić. In Vienna, Hanka became a regular contributor to *Prvotiny pěkných umění* (*First-fruits of the Fine Arts*, published 1813–1817), the Viennese periodical published by Jan Hromádko that filled the gap left by the much delayed *Hlasatel český*. In 1814 Hanka published, anonymously, a short article in which he called the Czechs to the collection and publication of their own songs:

> It would be highly desirable if some gentleman patriot would make the effort to collect for us our lovely folk songs [*národní písně*], so that the Czechs might be led back to Slavic song, from which, alas! we have strayed so far with harsh

sounds and the imitation of German songs, at least in the cities; and our old songs certainly deserve to be held up as models to today's new composers, for which nation can show us songs more majestic, more sublime and more sacred than our 'Otče náš milý Pane' [Dear Lord our Father]? Where can we find more amorous and humorous ones than 'Má panenka hezká je' [My lass is pretty] and 'Kdybys měla má panenko sto ovec' [If my lass had a hundred sheep]? The Czechs, widely famed in music and scattered all over Europe in all the capitals and at every court, ought to preserve that treasure of ancient singing too, not only for their descendents, but also for all nations, like Ivan Prač did for the Russians. He published "*Sobranie Narodnykh Russkykh* [*sic.*] *Piesen' s ikh golosami,*" that is, A Collection of Russian Folk Songs with their Melodies, from which the most famous musicians of our age, like Van Bethoven [*sic.*], draw themes for their compositions. Unfortunately we have no notes in our print shop in order to present our gentlemen patriots with a song; since that is impossible, we will set down here without notes at least one Russian and one Serbian song, along with Czech translations. Everyone knows that in folk songs [*v národních písních*] simplicity and innocence are the leading thing, and therefore that one cannot find in them sublime or artistic poeticizing. Even the Serbs outdid us this year in this, having published their folk songs in Vienna.[33]

Hanka here connects the Czech songs to the larger body of Slavic songs, placing them within a broader Slavic "national" context that is familiar already from Jungmann. And the national character of the folk songs is not in question—they are conceived as a route back to the ancient, common Slavic tradition. As noted earlier, the translation of Herder's terminology into Czech also contributed: *národní písně* is the Czech equivalent of Herder's *Volkslieder* and could as easily be translated as "national songs." Like Herder's and Bürger's, Hanka's concept of "folk song"—insofar as it can be determined from the small amount of data here—is broad and not at all equivalent to the oral tradition. Of the three songs he mentions, the first is an old and very popular Czech hymn that, whatever its relationship to a possible original oral tradition, had a long history in print.[34] The second is obscure, while the third—a humorous love declaration—is today still a part of the active repertoire of children's and folk songs. What Hanka holds up as a model, then, is not exactly folk songs, though it includes folk songs along with any other songs that can be linked to national tradition and an imagined and idealized national character. It is also worth noting that certain songs are models of particular poetic virtues, from the sublime to the humorous. One should not be surprised, then, when a few lines later Hanka notes, concerning his translations of a song from each of the two collections he mentions, that "everyone knows that in folk songs simplicity and innocence are the leading thing, and therefore that one cannot find in them sublime or artistic poeticizing." True folk songs as these were—note the term in Karadžić's title: "*prostonarodnja*"—still evoke the usual reservations concerning their aesthetic qualities. Though, in the spirit of Schiller's contrast between naive and sentimental poetry, "simplicity and innocence" (naiveté?) had become virtues and aesthetic qualities in themselves that Hanka would explore.

One should be cautious, however, in assuming that Hanka is here proposing folk songs as literary models; he suggests they can be models for *composers*. To be sure, in speaking of lyrics one might use such a term for writers as well as musical composers, but the example of Beethoven's use of Prach's songbook confirms rather the musical emphasis. If Hanka was here proposing the collection and publication of songs with musical notation for use by composers, then the fact that he himself never undertook a song collection is certainly less surprising than it has seemed to some commentators. On the other hand, Hanka does provide the song texts without the music, so that the aesthetic reservations and simultaneous offering of aesthetic models of simplicity and innocence refer here primarily to the song texts, rather than to the melodies.

A few words are in order here about Ivan Prach and his songbook. Ivan Prach/Jan Bohumír Práč/Johann Gottfried Pratsch (c1750–c1818) was a Silesian Czech by origin, a musician and clavichord master, who sometime in the 1770s went to St. Petersburg, where he lived in the home of P. A. Soimonov, presumably as a family music tutor. He also was appointed as a teacher of music at the Institute for Young Ladies of Noble Birth, where he worked from 1780 to 1790 and from 1791 to 1795.[35] Hanka's lament at all the scattered Czech musicians who were not working to preserve the treasure of ancient Czech song may, then, be a dig at Prach individually as well as a goad to the many other Czech musicians like him at the time.[36] Although Prach's name was the only one to appear on the collection in the first three editions (1790, 1806, 1815), the collection was in fact the work of Nikolai Aleksandrovich L'vov (1751–1803), who presumably hired Prach to transcribe the melodies and compose the accompaniment.[37] While not the first collection of Russian songs, it was the first to use the term *narodnye pesni*, thus calquing the title of Herder's *Volkslieder* by which it was directly inspired.[38] Nikolai L'vov was a noble landowner and the patron of an artistic salon that counted among its intimates leading poets and artists of the day, including Gavrila Derzhavin and Vasily Kapnist. He was also an early pioneer in advocating the use of folk songs as a model for artists of high culture. He himself penned a few imitations of Russian folk songs—decades before Merzliakov—and some of the opening choruses in his comic opera *Iamshchiki na podstave* (*Coachmen at the Relay Station*, 1787, with the composer Evstignei Fomin), in their imitation of the heterophonic chorus characteristic of the Russian folk genre of the *protiazhnaia pesnia* (a genre that L'vov first named and discussed), exceed in their faithfulness any other attempts in Russian art music for nearly a century.[39] His collection of folk songs not only introduced Russian music to Europe, where Beethoven made prominent use of its musical texts; it also defined Russian music for Russia itself, for in spite of the reservations of later generations of folklorists, Russian composers across the spectrum made use of its material.[40] Richard Taruskin concludes, "the collection, in other words, and uniquely, fulfilled the role its compilers (but particularly Lvov) envisioned for it, as a cultural uniter—indeed, as a creator—of the Russian nation."[41] To be sure, the preface to the first edition should be added to the list of possible sources for Hanka's national reading of the folk song (the title given by Hanka, which reads "narodnykh russkikh" rather than "russkikh narodnykh," clearly indicates Hanka had the 1790 and not the 1806 edition). There, L'vov expresses his preference for the aesthetic qualities of the "ancient songs" over the more recent compositions, offers folk song as a national treasure and a rich source for national music, and suggests that the origins of Russian music are to be found in ancient Greek music (which will be of more interest in chapter 7 than here).[42]

While Hanka did not collect songs, he did soon begin to "compose" song texts, with a particular emphasis on his own artlessness. In a note to one poem in his first collection, *Dvanáctero písní* (*Twelve Songs*, 1815), he observes that it was "the composer's very first song, when he still did not know anything about prosody."[43] But Hanka's papers show the poem to be far from his first (though it may indeed be his first "song"), and the poem is accompanied in the manuscripts by an annotation of its metrical form.[44] And in a "Reminder" in the 1819 edition of Hanka's *Songs*, he described his methods thus: "My desire for the songs was—mere song; for this reason the prosodists will not measure them either by stress or by quantity; my hearing alone was my guide, and sometimes I even slipped off its path, unable to overleap the constraints of the language."[45] By that time, the battle over Czech prosody had begun, and concerns of aesthetics and artfulness were at its center (see chapter 6). Hanka here poses as the naive poet whose songs do not conform to artful means of composition and cannot be measured by them. Though in fact, as Jan Máchal observes, one of the better compliments one can pay Hanka's songs is that they are rhythmically regular and correct in their syllabotonic prosody, which made them attractive to tune composers.[46]

In his pose, Hanka opposed himself to Jungmann and his followers and their striving after high art. But his literary methods share something fundamental with Jungmann's program. As already noted, Hanka translated songs from each of the two collections mentioned in his article, and soon he undertook a translation of eight Serbian and two Russian songs for his *Prostonárodní Srbská Muza, do Čech převedená* (*The Serbian Folk Muse, Led Over into Bohemia*, 1817). Rather than collecting Czech folk songs as he proposed, Hanka proceeded by the same means as Jungmann, using translation to "lead in" the desired artistic (or "natural") and linguistic values. In fact, the metaphor of his title can be read in two contradictory ways: it can be a Russianism or a Serbianism, a phonetic translation of the Russian or Serbian words for "translated," *perevedena/prevedena*—this would take the metaphor back to a more literal naming of what he is doing; or one can see it as a metaphorical resistance to translation, to using the word translation to describe what he is doing. It is almost impossible to decide between these two interpretations, because Hanka's practice of translation was so open to the Russian and Serbian languages that it was resistant to translating from them. The language of his translations was filled with Russianisms and Serbianisms, often leading to nonsense in Czech when words he translated only phonetically, thus leading them into the Czech language, already had entirely different meanings in Czech.[47] Here, too, Hanka is entirely true to the language ideology expounded by Jungmann—if the Slavic languages are actually but a single language that may reunite one day, then Russian and Serbian are not foreign languages but merely related variants of the Slavic language. Translation from Russian and Serbian involves not an encounter with an Other, but a discovery and reappropriation of a less familiar self. Taking words from Russian and Serbian is not appropriation of foreign goods, but internal trade and exchange. Hanka was less elegant than Jungmann, but he was also more direct, using Slavic borrowings in translations from Slavic languages, rather than in translations from English, French, or German, and by this means returning the Czechs to their native Slavic roots. The "in-difference" of the Slavic language(s) and nation(s)— that is, their presupposed common identity for Hanka, who ignores their differences—is also evident in his inclusion of two Russian songs (marked as such) in a volume dedicated to the Serbian folk muse. As Macura has observed, phonetic translation of this type became a common practice in translating Slavic texts in the Czech revival, especially for Russian and Polish texts—sometimes whole texts were only phonetically translated while at other times this was done more selectively. But it could also be used in translations from any prestige culture as a means of suggesting close genetic, ethnic, or linguistic ties, and the practice appears in translations from Greek in particular, but also in translations of Roman and Celtic texts.[48] Hanka thus participated in, and helped to establish, an important form of translation practice that aimed to raise the prestige of Czech language and culture by, in fact, appropriating foreign cultural currency, pretending it was not foreign.

In his "original" poetry, Hanka also helped to establish an important new literary genre. Here, too, his method both used and resisted translation. From the beginning of his poetic activity, the collection of Russian songs by Mikhail Chulkov (part 1, published 1770) provided Hanka with endless inspiration for his own love and pastoral lyrics.[49] From 1816 on, his use of the collection became more overt. Most often Hanka's songs begin with a direct translation of the opening lines of one of Chulkov's songs, followed by a freer adaptation of the following lines, and finishing with Hanka's own inventions, often quite distant from the Russian original.[50] Some songs are entirely paraphrases or adaptations.[51] Nowhere does Hanka acknowledge his source, thus hiding the fact of his translational method. In this manner, he created one of the most fertile poetic forms in the Czech revival, the "ohlas" or "echo" genre, which involves the composition of a poem in the spirit of a folk song. It is a genre based on the recognition that it was necessary to translate folk material into literary material, to alter it in order to make it acceptable to a more educated readership. Hanka's own method, though, and his results would be superseded as later poets looked beyond the simple surface of folk poetry in search of poetic means and values. Hanka was satisfied with a more superficial method, and so were readers, who made him one of the most popular poets of the decade. In one poem, which Hanka indicated was written "in the old-Czech spirit," he began with a song from Chulkov and ended with material from a Serbian song he had translated for his book.[52] The in-difference of the Slavic cultures is thus evident in his "echo" poems as much as in his translations. The example shows, further, that this Slavic in-difference had an important temporal dimension—contemporary folk songs from other Slavic cultures are taken as directly reflective of a distant historical layer, the old-Czech period when Slavic cultural identity was especially considered to be shared.

Hanka confirmed that he best knew what the old-Czech spirit and style was, or what his contemporaries thought it should be, by helping to counterfeit a series of manuscripts, "discovered" between 1816 and 1818 and claiming their origins in the ninth and thirteenth centuries. These texts, too, are products of the adaptive non-translation of other Slavic material on the assumption of cultural identity. This aspect of Hanka's activities will also be discussed in chapter 6.

THE RUSSIAN BALLAD DEBATE. In Russia there were also practitioners of the imitation of folk songs, but they were not able to move folkloric discourse into the center of literary attention in the manner of Hanka. Nikolai L'vov's collection of folk songs was more a musical than a literary event, and his innovative epic fragment *Dobrynia* (1796, published 1804), which took its hero from the Russian *bylina* (oral epic) and its tonic verse forms from folk songs, remained an isolated experiment without imitators for nearly as long as his musical imitation of folkloric heterophony. Merzliakov's imitations of folk songs were popular as songs and some even entered into the oral tradition (like some of Hanka's), but while Hanka was the progenitor of a highly productive genre in Czech literature, Merzliakov had no followers and his songs were not recognized as an important contribution to literature until their republication in 1830. When L'vov and Merzliakov were joined by Shishkov as advocates for the use of folkloric discourse, however, the question of folklore's place in the national literature became potential fodder for the constant debates between Shishkov's followers and the followers of Karamzin. This potential was realized in 1816 in debates over the ballad genre and its appropriate language style. The reader will not be surprised to learn that the competing ballads in the debate were translations.

As already noted, Shishkov first suggested in his 1805 edition of *Slovo o polku Igoreve* that old songs, proverbs, and tales (*skazki*) gave evidence of the high development of the Russian language before the introduction of Christianity.[53] He made the popular/folk language (*narodnyi iazyk*) a model for poetry and *krasnorechie* in his *Razgovory o slovesnosti* (*Dialogues on Slovesnost'*, 1811) alongside church books and chronicles.[54] Here the significance of the folk genres is directly connected to *Slovo,* because both are evidence of an older tradition of Russian poetics. Shishkov divides Russian poetry into two larger periods, before and after the poetic reforms of Trediakovsky and Lomonosov in the mid-eighteenth century. *Slovo* gives direct evidence of the older poetic tradition, while tales and songs preserve remnants.[55] Shishkov's description of the nature of the older poetic tradition is an early attempt to describe folkloric poetic discourse—he comments on various types of repetition; the use of epithets, diminutives, and the grammatical form of the short adjective; and the device of negative comparison.[56] The incorporation of folkloric discourse could thus be figured as the reincorporation of a native poetic tradition that had been lost to the imitation of foreign models.

In Russian literature of the first decade of the nineteenth century, the ballad, particularly in the new folk-derived form that English and German poets had recently developed, was an almost untried genre. This new form of the ballad had great potential for the incorporation of folkloric elements, but as already noted, folklore was having difficulty finding its way into Russian literary practices. Filipp F. Vigel' in his memoirs described the resistant literary atmosphere into which Vasily Zhukovsky tried to introduce the genre in 1808: "Satiated by the literature of the ancients and by French literature, its humble imitator . . . we saw something monstrous in his choices. Dead men, ghosts, devilry [*chertovshchina*], murders, all lit by the moon, well that all belonged to fairy tales [*skazki*] or perhaps to English novels; instead of Hero, awaiting the drowning Leander with gentle trepidation, to present us the madly passionate Lenore with the leaping corpse of her lover! It needed his wondrous gift in order to make us not only read his ballads without disgust but, finally, even to like them."[57] To satisfy the needs of such a reading public, the ballad genre and its folkloric elements had to be translated into a readable language, and Zhukovsky was just the translator for the job.

It is characteristic of Zhukovsky as a poet to move from translation to original poetry. As he observed later in life, "I have often noted that I have the clearest thoughts when I have to improvise them in expressing or supplementing others' [*chuzhikh*] thoughts. My mind is like a flint that has to be struck upon a stone in order that sparks fly from it. That is in general the character of my authorial creativity; with me everything is either another's [*chuzhoe*—"foreign"] or apropos of another's; and everything is, nonetheless, mine [*moe*]."[58] In particular, as the leading poet of the first two decades of the nineteenth century, Zhukovsky often used translation to open up new generic possibilities. His adaptive translations of Gray's "Elegy Written in a Country Church-Yard" (1802), Bürger's "Lenore" (1808), and Byron's "The Prisoner of Chillon" (1822) were especially notable new openings of genre practices for himself and for Russian poetry more generally. A. Ianushkevich has argued convincingly that Zhukovsky's intensive work in the ballad from 1808 to 1814 was an exploration of a romantic epic form as a part of his search for a form for a national epic.[59] At the time, however, those in Shishkov's camp were not terribly impressed by the genre or its national qualities in Zhukovsky's practice. A comedy by Aleksandr Shakhovskoi, a member of Shishkov's Colloquium of Lovers of the Russian Word, "Urok koketkam, ili Lipetskie vody" ("A Lesson for Coquettes, or the Lipets Spa," 1815), satirized Zhukovsky in the character of a sighing balladeer. The comedy became one of the primary impulses to the formation by Karamzin's followers, with Zhukovsky in the lead, of the Arzamas literary society, and the rapid sharpening of polemical spears.[60]

When Pavel Katenin (1792–1853) published his translation of Bürger's ballad "Lenore" in 1816 under the title "Ol'ga," it was intended and taken as a further attack on Zhukovsky's ballad practice. Perhaps to be sure that the strike would not be missed, Katenin managed to get the translation published in two journals, *Vestnik Evropy,* where Zhukovsky's version had appeared eight years earlier, and *Syn Otechestva.* Zhukovsky had called his Lenore "Liudmila" and given it the subtitle "Russkaia ballada" ("A Russian Ballad"), thus indicating his intention of founding the genre of the Russian literary ballad. Katenin was implicitly offering another possible foundation, another way of making a Russian ballad.

Zhukovsky had adapted Bürger's markedly folkloric ballad to his own poetic practices, which meant that what folkloric elements remained were smoothed over and incorporated into a seamless and light poetic idiom that is clearly of a higher style than Bürger's; the characteristic folkloric triple repetition of the dialogue between the dead fiancé and the heroine on the way to the cemetery was reduced to a doublet; Bürger's internal rhymes and sound play with onomatopoeia were diminished; and the heroine's laments were given an elegiac pathos: "The heart cannot love twice" (Dvazhdy serdtsu ne liubit'), "No, the past cannot be called back with fruitless prayers" (Net, besplodnymi mol'bami/ Ne prizvat' minuvshikh dnei).[61] In adapting Bürger's concrete historical setting (his hero was a participant in the Battle of Prague during the Franco-Prussian War), Zhukovsky opted for a very abstract Russian setting: he offers but one toponym (Nareva—the Lithuanian name for a tributary of the Narev river in Belarus), no historical markers, and a heroine whose name, Liudmila, was hardly in use in Russia at the time but belonged to a Czech saint. Katenin, on the other hand, made what he called a "free translation" rather than an adaptation, and followed Bürger more precisely both in plot and in his marked folkloric discourse (but of course, this was, in translation, a markedly Russian folkloric discourse). He also gave the ballad a precise historical Russian setting: the fiancé was away fighting the Swedes in the Battle of Poltava (1709) and the Turks thereafter (Turkey declared war on Russia in 1710).[62]

Nikolai Gnedich (1784–1833) responded anonymously in *Syn Otechestva* to Katenin's implied polemics with a defense of both the place of "Liudmila" in Russian poetry and Zhukovsky's method of making a Russian ballad.[63] His defense is founded on the necessity of adapting Bürger and the ballad genre for the Russian audience and thus manifests a resistance to translation, including the translation of folklore into the literary sphere. Gnedich opens his article by lamenting the fact that Zhukovsky, a superior talent, has so many followers, competitors, and enviers (implicitly casting Katenin as the latter). He despairs of the fact that, until another such talent emerges, "how many epistles [*poslaniia*] to friends will we have to read in which nothing is sent [*nichego ne posylaetsia*] except rhymes; [how many] romances and songs, which are sung by their Composer alone; and [how many] ballads, ballads—miraculous, unbelievable, but terrible!"[64] He even quotes from another comedy, this one by Zagoskin, in which a character had referred positively to Shakhovskoi's treatment of Zhukovsky and the ballad: "Indeed, 'only the beauties of Poetry could have excused the strange selection of material in this genre of composition (in ballads).'"[65] But for Gnedich, unlike for some of Shishkov's allies, Zhukovsky's poetry had indeed overcome the natural disgust that one felt for the thematic material of the ballad genre.

Zhukovsky could not have accomplished this had he merely translated the poem:

> "Liudmila" is a charming, original Russian poem for which only the idea was taken from Bürger. The poet knew that it was possible to make Lenora, a German popular [*narodnaia*] ballad, pleasant for Russian Readers in no other way than through imitation. But his imitation did not consist in replacing German proper names and city names with Russian ones. The colors of poetry, the tone of expressions and feelings that make up character and give the figures their physiognomy, turns of phrase, especially those that belong to the simple dialect [*prostoe narechie*] and distinguish the spirit of the Russian national language [*dukh" narodnago iazyka Ruskago*]—these are the means by which "Lenora" is transformed into "Liudmila." And since her singer has extraordinary talent, that's why I like his imitation in many places (in spite of the [appealing] German: *Hurre, hurre, hop, hop, hop* and *Klinglingling*) more than the work of Bürger itself.[66]

Gnedich defends Zhukovsky's shift in poetic means as a necessary step toward making the ballad pleasant for Russian readers. The goal of "pleasantness" (*priiatnost'*) and of producing a "charming" (*prelestnoe*) poem mark Gnedich's point of view as Karamzinian, though he was not part of the Arzamas circle. His opening doubts about the ballad genre show his distance from Zhukovsky's circle; he is trying to negotiate a position somewhere between the two warring camps.[67] But in so doing, in responding on behalf of the Karamzinians, he adds something new to their discourse. The strange new addition is his reference to the "turns of phrase, especially those that belong to the simple dialect and differentiate the spirit of the Russian national language." This takes seriously Shishkov's concern with the national/popular/folk language rather than dismissing it with Arzamasian laughter. Now such turns of phrase are far more abundant to the modern Russian ear in Katenin's translation. The question for Gnedich, however, is not their quantity, but their quality. They have to be properly incorporated into the Russian literary language so that they do not offend the critical criterion of taste. The true Russian literary language, as the Karamzinians had argued against Shishkov and his allies for over a decade, is one that corresponds to the tastes of the upper class. Gnedich sees Katenin's vocabulary as vulgar: "The words *svetik* [darling], *vplot'* [right up to], *sporo* [quickly], *svoloch'* [scum] and such certainly breathe simplicity, but won't this simplicity conflict with taste?"[68] Gnedich moves the discourse of the Karamzinians into new territory by allowing for the necessity of the incorporation of folkloric discourse while continuing to insist on letting taste govern that incorporation.

It is perhaps surprising to find Gnedich, known to Russian literary history for his translations and especially his *Iliad* (see chapter 7), here expressing such ambivalence about translation. It is also ironic to find his resistance to translation deployed in the defense of the Karamzinian camp after Shishkov had attacked its language as a hybrid product of translation. Gnedich opposes Zhukovsky's originality in his adaptation to Katenin's mere translation—he explicitly questions how "free" Katenin's translation is.[69] Zhukovsky's "Liudmila," he declares, "having introduced Russian readers to the ballad genre, will always be read as an original work of the fatherland's Muse."[70] He thus refuses to compare "Ol'ga" to it at all, instead making comparisons only to Bürger's text and finding errors in grammar, logic, and particularly taste. Mostly he objects to Katenin's insistently low style, but some of the "errors" he cites against grammar and logic are interpreted as altering the Russian language or culture on the model of the original work. For example, he objects that in Russia (where Katenin's translation is set) victorious troops have never entered a town to the tolling of bells.[71] Gnedich thus not only admits the importance of Shishkov's *narodnyi iazyk,* he also admits the threat of translation to cultural identity and defends the practice of adaptive translation as a better approach.

Aleksandr Griboedov (1795–1829) replied to Gnedich's criticisms of Katenin and supplied his own critique of Zhukovsky's poetics. Like Gnedich, Griboedov belonged to neither of the warring camps, though he was close to Katenin. In defending Katenin, he does not explicitly defend translation, but he does defend the place of folkloric discourse in literature and particularly in the ballad genre, appealing to the values of simplicity and naturalness throughout. He suggests that the "errors" of Katenin's translation are attributable instead to the faulty ear of the reviewer, whom he calls "an irreconcilable enemy of simplicity." He cites precedent for Katenin's vocabulary: "The word 'Turk,' which is often seen in both the model odes of Lomonosov and in folk songs [*prostonarodnye pesni*], is unbearable to the true ear of Mr. Reviewer."[72] Further, he defends the ballad genre against Gnedich and Zagoskin's doubts: "The strange selection of material, that is the wondrous, with which ballads are filled—I admit my ignorance: I did not know until now that the wondrous in poetry needed excuse."[73] He defends Katenin's vocabulary throughout as appropriate to the material and the genre. When he turns to Zhukovsky's version, though, he finds it "too pompous," "a bit flat," the graveyard shades "pleasant," the dead man "too kind: a living person could not be more amiable," and Liudmila's words so meek and humble that she could not deserve her punishment.[74] In other words, he finds Zhukovsky's seamless poetic idiom with its careful incorporation of folkloric elements to be too much of the same cloth, not diverse enough to deal with the thematics of the ballad. This is a strong argument for the further incorporation of folkloric discourse into the genre.

Perhaps because they did not belong to Shishkov's colloquium or to Arzamas, Gnedich and Griboedov were able to introduce something new into the already clichéd polemics over style. Together their opposing arguments amounted to a serious challenge to the Karamzinian camp to open up its poetic language to folkloric discourse—even Gnedich's defense of Zhukovsky assumed the value of the national/folk language. And while they continued to argue over style, the force of their polemics would help to turn the struggle over poetic language and verse culture into a struggle to define the proper means to embody Russianness in literature. For that reason, the 1820s debates on romanticism and the national literature would return repeatedly to this polemics, to questions of Zhukovsky and his originality, and to the place of translation in creating a national literature.[75]

6

Translatio Studii—Translatio Prosodiae I
Quantity as Quality in Czech Meter

The topos of *translatio studii et imperii,* the transfer of culture and power, was commonly invoked in medieval Europe. It expresses the historical idea that learning and political power move from one people to another, usually from east to west—from Greece to Rome to France to England, for example, though the particulars depended on the location and political loyalties of the writer deploying the topos. The transfer of culture, *translatio studii,* often prominently involved the translation of literature (in the broad sense as well as the narrow)—certainly this was true of Rome's appropriation of its Greek inheritance, but also of Renaissance Europe.[1] While the topos seems to largely disappear in the eighteenth century, an age of rising historicism, the idea of the transfer of cultural and political leadership survives in new forms. Hegel's ideas on the historical development of "spirit" through the particular spirits of nations are one of the more influential and important variations on this theme for nineteenth-century nationalist thought. But many of the late eighteenth-century German histories of culture and civilization also worked out analogous ideas, and the idea of transfer of leadership could also be imagined in more particular spheres. Friedrich Bouterwek's *Geschichte der Poesie und Beredsamkeit seit dem Ende des dreizehnten Jahrhunderts* (*History of Poetry and Rhetoric since the End of the Thirteenth Century*, 1801), for example, imagined European literary history as moving from Italian to Spanish, Portuguese, French, British, and ultimately, German dominance. This example is not a random one—Bouterwek's history inspired a young František Palacký (1798–1876), future historian of the Czech nation, to conceive of the history of modern aesthetics as consisting of an Italian period followed by periods of French, British, German, and—soon thereafter—Czech or Slavic dominance.[2]

Before examining Palacký's early program to ensure that inheritance, however, it is necessary to understand how the linearity of such developmental schemes was fundamentally altered in the aftermath of the Quarrel between the Ancients and Moderns and in the eighteenth-century German struggle to overcome French cultural dominance. Some writers in the Quarrel began to fundamentally question the progress and continuity implied in the Renaissance inheritance of ancient culture on the basis of new philological knowledge that suggested the reality was cultural difference and distance. The various layers of accretion to the ancient inheritance thus could be seen as deformation and devolution, the mediation of the ancients by the Italians and French as an obstacle rather than assistance. For the Germans, then, a return to the origins of culture, directly to the ancients without the mediation of French culture, became the means for their claim to the inheritance of cultural leadership—a direct *translatio studii* from the source, without all the intervening layers of mediation. As Berman has argued, the ancients became essential to the German concept of *Bildung* as the *Urbild* (original, archetype) and *Vorbild* (model) of culture itself. And while Johann Joachim Winckelmann made antiquity as a whole the model, it was clear to Goethe and others that Greek precedence was complete, that Greek culture was the *natural,* organic culture. Still, it was precisely the derivative and hybrid nature of Roman culture that made it attractive to the romantics, because it was closer in that hybridity to German culture.[3] The German program for the domestication of the ancient cultural inheritance was broad and had multiple fronts in art, philosophy, and literature, and translation was a central means. This included the remaking of the German literary language on the model of Greek. Herder's demands for a translation of Homer, the original poet, were fulfilled by Johann Heinrich Voss, who, among other things, aimed "at submitting the still 'unformed' German language to the 'beneficial' yoke of Greek metrical forms."[4] The remaking of the literary language and assimilation of Greek metrical forms was a very important part of the German bid for cultural inheritance and supremacy, but was far from constituting the entire program.

The Germans had changed the model of inheritance, so if the Czechs were to claim the next historical stage as their own, as Palacký hoped, they would have to do so by finding a better route back to the acknowledged origins in Greek culture. But in the general absence of Czech cultural life, such a broad cultural program as that pursued by the Germans was beyond their means. Jungmann, however, had shown how a program for the cultivation of the language could, in effect, be the engine for the revival of a broader cultural life. He had also suggested one way in which the Czechs might "out-Greek" the Germans.

Jungmann's program for the Czech national literature (outlined in chapter 4) had slowly gained ground in the decade following the first articulation of it in print, but had only ever been embraced in part by various writers and institutions. The journal *Hlasatel český* was programmatically oriented toward high literary art, but its editor, Jan Nejedlý, disagreed with Jungmann over the means to achieve this goal, preferring strict adherence to the language norm of the sixteenth century to Jungmann's Slavicizing and neologizing innovations. Václav Hanka embraced Jungmann's linguistic means and their embodiment in translations, but rejected high, modern literary art and rather pursued the simple forms of folklore. Most marginal of all were Jungmann's ideas on quantitative prosody: his 1804 letter advocating the quantitative system received almost no response and was not ultimately preserved. In the 1820s, Jungmann's program was adopted more fully and widely in no small part due to the ardent advocacy of it in *Počátkové českého básnictví, obzvláště prozódie* (*Principles of Czech Poetry, Prosody in Particular*), published anonymously in 1818, which placed quantitative verse or *časomíra* (literally: sound-measure) at the center of the program.

Počátkové, published in Prague and Prešpurk,[5] brought a shriller polemical tone to the advancement of Jungmann's program for the national literature. The work took the form of six letters on prosody, and its authors were, at the time, aspiring poets hardly out of their teens. Pavel Josef Šafařík (1795–1861) would go on to write a history of the Slavic literatures and lay the groundwork for Slavic ethnography and anthropology as one of the leading Slavic philologists of his day. František Palacký, after some explorations in aesthetics, went on to write the first monumental history of the Czech nation. Neither continued to write poetry for very long, but the principles they outlined in 1818 established the terms of Czech critical discussion for the 1820s and beyond. They argued that the embodiment of Greco-Roman quantitative prosody in Czech poetry, a system that the Czech language was capable of assimilating though most modern European languages were not, would enable the embodiment of a whole series of other values, including the *klasičnost* (classicality) of Czech literary productions along with their national aspect, and the *libozvučnost* (euphony, melodiousness) and *vznešenost* (sublimity) of Czech poetry.[6] In other words, *translatio prosodiae*, the translation or transfer of Greek prosody into the Czech language, would be the primary basis for the Czech claim to *translatio studii*, the inheritance of Greek culture and of cultural leadership. *Časomíra* would link the Czechs to the Greeks in ways the Germans could only dream of.

The program Šafařík and Palacký articulated for Czech literature in *Počátkové* in 1818 was quite bold in its competitive stance vis-à-vis German literature. The authors were inspired by the German efforts to assimilate classical verse forms, but were even more encouraged by recent German writers on metrics who critiqued the means of that assimilation. The German writer who served both as model and opponent in the imitation of Greek meter was Friedrich Gottlieb Klopstock, who had worked out a German prosody, using word stress as the equivalent to length, that allowed Greek metrical forms from hexameter and elegiac distich to Sapphic verse to be successfully used in German poetry. The epigraph to *Počátkové*, printed on the title page, is taken from Klopstock and describes the aim of his project: "Gesänge des höhern Flugs/ In dem Lautmaß der Natur" (songs of higher flights in the meter [literally: sound-measure] of nature). Klopstock's poetry aimed at the sublime, and his means was a metrical system that was natural to German, but could imitate Greek forms. The authors of *Počátkové* had the same aim, but argued that the nature of the Slavic language was equivalent to Greek, that there was no need to compromise the metrical system merely to imitate the Greek system using stress in place of vowel length. Letters one and two of *Počátkové*, written by Palacký, are also headed by epigraphs from Klopstock that represent his implementation of classical metrical forms. But for Palacký, Klopstock is exemplary above all else of the failure of good intentions. In the first letter he evaluates Klopstock in terms taken from the book's epigraph:

> Klopstock, god-inspired, intended to return to the more graceful and sensible playing of the Greek Muse, but seeing that the un-sonorous and quite rough German tongue would not bear the better Hellenic organization, with bold audacity, spurning the primary basis of that organization, position, he made the accent found in his natural language a rule for himself in quantitative

meter, and so, ignoring the heaviest consonant clusters, attempted to fly on new wings after that flight, so graceful and light. In fact, the distinguished [Bernard] Jenisch says, it was as if the heartfelt, moving compositions of Mozart were sung by the voice of an American savage; but he still constantly wants to consider it the boldest act on the literary stage in our times.[7]

Palacký notes the obstacles to the achievement of higher flights that was Klopstock's aim. All come down to an unfit language. His reference to expert opinion points up the disparity between Klopstock's reputation and an evaluation of Klopstock's achievement that is presented as more objective.[8]

Palacký makes a further appeal to contemporary German authorities in his second letter: "But the Germans after Klopstock, unable to conform to these laws [of rhythm] due to the characteristics of their language, began to innovate, deviating from the legitimate way. They could still be forgiven for this, since they did not sin against the eternal laws of rhythm in this as grossly as our countrymen; however, one should also consider the impartial judgment of more skilled [*umělejších*] Germans about this."[9] August Schlegel was one such German who spoke out at the time against Klopstock's imitation of Greek meters and demanded a strict quantitative prosody in German verse.[10] Palacký certainly knew much of Schlegel's work, but he did not need to reference it, for Šafařík soon provided all the German authority needed to back this assault upon Klopstock's reputation. Šafařík had in his possession a letter from one of the leading scholars on metrics, Johann Gottfried Hermann, from which he published excerpts in the fourth letter. Hermann was the author of *Handbuch der Metrik* (1799) and *Elementa doctrinae metricae* (1816)—Šafařík had made a stop in Leipzig to consult with him in 1817 on his way home from university studies in Jena.[11] Hermann encouraged the Czechs to pursue quantitative verse, which he considered far more civilized than its accentual (that is, syllabotonic) imitation. And Hermann himself cites additional authority to back his critique of Klopstock's achievement: "the fact that [German] accentual versification is simply out of need we are equally convinced by [Friedrich Heinrich] Bothe, [Johann August] Apel and others." Still, like Jenisch, Hermann is not dismissive of Klopstock, though he does look forward to something better: "We Germans can still brag of something, yes, and we can still introduce true quantitative meter into our poetry someday, although probably never in the High German dialect."[12] Palacký mirrors the judgments of these German authorities in his polemical use of Klopstock: Klopstock represents the highest achievement of German culture and thus sets the mark that must be surpassed, but that mark is clearly assailable for anyone who would remain true to the principles of prosody employed by the Greeks. Palacký had it on the authority of the most skilled Germans that the Czechs had the potential to exceed one of the Germans' highest attainments.

Recent Czech verse, however, was dominated by syllabotonic prosody, like German verse, thanks to the codification of this system by Dobrovský in 1795. In order to better understand the sense of the belligerent attack on this system in *Počátkové,* it will be useful to examine Dobrovský's innovation. Native Czech verse, in both learned and folk forms, involved the coexistence of syllabic and syllabotonic versification from the medieval period onward. Syllabic verse, however, was predominant in both the bookish and oral traditions, and that remained true in the eighteenth century.[13] As Karel Horálek has argued, while one can distinguish between the two systems, they did not stand in sharp opposition to one another. Syllabic verse tended to the alternation of stressed and unstressed syllables, that is, to either a trochaic or iambic rhythm, but without being strictly readable as either.[14] Horálek finds examples of more strictly defined syllabotonic verse in the early fourteenth century and in the rationalist Hussite period, but also in the folk tradition of Dobrovský's day.[15] Contact with Latin verse also led to the development in medieval Czech verse of a form of syllabotonic hexameter.[16] In contrast to these two native verse systems, quantitative verse was strictly a bookish tradition derived from classical models. It was introduced by Czech humanists in the sixteenth century when much of Europe was experimenting with the quantitative principle, though initially it was primarily used not for the translation of classical texts, as one might suppose, but for song composition—to harmonize the vowel length in texts with the music—and psalm translations. It remained a largely marginal phenomenon in Czech verse—it was used most by Czech Protestants—and was hardly in use by the late eighteenth century, though the tradition did survive among the Slovaks.[17] Horálek has argued that quantitative verse, too, was not strictly differentiated from syllabic verse in poetic practice.[18]

Into this potential chaos of three competing systems, only one of which—quantitative verse—had any support in theoretical treatises, Dobrovský brought order by strictly differentiating the syllabotonic system from the other two and giving it a set of rules. As a result, Czech literary verse, now cultivated by an emerging new class of intellectuals, made a sudden change from the syllabic system that had been long dominant to a system that had previously played a secondary role and was only alive at the time in folk verse.[19] Dobrovský's choice of syllabotonic verse was not at all random, but was founded on classical verse as the ideal model, in comparison with which syllabic verse appeared disordered, unmetrical, and unaesthetic. He further considered the attempts to employ the quantitative system in Czech improperly founded for their failure to consider stress and thus the difference between the classical and the modern languages.[20] His codification of the rules for syllabotonic prosody, then, has to be seen as an attempt to bring Czech verse into an explicit relationship with the ideal model of classical verse, based on the properties of the Czech language—to translate ancient versification into Czech. In this, his goals could not have been closer to the goals of the authors of *Počátkové*.

Dobrovský's system, however, had a major drawback, which he himself freely acknowledged. Because the stress in Czech always falls on the first syllable of a word, verse rhythms with a rising intonation—with the stress at the end of the foot—presented particular difficulties. This difficulty was magnified by the strict fulfillment of the metrical scheme demanded by classical versification. As a result, Dobrovský concluded that the metrical and rhythmical variety of ancient verse was unattainable for its Czech imitation.[21] In his "*Böhmische prosodie*" he asks explicitly, "Can we imitate the epic verse of the Greeks and Latins?" His answer is no. Because the language does not offer a sufficient variety of metrical feet and because caesura cannot be preserved, "the perfect harmony of Greek and Latin hexameter is unattainable for us."[22] And he continued to reinforce this opinion in reviews of Czech works in syllabotonic hexameter. He considered the hexameters of Jan Nejedlý's translation from the *Iliad* among the best, but observed that "it is obvious that the Czech translator must struggle with very many practically insurmountable problems if he wants to reach, to some extent, Homeric hexameters in his language. The blame lies with the language itself."[23] And of Puchmajer's *Chrám gnidský* (a translation of Montesquieu's *Le Temple de Gnide*) he wrote, "No Czech poet has ever written better hexameters than these, but they are not as flowing by far as the Latin ones, nor do they have even the variety of the German ones, and they *cannot* have it."[24] One must recall that the competition with the German cultural sphere was not so much directed externally, toward a foreign German literature, as internally, toward the hearts and minds of fellow countrymen. Every educated person who used Czech in speech and writing did so by choice, choosing Czech over German. To win converts, the Czech language had to at least demonstrate the *potential* to compete with the accomplished German tongue. In his evaluation of the potential for Czech poetry, Dobrovský was refusing to act as an ally. If Czech verse could not even measure up to German verse, let alone Latin, not to mention the original Greek, this would be a serious failure for the new, romantic form of classicism that strove above all to contend with the Greek standard.

To the authors of *Počatkové*, however, it was false to blame the language, for the lack of metrical feet and the ability to preserve caesura were products not of the language itself but of the syllabotonic system of prosody.[25] Palacký and Šafařík thus attacked Dobrovský and his system in the same spirit in which romantics in general attacked the authority and rules of classicism. Palacký describes the system in the first letter as a "cruel law" (*krutý zákon*) weighing on the neck of the Czech hippogriff, preventing his flight (recall the motif of flight from the book's epigraph).[26] They figure Dobrovský's reform as contrary to the spirit of the Czech language and but another example of the blind imitation of German culture.[27] Palacký observes with irony that once the Germans began to innovate, they deviated from the legitimate way of producing rhythm: "Here the Czechs came right behind them—for Czech and Germanomaniac have always been synonyms—wondering at the newly reborn German cockroach [*kakerlak*], they declaimed in favor of ushering it into their breed with hurried readiness, tending it, lying and dallying with it until in the end they had bred what they desired: a Germanoczech-overaccented monster [*německočeskopřepřízvučnou potvoru*]. Why? The Czechs could not be capable of anything themselves; if they were to have anything, it was naturally understood that they had to beg it off the Germans."[28] Palacký here is not really attacking imitation as such, but rather blind imitation, which fails to see the value of what is imitated. Blind imitation also fails to take into account the local context, and what is a progressive innovation in one literature may be much less so in another. Šafařík points this out in a comparison of Klopstock and Dobrovský in the third letter: "Certainly having seen that the syllables long in pronunciation in his language could not be any but accented and partially accented, [Klopstock] made better use of the properties of his language than that immortal discoverer of our stress, who, overcome with joy at such great and unexpected luck, out of thanks hitched the bonded Czech Muse to the German conductor in a Germanic yoke. But even that theory of Klopstock's, even that, the boldest discovery of human ingenuity, is poverty, not wealth."[29] If the Germans had to compensate for the inability of their language, the Czechs needed no such compromise. But the compromise had been made anyway: "The German began to limp on his one leg, [and] that is the only reason why the bonded Czech had to limp after him on both."[30]

Limping is not the only characterization used by the authors to describe contemporary Czech poetry. If Jenisch had described the German attempts to imitate Greek meters as the singing of Mozart's compositions by the voice of an American savage, Palacký could imagine what the Czech imitation of this might sound like: "Dear Mr. Jenisch! If you caught wind of the exploits of contemporary Czech poetry, you would hear not the coarse voice of an American, but the clatter of timber-wagons barreling down gorges."[31] Šafařík outdoes him, though, in the fourth letter, complaining of the lack of effort Czech poets make in their poetry:

> Our versifiers are ready with their trade, prosody and metrics—of poetics I'll not say a word, for whomever God does not favor, all the saints will not forge—in two hours, and if one is more slow-witted, in three; and then they puff up as great as you please; beginning to fly, they rain down from their Parnassus the most motley verses, which they call rhymes, like water through a colander, and they blow about poppycock as if it were leaking from a bag. But for that very reason, all of their odes, dirges, choruses, anti-choruses, chants, preludes, afterludes, final songs and unfinalized songs [*vítězozpěvy, truchlozpěvy, mnohozpěvy, málozpěvy, výzpěvy, prozpěvy, zázpěvy, dozpěvy a nedozpěvy*], and whatever else they might call them, no sooner than they appear, they wither and waste away, and like a bubble blown on the wind, before it even flies to the ground and the world in wonder turns to look on, they vanish in the air. Our classicality [*klasičnost*]![32]

The blame for these faults is placed not so much with the poets themselves, as with Dobrovský's prosody, which required little effort to master and consequently produced little of value, according to the authors.

Dobrovský's prosody is even at fault for the failure of the language to win more converts in the internal competition with German:

> The fate of our dear language is certainly lamentable and worthy of pity, that, just when it had been pulled out of the mould of disdain and should have gone to its powerful protectors and made itself beloved among them, it was immediately dressed in the harsh garb of accent. Certainly the main, if not the only reason why our language thus far is so little valued among the educated and great must be sought in this. But with almost the same degree of assuredness I can say, that if those who first recommended it to the higher estates in belletristic writings had better preserved the melodiousness [*libozvučnost*] and Hellenic beauties of our language, we would never have seen it so ignored, so foreign in its own homeland as reality itself unfortunately still shows us to be the case.[33]

The language itself is clearly not to blame. In Palacký's formulation here, the language is already endowed with Hellenic beauties and *libozvučnost*. These must simply be preserved in the practice of poets.

Where the Germans had to labor and invent to transfer some measure of Hellenic beauty into their language, the Czechs would only have to make use of the given properties of their language, which was of a type with the Greek. The affinity of Czech to Greek is brought out by numerous comparisons of languages and their properties. The thrust of these comparisons is generally to demonstrate how Czech is, if not identical to the Greek in its structures, at least much closer than German. The main concern is with stress and vowel length, the phonetic properties on which the competing prosodies are based. In the first letter, two of Palacký's four arguments against the syllabotonic system rest on the same observation: that stress in Czech is separate from length, whereas in German stress and vowel length coincide. "The stress in our language is not so strong as to paralyze all the following syllables by its strength or to resign them to being swallowed entirely, as with the German." He observes that the Greeks and Romans also had stress in their language, separate from length, and "with so much sensitivity for beauty," they never even considered making stress a principle in their meter. Rather, the principle is vowel length, and it must be followed if one wants to use the Greek meters. "The Germans held back here entirely, since length for them can only fall on the stressed syllable; and they can therefore make bold use of it."[34] The German accentual prosody, again, is a product of necessity. The Czech one is not, and in fact represents the choice of a lesser principle.

Šafařík, in the third letter, offers a reading of the national character of various nations based on the way in which stress is placed in their languages. This is more than a bit tendentious, but hardly surprising in the Czech context, in which language stood for so many things:

> To the Persians and Turks it was enough to separate word from word with it [stress], in order that they did not all grow together into one, to which purpose their accent invariably sticks to the first, last, or penultimate syllable; the subtle Greek marked the finest variations in his words with accent, for example ιδέ (see) and ίδε (saw), ειπέ (speak), είπε (spoke); the turgid-blooded Englishman loads up his words with a heavy accent especially towards the beginning; the ingenious German, constantly pondering, has to have the most sound where there is the most meaning, in the root of the word; his stress, which must be considered well, is logical stress. Slavic dialects in placing stress are still guided more by the place than the weight of a syllable, sometimes by

the subtle shading of differences in meaning, for example *okrasa* — ‿ ‿,
o kráse ‿ — ‿, in which too, as in everything else, they resemble the Greek
language more than the nordic ones.[35]

His grouping of all the Slavic languages together in terms of stress is highly
misleading and would lead to problems later, when Šafařík attempted to get
other Slavs to adopt quantitative prosody. His explanation of the principle
of Slavic stress is far from clear in any case. Czech stress almost always falls
on the first syllable of a word, and in this sense it is indeed "guided more by
the place than the weight" of a syllable. But to state this openly would link
it to Turkish and Persian, rather than Greek. Šafařík's aim is to link Slavic
to Greek in its subtlety, and not merely in its potential, but rather as a fact,
given in the language. This givenness proceeds from the origin of languages:
"With the first appearance of a language the difference in short and long
syllables between various nations occurred according to the degree in which
their feelings and thoughts expressed and marked the objects that awoke
them by suitably shorter or longer pronunciation of individual sounds."[36]
Similarities in language thus mark similarities in thoughts from the origin
of nations and national languages.

Other features of languages besides stress and vowel length could be used
to argue for the affinity of the Czech and Greek languages, and thus nations.
In the same letter, Šafařík appeals to the distinction between analytical and
synthetic (inflected) languages, or, in the terminology of the day, languages
"regulated by mere logical order (*ordo rationis*)" and those "governed
by imaginative power (*ordo imaginationis*)."[37] Jungmann had used this
distinction in 1814 to argue against a writer who had accused Czech of a
lack of abstract vocabulary. The distinction was very useful to the Czechs
because it placed the Czech language in a different category than German,
and in particular, into that category of languages that, supposedly, was more
poetic, as opposed to philosophical, in its nature. The Czechs would grant
the Germans their philosophy, but they would oppose them in poetry (or at
least in the poetic nature of their language). Jungmann noted that, while its
inherent poetic nature made it less suited for abstract discourse, Czech could
be cultivated to overcome this obstacle, just as the Germans had managed to
cultivate poetry in addition to philosophy.[38] Šafařík adds another distinction
to this division of languages: "the former we can call accentual, the latter
quantitative languages."[39] Greek, Latin, and Czech all belonged to the latter.

The only modern European language that joined Czech in having
properties allowing it to make use of quantitative versification was

Hungarian, according to the authors.[40] They were inspired, in addition to German metrical developments, by recent Hungarian experimentation with the quantitative principle, and especially the odes of Dániel Berzsenyi (1780–1836). Where the Hungarian quantitative movement was latinizing, though, Czech authors focused on the Greek.[41] Though the classical principles of meter were shared by Latin and Greek, the metrical forms had been originated by the Greeks and only borrowed by the Latins. The concern of the authors of *Počátkové* with origins and originality led to their favoring of the Greeks in the same way as it had for German authors before them.[42] For the most part, the Latins suffer mere neglect in *Počátkové*, only occasionally becoming obstacles to the Czech language coming as close as possible to the Greek. Dobrovský had compared the Czech language, with its lack of available metrical feet, negatively to Latin and German. With the quantitative principle, however, it would be second only to Greek: "With us long and short syllables alternate in the most various ways; we have plenty of all possible feet (*pedes metrici*) of every manner. Thus we can soar joyously and lively, make our way weakly and sadly, run lightly or stride along solemnly. In that fortunate ability our tongue even surpasses Latin, which learned only solemn steps from the solemn Roman." The Czech language "like Proteus takes all forms."[43] Quantitative prosody thus opens up all the possibilities that the syllabotonic system closed off.

These possibilities reflect on national character in a particular way. In Hermann's letter to Šafařík, he comments on previous attempts to embody the quantitative principle in modern European literatures: "For the fact that it was not successful, not always the language, but sometimes the character of the nation is at fault."[44] Hermann may have been indicating how a lack of critical thought, a lack of the ability to come to a true understanding of the ancient principles of prosody, had led to some failures. The German nation, studious in character, certainly could brag, then, at its success. But the distinction he draws here, perhaps in response to comments of Šafařík's, seems strange in the context of *Počátkové*, in which the national character is taken as embodied primarily in the language, in features such as accent and vowel length. And in the fifth letter, Palacký refers to this comment of Hermann's in a manner that twists it toward the Czech context: "It is also worth considering that, as the distinguished *** mentions in the letter recently shared with you, in many languages the language itself is not to blame for the fact that in the country's poetry quantitative verse does not reign, but rather the cultivators of language, poets."[45] Hermann's logic, which opposed national character and language, is replaced by a logic that opposes the possibilities of a language to the realization of these possibilities in poetic practice, a fundamental opposition for the argument of *Počátkové*. Language and national character could not be opposed, because they were intimately related.

If the national character, from its ancient origins, is embodied in the language, then the need for diligent study in the manner of the Germans is somewhat mitigated for the Czechs by the genetic ties to the Greeks.[46] In the sixth letter, Šafařík refers to the "spirit of Slavdom, full brother to the Greek."[47] The Czech character was closely related to the Greek character. And because of this, the attempt to return to the quantitative principle in Czech poetry was very much a program for the national literature that sought original, individual productions that would reflect the national character. Šafařík exhorts his countrymen in the same letter: "Let's not search foreign lands for goods of which we have plenty at home. Foreign goods are false goods. Let's not play at Germanomaniacs. The Slavic genius will confirm the Slavs' being, cultivation, and glory. . . . Our fathers worked without all the fuss and published not brochures but national works [*díla národní*]."[48] The sixth letter in general is in the form of exhortation, of biblical eschatological prophecy, in which Šafařík calls for a return to the tradition of the fathers (meaning the Czech humanists and their quantitative principle) in order to forge the future glory of the Slavic nation. He imagines the Czech lion breaking his bonds, shaking his mane, and issuing forth a roar that "... will echo in the quieted Czech valley like the voice of the angel's trumpet prophesying the raising of the dead."[49]

In contrast, the fifth letter, by Palacký, is the final, sober summary of the argument for quantitative verse and a clear outline of the goals for the national literature that this change will help to achieve. These goals can be summarized as a realization of the potential of the Czech language, or as Palacký prefers to express it, as the preservation of the qualities of the language, qualities he had already described as "the *libozvučnost* [melodiousness] and Hellenic beauties of our language."[50] If one replaces Hellenic beauties here with an approximate synonym, *klasičnost* (classicality), then one has two terms that represent qualities that were essential to the thinking of the authors. Both terms would become central in the literary critical discussions of the 1820s in Czech letters. It has already been shown how the quantitative principle, *časomíra*, is linked through the language to a programmatic pursuit of national works. *Časomíra* would also allow for the realization of the *libozvučnost* of the language and the *klasičnost* of the literature, which were also essential to ensure its national significance.

Palacký launches into his summary of the arguments for quantitative verse by insisting on its necessity for the goal of *klasičnost:* "It is not only possible to introduce quantitative rhythm into the Czech tongue, but even necessary if we want to have in our poetry anything excellent or classical."[51] Classical form, for the authors, was a necessary condition to achieve *klasičnost,* but it was not a sufficient condition. That is to say, it would not be enough simply to write verses in classical forms in order to rival the Greeks. The Czech humanist poets were sufficient example of this. Even as they proclaimed a return to this humanist tradition, then, the authors were aware of its poetic lacks and aimed at overcoming them. In the second letter, Palacký declares, "I will more reasonably remain with the venerable elders, even if they were not so original."[52] And in the sixth letter, Šafařík recommends, "Let's hold to our ancestors—and leave them be—where the light of the nineteenth century bids it. . . . Is it proper, because Nudožerýn erred, because Drachovský, Rosa, or Komenský erred, to reject the whole theory straight away? Is it proper, because *** is not a poet, because **, or * is not, to straight away pronounce the conclusion that there is no Czech poesy?"[53] One should hold to principles of versification, because a classical poetry for the Czechs was impossible without it. But that form was insufficient in and of itself. True poets were needed to embody that form.

And not only true poets, but poets who were willing to work at their craft. One should recall here Šafařík's ironic commentary on the ease with which the accentual poets mastered their prosody and flooded the world with their songs so that a quickly popping bubble represents "our *klasičnost!*"[54] Palacký then takes on the complaint that the quantitative principle is too difficult: "Only the half-educated can lament the unease and difficulty of quantitative versification. It is not at all as great as it seems to those who look upon it from afar, never having tried anything. The beginning of everything is difficult, but practice brings facility and—delight. Was that difficulty not just as great, or perhaps even greater, for the Greeks and Romans? Did their thoughts flow into their quantities of their own accord?"[55] In fact, the difficulty of the quantitative system was its advantage, for it would necessitate the kind of work at the craft of poetry that had not yet been required of Czech poets, the kind of work completed by the classical poets:

> But the technique of poesy by rights and naturally must be difficult: poesy should certainly be beautiful, excellent, and aesthetic, not common and trivial, both from the point of view of its spirit—thoughts—and from the point of view of its clothing, rhythm and meter. Both the former and latter require

an ingenious, creative head (Genie); for the latter, which is mechanical, one must also undertake prolonged and reasonable practice. That is how it was for the masterful Greeks and Romans; trained from their youth in the technique of poesy, they still put so much work into versification itself, polishing, correcting, reforming it, that it would seem extreme to us. But precisely through this they added to their poems such beauties and perfections that they will last as long as poetry in general, while the poets themselves will dazzle immortally.[56]

Poetic form, like culture in general, required cultivation. The question was, would Czech poets follow this difficult road to *klasičnost?* Palacký asks, "Do the sublimity and beauty of quantitative rhythm not deserve greater effort? Or are we going to want to enjoy without any effort that excellence which neither rhyme, nor accent, nor all of those Italian artsy [*kunstovní*] sonnets, triolets, and ottava rimas taken together can make easier?"[57] The pursuit of *klasičnost* here comes into conflict with a certain understanding of romanticism (as the forms and traditions of the modern European literatures), presented as the easier road, but one leading to less exalted rewards.

In evaluating this Czech clash between romanticism and classicism, it is worth remembering how different this Czech classicism is from the seventeenth- and eighteenth-century tradition of normative, universal, classicist aesthetics. With its striving for the sublime, its resolute aestheticism, its rejection of a certain system of rule-bound practices (even while prescribing new practices and norms), and its particularist, national conception of literature, it exhibits features that link it, in the broader literary-historical picture, to romanticism rather than classicism. It is closely related to Wilhelm Küchelbecker's conception of true romanticism. But where Küchelbecker and other Russians linked romanticism and classicism of this type, leading Czechs in the 1820s chose to oppose the historical narratives of romanticism and certain romantic poetic features in pursuit of a truer classical humanism. No doubt German "Weimar classicism" had an influence on this direction, for Schiller and Goethe were revered poets. But the lack of a developed Czech classicism, of a practice that could be labeled *classicism* more or less decisively at a sufficiently distant point in time to make it easily distinguishable from the newer practices, may be just as decisive. In any case, for years to come, "romanticism" became a largely negative value in Czech letters.

Palacký continues his assault·on romanticism and its historical narratives (without ever naming it) with an attack on rhyme, the most marked feature of the romantic national poetic traditions in contrast to the classics. Such an attack on rhyme was nothing new. In fact, Dobrovský himself poked fun at it in his own *Prosodie,* although he allowed that it was more necessary than it might seem, perhaps because of the ultimate inability of the Czech language to embody the Greek forms.[58] Palacký grants rhyme no redeeming value:

> There is a tremendous difference between quantitative rhythm and the vacuous rhyme of modern times. The former lightly rides its wings in the wind like an eagle, the latter near the ground, convulsively, like a stork, and jumps along as if shackled; and if we continue, the eagle hurries to its goal in a free flight, now faster, now more gently, sometimes higher, sometimes lower; the stork strains forward always with a long, weak, monotonous jump. And thus it is time for us, having finally disengaged ourselves from unaesthetic barbarism, to preserve and follow that which is beautiful and excellent, which carries on itself the clear mark of subtle feelings and sublime artistry, leaving behind the crude inventions of an uneducated age.[59]

The references to barbarism and the "uneducated age" clearly point to the traditional interpretation of the medieval period as the "dark" ages that romantic narratives of national literatures were trying to combat.[60] But Palacký was not entirely free of medievalism, albeit pre-Christian and thus, in the terms of the day, not romantic. He immediately continues: "Besides that, our tongue is not so bound to rhyme as German and all the Germanic tongues in general. . . . I am venturing to prove to myself that our most ancient ancestors, as well as those of all the Slavs, knew nothing of rhyme until the Christian Latins of the Middle Ages chased it into Slavic verses from their schools. But I will speak of that at another time."[61] To this is attached a footnote from the editor (nominally Jan Benedikti, but the note was more likely added by Šafařík and with Palacký's knowledge), indicating that his opinion had been confirmed by the discovery of fragments of ancient Czech poetry by Hanka that were without rhyme. This clearly refers to the Rukopis královédvorský (Dvůr Králové manuscript, hereafter, RK), which had been "discovered" by Hanka a mere two months before the final version of the book was at the censor.[62] He is well informed, then, of this most recent development, which represented longed-for evidence of an ancient Czech poetic tradition that would be useful in constructing a Czech literary narrative to rival the German. The effect of the RK for Palacký was immediate: it confirmed that, unlike in the Germanic languages, ancient Slavic poetry was unrhymed, placing the Czech language, once again, closer to the Greek than the German language was. In a later history of Czech literature, written between 1825 and 1827 for a German audience, Palacký would ascribe the attribute of *klasičnost* (*Classicität*) to the songs of this manuscript.[63] By then, perhaps, the forged manuscripts and other developments in Czech poetry had led him to reconsider the necessity of the quantitative principle for the project of creating a classical Czech literature, though classical form (at least in terms of a lack of rhyme) was still likely critical. Palacký's rejection of the historical narratives of romantic poetry and his pursuit of classicality, then, should be seen as part of an attempt to construct an alternative narrative of the Czech national literature that was just as romantic in its own way.

The final eleven pages of Palacký's fifth letter are dedicated to the question of *libozvučnost*. The topic was already a familiar one from late eighteenth-century and early nineteenth-century language defenses, which among other things, defended the harmony and euphony of Czech against its detractors.[64] The authors of *Počátkové* drew on these defenses in many ways, and this may have helped to determine their tendency to focus on the qualities inherent in the language. In addition to the theme of the sound qualities of the language, which was not exclusively focused around the term *libozvučnost* (or *Wohlklang,* the German equivalent), it was common in these language defenses to point to the similarities between Czech and Greek and Latin and to draw conclusions about the poetic qualities of Czech. In 1783, for example, Jan Alois Hanke z Hankenštejna wrote that the Czech language "for its *libozvučnost* and particular flexibility is just as suitable for poetry as Greek and Latin."[65] Palacký and Šafařík were also responding to Dobrovský, who had introduced *libozvučnost* into the discussion of prosody, though typically, he was not writing a language defense. He allowed that the length and shortness of vowels "certainly could . . . have an influence on the *libozvučnost* [*Wohlklang*] of verses, but could never do any damage to the main accent of a word."[66] He also noted that "*Libozvučnost* requires that one also take into consideration the extended [that is, long] and sharpened [short] vowels in the final rhymed foot."[67] Dobrovský thus neither asserts nor denies the inherent melodious qualities of the Czech language, but he does consider language aesthetics and grants a role to vowel length in achieving a harmonious sound, particularly in verse.[68]

The authors of *Počátkové* respond, then, both to continuing criticisms of the supposedly harsh sound of Czech coming from outside the narrow circle of Czech patriots, and to Dobrovský's treatment of the topic. In the tradition of the language defenses, they argue for the inherent *libozvučnost* of Czech, but they also blame the syllabotonic system of versification for the fact that contemporary Czech poetry does not preserve this quality. They had to balance between the defense of the language and their sharp critique of current poetic practice. In the third letter, Šafařík, about to launch his definition separating the synthetic and quantitative languages from the analytical and accentual ones, asserts that, "[t]he *libozvučnost* and un-*libozvučnost* of a language is a gift of the gods; just like rhythmical harmony. But not every language, no matter how *libozvučný*, is capable of the ancient rhythmical versification for that reason."[69] And he gives Italian as an example. *Libozvučnost* and the possibility of using classical versification do not always go hand in hand, but the Czech language is gifted in both ways. Palacký begins his discussion of the topic in the following way: "If we give the quantitative principle a place in our poetry, then one day that un-*libozvučnost* of Czech verses will end. Our poets, who should have made the language *libozvučný*, have so far only competed in disfiguring it. Our tongue [řeč] is truly *libozvučná*; but this virtue, like *libozvučnost* in general, is not sufficiently preserved by domestic writers and is falsely judged by foreigners and foes."[70] He thus carefully distinguishes between the inherent virtue and the expression of that virtue, which remains a project. This project cannot be fulfilled by Dobrovský's system of versification, in spite of his brief attention to the topic, because it does not order the language in a proper manner.

Palacký continues with a characterization of the types of people who malign Czech and then imagines a dialogue among the spirits of nations in which each argues that his own language is the most *libozvučný*. Such subjective opinions cannot be countered, he concludes, and no principled discussion on the topic can take place because no one has outlined the proper principles by which to judge the *libozvučnost* of a language. He proposes some principles. First he remarks on the different roles of consonants and vowels in a language:

> Consonants form the foundation and are like the receptacle of concepts or thoughts; vowels are nothing but the means of support and the vehicle for the consonants; the first are the bones, the foundation and support of bodily strengths; the second are the meat, covering the bones . . . . From which it is clear, since the meaning and substance of a word depends on its consonants, that the more consonants there are in a tongue, the pithier, more substantial, and richer it is; but the more vowels it has, the lighter and weaker and, to be frank, more prattling it is, since it lacks the sufficient substrate of concepts,

consonants. But there must not be too many consonants either, for they
could not be pronounced, lacking a vehicle.[71]

Czech had frequently been accused of having too many consonants and
clusters of consonants. Palacký grants to consonants the more important
role in language, and makes his first principle a sufficient balance of vowels
so that the consonants are pronounceable. Second, a language must have a
sufficient variety of sounds to express the variety of human emotions and
experience. None of the particular types of sounds should be excessive,
and "then, most especially, where there is need to create pleasantness, all
the harsh and dark sounds should be displaced by more pleasant ones, and
variety, which is in general the mother of pleasantness, should be preserved.
These are the main objective laws of *libozvučnost.*"[72]

    Judged on these principles, the Czech tongue "could not but be known as
libozvučná."[73] This verdict however was based on the form of the language
itself, not on how it was currently being used, for contemporary poets paid
no attention to its melodiousness. If Palacký had previously spoken of the
need to preserve this inherent quality of the language, perhaps under the
influence of the language defenses, his discourse now shifted to a more
contemporary metaphor essential to Jungmann's program: cultivating the
language. Again, the model is the Greek language, which "originally, as has
been shown by learned men, must have been very un-*libozvučná,* as can
also be seen from many harsh remnants; but in the years to come, it was
so polished by poets and the subtle people that no known language in the
world can equal it. Why could the same not happen with the Czech tongue,
which is equally pliant and perfectible?" Note that the inherent quality has
now become one that has to be attained. Palacký then suggests some means
by which poets could achieve a greater *libozvučnost*: first, by avoiding the
harsher sounds and replacing them with more pleasant ones—pointing
to the richness of Czech vocabulary as a resource, he has word choice in
mind here; second, by masterful alternation of words and adjustments in
word order; third, by making use of grammatical variation in choosing
more delicate word endings; and finally, by incorporating vowels into
unpronounceable consonant clusters to facilitate pronunciation.[74] Of these,
only the last suggests a willful intervention into the existing sound structure
of the language. This final suggestion is in concord with the general tendency
of Jungmann's generation to favor linguistic creativity; by making this the
last of several suggestions, however, Palacký places far less emphasis on
phonological intervention than others do.

But the primary means to greater *libozvučnost* was quantitative meter. Palacký does not make this argument explicitly here, but he has stated it previously and it is implied in his arguments against the syllabotonic system: "Our accentual measure does not require either sense or a greater efficiency of speech." "From a lack of rhythm, verse feet, caesura, from the failure to observe position and from the detestable shortening of long syllables and lengthening of short comes the unavoidable result: a supreme un-*libozvučnost* of verses."[75] In contrast, the quantitative system would result in true rhythm, would allow caesura and a variety of feet, and because it was difficult and required the careful ordering of words and vowel sounds, it would ultimately produce both better thought and a more harmonious sound. *Časomíra,* as the fundamental poetic principle, would thus be the means to both *klasičnost* and *libozvučnost,* and ultimately to a truly national Czech poetry.

The peak of the Czech Parnassus was nonetheless not entirely without any work of redeeming value. Palacký and Šafařík both refer to each other and to Jungmann and his close friend Antonín Marek (1785–1877), who had also made some attempts in quantitative verse, as the hope of Czech letters. But outside of this small circle of convinced quantitative versifiers, the author who receives the greatest praise (albeit not without reservations), and the only other author mentioned, is Milota Zdirad Polák (1788–1856) for his "Vznešenost přirozenosti" (The Sublimity of Nature), published serially in *Prvotiny pěkných umění* beginning in 1813. There was much in this poem to recommend it to the authors. By doubling up the usual trochaic tetrameter line and making use of a large number of four-syllable words, Polák was able to introduce some rhythmical variation into the syllabotonic verse line and break the close association of words and feet, at least in relation to the end of the word.[76] The longer line also produced a slower, more majestic rhythm in keeping with the genre of the piece: descriptive nature poetry in high style. The striving toward an elite poetic style embodied in a more varied rhythmical structure gave the authors of *Počátkové* reason to hope.[77] But a mere reform of syllabotonic verse still strictly tied to trochaic feet could not be enough, and other aspects of Polák's style came up for strict (albeit anonymous) criticism at other moments of their discourse.[78] For example, Šafařík's ironic list of genre titles, "vítězozpěvy, truchlozpěvy, mnohozpěvy, málozpěvy, výzpěvy, prozpěvy, zázpěvy, dozpěvy a nedozpěvy," has among its targets the titles for Polák's many lyrical insertions.

Šafařík's and Palacký's verdicts on Polák's work are worth citing at length, both for their interesting dynamic of praise and censure and because in the discussion of Polák they bring into closest relation their concepts of *libozvučnost* and *klasičnost, vznešenost* (sublimity), and their vision for the national literature. Palacký alternates expressions of the highest praise with those of deep dissatisfaction:

> To Polák perhaps, it seems to me, the spirit of the Bohemian lands could properly give the poetic palm of victory: up until now no one has given us so much genuine originality, *vznešenost,* and individual beauties—but why are we still left wanting? The entire form of his poem is very inadequate to excellence of thought. I will leave aside the insufficiency of poetic rhythm and lyrical unity; a greater *libozvučnost* is that which above all else I am seeking. In a few masterful places he proved that he has the ability to preserve it—but why are we still left wanting? If only by some happy chance my weak voice could reach him, thereupon I would rise up ardently and, listening to the sweet sounds of his lyre, would gladly sacrifice everything to the perfecting of this national work [*národní dílo*]! For his "Sublimity of Nature" is a national work; a work that the nation [*národ*] should boast of and will boast of in the future—the present common public pays no attention to it—it is national and not the work of an individual person.[79]

Polák's work already has national significance, but it is notable that what makes it a national work has nothing to do with popularity, as Palacký makes explicit.[80] Its importance lies rather in the direction in which it takes the national literature—in precisely that direction most desired by our authors, toward sublimity of expression. This is to be a common goal and to result in works that allow the Czechs to boast of their poetic prowess. Palacký speaks of the work here, in spite of its many faults, as if it already had fulfilled that ideal, but this is perhaps because he is imagining it as already perfected, having already responded to his critique: the greater preservation of *libozvučnost* would lead to works of national significance. Palacký here explicitly leaves aside questions of form, only for Šafařík to take them up in the next and final letter. In that prophesy on quantitative meter and the nation he intones, "It is high time for ... patriots whose Slavic flight could be a classical flight, like our fiery Polák and ingenius Marek, to attain to Greek *klasičnost.*" And he throws down a challenge:

> I am not an enemy of the muse of *libozvuky,* but show me among the thousands and thousands of Czechoslovak poets from master Dalimil, and if you like even from "Hospodine pomiluj ny," on down to the most recent accentizer, show me

just one Czech Homer or Petrarch or Camões or Milton or Klopstock. But no, no, no: my request was crazy; show me just one national tragedy or comedy worthy of patriotic boasts and the envy of foreigners, worthy of immortality, and I will carry the punishment for tarnishing the genius of the homeland with my insult, a punishment deserved by one who has betrayed his country. Do you think then that in Polák's songs the Czech spirit does not breathe with the same power as the Greek spirit in Homer, the Italian in Petrarch, the Portuguese in Camões, the English in Milton, or the German in Klopstock? Of course, but the flight of the poetic genius should be a classical flight![81]

The *klasičnost* that Polák is missing is clearly the classical form of verse. This is what would allow his national muse to attain to something of international importance. In the poetic ideal outlined by these authors, the features of the national language would be fully realized in classical poetic form, a form that would require the aesthetic organization of the sounds of the language and a sound organization of thought. Works that attained this ideal would not only embody the national spirit, through their perfect form they would raise that spirit to international significance.

THERE HAS BEEN SOME DISAGREEMENT concerning the impact that *Počátkové* had on the development of Czech poetry. It is well known that the tract failed to usher in the fundamental change in Czech prosody that it aimed at—Dobrovský's syllabotonic prosody remained the only major turning point in the history of Czech prosody. Quantitative prosody did experience a short revival following the tract, but it was mostly used for translations of ancient classics, occasionally for new works in ancient genres, and hexameter was by far its dominant verse form. (There will be more on the fate of *časomíra* in critical discussions in chapter 9.) Jan Mukařovský argued that, though it did not establish a new prosody in Czech verse, *Počátkové* did have an impact on the syllabotonic verse tradition by helping to free up verse forms, rupturing the identity between words and verse feet in Dobrovský's system, and by drawing attention to the importance of quantity as a rhythmical factor for syllabotonic verse as well. He further suggested that the wave of new poetic activity and new poetic forms that appeared in the 1820s was also attributable to *Počátkové*.[82] Horálek has shown, however, that the rupture of the identity between words and verse feet and some experimentation with quantity in syllabotonic verses had already happened without *Počátkové*. He argued, moreover, that much of the new poetic activity drew upon either the work of Hanka and his forged manuscripts or the new poetry of Jan Kollár for its inspiration and is not attributable to *Počátkové*.[83]

While Horálek's work admirably places *Počátkové* into the context of the variety of poetic experimentation that characterized the first two decades of the nineteenth century, it would also seem to reduce it to a phenomenon of no particular importance. For a history of the development of Czech verse, this may be an appropriate conclusion, but from the broader perspective of the development of Czech literature and its modernization, this misses the fundamental significance of the work. *Počátkové* was instrumental in establishing an entirely new relationship to the ancient classics and thus the identity of Czech literature as a modern national literature. The poetry of the Puchmajer school had been full of classical references, but their translations, forms, and classical commonplaces were the typical ornaments of those who had studied Latin in secondary school.[84] And Dobrovský's resignation to the inadequacy of the Czech syllabotonic system for embodying the beauties of classical verse did not challenge the decidedly derivative, implicitly parasitic role of Czech literature as eternal student and apprentice in relation to the classics. The authors of *Počátkové* in contrast insisted on the open possibilities for Czech literature and sought to define the relationship between the ancient Greek tradition and their own national language and literature as a means to clarify the central values of their own literature. By claiming the ancient classics as their own inheritance, through their own related language and culture, they also challenged the secondary role Czech literature played to German literature.

Moreover, it is not as easy to separate *Počátkové* from Hanka's folk song echoes or the forged manuscripts, and thus from certain trends in the new wave of Czech poetry of the 1820s, as Horálek implies. If the qualities of the Czech language that related it to the Greek and allowed it to embody quantitative prosody were established, as Šafařík argued, at the birth of the nation and language, then the use of quantitative prosody could be figured as a kind of return to ancient national origins. Palacký's appeal to a yet-to-be discovered pre-Christian Czech tradition in his attack on rhyme is further evidence of the connection between quantitative verse and the ancient national tradition, in particular as he found the desired confirmation of this in the unrhymed verse of the RK. The fact that hexameter verse became the dominant form of the quantitative versifiers is also evidence, in that it points to the particular importance of epic form. As Joep Leerssen has noted, epic form was considered to be closely related to folklore, and epic had a central role in early nineteenth-century conceptions of national literary history:

> The poetical production, edition, collation and cultivation of national epics . . .
> presupposes in each case a number of interlocking, underlying assumptions:
> a) that European literature is naturally divided into different traditions, each
> individually characterized by its separate language; b) that each of these
> 'national literatures' follows a parallel, stadial progression of development,
> from primitive national origin towards latter-day cosmopolitan refinement; c)
> that the primitive origin of each literature lies in an epic whose *topic* describes
> a formative episode in the nation's collective experience, and whose *form* is
> closely linked to the nation's anonymous, oral-collective traditions.[85]

In the context of such a conception of national literary history, the advocacy
of quantitative meter has to be seen as deeply related to the exploration of
folk poetry in that both sought ancient national origins.

Indeed, the authors of *Počátkové* were also actively involved in the
collection of folk songs. In early 1817, even as the letters of *Počátkové* were
being conceived, Šafařík published an article in *Prvotiny pěkných umění*
calling on the Czechs to collect their folk songs, just three years after Hanka's
call in the same publication. Unlike Hanka, though, he and his collaborators
did contribute to a collection, published by Jan Kollár in 1823 (see chapter
9). Šafařík noted the Serbian efforts in the area and the fact that P—[Palacký]
in Moravia and B—Jan Benedikti, the publisher of *Počátkové*] in Hungary
were collecting songs, so that only the Czechs had not begun, in spite of
the known value of such songs. He describes the value of these songs as
follows: "There is from the aesthetic standpoint a natural simplicity, and
their loveliness has to interest everyone who reads them with a pure heart,
everyone, no matter who you be, even if you are not Herder or Goethe,
for they were not ashamed of folk songs; everyone who drives the rules
of aesthetics out of his head, as one should, and will not look for artistic
creation where it does not exist."[86] Palacký's comments in *Počátkové* show
him to be in essential agreement with this: folk songs have aesthetic value,
but this is not the same as the aesthetic value of high art. They can have a
positive function, however, in helping one to overcome the rules of high art,
when such become an obstacle, and in pointing one toward more essential
values. For Palacký, the syllabotonic system was an obstacle that folk songs
could help to overcome by demonstrating the essential value of *libozvučnost*.
He notes that the Czech "pay so little attention to it [*libozvučnost*] that—
to their shame—even folk songs so outdo them in *libozvučnost* that they
could serve them as a perfect model."[87] He gives two short excerpts from
simple folk songs and concludes, "Admit it, does not a greater *libozvučnost*

rule in folk songs than on the top of the Czech Parnassus?"[88] This, of course, maintains the strict hierarchy of high and low art and limits the function of folk songs to serving as a corrective to high art.

Folk songs were, after all, only indirect evidence of the ancient national poetic tradition, its debased modern offspring. Russians like Shishkov could compare and contrast this indirect evidence with some recently discovered direct evidence, the *Slovo o polku Igoreve*. Well aware of this discovery, the Czechs longed for direct evidence of their own ancient epic tradition.[89] Indeed, as suggested earlier, the Russian *Slovo* may have encouraged Dobrovský's inquiries after "demonstrably old *Volkslieder*"—he received Shishkov's 1805 edition of it in 1809.[90] Hanka had already been composing songs in the "old-Czech spirit" and publishing them as his original songs. He confirmed that he best knew what the old-Czech spirit and style was, or what his contemporaries thought it should be, by helping to counterfeit a series of manuscripts that pretended to offer fragments of a lost old-Czech poetic tradition. The manuscripts were put into circulation by the careful staging of their discovery.

This began modestly enough. In 1816, Josef Linda (1789 or 1792–1834), a close friend of Hanka, claimed to have found in the binding of a book he had been using as a footrest a sheet of parchment with a short lyric in old Czech that would come to be known as the "Píseň pod Vyšehradem" ("Song under Vyšehrad Castle"). The major discovery would follow a year later. On September 16, 1817, while looking in a vault under a church in Dvůr Králové through artifacts said to date from the Hussite wars, including some of Jan Žižka's arrows, Hanka found a bundle of twelve sheets of parchment with writing in old Czech that would come to be known as the Rukopis královédvorský (RK), for the place of its discovery. It contained six epic songs (one of which was a fragment) and eight shorter lyrical or lyrical-epic songs and presented itself as a fragment of a much larger collection, namely as the 26th–28th chapters of the third book of songs. By all apparent signs, the manuscript dated from the late thirteenth or early fourteenth century. It thus provided evidence for a highly developed poetic culture in Czech, which included epic compositions, far earlier than had to that point (or ever after) been attested. The following year, another manuscript, consisting of four parchment sheets in booklet form, was sent anonymously to Count František z Kolovrat, the governor of Bohemia. It came to be known as the Rukopis zelenohorský (RZ), as it apparently had been found in the town of Zelená Hora. It contained a verse rendition of an episode from the Czech legendary past, "Libušin soud" ("Libuše's Judgment"), and judging by both this subject matter and its written form, the manuscript had to be assigned to a far earlier period, perhaps even the ninth century. Other manuscripts and documents would follow, including a new series of discoveries in the late 1820s, but these were less important, and several were more obviously inauthentic. Of the early manuscripts, even the skeptical Dobrovský doubted, and publicly denounced, only the RZ.[91]

Among Czech patriots, in spite of Dobrovský, these manuscripts were accepted as a "demonstrably old" part of the Czech literary heritage until the late nineteenth century and played a central role in the formation of the Czech national literature and its cultural myths.[92] They were used as the most ancient and authoritative documents in arguments on Czech prosody, aesthetics, and, of course, the national character. The manuscripts provide a picture of life in the ancient Czech pagan society and later kingdom, embodying all the ideals of democracy, bravery, and national individuality the Czechs could hope to find in their past, or realize in their future. Hanka himself was the author of the lyrical poems of the RK and of the first manuscript, the aforementioned song "Píseň pod Vyšehradem" ("Song under Vyšehrad Castle"). The method used in composing them was the same as for Hanka's original lyrics, based on the same Russian songs of Chulkov and with similar use of Russianisms.[93] Authorship of the more original epic poems of the RK is most reasonably assigned Josef Linda, though Hanka is assumed to have reworked the poems into old Czech. In part the epics are more "original" in that they draw on a much broader spectrum of sources and use those sources in a less straightforward manner. A short list of those sources would include *Slovo,* the Serbian oral epics collected by Karadžić, the poems of Ossian (via the 1792 Russian translation of Ermil I. Kostrov), Homer, Karamzin's Russian history, and the Czech chronicle of Jan František Beckovský, but also Milton and Chateaubriand in Jungmann's translations. By translating this broad array of historical and epic sources into Czech epic fragments, the forged manuscripts succeeded in placing Czech literature into a relationship with the national traditions of other nations, including the Greeks, in a far more convincing and comprehensive manner than *Počátkové.*

Within the context of Jungmann's general program, which mandated the creation of literary works for a non-existent Czech literary public with the goal of producing such a public, Hanka's mystifications stand out only for their boldness of conception and their resoluteness in pursuing the embodiment of all the revival ideals in a single corpus of work. Hanka's simulacrum of the ancient Czech past allowed the ideal of Slavness and romantic classicism to conjoin. Moreover, it bridged the gap between folk productions and artistic literature. The RKZ (that is, the RK and RZ together) marked the conjunction of Jungmann and Hanka's programs by embodying the artistic ideal of national poetry and allowing sublime monumentality and simplicity to meet.[94] The unfamiliar old-Czech and Russian language forms gave a poetic luster to the language of the poems. At the same time, the poetic forms used were mostly syllabic—including native eight-syllable forms and some imitation of Serbian ten-syllable epic—and unrhymed, and thus mark a radical break from the central competing prosodic forms as well as a sort of return to the predominant historical form of Czech verse.[95] Hanka's exploration of the values of folk songs and Šafařík and Palacký's advocacy of quantitative verse both had as their objective the rediscovery of the values embodied in the ancient national origins of the Czech language and Czech poetry. With Hanka's "discovery" of several "authentic" fragments of this ancient national tradition, this rediscovery had been achieved, for the texts embodied the values of *libozvučnost, klasičnost,* and *vznešenost* that the authors of *Počátkové* had expected to find and wanted to continue to pursue. If they failed to confirm that ancient Czech verse was quantitative, they at least contributed to the challenge to the dominance of syllabotonic verse forms, allowing Czech poets to continue to experiment with new and old verse forms of all types in pursuit of whatever values and cultural capital they carried with them.

7 *Translatio Studii—Translatio Prosodiae* II
The Greco-Russian Meter

The Russian language had its own ancient ties to Greek, through the Orthodox religious tradition, and the Russian cultural tradition that envisions Russia as the inheritor of Greek civilization is nearly as old as Russian literature itself. Russian Grecophilia, however, did not often manifest itself in the promotion of secular literary values. Russian variations on the topos of *translatio studii et imperii* emphasized the inheritance of Byzantine Greek religious culture and political power.[1] Most famously, it is embodied in the doctrine of Moscow as the Third Rome, for example in the formulation of Filofei of Pskov from the early sixteenth century, "All Christian monarchies have come to an end and have been gathered into a single monarchy of our Sovereign . . . , that is to say the Russian monarchy; for two Romes have fallen, the third stands, and a fourth there will not be."[2] A century later came the first attempt to introduce Greek meter into the Russian language sphere, Melety Smotritsky's grammar of the Church Slavonic language (1619). Using the Greek and Latin quantitative principle to describe the prosodic properties of the language, it can be seen as part of a Ukrainian defensive against the intrusion of Polish syllabic poetry in an attempt to maintain the distinctiveness of Orthodox culture, and thus also as a part of the same complex of ideas on religious inheritance.[3] The attempt was also a belated echo of European Renaissance interests that introduced quantity into Czech verse. It remained, however, a purely grammatical act that had no following in poetic practice. The later successful reform of Russian prosody undertaken by Vasily Trediakovsky (1703–1769) and Mikhailo Lomonosov (1711–1765) in the second third of the eighteenth century, even as it made use primarily of German syllabotonic developments, had as its subtext the attempt to gain classical, *secular* poetic values and forms for the new Russian literature.[4] The reform of Russian verse can thus be seen as a part of the general renewal of the topos of *translatio imperii* in eighteenth-century Russia, which also included the translation of a large number of Roman histories into Russian and the metaphorical translation of Russian history into the Roman form, as in Lomonosov's periodization of Russian history, based on the Roman.[5] But, the verse reform introduced something entirely new to *translatio studii* by emphasizing classical poetic culture over Byzantine religious culture. In the second decade of the nineteenth century, interest was renewed in this aspect of the reform and in particular in the possibilities for the imitation of classical hexameter in Russian verse. One young critic, Sergei Uvarov (1786–1855), even suggested that the independence of the Russian national literature rested upon the possibility of this inheritance. The alternative offered by Vasily Kapnist (1738–1823) of a return to ancient Russian verse culture as embodied in folk songs ultimately derived from an alternative, idiosyncratic theory of the origin of European civilization and its verse culture and thus constituted a different conception of cultural inheritance.

Many of the features of the Czech reformers' discourse were already present in the Russian eighteenth-century reform: the attack on the false and foreign system, the figuring of the reform as a return to an ancient and true system, the attack on rhyme and the associated dismissal of the (Catholic) barbaric Christian age, and the characteristic messianic pathos. Most of these features are manifested or at least adumbrated in just a few lines of Lomonosov's initial "Pis'mo o pravilakh rossiiskogo stikhotvorstva" ("Letter Concerning the Rules of Russian Poesy," 1739):

> In all correct Russian verses, long and short, one should use feet proper to our language based on a particular number and order. . . . That unfounded practice that was brought into Moscow schools from Poland cannot give to our versification any laws or rules. . . . The French, who wish to proceed

naturally in everything but almost always act against their intentions, cannot be an example to us in what concerns poetic feet: for, relying on their fantasy rather than on rules, they glue together words in their verses so aslant and askew that it can be called neither prose nor verse. . . . Someone depicted French poetry with quite an appropriate symbol, showing it in the theater in the guise of a woman who, hunched over, legs spread wide, dances to music played on a fiddle by a satyr. I cannot rejoice enough that our Russian language not only is not inferior to the Greek, Latin and German in vigor and heroic ring, but also can have a versification similar to theirs that is at the same time natural and peculiar to itself.[6]

The religious subtext of the dismissal of Polish syllabic versification is not realized here. But it becomes explicit in Lomonosov's "Predislovie o pol'ze knig tserkovnykh v rossiiskom iazyke" ("Foreword on the Utility of Ecclesiastical Books in the Russian Language," 1757): "The Poles, converted to the Catholic faith in ancient times, conduct their services according to their ritual in the Latin language, in which also their verses and prayers were composed in the barbarian times for the most part by bad authors, and therefore neither from Greece nor from Rome could gain such advantages as in our language were acquired from the Greek."[7] This later article, then, which was to become so important to Shishkov's ideology of the Slaviano-Russian language, links the reform of Russian verse culture, with its implicit striving toward a classical ideal, to the broad Russian orthodox religious and political tradition of the Greek inheritance.

The other reformer of Russian verse, Trediakovsky, was somewhat less explicit on the ideological structures that subtended his reforms, preferring to maintain a professional, philological mode of discourse.[8] But his increasingly Slavonic linguistic usage and his highly speculative philological work concerning the origins of verse tend to link the most ancient Russian/Slavic forms to those of the Greco-Roman classical world. Unlike Lomonosov, who emphasized the innovative aspect of the verse reform, Trediakovsky insisted that the syllabotonic form was in fact a return and renewal of the most ancient Russian forms. For Trediakovsky, the Russian verse tradition had been interrupted first by the advent of Christianity, which chased out the ancient pagan verse tradition (compare Palacký's ideas on the ancient Czech tradition), and later by the introduction of Polish verse forms. He outlines this history of Russian verse in his article "O drevnem, srednem, i novom stikhotvorenii rossiiskom" ("On Ancient, Middle, and New Russian Versification," 1755), which is both a defense of his priority in the verse reform over Lomonosov and a defense of that marked innovation as a renewal of the ancient system.

Trediakovsky admits that it is not possible to have direct knowledge of the Russian pagan verse tradition, because it left no monuments. But folk songs (*prostonarodnye pesni*) constitute sufficient evidence, for it seems likely that the church allowed the pagan poetic tradition to live on in harmless entertaining songs even as it wiped out the hymns to false gods. Such evidence showed the ancient tradition to be based on a "tonic" prosody (*tonicheskoe kolichestvo*), to involve the use of a variety of feet, and to be without rhyme.[9] There was little doubt for Trediakovsky that the secular folk songs had inherited the ancient pagan sacred forms (which he assumed to have existed), for that was the nature of poetry itself, developed everywhere as a sacred language first, only to undergo secularization later. Such an opinion was both formed on and confirmed by the Greek and Roman examples: "The popular (*narodnyi*) structure of verses is a direct copy (*podlinnyi spisok*) from the hieratic (*bogosluzhitel'skogo*) one: the Greek and Roman nations demonstrate this; and all others with whom verses are in use can also demonstrate it."[10] Trediakovsky's speculative inquiry into the origin of verse here anticipates the inquiries of Herder and others that stood at the foundation of later German romantic narratives of the histories of national literatures, and could be similarly used for later Russian national literary histories. Tredkiakovsky's thesis concerning the origins of Russian verse draws upon advances in classical philology and responds to the Quarrel between the Ancients and Moderns by drawing a parallel between the development of verse in ancient Greece and in ancient Russia. Tredkiakovsky had developed this thesis just a few years earlier in his "Mnenie o nachale poezii i stikhov vobshche" ("Opinion on the Origin of Poetry and Verse in General," 1752), which is a highly speculative gloss on Charles Rollin's discussion of poetry's origins from the opening of volume 12 of his *Histoire ancienne*.[11]

Trediakovsky's "renewal" of the ancient Russian verse form, then, is based on a reconstruction of the form that was created on a parallel with the development of the Greek and Roman poetic traditions. Moreover, what the discovery of the "tonic" basis of Russian verse in folk songs leads to is not the imitation of folk verses; rather, it makes possible the imitation of Greek and Roman verse forms from hexameter and elegiac distich to Sapphic and Horatian stanzas.[12] The "renewed" verse system creates an idealized classicist version of ancient Russian poetics. Like some of Trediakovsky's other gestures (discussed below), this argument for syllabotonic verse is at once classicizing and modernizing, a compromise between the extremes of the "Ancients'" and "Moderns'" positions.[13] This verse system founds an entirely new, modern, secular poetic tradition in Russia, but it does so on the basis of an ancient classical model, and it mitigates the contradictions inherent in such an approach by a mythologizing assertion of the identity of the native tradition and the classical one. This conflation of the forms of Russian folk poetry and of classical poetry would have important consequences for the discussions taking place in the 1810s.

Of all the verse forms offered by the Greco-Roman tradition, the one that concerned Trediakovsky the most was hexameter, the verse form of the highest poetry, epic, and, to a certain extent, tragedy. Tredkiakovsky's first attempt at verse reform, the "Novyi i kratkii sposob k slozheniiu rossiiskikh stikhov" ("New and Short Method for Composing Russian Verses," 1735), was largely limited to a discussion of heroic verse, which the writer formed as a compromise between the thirteen-syllable verse of the existing Russian tradition (based on the Polish) and hexameter, creating a syllabotonic organization of those syllables into a kind of rough hexameter. The inadequacy of this reform was quite apparent, and Lomonosov (in his 1739 letter) suggested a dactylo-trochaic imitation of Latin hexameters. In his poetic practice, however, Lomonosov followed the French use of Alexandrines for heroic verse, and it was left to Trediakovsky to develop the Russian imitation of classical hexameter. His revision of the "New and Short Method," published in his collected works in 1752, gives a full treatment of the dactylo-trochaic hexameter form.[14]

The apogee of Trediakovsky's work on hexameter is his translation of François Fénelon's *Les aventures de Télémaque, fils d'Ulysse,* which Trediakovsky prefaced with a long introduction, "Pred"iz"iasnenie ob iroicheskoi piime" ("Explanatory Foreword on the Heroic Poem," 1766). The introduction is divided into four parts: (1) the matter of epic, (2) the plot form of epic, (3) the didactics of epic, and (4) the metrical form of epic. Trediakovsky concludes with a discussion of prior Russian translations of Fénelon's novel and his own approach to the translation. The most striking aspect of Trediakovsky's translation is the transformation of Fénelon's prose into Russian hexameter. The introductory reflection on the epic, with its extensive discussion of meter, shows that Trediakovsky wished his translation to be read in the grand epic tradition and to be seen as an improvement of Fénelon's work for having translated it into the proper form. At the end of the introduction he makes this nearly explicit, indicating that he hoped through his translation "to lead readers to a level from which they could see themselves how worthy of admiration and reverence are the Hellenic poet Homer and the Latin Virgil: for Fénelon's *Télémaque* presents them with all their beauty, stateliness, and pithiness [*del'nost'*], while my *Tilemakhida* pours forth all their smoothness and pleasantness with the same sweetness, being of similar flow of words."[15]

Flow is a key word, because liquidity is the central quality of the hexameter line that makes it the appropriate vehicle for epic, according to Trediakovsky. He resorts to an extended river metaphor to describe the nature of the epic verse line.[16] A verse form that flows beyond the borders of the line is necessary to the extended narration of epic, and this flow must be able to embody all the variety of nature, the object of imitation. Rhymed verses, then, which emphasize the ending of each verse line, are inimical to the epic:

> Such verses are not rivers, flowing downwards, uninterrupted and undiverted, to their distant end: they are some kind of fount [*studenets*] bursting upwards and, having reached its close-by limit, breaking off and returning headlong downwards; so, every line has its own rapid and makes a racket on it. No matter how much lines with rhyme might ring out with a manly trumpet in their beginning and middle, in their end they merely squeak and squeal with a childish whistle. Rhyme is an adolescent toy unworthy of masculine ears. This frozen invention is Gothic and not the Hellenic or Latin ending, glittering and warming with noble heat.[17]

Trediakovsky here demonstrates his solidarity with other classicizing critics of rhyme. He employs a variety of metaphors to dramatize his critique: rivers versus sputtering founts, trumpets versus whistles, and heat versus cold (even the word he uses for fount, *studenets,* is derived from a word for cold).

Any language whose verse culture was dependent upon rhyme, then, met with an especial difficulty when it came to the epic. Trediakovsky singled out the Italian, Spanish, French, and Polish languages in this regard (he also included the English, clearly unaware of innovations in blank verse that had resulted from Renaissance experiments in quantitative verse). Fénelon, therefore, had to overcome this difficulty in composing his epic. Trediakovsky suggests that he wrote in prose because French verse was inappropriate to the epic and incapable of imitating the Greek and Latin hexameter, being rhymed.[18] A Russian translation, however, need not be hampered by this inability. Trediakovsky remarks that the existing prose translation by A. F. Krushchov flows with a *historical* and not a *heroic* river of narration, just like the author's, for whom however it was unavoidably necessary to prozaicise, being entirely without a heroic meter; but for us, enriched with such a verse by natural fertility in our literature—which is smoothly flowing, burning with heat, and aptly and sublimely flexible in all directions—it would be inappropriate, I think, to ignore it and to willfully appear poor in our abundance, just like one standing in water up to his mouth who is unable to quench his thirst. Finally, we have had this high heroic verse since ancient times; and *Télémaque* is an epic poem, which requires Homer's or Virgil's trotting gait.[19]

He later connects the ability of the Russian language directly to Greek and Latin: "Nature gave it all the abundance and sweetness of the Greek language and the seriousness and stateliness of Latin."[20] His translation would not be guilty of such an error. Rather, it would mark the return of Russian verse to its proper origins: "Therefore this type of verse, begun by me a few years back, and now commissioned for common use in this weighty poem, should not seem to us new and strange: it is a return from a strange, childish, and incorrect versification to our ancient, stately, proper, and appropriately perfect one; a return, I say, just like the return from Gothic architecture, lasting from the thirteenth through the sixteenth century, to the excellence of the Hellenic original form, alone grandiose and excelling in all proportionality."[21]

Trediakovsky's discourse on Russian versification shares many features with the Czech discourse in the 1810s. However, certain of Trediakovsky's statements also mark important differences from the attitudes of the later Czechs and also, as will be seen, from his Russian followers. Almost all of these differences in attitude can be linked to changes associated with the development of the national perspective on literature. For example, Trediakovsky exhibits a good classicist universalism. He begins his article on the history of Russian verse with the observation that poetry is "one and the same, according to its nature, in every century and in all places with the human race," allowing only that the form of versification differs with each nation.[22] But the national perspective on literature develops from the historical observation that something essential about poetry changes from place to place and time to time. Where Trediakovsky observes that Fénelon's *Télémaque* "is a poem of all races, tribes, classes and ages,"[23] later critics would be more interested in what marked a poem as belonging to its particular place and time. And while the Czech Palacký would still attack the early Christian era invention of rhyme, he and his contemporaries would have been unlikely to extend the critique to Gothic architecture, which had been rehabilitated as a unique European tradition as early as 1762 by Richard Hurd and had had its praises sung by Goethe.[24]

Another telltale eighteenth-century attitude is Trediakovsky's decidedly conservative take on the epic. His definition of the epic limits the subject matter to the heroic age and the meter to hexameter and thus leads him to number true epic works in general at four: Homer's two, Virgil's, and now Fénelon's.[25] He grants no place whatsoever to the European epic tradition, to Dante and Tasso or Milton, writers so essential to the narratives of the romantic, national critics. His inclusion of Virgil is also telling. Trediakovsky makes little to no distinction between Greek and Roman literatures. In bringing Fénelon's prose closer to the epic tradition, Trediakovsky made liberal use of epic formulaic additions to the text. Most often the formulae come from Virgil.[26] And even his compound adjectives, which seem to hark back to Slavonic borrowings from Greek, are actually most often from the Latin.[27] Trediakovsky's functional model for epic verse was Virgil, who had been the ideal model among European poets for centuries. But the German and English rehabilitation of Homer was at the expense of Virgil, who became exemplary of Roman literature's epigonic and imitative nature. The later Czech and Russian adepts of the hexameter line are explicitly pursuing Homer and not Virgil, who rather represents the imitative nature of their own literatures, which they hoped to overcome.

Trediakovsky's gesture of translating Fénelon's *Télémaque* into hexameters is distinctly classicizing, and yet that gesture and the arguments for it were of considerable help in the modernization of Russian literary discourse. Fénelon did not really choose prose out of a lack of a heroic meter in French, but as a compromise in the Quarrel between the Ancients and Moderns. Perrault had suggested that prose was a more exact medium than verse, so Fénelon used a modern form—a moral poem in prose—for his imitation of the ancients.[28] The publication of the novel in 1699 is often said to mark the end of the first phase of the Quarrel.[29] Trediakovsky's translation thus undoes Fénelon's compromise by attempting to outdo him in classicizing.[30] At the same time, however, this gesture might best be seen as an attempt to finally bring a modern literature up to the achievements of the ancients.[31] In the early nineteenth century, a return to ancient sources would also be an important strategy in literary modernization.

The Napoleonic Wars, and particularly the invasion of Russia in 1812, were a strong impetus to the re-evaluation of Russian literature and culture in relation to French culture. A striking example of this can be seen in the letters of I. M. Murav'ev-Apostol (1765–1851), a senator and member of the Academy of Sciences and an active member of Shishkov's colloquium. Murav'ev-Apostol published ten "Letters from Moscow to Nizhnii Novgorod" in *Syn Otechestva* in 1813 and 1814 in which he called for educating the Russian nation and its literature on the ancient classics, as opposed to the French classics. Like many others, Murav'ev-Apostol had fled Moscow for Nizhnii Novgorod with Napoleon's approach. His letters, written upon his return to a destroyed Moscow, unapologetically rail at the French nation for its godless actions, from the French Revolution to the burning of Moscow. Imitation of the French is no longer an attractive option, and instead, in his first letter Murav'ev-Apostol imagines the city of Moscow addressing the Russian nation (*narod Rossiiskii*) and calling it to be true to its church, its tsar, and itself: "Know yourself, and throw off from your powerful neck the yoke that has enslaved you—giant!—to the imitation of pigmies who have exhausted all their spiritual energy by centuries of vice. Know yourself!"[32] The recurring theme in the letters is the fundamental problem with the education of Russian nobles, especially the domination of education by French models and French tutors and the preference given to the French language, French literature, and French fashions. At the end of his third letter, Murav'ev-Apostol suggests that this preference for all things French is also the cause of the lack of progress in literature (*slovesnost'*), and he takes up the topic of literature in depth in the fourth letter.[33]

There, Murav'ev-Apostol presents a fictional "dialogue" between two characters, Neotin and Arkheonov. From the names, a present-day critic might expect them to be representatives of the two sides from the debates of the previous decade, in Tynianov's terminology, an innovator and an archaist. And indeed, Murav'ev-Apostol clearly sides with Arkheonov, to whom he gives the second and final monologue (there is nothing dialogic about Murav'ev-Apostol's presentation). But Neotin is an unrepentant neo-classicist of an eighteenth-century stamp, for whom French writers alone remain models, above any possible ancient models. There is nothing at all "new" in his views, which are far behind the developments in the Karamzinian camp with Zhukovsky as the leading poet. On the other hand, Arkheonov dares to articulate a new point of view on literature that he fears may be seen as heretical, without mention at all of the necessity of maintaining the "old style" that so dominated Shishkov's position. The "heresy" that Arkheonov proclaims is that he does not find genius in even one of the French writers.[34] This has its rhetorical effect, but what is more interesting is Murav'ev-Apostol's insistence on a certain relativity of literary values. The question of where tragedy truly flourishes "is not one of that taste for the elegant that unchangingly belongs in general to all ages, to all enlightened nations, but of that taste that particularly forms according to the character of each nation, its moral traits and its form of government." How, then, can one suggest that the English are wrong if they prefer Shakespeare to Racine, the Germans Schiller, or the Italians Alfieri? One cannot argue with "national taste" (*narodnyi vkus*).[35]

Such considerations, in the context of the question of education, do not lead Murav'ev-Apostol to conclude, as Venevitinov would a decade later, that Russia should do all it can to develop on its own resources (see chapter 11). Instead, Murav'ev-Apostol defends the role of imitation and even translation in the creation of works of genius: "Won't you agree that Tasso is the only poet who can stand alongside the ancient creators of the epic and that his epic [*poema*], in consideration of its plan and plot, is the equal of the *Iliad*, and in the character of its heroes it exceeds the *Aeneid*. One cannot but agree, however, that Tasso borrowed the majority of his characters from Homer, and that in many places one finds not merely imitation but even translations of Virgil."[36] The question then remains: who to imitate? The answer is in the conclusion to the fourth letter: "Not one of the modern literatures perfected itself, as you maintain, by the imitation of modern ones: all of them, without exception, drew their beauties from the single and endless font of all elegance—from the Greeks and Romans. For that purpose it is long time that we too undertook the genuine task, and therefore I will boldly say and will always repeat, that until we study, that is, dedicate all of the time of the early period, from 7 to 15 years, to the learning of the Greek or at least the Latin language, along with the Russian, fundamentally, aesthetically—until then we, the greater part of the crowd, will not speak, but chatter, not write, but merely ruin paper."[37] For Murav'ev-Apostol, imitation and translation of the ancients have a fundamental a role to play in the creation of a national literature and the education of a national taste, although he gives no special attention to Homer and the hexameter form.

But if the translation and imitation of the ancients were essential to the formation of a modern literature, then the hexameter form pioneered by Trediakovsky and his discourse in its defense could be of great use. Trediakovsky's example, however, was not seen as a positive one. In the harsh polemics of the eighteenth century, he had been painted as a pedant and talentless poet, cast in the role of the "fool" of modern Russian literature.[38] His high hopes for the *Tilemakhida,* for lessening the gap between the achievements of the ancients and the moderns, were not confirmed by the reception of this work, which made it the primary example of bad Russian poetry, a role that it continued to play into the nineteenth century. To take one example, Semen Bobrov, in the "Proizshestvie v tsarstve tenei" (examined in chapter 4), has Lomonosov sentence the Frenchified dandy Gallorus to an eternal punishment consisting in the reading and analysis of the *Tilemakhida*.[39] This appropriately makes punishment in the heavenly spheres mirror the favored punishment in the highest earthly spheres: in Catherine II's court, the worst punishment in the game of "forfeits" was to have to read a page of the *Tilemakhida* or commit some verses from it to memory.[40] If hexameters were to find a place in Russian verse, then they would have to be rescued from Trediakovsky's shadow.

Aleksandr Radishchev (1749–1802) records precisely this complaint in the "Tver'" chapter of his *Puteshestvie iz Peterburga v Moskvu* (*Journey from Petersburg to Moscow*, 1790). There his narrator's interlocutor over dinner laments the lack of metrical variety in Russian verses, blaming Lomonosov and Sumarokov for not giving a greater variety of examples. In particular, the character observes, "I would have liked for Homer to appear among us not in iambs but in verses similar to his own, in hexameters; and Kostrov, though he is not a poet but a translator, would have begun a new epoch in our versification, having speeded the arrival of true poetry by a whole generation."[41] E. I. Kostrov's translation of the first six books of the *Iliad*, in Alexandrines, had appeared in 1787. The character continues, "But Lomonosov and Sumarokov did not halt Russian versification alone. The indefatigable toiler [*vozovik*] Trediakovsky assisted in no small way with his *Tilemakhida*. . . . Whoever takes it into his head to write in dactyls is immediately assigned Trediakovsky as a foster-father [*Trediakovskogo pristaviat diad'koiu*], and the most beautiful offspring will long appear to be a monster, until a Milton, Shakespeare, or Voltaire is born. Then they will dig Trediakovsky out of his grave, overgrown with the moss of forgetting, will find good verses in the *Tilemakhida,* and will make them examples."[42] Radishchev himself would later attempt this disinterment.

With the publication of his collected works in 1811, there appeared in print for the first time Radishchev's "Pamiatnik daktilokhoreicheskomu vitiaziu" ("Memorial to the Dactylo-trochaic Knight"), which had been written around 1801. The work as a whole is not so much an attempt to defend Trediakovsky or the *Tilemakhida* as it is an attempt to name precisely their failings and to absolve the hexameter from any guilt for having contributed to those failings. The "Pamiatnik" is a parody of Trediakovsky's translation, but its primary target is Fénelon's novel and its moral-didactic plot of an uncle instructing his nephew, out of which Radishchev makes hilarious parody in the middle section of the work. In the dialogues that frame the narrative, the character *B*, who is defending the hexameter form, suggests that "the very idea to translate *Télémaque* in verse is something infelicitous," perhaps because it contains matter "unnecessary and inappropriate to a heroic song."[43] This is half of the problem of the *Tilemakhida,* the other half being Trediakovsky's failings as a poet. "Trediakovsky understood very well what versification is, and . . . wrote in verses like those in which the Greeks and Romans wrote, that is, for the Russian ear, in entirely new ones; but, knowing Virgil's language better than his own, he thought that one could make the same kinds of word order transpositions in Russian as in Latin. His misfortune was that, being an educated man, he had no taste. He was so nourished by the reading of the rules of verse used by the ancients and knew so well the beauties of their harmony [*blagoglasie*], that he clearly imitated that."[44] *B* thus defends Trediakovsky's innovation in verse form, even as he recognizes his numerous failings in the execution of that verse.

In spite of all these failings, *B* insists that the *Tilemakhida "is not entirely worthless."*[45] He analyzes and defends the exemplary value of a certain number of verses in the work, while admitting that such verses are in the overwhelming minority. The key term in this defense is *"blagoglasie"*—harmony—a very close analog to the Czech term *"libozvučnost"* that was a part of Šafařík and Palacký's argument for quantitative verse. It looks like a comparable Slavonic calque of the German term *Wohlklang,* which Radishchev would have encountered in Klopstock's essay on the hexameter, an essay that Radishchev drew upon for his analysis of Trediakovsky's hexameter verse.[46] But whatever the inspiration for the term, Radishchev had made it his own as a central term in his literary criticism and an integral part of his aesthetic philosophy, outlined in the tract "O cheloveke, ego smertnosti i bessmertii" ("On Man, His Mortality and Immortality"), where it joined comparable terms for the human aestheticization of the senses, such as *"blagovonie"* (pleasant scent) and *"blagoobrazie"* (pleasant appearance).[47] In defending certain of Trediakovsky's verses in the *Tilemakhida* in terms of *blagoglasie,* Radishchev pays attention not so much to rhythmical harmony alone, but especially to metrical and sound combinations that support the sense of the verses, to combinations of sound and sense.[48] Where the Czechs argued that the quantitative form itself would lead to a greater *libozvučnost,* for Radishchev the argument is in the opposite direction: the hexameter form used by Trediakovsky is not an obstacle to *blagoglasie.* When *B*'s interlocutor suggests that certain verses are laugh-inducing, *B* responds, "Of course; but why? Not from the dactyls and not from hexameter [*shestistop*], but from awkward words. . . . And Trediakovsky is not made humorous by his dactyls, but because he did not have taste."[49] Unlike for the Czechs, then, when the arguments are made in the second decade of the nineteenth century for the necessity of hexameter in the development of the Russian national literature, the inherent *blagoglasie* of the hexameter form is not a part of the argument, and the term is not used.[50] But Radishchev helped to raise the question of the appropriate meter for epic works in the later eighteenth century with his *Puteshestvie*, and the publication of his "Pamiatnik" in 1811 drew renewed attention to the example of Trediakovsky's hexameters as a possible model for epic verse at a time when the need for a national epic beyond French influence was beginning to be felt more acutely.

Radishchev can thus be given some credit for the rising interest in Trediakovsky, especially around 1811 and the opening of Shishkov's Colloquium of Lovers of the Russian Word.[51] And in fact, both sides of the archaist-innovator debates made use of Trediakovsky's work, but polemically it was far more appealing to accuse one's opponent of having Trediakovsky as a foster-father, as Radishchev had suggested, than to admit that one had learned something from him.[52] The revulsion-attraction dialectic is nowhere more visible than in the debates over Russian hexameter. Like the Czech debate over quantity, the Russian hexameter discussion was more centrally concerned with the national qualities of Russian literature than with technical questions of versification.[53] And although Trediakovsky did not think of a national literature, or even a nation, in the characteristic ways focused on here, his work was easily adaptable to such ends.[54]

Aleksandr Vostokov (1781–1864), who would become Russia's leading Slavist but was a translator with the Commission on Law Making at the time, can perhaps be credited with the more immediate stimulation of the debate over Russian hexameter. His "Opyt o russkom stikhoslozhenii" ("Essay on Russian Versification,") published in 1812 in the *Sanktpeterburgskie vedomosti,* contributed to both sides of the debate. It is also exemplary in its treatment of Trediakovsky. The essay is a continuation of Trediakovsky's inquiries into the older tonic forms of Russian verse that makes use of Trediakovsky's terminology, periodizations, and polemical strategies. But Vostokov never acknowledges his debt to Trediakovsky, preferring to deride him at every opportunity.

Vostokov in general was publicly derisive about the quality of Trediakovsky's philological work, which of course failed to meet the standards of the new century.[55] He aimed in his "Essay on Russian

Versification" at "analyzing [the older tonic versification] with greater precision than my predecessors."[56] He begins with a discussion of three basic types of versification: "metrical," syllabic, and tonic. By "metrical," he means verses formed on the basis of feet, that is, syllabotonic. "This in fact belongs to the Greeks; was borrowed by the Romans from them. . . ."[57] The implied narrative of Greek priority and Roman imitation already represents one "improvement," in the understanding of the time, in relation to his predecessor Trediakovsky. His attitude toward syllabic verse, however, is entirely familiar: "It is used by the Italians, the French, the Poles and others whose languages, given the limitations of their prosody, are little or not at all capable of versification."[58] And while Vostokov kept to Trediakovsky's periodization of Russian versification, he explicitly separates the older tonic forms of verse found in folk songs from the innovation (which he credits to Lomonosov) of using stress in place of length in order to imitate Greek metrical versification. Trediakovsky's strange identification of the ancient or folk forms of Russian verse with classical forms is thus negated and each is understood as a separate system—another improvement over Trediakovsky's lack of distinction between true tonic verse and syllabotonic. Trediakovsky had used this sleight-of-hand identification in order to justify the introduction of Greek verse forms into Russian. Vostokov's separation of the two would have important consequences for the debate on hexameter to follow. But Vostokov aimed at technical reform without the national pathos of what followed.

Before treating Russian tonic versification, the subject of his study, Vostokov first deals with the "metrical" and syllabic forms. In versification, according to Vostokov, the Greeks are our teachers just as in all of the other fine arts. "For that reason we will say ahead of time that the two forms of poetry that will be examined hereafter cannot compare with [Greek metrical verse] in any aspect."[59] Though Vostokov intends to analyze and recommend the use of the Russian tonic meters, his recommendation of Greek meters is much stronger. And the greatest of the Greek forms is hexameter: "It is properly considered by experts to be the most perfect of all existing forms of poetry, uniting in itself the two primary conditions of harmony, variety and unity, in the greatest degree possible."[60] In contrast, the Russian epic verse form (tonic), with three stresses and a dactylic ending, presents so much variety (more than 100 possible combinations of long and short syllables) that any unity in the verse line is lost. Vostokov recommends the verse form, but suspects it will be used more for romance than for true epic, its aura having been spoiled by lowly folk usage.[61]

Greek metrical forms, however, were out of the reach of most languages as far as Vostokov was concerned: "Of the newer polished languages not one has been capable of all the forms of Greek versification due to the lack of quantitative prosody. Only the German language, as far as I know, and also of Slavic dialects related to ours, Bohemian, having prosody in part corresponding to the Greek, can successfully imitate Greek meters."[62] He goes on to emphasize the limitations of this ability for each language.[63] Then he cites the major difficulty for the Russian language: a lack of spondees. For him the lack of spondees means that "we are obliged to reject the majority of Greek meters based on [them]."[64] Unfortunately, this includes hexameter.

Trediakovsky championed the dactylo-trochaic meter as a Russian equivalent of Greek hexameter. Vostokov is no less a champion of this meter for epic forms, but he is determined to avoid the stigma of association with Trediakovsky. His transition from the impossibility of spondaic meters to advocacy of dactylo-trochaic meter is thus a fascinating example of careful literary affiliation and myth making. He continues with the observation that Russian is more fortunate than most languages in the variety of feet that it does have and laments the fact that "habit and imitation" have limited the number of feet Russian poetry uses.[65] His primary example of this is the use of the Alexandrine in Russian for epic, elegiac, and dramatic poetry, introduced by Lomonosov and Sumarokov "only because it was used so by the French and Germans."[66] He notes that Lomonosov was aware of the possibilities of the dactylo-trochaic meter and quotes from that part of Lomonosov's "Pis'mo o pravilakh rossiiskogo stikhotvorstva" in which Lomonosov gives an example of the meter. Vostokov adds that "[h]e certainly would have been able, on the strength of his talent, to introduce this meter among us, and in doing so would have widened the borders of our poetry in no small way." This potential was not realized, however, and instead "he hindered for [the Russian Muse] the free stride of the epic by the most monotonous of all verses, the Alexandrine with rhymes."[67] Vostokov excuses Lomonosov for this error, given that he was a lyric poet and not an epic poet or tragedian. But other epic poets followed his example, "and dactylo-trochaic hexameter unfortunately from the very first fell into the hands of Trediakovsky, who also had the courage to undertake new things, but did not have that talent and taste at all for the attractive teaching of his innovations; and thus with his infamous *Tilemakhida* he defamed also the meter in which it is written and long turned the public away from it."[68]

Vostokov has entirely turned the tables on Trediakovsky. Lomonosov has been made the virtual father of the meter while Trediakovsky, who actually advocated, practiced, and developed the meter, is blamed for its absence in Russian poetry. Vostokov has cleansed the meter of Trediakovsky's unhealthy aura and placed the beneficial Lomonosov at its head, so that he could advocate it without embarrassment. And yet, throughout the essay Vostokov silently invokes Trediakovsky. His division of Russian poetry into three periods, ancient, middle, and new, corresponding to three different verse forms, tonic, syllabic, and syllabotonic, is exactly Trediakovsky's division. The same source modeled his invective against the use of the Alexandrine in epic and his suggestion that French syllabic verse proceeds from an essential lack in the French language of proper prosody. This was the aspect of Trediakovsky's discourse that was most attractive to advocates of an independent Russian national literature, contrasting the inability of the French language to the ability of the Russian and thus making absurd the further imitation of the French practice. Vostokov, however, like Radishchev does not tie his advocacy of hexameter to the concern with the national qualities of Russian literature. In the debate that followed, this was a central concern.[69]

The victory in the debate over hexameter already belonged to hexameter's advocates before the first letters were published in 1813. Nikolai Gnedich had begun a translation of Homer's *Iliad*, with the encouragement and patronage of Vasily Kapnist, in Alexandrines. The translation was to be a continuation of the work of Kostrov, who had published his translation of just the first six books. Gnedich published his translations of books VII and VIII in 1809 and 1812, and he was encouraged by Kapnist to continue the important work.[70] But in his reply to Sergei Uvarov's letter advocating the use of Russian hexameter for the translation, published in the same issue of the journal of Shishkov's colloquium in 1813, Gnedich began with the following acknowledgment: "I have long felt, dear sir, the disadvantages of the Alexandrine verse for the translation of ancient poets, demonstrated quite correctly in the letter with which you have honored me. . . . Encouraged by A. N. O[lenin]'s and your flattering advice, I have dared to undertake a larger experiment with hexameter in order to present it according to the wishes of your esteemed society the Colloquium."[71] Uvarov's arguments for the meter and Gnedich's explanation of its forms should be seen, then, as an attempt to prepare the public for the change of form Gnedich's translation was taking, to head off possible objections to the use of this notorious meter. In his reply to Uvarov, published two years later in the same journal, Kapnist—clearly annoyed by the derailment of a promising project he had patronized—did not fail to raise the specter of Trediakovsky: "All of

Portrait of Nikolai Gnedich. A lithograph by Mosharskii (1911), based on the drawing by A. M. Kalashnikov, 1836. Courtesy of The State Literary Museum, Moscow, Russia.

a sudden with your cunning and vain philosophizing [*khitrospletennym suemudrstvovaniem*] you turned him to a path trod by the author of eternal, heavy versifying memory, of the *Tilemakhida!* A particularly evil-minded act for me and for Mr. Gnedich, but most of all for his readers."[72] Rather than defending the Alexandrine form, however, Kapnist offered an even bolder design. If the translation of Homer into Russian were really to mark a return to the ancient forms of Russian versification, as Uvarov had argued, then those forms were not to be found through the imitation of Greek meters, but rather in the meters of Russian folk songs.

Ultimately, the meters advocated by Uvarov and Kapnist played a part in the strategies for *translatio studii,* for claiming a cultural inheritance and cultural leadership, with the different meters reflecting very different conceptions about the origin of European culture and especially literature. Between 1810 and 1818, Uvarov was developing a philosophy of history that would ultimately underlie his approach to Russian education, as Nicholas I's minister of education, under the slogan of "Autocracy, Orthodoxy, and *Narodnost'*."[73] He saw historical progress as an organic process that developed within nations and civilizations, so that each nation or civilization had a life cycle, periods of infancy, youth, maturity, and old age. The greater progress of the "*esprit humain*" was an upward spiral, with each nation or civilization contributing and then passing its "spirit" or "torch" on "to another part of the globe."[74] If European civilization was mature, it was also sick, and in this conception, Russia's "youth" was an advantage, for it was poised to inherit European civilization and bring it to its full maturity, just as the Roman Empire had done in antiquity.[75] Russia's maturity, embodied in a future constitutional monarchy and with a secure sense of national cultural identity, would be the maturity of modern civilization. Uvarov's arguments for the use of hexameter in 1813 reflect this broader historical conception.

In 1809, Uvarov returned from two years as an attaché in Vienna with a sense that the old world was dying, but inspired by the possibility for its renewal through a return to the ancient sources of European civilization in the Orient.[76] In 1810, he published his essay, "Projet d'une académie asiatique," in which he proposed the establishment of an Asian academy in St. Petersburg, so that Russia, ideally situated between Orient and Occident, could become the leader of the latest renaissance of the exhausted European civilization. Study of the oriental sources, which gave rise to all civilization, ancient and modern, would also enable Russia to avoid the "European contagion" and "premature old age" in developing its own cultural identity.[77] If the sources of religion and philosophy were in India, though, Greece remained the birthplace of literature, and in his "Projet," Uvarov advocated a return to this source as well:

> Russia has an infinite advantage over the rest of Europe. She can take Greek literature as the basis for her national literature and found a completely original school. She should imitate neither German literature, nor the

French spirit, nor Latin erudition. The thorough study of Greek will open an inexhaustible source of new ideas, of fecund images for Russia. It will give to history, to philosophy, to poetry the purest forms and those closest to the true models. Further, the Greek language is tied to the religion of the Russians and to Slavonic literature, which appears to be formed from it.[78]

As it was for the Czechs and Germans, for Uvarov the return to the ultimate sources was the means to claim Russia's cultural inheritance.

In his memoir, written years later, Uvarov acknowledged that the salon of Aleksei Nikolaevich Olenin (1763–1843), known to his contemporaries as the Russian Winckelmann, was the main influence on his literary views and the source of his new interest in Russian culture.[79] Olenin was director of the Imperial Public Library in Petersburg, where Uvarov was employed beginning in 1812 and where Gnedich also had begun to work, in 1811. Olenin was also the patron of the most prominent salon in Russia in the first three decades of the nineteenth century and a tireless supporter of Russian culture.[80] As "Russia's foremost Hellenist," Olenin, who had been deeply influenced by the writings of Winckelmann during his studies in Dresden, seems to be the source of programmatic attempts to develop Russian national cultural traditions on the basis of Greek models.[81] In addition to his support of the hexameter form for Gnedich's translation, acknowledged by Gnedich in his letter, Olenin encouraged and contributed to the dramatic work of Vladislav Ozerov, which moved towards a synthesis of national and classical forms and motifs.[82] It was Uvarov, however, who made the public case for hexameter.

Uvarov opens by stating that his delight in Gnedich's translation "has prompted my desire to communicate some observations about our versification, in particular in relation to the ancient languages."[83] In delineating this relationship, Uvarov follows Trediakovsky rather than Vostokov. Where Vostokov separated Russian verse forms from Greek forms like the hexameter, Uvarov, like Trediakovsky, prefers to elide any difference in order to justify the use of hexameter in Russian. "Individual fragments of our country's poetry show that our language contains all the shades of a *systematic prosody*. The first works of our poetry present a particular character, based on quite a distinct pronunciation of *long* and *short* syllables."[84] Which fragments and works these are and the proof of these assertions are left to the imagination of the reader. He continues by observing that these native resources were not developed: "Rather than pursuing this and gradually perfecting Russian prosody, our first and best poets deviated entirely from this rule. The history of our poetry shows us that blind imitation with which we adopted not only foreign *ideas,* but even foreign *forms.*"[85] Even Lomonosov joined the French in the general trend of writing epics in Alexandrines. Here Uvarov follows Vostokov and Radishchev.

This argument against the imitation of foreign forms is potentially dangerous, to say the least, when one is advocating the adoption of an imitation of a Greek metrical form! Uvarov adopts the double strategy, then, of arguing that the Greek form is an essential and original form upon which the metrical forms of all other languages are built, and of implying, as already noted, that native Russian forms share something essential with the Greek forms. This allows the imitation of Greek forms to represent, at the same time, the development of native forms. After observing that the influence of ancient poetry on Russian has been regrettably small, Uvarov asserts that "one of the greatest beauties of Greek poetry is its rich and systematic versification," which used distinct poetic forms for each genre.[86] This was recognized by the Romans: "When the Romans conceived of the desire to refine their coarse language, antagonistic to the Greek spirit, they made their primary efforts in devising metrical forms. The Romans borrowed all of them from the Greeks because they acknowledged them as the most perfect and the Latin language as not terribly made for poetry. All the experts are agreed that Latin poetry succeeded in assimilating to itself hexameter better than all other parts of the Greek metrical system. The Romans never undertook to write an epic other than in hexameter."[87] Rome's imitation of Greece is, for Uvarov, exemplary, because it founds its poetry on the true source. And even the Romans recognized the necessary connection of the epic and hexameter.

Beginning with the Italians in the Renaissance, the modern European languages also looked to the ancient sources as the foundation of their literatures: "From that time on, every European nation developed its own literature [*obrazoval svoiu slovesnost'*], and each of them has its own character. Poetry differed everywhere by newly discovered forms, *natural,* so to speak, to those languages. Italy, Spain, Portugal, France, and finally England and Germany each entered in the field of literature. Each attained by its own path a degree of formation and ornamented itself with many famous works."[88] Here one sees a reflection of Uvarov's conception of cultural history as a kind of relay race, and in fact, to digress briefly, this passage points to another source of Uvarov's historical theories that has not, to my knowledge, been previously noted. The series of leading nations in literature enumerated here is the very progression outlined in Friedrich Bouterwek's *Geschichte der Poesie und Beredsamkeit seit dem Ende des dreizehnten Jahrhunderts*—that is, the same source that inspired František Palacký to conceive of a similar progression in aesthetics, to be completed by a Czech or Slavic period. Bouterwek was a professor in Göttingen, where Uvarov studied from 1801 to 1803, and while very little is known about Uvarov's studies, it is likely, given his interest in German literature, that Uvarov would have been familiar with this important history of literature published in 1801.[89]

The fact of this progression is not as important to Uvarov, though, as the fact that in the process, each nation created its own poetic forms. French literature was no different. Like both Vostokov and Trediakovsky, Uvarov takes the French Alexandrine to be a form that is a result of the inadequacy of the French language: "When the French began to write correctly, to translate the ancients and to imitate them, they were forced to create for themselves a particular *system of versification*. Their language, for all its dignity and beauty, was quite unfit for poetry. . . . Thus the French invented the Alexandrine verse as the most fitting, given the lack of prosody in the French language, and the most in keeping with the rules of poetry."[90] In imitating the French, then, rather than going to the Greek source, the Russians had adopted a form that was derived from the Greek source in a manner inappropriate to their own language. "Is it appropriate for us Russians, having, fortunately, an abundant, metrical language full of prosody to follow such blind prejudice? Is it appropriate for us, having in our language such excellent qualities, to borrow from foreigners the most impoverished aspect of their language, the prosody, entirely improper to us?"[91] The results of such borrowings are absurdities: "When instead of the smooth and majestic hexameter I hear the meager and dry Alexandrine verse, decorated with rhyme, it seems to me that I see the divine Achilles in French dress."[92]

These absurdities are not mere failures of taste. For Trediakovsky, hexameter was the essential form of the epic as a distinct and well-defined classical genre. For Uvarov, the argument of form goes beyond the question of genre and touches upon the natural and distinctive essence of any national literature, the forms of which are always built upon a direct relationship to the Greek forms: "[I]f we want to raise the dignity of our language, if we want to aspire to having a *national* literature [*slovesnost' narodnaia*] truly proper to us, then let us stop writing or translating the epos in Alexandrine verses; let us stop weighing down the youth of our literature with the heavy chains of French taste. If we do not return to the true character of our language; if we do not create a metrical system based on the very spirit of the language; if we will not have the means to resurrect the *prosody* of our ancient versification, then without a doubt there is reason to fear that in a very short time our poetry will resemble an infant bearing all the signs of decrepitude or a withered youth."[93] The metrical form that the translation of Homer will take in Russian will either hinder the formation of a national literature or contribute to it by employing and developing the natural and proper forms of the language of that literature. In his conclusion, Uvarov again implies that those natural and proper forms were closely related to the Greek forms. A return to the sources, in ancient Greek and Russian versification, will prevent the youthful Russian literature from aging prematurely and enable it to mature properly into its role as the new leader of European literature.

Kapnist could only agree with the proposal to "resurrect the prosody of our ancient versification," but was unable to agree about the means. He cited the passage from Uvarov's just examined conclusion and continued, "Everything you said to this point was entirely in agreement with my thoughts; but with what amazement did I see, reading on, that in consequence of the truths you had stated you advised Mr. Gnedich to translate the *Iliad* in hexameters!"[94] For Kapnist, Greek hexameters were as contrary to the spirit of the Russian language as any iambs, trochees, or anapests that formed contemporary poetic practice. To make this argument, he insisted that Greek hexameters were formed with dactyls and spondees—not trochees, noted the well-known fact that the Russian language is poor in spondees, and proceeded to demonstrate the complete awkwardness of the dactylo-spondaic meter by retranslating eleven lines of Gnedich's translation—the first eleven lines of the sixth book— into that meter. The two stresses that end every line in his example indeed slow down the end of these lines and break any rhythmical harmony, and Kapnist challenges anyone to try to translate Homer into correct hexameter in a way that preserves the "purity and *blagozvuchnost*' of style" that one would prefer.[95]

If Gnedich was going to deviate from a proper Greek hexameter anyway by substituting trochees for spondees, "I [Kapnist] repeat my question, what prevents us, in keeping with your own opinion, from trying to devise for the epic, just as for other genres of verse, meters proper to our language?"[96] Kapnist proposes folk songs as a source, but the manner in which he does so is very revealing of what Kapnist, a representative of the older generation, thought the reading public was prepared for: "So, I admit openly, not fearing, out of love for the fatherland's language, even the mockery that I may subject myself to for the novelty of my proposal, that I would like to encourage the lovers of our literature who are more accomplished in it than I to seek in the meter of our folk songs [*narodnye pesni*] a metrical versification proper to our language."[97] In fact, the idea of using folk song meters was far from new, and Kapnist cites the examples of Karamzin's "Ilya Muromets" and Kheraskov's

Translatio Studii–Translatio Prosodiae II **157**

"Bakhariana" as having given him the courage to face the mockery, this time. He himself had long ago begun to experiment with folk verses—he cites his own translation of a song of Ossian, which he had done in the early 1790s and which made use of a number of folk verse forms in addition to some more standard syllabotonic forms of literary verse, but which he had never dared to publish. (In fact, he had published a fragment in 1796, but one composed in eight-line stanzas in a canonical iambic tetrameter.)[98]

If there was anything in Kapnist's position that was laugh-inducing for his opponents, it was not the author's defense of the value of folk poetics. Rather, it was his historical argument for the primacy of Russian folk meters that even some of his friends described as "nonsense" (*bred*).[99] If Russian writers were to take up the variety of meters "that remained, obviously from deep antiquity, in our folk songs" then "perhaps we would hear in their imitations echoes of Boian, that late descendant of the celebrated Hyperboreans, of whom even the extremely proud Greeks relate that Apollo, who visited them every year from the spring equinox until the rise of the Pleiades, taught them music, and doubtless, also versification, inseparable from it in ancient times."[100] Kapnist here alludes, in a highly condensed form, to his Hyperborean thesis, an idea he had been working on since the late 1780s but would finally publish in the very next issue of *Chtenie v Besede* as "Kratkoe izyskanie o Giperboreanakh: O korennom rossiiskom stikhoslozhenii" ("A Short Inquiry Regarding the Hyperboreans: On Native Russian Versification"). Kapnist had been introduced to Russian folk meters by Nikolai L'vov and had been encouraged in his translation of Ossian into folk meters by L'vov, whose own experiments have been previously noted.[101] In the introduction to the collection of folk songs L'vov published with Ivan Prach, L'vov had suggested, on the basis of some recently discovered ancient Greek music, that Russian folk songs had inherited their heterophonic chorus structure from the Greeks.[102] Kapnist cites this evidence in his own discussion, but comes to the opposite conclusion regarding the direction of cultural inheritance.[103] On the basis of Greek historical and mythological sources, Kapnist determines that the source of Greek culture and learning, including versification, was the culture of the Hyperboreans, a branch of the Scythian nation and ancestors of the Russian nation.[104] Russian folk songs, then, were the direct descendants of the music from which the Greeks had themselves learned music, so there was no need to use Greek intermediaries: "In the fatherland's soil there still remains a precious seed, scorned to this day. It is time, it seems, to grow it, and enriching our language with new *blagoglasie* of versification, demonstrate that we are not inferior, in any form of perfection, to either contemporary or ancient nations, so highly regarded throughout the universe."[105] Kapnist would oppose Uvarov's oriental and Hellenic renaissance with his own Scythian-Hyperborean renaissance.

Kapnist thus rejects, in his letter to Uvarov, the dominant tradition of *translatio studii* from Roman times onward, which takes Greek literature as the ultimate source and the adaption of Greek forms to a new language as a source of eternal fame: "Horace's vanity of this sort is known to all: he considers the introduction of alcaic verses into the Latin language a feat that surpasses the edifice of the Egyptian pyramids! For us, in contrast, it suffices to merely open the still-scorned ark of the native treasure and we will find in it a great number of models not inferior to the Greeks' in beauty."[106] The reference is to Horace's "Exegi monumentum," ode 30 of book III, which also had its Russian tradition: Lomonosov's translation of the ode in 1747 can be seen as part of his claim to have introduced classical meter into Russian poetry. Here, too, Kapnist is owing to L'vov: in his "Dobrynia," L'vov had argued that Russian words did not fit into the Greek frames and had suggested that the Russian spirit would be crowned with greater laurels than those claimed by Horace.[107]

In offering an alternative to the Russian syllabotonic tradition, however, Kapnist, once again out of fear perhaps, does not go far enough. L'vov gaveexamples of tonic measures and Vostokov suggested the three-stressed tonic measure of the Russian *byliny* as an alternative epic meter, but Kapnist gives no indication that he is familiar with Vostokov's essay—in spite of the fact that the distinction he drew between Russian verse and Greek verse would have been very valuable to Kapnist. Instead, when Kapnist steps "out on stage in an undyed wool peasant caftan, in a red calico shirt, and with my cap in my hand in order to proclaim Homer's verses in a Russian meter," the translation he offers, again of the first eleven lines of book six of the *Iliad,* while based on a folk song meter, is hardly a radical departure from the syllabotonic tradition or even the hexameter imitation of Gnedich. He uses a six-foot line composed of five trochees and a dactylic ending—another form, then, of a dactylo-trochaic hexameter![108]

Uvarov responded in the same volume of *Chtenie v Besede.* A much more advanced Hellenist than Kapnist, Uvarov quickly dismissed the limitation of the final foot of hexameter to the spondee with reference to ancient authority.[109] But he also no longer claimed the identity of ancient Russian meters with Greek meters. Instead, the emphasis in the second letter is on the difficulty of the appropriation, for which the lack of spondees is but one obstacle. "In German prosody the same difficulty exists; but their poets arrived through their fortunate obstinacy and diligence at the point of having quite a proper hexameter. True, they sometimes use a *trochee* instead of a *spondee* even in the middle of a line, which, of course, is against the rules and which the Greeks never did; but German writers contend, and it seems quite soundly, that it is better to sacrifice a certain metrical strictness than to entirely give up hope of having a superior versification, a true echo of ancient poetry. We are forced to carry out by means of art those activities that for the Greeks sprang from the spirit of their language and their own nature."[110]

The schooling of all of the modern literatures upon the Greek models continues to justify the pursuit of a Russian equivalent to the hexameter form for epic poetry in the second letter, but Uvarov adds to that some considerations of translation theory. "We are obliged to try to confirm the impression produced by reading [ancient authors] on all enlightened minds: consequently, to present a *fragment* [*otlepok*] of Homer's creations in the spirit of the original, with its forms and with all the shades of meaning, so that we have before our eyes not Kostrov, not Gnedich, but Homer—Homer in the purest reflection of his natural beauty." In order to do so, "it is absolutely necessary to take as the first rule that *forms* in poetry are indivisible from *spirit;* that the same mysterious connection exists between the forms and spirit of poetry as between the body and soul."[111] Like his acquaintance August Schlegel, who similarly argued for metrically equivalent translations, Uvarov insists that Homer is not Homer without his hexameter form.[112]

For Uvarov, it was more important to have this equivalent than to make Homer over into a kind of bard of ancient Rus'. And he expresses this, once again, in the language of fashion: "Homer in a Russian home spun coat [*zipun*] is just as disgusting to me as in a French caftan. To translate the *Iliad* in a Russian folk meter is even worse than in Alexandrines: for the latter verse, after much use, belongs to *everyone* and takes the place of heroic meter in almost *all* the modern languages."[113] Russian literature had first to become a literature able to match what had been done in other model literatures. All of the modern European literatures had come through the school of the classics and it was essential that Russian literature do so as well. A translation of Homer that accurately conveyed the original was one means of obtaining such a schooling. Uvarov sums up his argument by returning to the benefit this education will bring to the Russian national literature: "Without fundamental knowledge and extensive labors in ancient literature no modern one can exist; without close acquaintance with other modern ones we will be in no condition to embrace the entire realm of the human mind—a wide and glittering field in which all prejudice should perish and all hatred fade; but without our own forms proper to our language we will never have a truly national literature [*narodnaia slovesnost'*]."[114]

Gnedich was clearly convinced by Uvarov's argument about national forms. In 1804 he had, like Kapnist, translated some Ossianic poems into the "russkii sklad" (Russian form), the same folk verse form used by Karamzin for his "Ilya Muromets." At the time, he noted that "no harmony of verses is so appropriate to the songs of Ossian as the harmony of Russian verses."[115] In a letter in 1818, however, he regretted that he had dressed Ossian's muse in the unbefitting "rural clothes of the Russian muse." He added, "The meter of a verse is its spirit; and the more the poetry of a nation is original, the more the forms of its meters are distinguished by their particularity, defining the nature of the verses and their appropriateness. That is why, it seems to me, Russian folk verse, which has a distinct, sharp particularity, is inappropriate to the bard of Scotland."[116] On the other hand, when he published his translation of contemporary Greek folk poetry in 1826 (*Prostonarodnye pesni nyneshnikh grekov*), Gnedich saw affinities between Greek and Russian folk poetry—but he emphasized the differences between the contemporary Greek folk poetry and ancient Greek poetry.[117]

The debate over Russian hexameter and its use in the translation of Homer continued into the late teens.[118] Like the ballad debate, which it preceded, the debate over hexameter helped to move the question of the national literature beyond the stylistic arguments that had occupied the first decade and into more complex questions of genre, form, appropriate models for imitation, and the proper approach to creating a national literary tradition. The translation of Homer proved, as it had in the Quarrel between the Ancients and Moderns, to be an ideal site for the exploration of modern literary values, and this debate, like the Czech one over prosody, helped to establish a fundamentally new relationship to both modern and ancient literatures. Unlike quantitative verse in Czech literature, the hexameter form was developed widely in Russian poetry and was used for original verse as well as translations from modern and ancient literatures. One of its most active developers was Vasily Zhukovsky, who had also encouraged Gnedich's pursuit of a hexameter translation, though not as a part of the public polemics.[119] Zhukovsky later added his translation of Homer's *Odyssey* to Gnedich's *Iliad,* and both works were received as original contributions to the Russian national literature.

CODA: THE GHOST OF ANDREI TURGENEV. In 1818, in an article in the Petersburg *Le Conservateur Impartial,* Wilhelm Küchelbecker (1797–1846) celebrated the turn in Russian letters away from French rules to better models more in keeping with the Russian spirit. His particular praise for Gnedich and Zhukovsky brought together the debates on hexameter and the ballad and suggested that they had helped move Russian literature to a new stage. Aleksei Merzliakov disagreed. In an incident on February 22, 1818, Merzliakov read aloud at a meeting of the Obshchestvo liubitelei rossiiskoi slovesnosti (Society of Lovers of Russian Literature), with Zhukovsky present, an anonymous "letter from Siberia" (of which he was clearly the author) that denounced "two innovations, and namely: hexameters and ballads."[120] He couched his criticism in language that would have made it clear to Zhukovsky, if not to all of the other listeners, that his criticism was founded in Andrei Turgenev's speech from 1801 (see chapter 2), that he, Merzliakov, was continuing the legacy of their mutual friend, while Zhukovsky had come to occupy a place in Russian literature that corresponded to that of Karamzin in 1801.[121] He was continuing to pursue the program of that speech, in his own way, and in so doing, he inserted some more of the language and rhetoric of Turgenev's speech into public debates on the national literature.

Merzliakov's critique of the ballad genre follows Turgenev's critique of Karamzin's poetic trifles, finding the harm in the temptation of young authors to imitate: "Our poets dress up their ballads beautifully, there is no doubt, but what do their numberless imitators do? For them there are no limits. . . . Let us quickly and openly admit . . . that this genre is quite tempting, especially for us simple, uneducated readers and for our children, young poets."[122] And the danger continues to be to the national spirit of the literature: "The *Conservateur Impartial* asks us to celebrate and take joy in some kind of transformation of the spirit of our poetry. He [It] congratulates us for being filled with the spirit of German poets and for that spirit being kin to us. —Ladies and Gentlemen! Allow me to ask, has our poetry as yet had any spirit, under Lomonosov, Sumarokov, Derzhavin, and Dmitriev?"[123] The list of names and the iconoclastic question echo Turgenev's speech clearly.

Another such echo will be heard in the introduction to Pushkin's "Fountain of Bakhchisarai" by Petr Viazemsky, in the following chapter. Nearly twenty-three years after Andrei Turgenev's speech, Viazemsky would repeat his opening two rhetorical moves in order. Is this echo a mere coincidence? Perhaps Merzliakov's willful repetition of Turgenev's speech—which represented *his own* literary program in its dearest form, as it proceeded from the mouth of his friend of most beloved memory— makes this belated echo far from uncanny. Merzliakov had pursued, if in a sometimes muted fashion, the program of that speech and had given it to Russian critical discourse in a way that prepared the debates of the 1820s.

Part III

TERMS IN CONFLICT

Narodnost' Invented and Deployed

In the 1820s, a new term entered into Russian literary criticism and quickly became a major focal point of discussions of the national qualities of Russian literature and its relationship to romanticism and classicism. The precise content of the term, *narodnost'*, was and is very difficult to define, but its productivity in many ways derived from exactly that quality. Functionally, in its use in Russian criticism, *narodnost'* operated as a collector of all those qualities that marked the national individuality of Russian literature—just what those qualities were was the subject of much disagreement. But the wide discussion of the term and the evaluation of authors and works in relation to it suggest that in Russian literary criticism, the nation had become the new foundation of literary value. The paradigm of "national literature" was becoming the new standard. The general sense of "nationalness," which allowed the term to collect those qualities that mark a work or literature as belonging to a particular nation, that pervade the literature of a nation and mark it as independent from other literatures, made *narodnost'* a term whose necessity everyone could agree on.

The noun *narod*, as already presented (chapter 5), could refer at the time either to the "people" (the folk) or to the nation. The term is formed from the adjectival stem *narodn-*, by adding the derivational suffix *-ost'*, similar to the English "-ness." Potential senses of the abstract term, then, included "popularity," "folksiness," "nationhood," "nationality," or even "nativeness." In Russian word derivation, *-ost'* is a productive suffix for the formation of abstract nouns, so the term had the potential to be formed at any point in the history of the Russian language. It seems not to have been used, however, with any frequency before the nineteenth century. While the *Slovar' russkogo iazyka XVIII veka* does not record any instances of the word in the eighteenth century, Radishchev did use the word in an early letter from his Siberian exile in Ilimsk.[1] Radishchev describes, in a letter dated February 17, 1792, the discovery of the natural man within himself: "Living in the great Siberian forests, among wild animals and peoples [*sredi dikikh zverei i narodnostei*] . . . I believe that I can become a happy person in the manner of Rousseau and begin to walk on all fours."[2] Here the word is close to one of its more common senses in the later nineteenth century, when it was used to refer to the smaller ethnic groups in the Russian Empire. The earliest occurrence of the word recorded by Lotman and Uspensky is from 1807, from the diary of S. P. Zhikharev in an entry on January 9, in which he notes his impressions upon meeting Admiral Shishkov for the first time: "With great curiosity I looked over the venerable figure of this man, whose children's verses had achieved such popularity [*poluchili takuiu narodnost'*]."[3] Here, for perhaps the first time, the word is needed to describe a form of literary success.

   Credit for "inventing" the word as a term of literary criticism, however, has been traditionally assigned to Prince Petr Viazemsky (1792–1878).[4] Writing to Aleksandr Turgenev (younger brother of Andrei, introduced in chapter 2) in 1819 from Warsaw, where he was stationed in governmental service, Viazemsky was trying to sell Turgenev on the merits of his latest poem, "Pervyi sneg" ("The First Snow"):

> In my opinion, these verses are my monsters [*moi vyrodki*]. There is a Russian coloring here that does not exist in almost any of our verses. One cannot recognize a Russian poet by his physiognomy. All of you are not convinced of that sufficiently, but I remember, once you laughed at me when I called myself a distinguishably Russian poet or verse-scribbler; this is not a question of merit, but of a particular imprint; not of eloquence, but of accent [*o vygovorie*]; not of harmonious movement, but of the *narodnost'* of a few indigenous wonts [*niekotorykh" zamashek" korennykh"*]. Why not translate *nationalité* as *narodnost'*? After all, the Poles have said '*narodowość!*' The Poles are not as fastidious as we, and words that do not voluntarily skip over to them, they drag in by the hair and are done with it. Excellent! The word, if it is needed, will take root.[5]

And take root it did, with vigor. It is now easily one of the most storied terms in Russian literary and political history. Following the debates of the 1820s, it entered into official public discourse in the 1830s with the slogan of Tsar Nicholas I's minister of public education, Sergei Uvarov, the former advocate of hexameter: "*Pravoslavie, Samoderzhavie, Narodnost*'" (orthodoxy, autocracy, *narodnost'*).[6] And it remained a central term for Russian criticism throughout the nineteenth century and even into the twentieth, when it again joined official discourse in the Soviet triad: *partiinost', narodnost'*, and *ideinost'* (party-mindedness, *narodnost'*, and ideological commitment).[7] Along the way, the term has accumulated a load of interpretive baggage, much of which one must leave behind in approaching the word in its infancy. Lauren Leighton noted the tendency of Soviet scholarship to link the term with a certain conception of realism, though in the romantic 1820s, such an interpretation involves flagrant anachronism.[8] Another difficulty is the by-now standard connotation of a certain folklorism and elevation of the common people. But such a positive concept of the folk was still in its formative stages in the 1820s, and folklore and the folk long remained contested and ambiguous categories in their connection to *narodnost'* as well as within the broader discourse on the Russian nation. In this chapter and those that follow, some of the first uses of the term will be read closely and contextually to specify, as precisely as possible, what sense or content each writer ascribes to the term.

Viazemsky needed the term—he explicitly performs the act of coining the word here (never mind that he was not really first, for the word was clearly not much in circulation)—to serve as a Russian equivalent to the French *nationalité*. His overall concern in this passage is quite close to that of his correspondent's brother, Andrei, some eighteen years earlier: the readability of a kind of Russianness in the productions of Russian writers.[9] In addressing this concern, the term *narodnost'* plays a relatively minor role. What makes a writer readable as a Russian, for Viazemsky, is a kind of Russian coloring (*russkaia kraska*) or physiognomy, readable as an imprint (*otpechatok*) in the writer's work. This could be constituted by a certain accent or way of speaking (*vygovor*) or by the nationality (*narodnost'*) of certain ways of acting. The term is used to name one part of what potentially could make a Russian writer readable as such. One has to read here against the way the term would come to be used later, when it was adopted as a catch-all term for all the qualities that made up the readable nationality of a literature or writer. Viazemsky speaks here, not of the work's *narodnost'*, but of its Russian coloring, not of the writer's *narodnost'*, but of the writer's Russian physiognomy. These are the general terms in his discussion, and *narodnost'* marks the national quality of certain native habits that potentially help to create that more general Russian picture. Viazemsky is struggling to name what it is exactly that makes a literature readable as a national literature. At this point, *narodnost'* had not yet become the one-word answer to that question, but it was a part of the answer.

Instead of *narodnost'* Viazemsky might have said *natsional'nost'* to translate *nationalité*. That was, after all, a term Denis Fonvizin had used.[10] *Narodnost'* then could have been limited to the sense of *popularité,* as it was in Zhikharev's usage. In 1824, after Viazemsky began to use his term in published criticism, Mikhail A. Dmitriev (1796–1866), a minor poet and critic, took Viazemsky to task for conflating the two senses and thus introducing ambiguity, rather than clarity, into his terminology: "*Popular* [*narodnaia*] Poetry can exist even among an uneducated people [*narod*]: the proof of this is our ancient songs. But *national* [*natsional'naia*] poetry exists only among those peoples whose political being is closely united with civic enlightenment and each finds its essential support in the other; [it exists] among peoples that have, along with education that is in common with other peoples, their own mores, their own customs, not effaced, but merely softened with time, and their own legends, which history perhaps may not recognize, but which the spirit of the nation [*natsii*] believes in."[11] Viazemsky, however, rejected this criticism, insisting that Russian discourse deal with the ambiguity of *its own* terminology: "Anyone who is literate knows that the word *natsional'nyi* does not exist in our language; that for us the word *narodnyi* alone corresponds to two French words: *populaire* and *national;* that we say '*piesni narodnyia*' [popular/folk songs] and '*dukh narodnyi*' [national spirit] where the French would say '*chanson populaire*' and '*esprit national.*'"[12] Viazemsky refused to make use of a borrowed word as a term for the discussion of national identity in literature. The ambiguity he insisted on had already marked Russian discussions of *Volkspoesie* and *Nationalliteratur* and would continue to mark discussions of *narodnost'* for years to come.

While Viazemsky can be credited with coining the term in connection with the concern for a readable national identity in literature, he was slower than others to deploy the term in public discourse. Instead, before 1824, he discussed the new literary trends in terms of "Romantic poetry." Aleksandr Bestuzhev (1797–1837) was to become no less a propagator of romanticism in Russia, but in early 1823, in the first of his three survey articles for the almanac *Poliarnaia zvezda* (*Polar Star*), he did not use the term romanticism, preferring rather to discuss the "new school" of poetry, led by Zhukovsky, Konstantin Batiushkov, and Pushkin. Bestuzhev apparently did not entirely identify this school with romanticism.[13] He did, however, use the term *narodnost'* as a term of praise in discussing older writers, becoming perhaps the first to use it in public literary criticism: "Fonvizin, in his comedies *The Brigadier* and *The Minor,* was able to capture features of *narodnost'* in the highest degree and, like Cervantes, bring into play the petty passions of the provincial nobility." "I. Krylov raised the Russian fable to its original classical merit. One cannot give more simple-heartedness to narration, more *narodnost'* to the language, more palpability to moral instruction. Russian common sense can be seen in his every line."[14] As is the case with so many other later writers, it is difficult to make explicit what exactly Bestuzhev had in mind for the term *narodnost'*. For Fonvizin and Ivan Krylov, who wrote in the lower genres, the term seems to gravitate toward the "popular" rather than "national" end of the spectrum, as these writers made use of colloquial language and features of popular character and thought. The emphasis is on features that derive from or connect to the people. Of course, the step from "the people" to "a people," as in a nation, is never very far, but this potential meaning does not seem to be actualized by Bestuzhev and does not seem to interest him at this point. *Narodnost'* is a positive value—it is used as a term of praise—but it does not stand out above other terms of praise and is not a central value to the national literature yet for Bestuzhev. His goal in this short article was no less than a history of the Russian language and literature. The quality of *narodnost'* appears at moments, with particular authors, in that history, but is not connected to the question of the independence or originality of that national literature.

If Bestuzhev did not link romanticism, *narodnost'*, and the national literature, and did not make of *narodnost'* a central value, Orest Somov (1793–1833) can be credited above all with doing exactly that, and thus with setting the terms of the debate to follow. Somov is known to literary history as a journalist and critic, particularly for his collaboration with Pushkin on the *Literaturnaia gazeta* and as an author of Ukrainian tales who preceded Nikolai Gogol. His essay "O romanticheskoi poezii" ("On Romantic Poetry") was published in 1823 in the journal *Sorevnovatel' prosveshcheniia i blagotvoreniia,* as well as in a separate book edition in the same year. Somov made a deliberate attempt in this essay to introduce *narodnost'* as a literary-critical term, to use the abstract noun, marked as terminological, in a specific and limited way. He employed the term only four times in over ninety pages of text, but the term marks critical moments in his discourse.

In his essay, Somov attempted to place Russian literature within the historical narratives of romanticism developed by European theorists. Those writers to whom he responded, Friedrich and August Schlegel, Madame de Staël, Jean Charles Léonard Simonde de Sismondi, and Jean-Pierre-Frédéric Ancillon, would become central to the Russian debates on romanticism and the national literature. Some had been translated into Russian in fragments before Somov's essay. Fragments of the works of all would be translated and repeatedly deployed in the Russian debates for many years to come.[15] What these writers on romanticism and literary history have in common is a historical perspective that centers on national particularity and originality. Their narratives created certain problems for Somov and others in fitting Russian history and literary development into their schemes, but the accomplishment of such a feat held the promise of giving Russian literature a place among European literatures and the potential to rise to a more visible place. While the first four remain well-known or relatively well-known among students of European literatures today, the last, Jean-Pierre-Frédéric/ Johann Peter Friedrich Ancillon (1767–1837), is obscure. Ancillon was a relatively minor Prussian aesthetic philosopher and a popularizer of the ideas of Friedrich Schelling.[16] He was of central importance, however, to the Russian debates of the 1820s, in no small part because of the way in which some of his ideas helped to deflect problematic aspects of the historical narratives of the other writers and to define *narodnost'* in ways that were useful in the Russian context.[17]

Somov's essay is divided into three parts. In the first he discusses the imagination and its craving for novelty as a key to the spirit of poetry and takes French literature to task for ignoring, with its rules, this essential aspect. In the second, he distinguishes between the classical and the romantic and narrates a history of European literatures in relation to romanticism. In the final part, he argues the necessity of Russian literature's making use of available resources and the possibility of its thus becoming more national in its aspect. In his narrative of the development of romantic poetry, Somov plays various European writers off against one another in order to keep open the possibility of Russia's inclusion in this history. He begins his narrative by noting that "the first nation that had a Romantic Poetry was unquestionably the Arabs or Moors. This nation, in the period of its short reign over Europe, made use of the barely revived arts and sciences of that part of the world, made quick progress in them, and to its glory, first showed the Europeans that it was possible to have a national [*narodnaia*] Poetry, independent of the traditions of Greece and Rome."[18] In this assertion, he follows Sismondi's *De la littérature du midi de l'Europe*. Sismondi was countering the arguments of August Schlegel, who had rather proposed a northern origin for romanticism, among the German tribes, with a narrative of eastern influence in southern Europe. This initiated the north-south debate in romanticism, and it attracted the interest of Russians, like Somov, because of its potential for creating narratives of Russian romanticism. Russia had experienced periods of both northern influence (with the establishment of the Kievan state by Normans) and southern/eastern influence (with the Tatar domination).[19] Somov leans toward the southern/eastern narrative here, but he does not go that route entirely. In the first section he challenges the link between the Arabs and the French troubadours and the claim of troubadour poetry for romanticism that was essential to the continuity of Sismondi's narrative.[20] The finished quality of narratives like Sismondi's and Schlegel's closed them off to the incorporation of further material, like the history of Russian literature, and Somov's breaking of this continuity, his final unwillingness to side entirely with any given narrative, is an effective tactic to leave the history of romanticism open to a Russian narrative.

This tactic is nearly laid bare in the opening of part two of Somov's essay. He notes the common division (supported by Schlegel, de Staël, and Sismondi) of poetry into classical and romantic, where the former is the ancient, pagan, mythological poetry of the Greeks and Romans and the latter is the medieval, Christian, chivalric poetry of European nations. He observes:

> This division is quite clever, but not entirely correct for the following reasons. First, conceptions appropriate to the age of chivalry are no longer appropriate to our enlightened age, and for this reason we ought to separate all modern Poetry from the first centuries of Christianity to the twelfth and thirteenth. Secondly, not even all European nations participated in the ideas, way of life, and deeds of the ancient Italians, Spanish, French and Germans during the age of chivalry, and consequently the Poetry of many of them, especially the peoples of the Slavic race, would be deprived of the main charm for compatriots: *narodnost'* and locality [*mestnost'*].[21]

The subjunctive mood of the final sentence clarifies the nature of Somov's argument. He is not saying that a lack of chivalry in the Russian context would keep Russia from enjoying a literature marked by national and local traits. Rather he is arguing against narratives that place the origin of romanticism and national literatures in Europe in chivalric culture, because such narratives would seem to deny the possibility of a national literature to Russia and therefore cannot account for the national and local qualities felt in their literature by Russians (this use of the term *narodnost'* will be discussed later). Still, the chivalric thesis was the leading account of romanticism's development, and Somov felt compelled later in his essay to offer a Russian parallel to the European development: "The age of chivalry was replaced in Russia by the age of the bogatyrs."[22]

Somov's first objection, though, offers another possibility: by marking a discontinuity between the poetry of the Middle Ages and modern poetry he challenges any narrative of continuity. The lack of organic continuity in Russian literary development was a significant problem to be overcome by the Russian romantics, and if it could be argued instead that modern national literatures were more a product of modern nations than of the Middle Ages, then the late arrival of Russian literature to European discourse would present no obstacle to its taking a place among them. Ancillon was an ally in this regard. In his *Analyse de l'idée de littérature,* he argued the necessity of first developing the characteristics of a modern nation before it was possible for a people to create a truly national literature.[23] Such a distinction was of great potential use to Russian critics. In fact, it is behind M. Dmitriev's objections cited above to Viazemsky's terminology, his failure to distinguish between the popular (*narodnoe*) and the national (*natsional'noe*), on the basis that only a modern nation could have a national poetry. Dmitriev continued, "That is my opinion, which, by the way, is nothing other than the fruit of considerations taken from the observations of the best-known aestheticians. Among them, Ancillon approaches the definition of national [*natsional'naia*] Poetry in the most reliable way: he first defines what a nation [*natsiia*] is."[24]

But Somov did not draw such terminological conclusions from this thesis. On the contrary, his essay played a critical role in establishing *narodnost'* as a term in the debate on romanticism and national literature, and *narodnost'* clearly carries the meaning of nationalness or nationality. (One should also note that, in his essay, any discussion of "*narodnaia poeziia*" clearly refers not to anything like *Volkspoesie* but rather to something like *Nationalliteratur.*) Somov's essay overflows with the related adjective and noun forms *narodnyi* and *narod,* and these words take on a wide variety of inflections that cover the spectrum from popular to national, outlined by Viazemsky, and they include the overtones of naturalness or even common folksiness that were part of Bestuzhev's usage. But, as already observed, the abstract noun *narodnost'* appears only four times in Somov's lengthy essay.

This suggests, most probably, a certain care on Somov's part to reserve the abstract noun as a term, to employ it in a specific and limited way in his discourse.[25] Three of Somov's four usages are connected to the work of particular authors and are thus similar to the usage of Bestuzhev in that they employ the term in evaluating and canonizing certain practices. But Somov applied the term in his essay exclusively to German authors, and specifically to Goethe, Schiller, and Bürger.

In his treatment and evaluation of German authors, Somov followed entirely the work of Madame de Staël in *De l'Allemagne,* translating, rearranging, and condensing her work. Her chapter "*De la poésie allemande*" opens with the following evaluation of these three authors: "the German detached poetry, it seems to me, is more remarkable than the poems, and it is especially on this genre that the seal of originality is imprinted: it is also true that the authors most cited in this regard, Goethe, Schiller, Bürger, etc., are of the modern school, and *this school alone has a truly national character. Goethe has more imagination, Schiller more sensibility, and Bürger is, of them all, the one that possesses the most popular talent.*"[26] These three authors represent the most truly original and national German literature, and thus present themselves as models to Russian writers who wish to create a truly national Russian literature. But each of them achieves this in a different manner, with different talents. The term *narodnost'*, as it is attached to each of these authors in Somov's essay, points to a particular way of creating an original national literature, different in each case. Somov thus moves beyond the more limited uses of the term by Viazemsky and Bestuzhev by making *narodnost'* the term under which he collects a number of different practices or methods that form a national literature. Somov wants to place Russian national literature into the European discourses on original national literatures, and he deploys the term *narodnost'* to mark various practices by successful German authors who have been recognized (by de Staël) as representative of that literature's national qualities.

Unlike Bestuzhev, then, Somov is not canonizing Russian authors and their practices, but rather the practices of some outstanding German authors that are loosely related to their own distinguishing qualities, that is, Goethe and his imagination, Schiller and his sensibility, and Bürger with his popular talent. As Somov applies the term *narodnost'* to Bürger, in fact, it is a translation of this evaluation of de Staël's: "Bürger, among the German Poets, stands out for the *narodnost'* of his works; in beautiful verses he revived the traditions of the old times and the superstitions of his countrymen."[27] Somov here combines de Staël's initial evaluation of Bürger with the opening of her discussion of his ballad "Lenore": "Bürger is, of all the Germans, the one that has better seized this vein of superstition, which leads far into the depths of the heart."[28] But Somov has changed the phrasing, so that it is no longer Bürger's popular talent that separates him, but the *narodnost'* of his works. *Narodnost'* here is not exactly a translation of the adjective *populaire*, then, but it does retain a relation to that word, reinforced by the popular traditions and superstitions incorporated into Bürger's works. Somov thus turns from de Staël's evaluation of the unique talent of Bürger to a particular practice or method that can be imitated, shifting the discourse from a descriptive to a prescriptive mode.

Goethe's talent cited by de Staël, imagination, is less reducible to a method. Neither is his imagination entirely reducible to German nationality. In fact, his particular talent, in de Staël's and Somov's discourse, is the ability to recreate with his imagination the particular characteristics of distant nations and places and incorporate himself into them. One should note here that this particular talent is entirely dependent on the consciousness of historical and cultural alterity that proceeds out of the Quarrel between the Ancients and Moderns—Goethe's talent is a distinctively modern talent. Somov writes, "In his Elegies, written in Rome, he makes us breathe, it seems, the air of Italy, narrates his pleasures and it is as if he becomes a Roman. If he speaks of Greece, in his verses you feel some kind of co-presence of the ancient sons of Hellas with their beliefs, customs, and superstitions."[29] The term *narodnost'* appears in the discussion of his drama *Iphigenie auf Tauris,* connected to an ancient song sung by Iphigenie: "The horrible images and the meter of the verse, which agrees with the feelings, give this fragment the colors of *narodnost'*. The most supreme efforts of talent are needed in order to, so to speak, make oneself kin in such a way with antiquity, in order to capture features that were common to the people [*narodnye*] among the Greeks and to make with them, through that immense separation of ages and mores, such strong and fresh impressions."[30] This is a fairly exact translation of de Staël: "Les images les plus frappantes, le rhythme qui s'accorde mieux avec les sentiments, donnent à cette poésie la couleur d'un chant national. C'est le plus grand effort du talent que de se familiariser ainsi avec l'antiquité, et de saisir tout à la fois ce qui devoit être populaire chez les Grecs, et ce qui produit, à la distance des siècles, une impression si solennelle."[31] While the adjective form *narodnyi* translates the French *populaire*, "the colors of *narodnost'*" stands in for "the color of a national song." Just as it was not exactly a translation of the adjective *populaire* in the evaluation of Bürger, here *narodnost'* is not exactly a translation of *national,* but both meanings color the term.

At first glance it is difficult to see what a talent like Goethe's has to do with the making of a national literature. But it is this indirectness, perhaps, that also makes the question so intriguing. Goethe's ability to enter into other cultures and times with his imagination is a unique talent and marks his own originality as well as the originality of German literature. Through him, German literature is able to incorporate the ever-important Greek nationality, as well as any other national character to which he would set his mind. This synthetic model of forming nationality proved actually to be quite attractive to certain elements of the Russian educated classes later, and the common evaluations of Goethe's protean genius adumbrated here by Somov find echoes in Kireevsky's article on Pushkin, Gogol's discussion of Zhukovsky's translations and Dostoevsky's Pushkin speech—key moments in the articulation of Russian national character.[32] It is striking that Somov uses the term *narodnost'* in a way that connects to national features but is enigmatic in its connection to the project of a national literature, since those national features belong to other nations. The result is quite suggestive, pointing beyond the method he associates with Bürger, which could lead to a kind of "kvass patriotism," as Viazemsky would later term it, too focused on the particular and common traits and traditions, to a broad-ranging imagination that is not exclusive in its national focus, but nonetheless marks the literature of the nation with its unique stamp.

While the term *narodnost'* is loosely connected for Bürger and Goethe to their special talents as described by de Staël, the term in Schiller is rather displaced from his "sensibility."[33] It comes at the beginning of Somov's discussion of one of his tragedies: "Now we intend to expand a bit on just one of the Tragedies of Schiller, *Wallenstein,* a Tragedy that, for Germans, has the merit of *narodnost'* over others."[34] The corresponding place in de Staël reads, "Wallenstein is the most national tragedy that has been performed in the German theater."[35] Here again, *narodnost'* is not simply a translation of the adjective *national,* but a transformation of the discourse, turning from the descriptive, historical discourse of de Staël to a prescriptive, future-oriented discourse (as will be seen, Somov is centrally concerned with Russian literature becoming national). Instead of Schiller's sensibility, Somov focuses attention on the merits of his drama, and in particular on those qualities that mark it as national. His discussion of the tragedy emphasizes the German historical setting of the action and Schiller's ability to make the setting and characters come to life—the latter would connect him to Goethe in the ability to bring a distant time to life. The method of making a national literature that Somov has Schiller model for his audience here already had a lengthy history in

Russian letters: the incorporation of national historical themes into drama. But the results had been far from satisfying (recall Turgenev's critique of the Frenchmen striding onto the Russian stage pretending to be Russian historical personages). Somov does not, therefore, stop with the historical setting, but emphasizes the veracity and appropriateness of Schiller's characters and the unusual three-part form he embodied it in. Pushkin would pursue a more original Russian historical drama in this vein with his *Boris Godunov* in the following years (see chapter 10).

Now to return briefly to the first occurrence of the term *narodnost'* in Somov's essay, to his objections, cited above, to narratives that place the origin of national literatures in chivalric culture: "Secondly, not even all European nations participated in the ideas, way of life, and deeds of the ancient Italians, Spanish, French and Germans during the age of chivalry, and consequently the Poetry of many of them, especially the peoples of the Slavic race, would be deprived of the main charm for compatriots: *narodnost'* and locality [*mestnost'*]." Here, Somov is trying to keep open the possibility of the inclusion of Russia and its literature into European discourse on the origins and development of national literatures. If Russian literature has *narodnost'*, features that mark it as national, specific, belonging to the Russians, then it will have to be included in any such narrative. Somov seems to imply that it does have such features: *narodnost'* and *mestnost'* are the main charms of the literature for his compatriots. However, his use of the term further in the essay points to programmatic ways to increase the national originality of Russian literature by following methods derived from German poetry, such as Bürger's incorporations from popular belief, Goethe's synthetic imagination, and Schiller's nationalized drama. Such a program for *narodnost'* points rather to a lack, to the need to increase the national originality of Russian literature in ways that move beyond simple local and national features, the minimal *sine qua non* for the existence of a Russian literature.

Somov moves consistently from the idea that a literature naturally reflects the features of the people or nation that produces it to proposals for Russia to increase the national qualities of its literature. This is also the movement of the entire third part of his essay, which begins, "The literature of a nation [*narod*] is a talking picture of its mores, customs, and way of life. In every Writer, especially in a Poet, national [*narodnye*] features force their way through almost unwittingly. Thus it is almost possible to guess the work of a German, Englishman or Frenchman, even if it be in a translation, even if the translator hid the name of the Author and kept secret which language the work was translated from."[36] This recalls Andrei Turgenev's opening (chapter 2), which led him to question the existence of Russian literature of a similar character. Somov, though, first moves on to a more detailed explication of the features of national character that are readable in those three literatures, and only then raises the issue of Russian literature: "I have frequently heard judgments that there cannot be a national [*narodnaia*] Poetry in Russia; that we began to write too late, when all the principalities on Parnassus had been taken; that the landscape of our Fatherland is flat and monotonous . . . and so our nature does not inspire Poets; that we did not have an age of chivalry."[37] He places these doubts on others because he wants to argue for the possibility and even the necessity of Russia having such a poetry. After refuting all the arguments, such as the lack of distinct customs, of inspiring nature, of traditions, and so on, with extensive examples to the contrary, Somov concludes with the necessity of Russian literature's moving in this direction: "It has been my intention to show that it is imperative for the Russian nation [*narod*]—famed for its martial and civic virtues, dreadful in its power and magnanimous in victory, occupying the most vast kingdom in the world, which is rich in nature and memories—to have *its own national [narodnaia] Poetry, non-imitative and independent from the traditions of others*."[38] Implicit in his argument, then, is the idea that Russian literature does not yet exist as such a literature, or at least not in the measure of which it is capable. Romanticism, properly understood, provides a program for achieving such an original and national literature in full measure.

Romanticism, properly understood by readers and literary critics, is Somov's goal. Somov is quick to remind his audience, after his long exposition of the natural and cultural resources of Russia, that the point is not to focus exclusively upon these resources either: "But let no one think that I would restrict Russian Poetry to *recollections, legends and images of our Fatherland*: that would be like placing new fetters on Genius, and Genius does not endure fetters."[39] Such a restriction would not allow room for the genius of Goethe, for one, and Somov began his work on romantic poetry with the word "imagination," the word that characterized Goethe's genius for de Staël. In defining romantic poetry in the second part of the essay, Somov made the freedom of the poet primary: "A poet must not be confined within the bounds of place or event, but must be given complete freedom of choice and exposition; this, it seems to me, is the primary goal of the Poetry that we call Romantic."[40] True romanticism, then, would produce a national literature without reducing it to a narrow and isolating patriotism.

The term *narodnost'* does not appear at all in this third section of Somov's essay, which indicates how cautiously he used this abstract noun; however, the questions of the features that mark the national qualities of a literature and programmatic ways to increase national originality, to which Somov attached the term, are very much in play in this final section. While he used the term *narodnost'* with care, the effect was to attach it to the discussion of originality versus imitation, of imagination, of national spirit and character, and of the historical development of literature. Somov's contribution was to initiate a discussion of the Russian national literature within the European discourse on romanticism, with the effect of transforming that descriptive, historical discourse into a prescriptive discourse on the future of Russian literature, and to make *narodnost'* a term to gather together these prescriptions. Subsequent Russian writers would follow his lead in this and invest the term with their own contents, using the term far more freely, so that it became an essential part of the Russian discourse on the national literature, a more vital term than even "romanticism" or "classicism."[41]

BEFORE RETURNING TO VIAZEMSKY and the manner in which he began to deploy the term *narodnost'*, it would be helpful to briefly address the question of literary imperialism as it relates to Somov's essay, to the term *narodnost'*, and to the problem of translation. Harsha Ram, in the context of analyzing a pair of little-read works by Küchelbecker, writes, "Anticipating Küchelbecker's article of 1824, we might read the problem of poetic translation as a literary instantiation of the broader problem of Russian imperial nationhood. Far from being focused exclusively on the national, the Decembrist vision of Russian culture actively promoted the absorption of the foreign, even as it insisted that the foreign be translated and thereby subordinated to a national idiom. National self-affirmation was thereby linked to imperial hegemony, and this became an essential tenet of Decembrism, in literature no less than in politics."[42] As an example of Decembrist political discourse one can take the underground constitutional project of the leader of the Southern Society of the Decembrists, Pavel Ivanovich Pestel' (1793–1826), the project known as *Russkaia pravda,* which will also allow the reader to compare the use of the term *narodnost'* in Decembrist political discourse to Somov's use of the term. Pestel' was developing his ideas in 1822–1823, but apparently only put them into written form in 1824.[43] In the first chapter, Pestel' considers and weighs two conflicting rights, the right of various tribes and peoples to independence and separate political existence, the right of nationhood (*pravo narodnosti*), and the right of a large state to security (*pravo blagoudobstva*). The Russian nation is identified with the state as the ruling nation (*narod gospodstvuiushchii*) and the state's right to security is not in conflict with that nation's right of nationhood. For all other groups, including many on Russia's expanding imperial borders, Pestel' weighs the viability of their separate existence, considers their historical political independence, and determines that only for the Polish nation should the right to nationhood outweigh Russia's right to secure its borders. For the smaller nations, "it will be better and more beneficial for them themselves if they unite in spirit and society with the large State and completely merge their *Narodnost'* with the *narodnost'* of the Ruling Nation, making with it but a single Nation and stopping vainly dreaming of Things Impossible and Unattainable."[44] Pestel"s guidelines for a post-insurrection government are thus not only compatible with Russian imperial expansion,[45] they also explicitly advocate a form of national cultural imperialism. The suggestion that the smaller tribes "unite in spirit and society [*soediniatsia dukhom i obshchestvom*]" colors how one reads the term *narodnost'* in this passage. In the legal discourse presented by Pestel', *narodnost'* is generally far more effective as an unambiguous technical term than Somov could make it in his literary-critical discourse: it refers to the political concept of nationhood, implying an independent, self-determined, and separate political existence. In this passage, however, the reference to "spirit and society" invokes something beyond political existence, "nationality" as a form of cultural identity rather than "nationhood." Pestel' concludes his second chapter, which considers in detail all of the different national and ethnic groups in Russia, with the suggestion that "the Temporary Government, in relation to the various Nations and tribes inhabiting Russia, must constantly have in mind the indispensible goal of creating from them all only *One* Nation and merging all the various nuances into a single common mass in order that the residents of the entire stretch of the Russian State *all* be *Russian* [*Russkie*]."[46] Pestel' thus makes cultural assimilation an important goal.

Orest Somov was close to Decembrist circles, in particular to Bestuzhev and Kondraty Ryleev, and was arrested after the uprising, but the investigation showed he was not a member of the secret societies. He was from the Kharkiv district of Ukraine and had studied at the university there before coming to St. Petersburg in 1817. Somov's work as a writer seems to align itself with the imperial conception of Russian national identity outlined by Pestel'—his major contribution to Russian narrative literature involved the development of Ukrainian thematics, the literary assimilation of Ukraine for Russian culture. Like Küchelbecker, whose father had been granted Saxon nobility before coming to serve in Russia in the 1770s, Somov is an example of a writer of non-Russian ethnicity who contributed greatly to the project of defining Russian nationality and seems to have identified with that project fully. In the third part of his essay, Somov claimed the breadth of the Russian Empire for the creation of a Russian national poetry: "How many diverse peoples [*narody*] have merged under the name Russians [*Russkie*], or are dependent on Russia [*Rossiia*], not separated by the space of foreign lands or distant seas! How many various demeanors, mores, and customs present themselves to the searching look within the scope of Russia taken all together!" He suggests that the Ukrainians already represent differences in mores and appearance, though they share the same faith and fiery love of the fatherland, and then asks, "what if we cast our glance at the borders of Russia, inhabited by the passionate Poles and Lithuanians, by peoples of Finnish and Scandinavian extraction, by the residents of ancient Colchis, the descendants of settlers who witnessed Ovid's exile, by the remnants of the Tatars who once menaced Russia, by the diverse tribes of Siberia and the islands, by the nomadic generations of Mongols, by the wild residents of the Caucasus, the northern Laplanders and Samoyeds? . . . I leave it to the reader to consider [*delat' soobrazheniia*]." A modern reader might consider that the chance of all of those diverse peoples merging under the name Russians was mighty slim, but Somov does not. "And so, Russian poets, without leaving the borders of their homeland, can fly from the stern and gloomy legends of the North to the luxurious and brilliant fancies of the East; from the educated mind and taste of Europeans to the crude and unaffected mores of hunters and nomads; from the physiognomy of the beau monde to the demeanor of some half-wild tribe, all stamped with a single common feature of distinction."[47] Not surprisingly, he does not define the nature of that common feature.

That all of this national and ethnic diversity belongs to the Russian nation and to Russian poetry certainly concords with the conception of Pestel' regarding Russian nationality. This conception of Russian poetry also owes its debt, as Katya Hokanson has argued, to Pushkin's poem "The Captive of the Caucasus," but also to other poetry, like Batiushkov's works on Scandinavian themes, that engaged Russia's imperial borderlands.[48] The imperial context shaped Somov's conception of Russian nationality and Russian poetry in undeniable ways, but in his conception of romantic poetry and in his use of the term *narodnost'* there is also something that exceeds the imperial limits and context. One might recall that Somov concluded his enumeration of all the riches of the imperial fatherland by explicitly refusing to limit Russian poetry to that material because doing so would place new fetters on "Genius." He continued, "The entire visible and dream world is the property of the poet: he gathers his flowers everywhere, everywhere drinks life and power, and in his mysterious inspiration, presents to the mind's eye an unseen and strange world."[49] True romantic poetry is never merely a poetry of empire. One also needs to recall here Somov's example of Goethe, whose special talent was an imagination that allowed him to embody distant places and times (the whole world, visible or invisible: ancient Greece represents a particular type of invisibility), and that this is also a method of making a national literature for Somov, marked by the term *narodnost'*.

In transmitting the German myth of Goethe as a protean poet, via de Staël, Somov made available a cultural paradigm that would be mobilized in the creation of the myth of Pushkin as a protean poet and a representative of the protean Russian nation.[50] Andrew Wachtel has argued that this synthetic conception of Russian nationality, of which he saw early "hints" in Somov's essay, is a "peculiarly Russian cultural theory which insists that imperialism and translation not only can but also must be connected, for they are the basis of the national definition."[51] But as we have seen, this is not a peculiarly Russian theory at all: the German concept of *Bildung* linked German cultural development and identity to a broad project of cultural translation (chapter 5), and translation has long been a significant aspect of European attempts to claim the inheritance of the western tradition, including Czech and Russian appropriations of Greek metrical forms (chapters 6 and 7); moreover, as will be seen in the next chapter, Jan Kollár argued that the Slavic nation was destined to synthesize the entire western tradition long before the myth of Pushkin and the protean Russian nation were formed in Russia. This raises the question of the connection of such a cultural theory to imperialism. If Pushkin's appropriation of the Caucasus for Russian poetry is imperialist (and it may well be), what about his re-embodiment of Spain and Greece (also cited by Gogol alongside the Caucasus in defining Pushkin's protean nature), what about his translations of André Chénier, his imitation of South Slavic oral epics? What about Gnedich's and Zhukovsky's Homer?

In analyzing Batiushkov's works on Scandinavian themes, Jacob Emery suggests that it is possible to distinguish between the ideological and rhetorical principles employed there from those involved in appropriations from western European culture or the Orient (including the Caucasus).[52] But the distinction that he offers for Batiushkov's corpus between the genetic ties he articulates for the Scandinavian material versus the mere mimetic ties for the classical material does not hold up more generally.[53] It has already been seen how genetic ties could be imagined (by Trediakovsky and Uvarov) for the justification of appropriations of classical Greece as well. While Emery's analysis is admirable and his attempt to draw such distinctions is very important, it may be that the styles of cultural appropriation from different regions will prove to be difficult to distinguish at the level of broader cultural practice (though it looks fruitful for the analysis of individual authors). Europe could also be considered the object of colonial ambitions. Küchelbecker, for example, in his *Evropeiskie pis'ma* (*European Letters*, 1820) imagines an American traveller in Europe in the twenty-sixth century, when Europe has been effectively colonized by the later powers of Russia, America, Asia, and Africa.[54]

Is what makes the Russian forms of cultural appropriation "imperial" only the sociopolitical fact of power and domination? It seems so. In justifying his exclusion of German material from his study of orientalism, Edward Said does not suggest that there is a qualitative difference to the German material, but rather that the colonial interests of France and England led to a greater quantity of orientalist material and a more actual, as opposed to scholarly, interest in the topic.[55] Distinguishing, then, between imperial and non-imperial forms of cultural appropriation, then, would be a facile exercise, revealing little about the forms of appropriation, when they are common to the *Bildung* of all cultures.[56] But important distinctions can still be drawn between different forms of cultural appropriation, and in this, translation theory can be a guide. Antoine Berman has noted that "translation occupies an ambiguous position" in cultural practice, because every culture needs the fertilization of translation even as it resists it in an ethnocentric drive to imagine itself as a self-sufficient whole. "Every culture wants to be self-sufficient and use this imaginary self-sufficiency in order to shine forth on the others and appropriate their patrimony. . . . On the one hand, [translation] heeds this appropriationary and reductionary injunction, and constitutes itself as one of its agents. This results in ethnocentric translations, or what we may call 'bad' translations. But, on the other hand, the *ethical aim* of translating is by its very nature opposed to this injunction: The essence of translation is to be an opening, a dialogue, a cross-breeding, a decentering. Translation is 'a putting in touch with,' or it is *nothing*."[57] In analyzing translation and other forms of cultural appropriation, then, one can distinguish between approaches that respect and engage alterity and those that take without leaving an opening for the transformative power of the experience of the other.[58] This requires literary analysis of the utmost rigor that closely examines particular texts and moments of translation and cultural appropriation for the subtle traces in language, literary structure, and other cultural forms that are evidence of cultural dialogue. While such analysis has not been entirely absent in the study of Russian literature, it seems that the question of the nature of Russia's cultural imperialism would benefit greatly from an intensive effort to ground the discussion in such analyses.

WHEN VIAZEMSKY NEXT HAD the opportunity to introduce one of Pushkin's southern romantic poems, he addressed the topic of the national literature and romanticism, and in the wake of Somov's treatise, he also addressed the growing question of *narodnost'*. His introduction to Pushkin's "Bakhchisaraiskii fontan" (published in March 1824) was written in the form of a dialog between the publisher (himself) and a classicist. The publisher defended contemporary writers from the accusation that they were more indebted to foreign influence than their "classical" forebears, and this led to the question of the Russianness of the literature in general in a passage worth quoting at length:

> [*Pub.*] Poets who are our contemporaries are no more to blame than their poet predecessors. We do not yet have a Russian cut [*pokroi*] in literature; perhaps one will never exist, because there is none; but in any case the newer poetry, so-called romantic, is not less congenial to us than the poetry of Lomonosov or Kheraskov, which you endeavor to put forward as classical. What is there of a national nature [*Chto est' narodnogo*] in the *Petriada* and *Rossiada* besides names?
>
> *Cl.* What is *narodnost'* in literature? That figure does not exist in either the poetics of Aristotle or that of Horace.
>
> *Pub.* It does not exist in Horace's poetics, but it does in his works. It is not in rules, but in feelings. The imprint of *narodnost'*, locality [*mestnost'*]—that's what makes up, perhaps, the main and most essential merit of the ancients and affirms their right to the attention of posterity. There is a reason why the deep thinker Müller in his *General History* singled out Catullus among his sources and mentioned him in his characterization of the times.
>
> *Cl.* It seems that you want to recruit even the ancient classics into your band of romantics. You'll end up saying that Homer and Virgil were romantics.
>
> *Pub.* Call them what you will; but there's no doubting that Homer, Horace, and Aeschylus have far more similarity and relation with the heads of the romantic school than with their cold, servile followers who endeavor to be

Greeks or Romans retroactively. Did Homer really create the *Iliad* guessing in advance what Aristotle and Longinus would write and in observance of some *classical conscience,* still not conceived of at the time? And let me ask myself and your elders, has there been an exact definition of what the *romantic type* is and what relations and opposition it has to the *classical?* I will admit, at least for myself, that I have not had the occasion to find in books, nor in my own mind, no matter how much I have read about it, no matter how much I have thought about it, a full, mathematical, satisfying solution to that problem.[59]

Viazemsky can hardly be accused of defining anything here. He "admits" that he cannot produce a satisfactory definition of the "classical" and "romantic" that would distinguish between them precisely, and his gloss of *narodnost'* also leaves much unexplained: it is an imprint, similar to a kind of local color that somehow exists in feelings (*v chuvstvakh*). The vagueness of this definition is in strong contrast to the value he assigns to the category: he claims it is the most essential merit of the classics.[60] And insofar as the romantic poets also embody *narodnost'* in their works, they come closer to the classical authors than those who would attempt to imitate the ancients by following rules. The problem with classicist method is its reliance on rules derived from ancient books of poetics, so such classicists fail to see anything the ancients failed to see, such as the essential value of *narodnost'*. In fact, it is romantic practice, also not derivable from ancient poetics, that allows one to see it. The imprint of *narodnost'* becomes the link between the ancient and modern poetic practice, the highest literary value, unachievable through classicist methods. To that extent, at least, Viazemsky proposes to have solved the relationship between the classical and the romantic, and he has hit upon the other side of the definitions such as Schiller's, A. Schlegel's, and Ancillon's of the differences between ancient and modern poetry: along with essential differences come essential similarities that allow one to continue to claim the ancient heritage. The vague category of *narodnost'* allows Viazemsky to claim the aesthetic cache of the ancients in support of the practices associated with the new romantic school, though the terms *classical* and *romantic* here start to become subordinate to the principle that unites them. His usage of the term is, again, determinedly vague, in contrast to Somov's vain attempt to limit the term. As the reader will see, other writers would tend to follow Viazemsky rather than Somov, and metaphorical language, associative shifts, and conflation of ideas were highly characteristic of the discourse on *narodnost'*.

This principle or merit, *narodnost'*, was nonetheless not without content for Viazemsky. The reference to Müller is a clue to the political or civic content that Viazemsky attaches to the term. If Catullus is an important source for the study of Roman history and can be used to characterize the times, it is because his works reflect contemporary society. This readable imprint of place and time is a reflection of larger social and political developments. That same year, Viazemsky was also involved in polemics over his 1823 article on the fable poet I. I. Dmitriev (the uncle of the critic Mikhail Dmitriev). The value of the poet Dmitriev, according to Viazemsky, was in his baring of social and political truths in the genre of Aesop, the fable. This is also why Viazemsky appreciated the satires of Dmitriev. He praised one of them alongside Fonvizin's comedy *Nedorosl'* (*The Minor*): "*Nedorosl'* and *Chuzhoi tolk* carry the imprint of *narodnost'*, locality [*mestnost'*] and the times, which, aside from the author's art, gives them outstanding value."[61] Faddei Bulgarin objected to this characterization of Dmitriev, and especially to placing Dmitriev above the other fabulist, Krylov, known for his colloquial style—recall that Bestuzhev had praised the *narodnost'* of Krylov's language alongside that of Fonvizin. The problem is that Viazemsky was not referring to a particular quality of Dmitriev's *style* when he used the term *narodnost'*, but rather to the social content. Moreover, ever the aristocrat, he was far from enamored with Krylov's low language or, for that matter, with his politics.[62] In his reply to Bulgarin, he exhibits aristocratic cosmopolitan disdain for the sort of tendentious nationalism he sees behind the support for Krylov and his style: "Above all a fable should contain a moral truth [*istina*], common to human kind, and not a local, personal, agreed-upon truth [*pravda*]. One can say that the language of one fable writer has more *narodnost'*, or to say it better, folksiness [*prostonarodie*] than that of another; that is another matter. But such praise is not absolute, and it has its advantages and disadvantages alike."[63] For Viazemsky, *narodnost'* had nothing to do with being of the people, the *narod*. Instead, he emphasized the national side, and specifically the civic content of literature, which links him once again to Andrei Turgenev, but also to certain members of the growing Decembrist conspiracy like Kondraty Ryleev.[64]

The shift in the place of *narodnost'* in the question of the national qualities of Russian literature from Viazemsky's letter, when he coined the term, to his introduction to Pushkin's poem is striking. *Narodnost'* went from being but one of the markers that made up the national aspect of the literature to being the term that gathers together everything that creates the national aspect, an essential merit that ties together ancient and modern poetry. Somov had made *narodnost'* a collector of the methods that prominent German romantic authors had employed to create a truly national literary tradition.

He had his own doubts about the distinctions being drawn between classical and romantic poetry and connected *narodnost'* to those doubts, but not in a very effective manner. In Viazemsky's introduction, the term *narodnost'* became the one-word answer to what makes a literature national and what ties together the ancient and modern literary traditions. Other writers would contest the connections to classicism or romanticism, but *narodnost'* would largely remain the essential term for discussing everything that makes a literature national.

9 The Fate of Quantity, *Libozvučnost,* and *Klasičnost* (with a Sideways Glance at Romanticism)

Viazemsky and Somov introduced the term of the day in Russian criticism. In Czech letters, it was Šafařík and Palacký in their *Počátkové* who defined the terms of the critical discussion of the 1820s (chapter 7). Their rearrangement of the hierarchy of values in Jungmann's national literary program, which placed quantitative verse at the center in a constellation of values that also included *libozvučnost* (melodiousness, euphony) and *klasičnost* (classicality), was embraced by Jungmann and others. But their program of quantitative verse was not realized, and others introduced new conceptions of values while appropriating their terms, so that, before the end of the decade, Jungmann was forced once again to rearticulate his program and its hierarchy of values, in an attempt to rescue the concept of *klasičnost* from the failure of quantitative verse and the dangerous new associations that had been attached to *libozvučnost.*

Počátkové had a significant impact on Czech letters, some of which was already examined in chapter 7. The most immediate impact, perhaps, was on the work of Polák, whose work had come up for such high and yet reserved praise. Palacký's voice, calling out to him to perfect his poem with a classical form, did reach him, and it was not by chance. After *Počátkové* came out, he began to prepare a revised and greatly expanded edition of his "Vznešenost přírozenosti" ("The Sublimity of Nature") for book publication with the collaboration of Jungmann.[1] Jungmann first of all edited the language of the poem, bringing the work gramatically into line with literary norms, lexically allowing and even further encouraging the use of neologisms, like the four-syllable words so central to the work's structure.[2] The title, for example, was improved by the use of a Russianism: "Vznešenost přírody." In addition, Jungmann collaborated on the writing of a new introduction (*vprovod*) to the poem, written largely in quantitative hexameter.[3] The bulk of the poem, however, remained in the eight-foot trochaic line with lyrical insertions of trochaic lines of varying length. This new version of the poem was published in 1819 and was almost immediately canonized by Jungmann in the literary handbook he published in 1820, *Slovesnost*. Jungmann's book was a primer in literary theory and style and a collection of Czech examples, a kind of Czech secondary-school reader. Jungmann included among his examples of descriptive poetry the "Introduction" to Polák's poem, on which he had collaborated, thus placing the work into his Czech literary canon.

As if that was not enough, Jungmann also reviewed the work for the new journal *Krok* in 1821.[4] His review was entirely programmatic, praising the work for the ways in which it furthered his program for the national literature and encouraging further work in areas where it fell short. His discussion of Polák's poetic diction, for example, praises the neologisms as a means to the creation of a distinct poetic idiom.[5] He did not even hesitate to express the desire that the whole poem be reworked into quantitative verse, like the "Introduction" (which took such form thanks to his collaboration): "The fact that, in the same poem, for the introduction he used quantitative, and for the remainder accentual verses, by this he suggests to us what we should of course desire for the perfecting of his praiseworthy work: that he should take it into his heart to present the entire poem in the same rhythmical form as the introduction carries or in another, and so leave behind himself a work that, already excellent in its content and style, could be the boast of the nation for ages, presenting *klasičnost* also by its internal form [*doba*]."[6] Like the authors of *Počátkové,* Jungmann here envisions a kind of national *klasičnost* that is intimately tied to quantitative verse form—he thus embraces the subtle changes they had introduced into his program.

The journal *Krok* was begun in 1820 in an effort to realize some of Jungmann's visions for the national literature, and in particular for the development of learned discourse in Czech, with philology and aesthetics in the first place among those. The question of quantitative verse occupied a very prominent place in the first several issues, in multiple articles by Jungmann and Šafařík. (Palacký undertook work in aesthetics, producing several articles.) In addition to classical meter, Jungmann drew attention to the quantitative principle in ancient Indian meter, and the first issue of the journal was led by Jungmann's poem "Krok," written in a quantitative Indian metrical form. Mukařovský reads this as an attempt by Jungmann to separate the question of the quantitative principle from the imitation of classical meters in order to further propagate quantitative verse as a living principle and a necessary reform for the internal development of Czech verse.[7] As his review of Polák demonstrates, however, Jungmann continued to be very interested in the imitation of classical forms. Rather, it seems that he is broadening his conception of the ancient classical verse forms to include those of ancient Indian literature, research on which was rapidly expanding, to further pedigree the Czech language and literature by linking them with the most prestigious of models through versification.[8] Jungmann's exploration of Indian metrics can serve as another example of how the decentering of the Greco-Roman classical tradition in the wake of the Quarrel between the Ancients and Moderns opened up the exploration of other ancient and "classical" poetic traditions.

A major response to *Počátkové* was written by Šebestián Hněvkovský (1770–1847) in defense of the old school, entitled *Zlomky o českém básnictví* (*Fragments on Czech Poetry*, 1820), also in the form of six letters. What Hněvkovský defends, however, is more the efforts of his generation than its prosodic principle. Hněvkovský in fact offers a kind of compromise, allowing the quantitative principle for high forms of poetry. He also considers the difference between ancient and modern poetry, following the analyses of Schiller and others like him, and defends the different spirit of modern European poetry (including its rhyme).[9] Czech poetic practice in the early 1820s quickly developed a prosodic split along these lines. The quantitative principle was realized primarily in translations from ancient poetry, in new poems in ancient genres (elegies, odes, epigrams), or in new poems that aspired to the sublime (Polák's hexameter "Introduction" and Kollár's "Prelude" to *Slavy dcera* in elegiac distiches). Sonnets and other European lyric genres remained syllabotonic in form while imitations of folk verse often used the syllabic or tonic forms of the verse they imitated.[10] The distinction between "classical" and "romantic" poetry was thus realized in different prosodic systems in Czech letters.

Libozvučnost was a central quality ascribed to the Czech language by patriots in the 1820s, and defenses of Czech on this account continued to appear (such as in one of Palacký's articles on Czech literary history, intended for a German magazine but never published).[11] In his literary handbook *Slovesnost*, Jungmann also treats the concept of *libozvučnost*, within a discussion of the elements of style. The final element of style is "*skladnost*," which he glosses as *compositio*.[12] The two terms discussed under this heading are "*libozvučnost*, coming from the proportional placement and alternation of vowels and consonants most appropriate to the expression of all kinds of great feelings, positive or negative," and "*měrnost (numeri)*, the regular succession of long and short sounds."[13] His definition of *libozvučnost* here is very close to that provided by Palacký in *Počátkové*, and by discussing it together with meter Jungmann recalls that prior discussion and promotes it as normative.[14] Jungmann is tendentious here even in his terminology: for a Czech term for "prosody" he chooses "*časoměří*" (time-measure), practically the same term used in *Počátkové* for the quantitative principle: "*časomíra*." Jungmann appends a long footnote to this section (his usual manner of adding specifically Czech material to the discussion he translates from his sources), outlining the history of Czech prosody, beginning with the RKZ and ending with the rules from *Počátkové* for quantitative verse, the only rules he cites in detail.

It was Jan Kollár's peculiar approach to *libozvučnost*, however, that made that term problematic and controversial *within* the Czech literary realm (like *časomíra*, which was highly contested by advocates of the syllabotonic system), instead of merely a defense against the outside. Kollár (1793–1852) challenged the orthodoxy of Jungmann and his followers, not by taking issue with particular aspects of their program, but rather by enthusiastically embracing the program in a way that often combined aspects that remained separate in Jungmann's writing and by insisting on active work on projects that, for others, existed largely as utopian dreams. In his approach to *libozvučnost*, Kollár integrated the Slavism that was programmatically central in the new journal *Krok* and specifically suggested deliberate intervention in the Czech literary language to work toward both greater *libozvučnost* and the often-stated ideal of a common Slavic literary language. His article on the topic, entitled "Myšlénky o libozwučnosti řečj wůbec, obzwláště českoslowanské" ("Thoughts on the *Libozvučnost* of Languages in General, the Czechoslav Language in Particular), was published in the third number of the first volume of *Krok* (1823).

Portrait of Jan Kollár, by Jan Vilímek, 189?. The original is held by the National Library of the Czech Republic.

Kollár begins by distinguishing between the aesthetic and logical properties of a language: "The perfection of a language is based on two elements: the aesthetic, which leads to *libozvučnost,* and the logical, which leads to regularity."[15] Šafařík and Jungmann had used this distinction in the past to separate Czech from German, placing Czech on the aesthetic side and German on the logical side. Kollár takes a different tack: "The so-called original languages have more logicality as their basis; the daughters born from them more aesthetic properties [*aisthetičnost*]."[16] He places Slavic (and Czech) *with* German among the logical languages instead of among the aesthetic languages. The reason for this line of argument is not difficult to decipher: Kollár wants to propose specific changes to the Czech literary norm to increase its *libozvučnost,* so he cannot begin, as do Šafařík and Palacký, from the language's inherent *libozvučnost.* Rather, he must argue for the need to cultivate this quality: "The aesthetic qualities [*aisthetičnost*], the musical basis of a language or its pleasant effect on the ear (*libozvuk*) depends on its *matter,* the logicality of a language on its *form.* The matter of a language is *consonants* and *vowels. Libozvučnost* proceeds from the nature, degree, and variety of these two. Consonants in original and cultivated languages are almost untouchable; if one of these languages lacks *libozvučnost,* then the lover of it must turn his attention especially to the vowels."[17] Thus, Kollár's conception of what leads to *libozvučnost* is very close to that of Palacký: he stresses the variety of sound, and vowel sounds in particular. Because he proceeds from a different conception of the nature of Czech, however, his recommendations for how to achieve it are far more interventionist than Palacký's.

Kollár's interventionist attitude also likely draws on a reading of Dobrovský's 1815 article on *libozvučnost.* In keeping with contemporary theories of historical language change, Dobrovský attempted to explain the phonological development of Czech through the principle of euphony.[18] As Palacký noted, his discourse was not really aesthetic, but rather grammatical and, one might add, historical and descriptive. Kollár, however, clearly read it in terms of aesthetics, and he took issue not with the changes described, for these were historical fact, but rather with Dobrovský's aesthetic judgment. He was particularly bothered, for example, by the results of the Czech vowel shift that had occurred in the fourteenth century and marked the major separation of the Czech and Slovak dialects. To Kollár's Slovak ear, the result was anything but a more pleasing sound, and it also failed the important test of variety: it led to a far greater occurrence of the "e" and "i" sounds in Czech and a reduction in the more open "a" and "o" sounds, which Kollár valued more highly in any case. He thus repeatedly questions the greater aesthetic quality of the result and suggests that this historical change be reversed, particularly in those grammatical cases where the sound change led to some ambiguity in the declension of nouns.[19] Most of Kollár's suggestions for improving Czech *libozvučnost* are thus aimed at the sound structure of Czech and at the reversal or mitigation of historical changes (some of them ascribed to Germanization)[20] that led to a lesser, rather than a greater, *libozvučnost* in his opinion. These concerns, like his title, show that Kollár is responding more to Dobrovský than to Palacký, who proposed choices of poetic diction and word order as the primary means to greater *libozvučnost*. Although Dobrovský's discourse was primarily historical and descriptive, in Kollár's reading and response, it becomes prescriptive and programmatic.[21] The aesthetic principle is used, not to explain historical changes in the sound structure of the language, but to argue for programmatic intervention into that sound structure in the present.

Kollár further justified his proposals by the contribution they would make toward the national unity of the Czechs and Slovaks and ultimately of the Slavs in general. The reversal of the historical phonetic changes would bring literary Czech closer to its Slavic roots. At the same time, it would be more inclusive of the Slovaks and would draw them more firmly into the Czechoslav nation. The Czechoslav ideal was already being challenged by the separate codification of literary Slovak by Anton Bernolák, and Kollár is adamant that his suggestions do not amount to a compromise with Bernolák, but are rather a defense against such separation: "Thus the Czech, along with his tongue, will become more the Slav, and the Slav, especially the Slovak, will become more the Czech."[22] His proposals are thus conceived as a step in the direction of the goal that Jungmann had so clearly envisioned in 1806: a common Slavic literary language. Jungmann had also encouraged and practiced innovation in the Czech language, particularly the borrowing of vocabulary from other Slavic tongues. Yet Jungmann's borrowings were aimed primarily at diversifying Czech vocabulary and creating poeticisms and terminology. Kollár puts his linguistic innovations (conceived as a return to a Slavic origin) into the service of the larger project of developing a Slavic nationality.

In fact, the use of Czech as a written language among the Slovaks, often with a healthy admixture of Slovak phonetic, morphemic, and lexical elements, had a long history, beginning in the fifteenth century. In the western Slovak towns in the sixteenth and seventeenth centuries a regional administrative koine, today termed "cultural Western Slovak," developed on this basis. And the Catholic Counter Reformation gave further impetus to this mixing by using a Slovakized Czech in its attempts to win over the Slovak population. Bernolák's codification of literary Slovak (1787, 1790) derives from these traditions.[23] But Kollár came out of the Slovak Protestant tradition, which used a somewhat purer form of literary Czech, based on the Kralice Bible—a tradition that also included and integrated many Czech Protestant immigrants who settled in upper Hungary among the Slovaks after the defeat at White Mountain in 1620. In the later eighteenth century, among these Slovak Protestants, there were attempts to both purify the written language from Slovak elements (Bohuslav Tablic) and to codify special variants of Czech for Slovak use (Pavel Doležal).[24] With the conscious attempts in the Bohemian lands to revive Czech as a literary language, however, and with Dobrovský's codification of Czech grammar, based on the norms of the same period that produced the Kralice Bible, tolerance for variant usage in writing, whether that of the developing norm of spoken Czech (*obecná čeština*) or the Slovakized norm, disappeared.[25] Slovak writers found that their contributions to Czech journals were edited to remove any such impurities, sometimes without comprehension and in ways that altered the meanings of their texts.[26] It was into this context that Kollár tried to insert an entirely new norm, without any historical foundation in common usage, but with an ideological basis that everyone shared. His innovations would be rejected, along with similar suggestions coming from the Moravians F. Trnka and V. Žák.[27]

Like Palacký and Šafařík, Kollár constructed a new hierarchy and constellation of the constant values of Jungmann's program, placing Slavdom, rather than *časomíra* and high poetry at the center.[28] His vision of a Slavic poetic program also involved a different relationship to romanticism. In the terminology of the day, the history of the European literatures was the history of romanticism. But romanticism was also linked with a whole conglomerate of recent literary styles and practices. The Czechs and Russians differed greatly in what aspects of romanticism they admitted to their literatures. As already seen, Orest Somov was the first in Russia to confront the European narrative histories of romanticism, to play competing narratives against each other in an effort to leave the possibility open of the inclusion of Russia in those narratives. This contributed to a growing fashion for the historical survey of Russian literature in journals and almanacs and the preoccupation of Russian criticism with literary history.[29] Somov also helped to establish *narodnost'* alongside romanticism as a term in this discourse on the Russian national literature, and *narodnost'* turned out to be a more appealing term even than romanticism for many writers. Because the semantics of the term were so flexible, its meaning required special discussion and many authors were able to turn the term into a kind of bridge between romanticism and a new, national conception of the ancient classical literatures, as Viazemsky had suggested.

The initial Czech reaction was to reject the historical narrative of romanticism, to deny its universal validity and to oppose to it the enduring values of the ancient classical literatures. Palacký and Šafařík opposed *klasičnost* to romanticism, with its barbaric rhyme, and proposed to outdo the Germans in their Grecophilia by realizing the inherent properties of the Czech language, brother to the Greek. This was not, however, a rejection of the national perspective on literature, for they too shared the new perspective in relation to the classics, and the realization of classical meter meant the realization of the true properties of the Czech language and thus a national literature.

The German narratives of romantic poetry were built on the essential difference between classical and romantic poetry or ancient and modern poetry. For both the Russians and the Czechs, this essential difference had to be combated: for the Russians because they had discovered *narodnost'* as a link between the two, for the Czechs because it denied the validity of their attempts to achieve classicality. Wilhelm Küchelbecker, as will be seen, would follow Viazemsky in proposing that true classicism and true romanticism had in common their *narodnost'* and a true realization of the nature of poetry. In his survey of the history of aesthetics (1823), Palacký responded to the classical-romantic distinction in the work of A. Schlegel in a manner similar to that of Küchelbecker and Somov: "That very sharp difference of his between ancient and romantic art that is spreading now throughout almost all of Europe, does not seem to me to be true or adequate either philosophically or historically. . . . For just as humanity is one and the same, so is its poetry one, no matter how various it appears in all kinds of nations and ages. Also, do ancient Asian and ancient Slavic poetry belong to classical or romantic poetry?"[30]

Küchelbecker and Palacký gestured toward true poetry and its nature as the unity between the classical and the romantic. But unity could also be achieved through a synthesis of these different modes of poetry. Jan Kollár pointed to a Hegelian-style synthesis of classical and romantic poetry as the mission and eventual contribution of the Slavic nation to European civilization. For Kollár the striving toward a common Slavic literary language, to which his reforms in the name of *libozvučnost* also contributed, had its justification and philosophical founding in the historical role to be played by the Slavic nation. He outlined this justification and presented his vision of the historical role of the Slavs in an anonymous introduction to *Písní lidu slovenského v Uhřích* (*Songs of the Slovak People in Hungary*), a collection of folk songs he published with Šafařík and Benedikti the same year as his treatise on *libozvučnost* (1823). Because these songs were published in their original Slovak dialect, they required an introduction that defined this *not* as a contribution to a separate Slovak literary idiom, but rather as a contribution to a common Czech and Slovak and, ultimately, Slavic literary norm. The introduction begins, "One of the greatest obstacles in the progress of the Slavic nation toward enlightenment is its multi-dialecticality or the differences in dialects and sub-dialects [*nářečí a dialektů*], by which perhaps no other nation is so burdened and broken into pieces."[31] He describes, over the course of the next several pages, the many Slavic dialects, with particular attention to the varieties of Slovak, but the idea of writing in each of these dialects is, in his view, counterproductive. "A national literature is the more successful the wider its compass and the more freely it can fly on its wings far and wide, from shore to shore and mountain to mountain. It certainly finds more support and more stimuli in this way, and it develops a character that is not one-sided, but great, sublime, and purely human, that reflects not the rays of villages, towns, schools, guilds, and parties, but regions, nations, and humanity."[32] In order for the Slavic nation to become enlightened and fulfill its mission to humanity, then, it must overcome its division into dialects. "No sacrifice of a dialect need be difficult for us, for a great advantage can be won through but a small loss."[33]

This approach to the ideal of a common Slavic literary language, made concrete by Kollár's literary practice and demands that Czech change to accommodate and incorporate the Slovaks, caused Jungmann to rethink the whole ideal. In 1827, when the prospect was raised in an article in *Krok*, Jungmann, as editor, added the following footnote to temper any enthusiasm it might engender in readers:

> The idea of a general Slavic literary language has already occupied more than one head. Only two roads lead that way, either the selection of one dialect as common or the conjoining of all the dialects in one. The first is not possible, insofar as it would not be allowed by the national pride and love of each people [?] of its own dialect [láska každého *názwu* ke swému dialektu], and the development of both dialects, the domestic and the common, at the same time would be difficult. The difference among the Slavic dialects is significant, and while their various forms can be understood etymologically, they can in no way be joined. Someone once said that to become a Russian one must stop being a

Pole; and we say that whoever wants to be a Russian, Serb, or Pole has to stop being a Czech. That can only happen by force and to the detriment of Czech. So one cannot think of the joining of dialects, but only of their perfection through good common use, in which we entirely concur with the contributor.[34]

Kollár recognized what the loss of a dialect (that is, a language) would mean. The collection of folk songs is justified in part as a way to preserve this material before its final disappearance.[35] But the Slovak dialect should not disappear without having contributed something to the common language it adopts. Kollár consistently conceives of the conjoining of the Slavic dialects and nations as a synthetic process, one of incorporation and mutual compromise. After giving a handful of reasons why the Slovaks should use Czech as their literary language, he qualifies his recommendation thus: "By this, however, I do not advise that the Slovaks, in number nearly equal to the Czech, should forget about themselves entirely and give themselves, destroyed, entirely to the Czechs. The Czechs themselves, indeed, would have no cause to rejoice at such naked guests and allies. Let the Slovaks give something to the Czechs and the Czechs to the Slovaks if there is to be a place for a single literature among them, that is, a Czechoslovak literature."[36] In particular, Kollár suggests that Slovak has some beauties that it could lend to the Czech, including, as already seen, a greater variety of vowels, but also a greater number of long vowels, making quantitative verse more easily realizable.[37] The folk songs, then, can serve the linguistic goal of providing material for a desired linguistic integration.

Linguistic integration, however, is only a small part of the synthetic cultural integration of the Slavs: "The songs of the common people are precious and useful, not only linguistically, but also in regard to aesthetics and ethnology. They are images in which each nation paints and presents its character most faithfully; they are the history of its internal world and life, the keys to the sanctuary of nationality [*národnost*]; and whoever is unable or unwilling to open it with them will never know even what humanity, which is manifested in pastoral songs no less than in the Egyptian pyramids, is like."[38] Once again here, Kollár works his way up the levels of synthetic integration, from local to national and from national to international. The nature of humanity is nothing but the synthesis of the various natures manifested in specific localities and in specific nations. Aesthetically, these songs represent one face of humanity. This would be a minor role, except that this particular Slavic face has a great role to play in humanity, a role that is reflected in the nature of these folk songs.

Before examining that role, however, one should consider Kollár's judgment of the aesthetic value of the folk songs: "Even lovers of poetry and the fruits of aesthetics in general will frequently find healthier pasture in such collections than near many Parnassian volcanoes, which, particularly in these times, have nearly deafened us with their cracks and booms, nearly buried us in their ash and stone."[39] This is as much a shot at the high pathos of the polemics around quantitative verse as it is a promotion of the simpler aesthetics of the folk song. But Kollár also headed his introduction with an epigraph from Montaigne that compares the natural beauty of folk songs to that of the most perfect artistic poetry and finds them equal. Kollár seems to agree. But he immediately continues, "As far as the character of these songs is concerned, we do not want to overrate them."[40] They manifest the character of the aesthetics of their nation "only in its first fruits and buds."[41] They are useful, then, in the evaluation of that character and the role it can play, but do not represent the highest possible achievement, the fulfillment of that role.

In this careful delimitation of the aesthetic value of folk songs, Kollár steps only slightly beyond the opinions earlier expressed by his collaborator in the collection, Šafařík (see chapter 6). For Kollár, too, in spite of the epigraph from Montaigne, the aesthetic value of folk songs was strictly limited. But what a character they reflect, and what a role they project! In a key passage, Kollár reverses his hierarchy of synthesis, so that humanity is not the synthesis of all the various nations, including the Slavic nation, but instead, the Slavic nation acts as the ultimate synthesis, most fully embodying humanity:

> One whose head is filled with poems of dragons, lizards, knights, wizards and other romantic monsters, should not even pick them [the songs] up. The character of such poetry is foreign to all of Slavic poetry, and especially its folk poetry. With other nations, usually one of the faculties of the soul is, if not the suppressor of all the others, at least the outrunner [*předběhuně*]; among the Slavs, all seem to have equal rights and to tread at the same pace; with others the head and heart are often so estranged that a reader's wings become tired flying from one to the other. The Slav feels thinking, and thinks feeling. In the temple of Slavdom these two spirits of human nature have so fallen in love that their harmonious marriage will no doubt give birth to the new, perfect life of the entire spiritual future, realizing and representing the ideal of humanity in its greatest possible fullness. And that seems to be why our nation has progressed so belatedly and slowly in learning: it is carrying to Olympus together in a single basket all the gifts and talents that heaven loaned it and that others return only

in part. The spirit of poetry inclines among other nations either more toward adventure (the Spaniards), or toward passion (the Italians), or toward wit and politesse (the French), or toward agitation and sentimentality (the English), or toward cogitation (the Germans). Among the Slavs, poetry seems to be a fruit in which all the faculties of the soul have an equal share under the flag of imagination. A strange, dark, monstrous, delirious, overstrained, in a word a one-sided poem has never been heard so far in our literature.[42]

The Slavic nation has a tremendous, messianic role that can be read out of the aesthetic nature of the Slovak folk song. The synthesis of all of human nature for Kollár also means a resulting balance that rules out any sort of extremes. This rules out "romanticism," or at least certain, more marked aspects of it. Certainly Kollár is not interested in any individualism, in any exploration of psychological deviancy, or in fantastic representations that have their origin in medieval traditions and the type of folklore that had been ruled out of the folk song collection.

Still, Kollár's synthesizing approach leaves him far more open to romantic poetry, in the sense of the European poetic tradition, than the authors of *Počátkové*. He had already published in 1821 a collection of poems that included a great number of syllabotonic sonnets in addition to quantitative elegies, odes, and epigrams. Many of these sonnets became a part of his *Slavy dcera* in 1824, which opened with a prelude in quantitative elegiac distich. The incorporation of both modern and ancient forms, each with its appropriate versification, points to the kind of synthesis that he hoped to achieve, as does the marked decrease in the erotic and elegiac qualities of his poems in *Slavy dcera,* where such individual feelings are allegorized and sublimated into national myth. Romanticism as a certain historical collection of forms was permissible and necessary to the synthesis, which had to embody national, not individual, aspirations.[43] As he wrote in his *Výklad čili přímětky a vysvětlivky ku Slávy dceře* (*Explication or Notes and Annotations to Slavy dcera*), to accompany the second, expanded edition of the poem (1832), "The Slavic, and particularly the Czech tongue, is so fortunate as to be able to move freely in all poetical forms, old and new, classical and romantic: hexameters and alexandrines, pentameters and ottava rimas, Sapphic verses and sonnets, rhythm and quantity and rhyming—everything flourishes in it."[44]

The appeal of, and the problem with, Kollár's conception is in the fact that he systematically combined all the separate methods and ideals of Jungmann's national literary program into a single whole. In this way, he proved to be the program's most ardent enthusiast and at the same time its greatest challenger.

Kollár's use of the term *libozvučnost* places it into relationship with a utopian project of Slavic linguistic and cultural reunification that is seen as the messianic mission of the Slavic nation to humanity. He responds primarily to Dobrovský's use of the term in a historical account of the separation of the Czech and Slovak "dialects" and proposes a programmatic reversal of this separation. In his writing, the term is not connected, as it was by Palacký and Šafařík, to the quantitative reform of the Czech prosodic system and the classicality of Czech letters that was to result. While high poetry plays no small role in Kollár's synthetic vision, *časomíra* is only one of the prosodic possibilities of the Slavic language(s) that should be joined by syllabotonic verse in the final unifying synthesis of Slavic literature, which would also overcome the classical-romantic cultural divide.

Kollár's concept of a Slavic synthetic embodiment of all of literary history helped to balance out the overemphasis on ancient classical forms and allow romanticism a certain limited entry into Czech culture. But it also, by pointing up their impracticality, forced a reconsideration of the very ideals and methods that drove it. Kollár's proposed innovations in the sound structure of Czech, which he began to put into practice in his poetry and prose in the late 1820s and 1830s, were seen not in the light of this project of Slavic synthesis but instead as a threat to the identity and historical continuity of the Czech literary language, which had only recently begun to develop a modern identity out of the chaos of neglect and multiple centers and norms. This soon led to open disagreement between Jungmann and Kollár, and Jungmann and Palacký began by the late 1820s to emphasize the necessity of stablizing the Czech literary norm to combat a continuing tendency toward linguistic innovation. Insofar as *libozvučnost* was now connected to this type of linguistic innovation, it became a term to be avoided for Jungmann, who was forced to rearticulate his program in response to the enthusiastic challenge of Kollár's embrace, to the gains that had been made in the 1820s, and to the limited place that quantitative verse had won for itself in Czech letters.

He did so in an article in the first issue of the *Časopis českého musea* (*Journal of the Czech Museum*), edited by Palacký (1827). The article, entitled "O klasičnosti literatury vůbec a zvláště české" ("On *Klasičnost* of Literature in General and Czech in Particular"), redefines *klasičnost* for a national literature in a way that is no longer so dependent on ancient classical literature and its verse forms, but moves it much closer to Dobrovský's image of a fully developed literary culture, the image that had inspired Jungmann's program in the first place (see chapter 4).[45] Jungmann thus tried to rescue a place for *klasičnost* in Czech letters in a way that separated it from both quantitative verse form and from the dangerous interventionist linguistic creativity now implied by *libozvučnost*. *Klasičnost* has become a dividing issue, Jungmann notes, and he proposes to clarify the issue "making use to that end of what one of the better German writers said about it."[46] This writer turns out to be Karl Heinrich Ludwig Pölitz, the same writer Jungmann had used so extensively for his *Slovesnost*.[47] Pölitz was a productive writer but can hardly be said to occupy a prominent place in German criticism today, and even at the time, Palacký, for one, considered him a shallow aesthetician. In his "Přehled dějin krásovědy a její literatury" ("Survey of the History of Aesthetics and Its Literature"), published in the fourth issue of the first volume of *Krok* (1823), he limits mention of Pölitz to a single short sentence: "The eclectic Pölitz remained more on the surface."[48] But Pölitz was of great value to Jungmann within the Czech context, for Pölitz's approach to the problem of developing a national literature corresponded in many ways to Jungmann's practice. Jungmann strategically employed the German's theoretical discussions to promote ideas and practices that he thought were necessary for the development of Czech literature.[49]

The role that Pölitz played for Jungmann is analogous to the role Ancillon played for the Russian critics who addressed the problem of Russia's inclusion into narratives of romantic literary history, or Charles Rollin for Trediakovsky's response to the Quarrel between the Ancients and Moderns: that of a historically minor critic who nonetheless offered important ideas to their particular literature. Czech and Russian writers were often very aware of the work of the more original European thinkers, but chose to translate and respond to the work of these minor critics for a variety of reasons, from personal ties (Rollin had been Trediakovsky's professor) to the way that the ideas of these writers engaged the current situation of Czech and Russian literatures. Jungmann's choice of Pölitz also reflects the significant ties between Prague and the university in Leipzig, where Pölitz studied and taught. Jungmann's influential professor of aesthetics in Prague, August Gottlieb Meissner, had been educated in Leipzig.[50] Šafařík, too, in the *Počátkové* volume, made use of Pölitz's writing for general questions of aesthetics; moreover, he stopped in Leipzig on his way back from Jena in 1817 to see Johann Gottfried Hermann, who provided him with ammunition in his attacks on the German syllabotonic system. It would be far more surprising if the Czechs had responded to Ancillon, a Prussian. The Russian interest in Ancillon may have had to do with his position as royal Prussian historian, analogous to that occupied by Karamzin in Russia, and his prominence in the negotiations following the defeat of Napoleon.[51]

As with his *Slovesnost,* then, Jungmann's originality in the article on *klasičnost* lay in his strategic use of Pölitz, his selection of a small amount of material that would be most effective in promoting his own ideas.[52] The material from Pölitz makes up approximately one-half of the article on *klasičnost,* and it is taken from a few pages of the introduction to Pölitz's four-volume *Das Gesammtgebiet der deutschen Sprache* (1825).[53] It addresses the Czech situation quite effectively, and especially the central issue of *klasičnost* (*Classicität*). The translation and adaptation of this text for Jungmann's purposes required not only the selection of material that would address his goals but also the suppression of ideas or concepts that were contrary. For example, Pölitz discusses the process of cultivating a language (an idea dear to Jungmann), and suggests that the first to begin this process are the poets, who emerge from among the people "und der Sprache Reichthum, Neuheit der Wörter und Wortbildung, Wohlklang und Volkstümlichkeit geben."[54] In Jungmann's translation, the poets "bestow on the language richness, newness in words and phrase, *blahozvučnost* and *národovost.*"[55] By using a close synonym, *blahozvučnost,* he avoids the loaded term *libozvučnost,* the usual translation of *Wohlklang,* and thus possible implications of innovation in the sound structure of the language.[56] In the same vein, he translates *Wortbildung* (word formation) as "*spojování*" (joining) to avoid what could be taken as a direct statement of the same thing. He thus avoids lending any support to Kollár's language innovations either implicitly or explicitly in his translation, even as he still justifies the neologizing that had been central to his own practice.[57]

Since he had first articulated his literary program, Jungmann had struggled with those who, like Jan Nejedlý, held strictly to the language norm of the sixteenth century, which Dobrovský had named the golden age of Czech literature. For Jungmann, this prevented the kind of innovation in language that was essential to the embodiment of the new poetic values and new developments in the sciences of the nineteenth century. In his own *Historie literatury české* (1825), Jungmann declared the first period of Czech literature (up to 1310) the golden age, on the strength of the forged manuscripts. In spite of the assumed age of these documents, this revaluation of Czech literary history brought a greater focus on *contemporary* literary values.[58] But this age, from which so little had been preserved (and for which little enough had been invented), did not entirely satisfy the criteria outlined by Dobrovský for a golden age, for it did not reflect the broadest possible literary culture.

The material from Pölitz's introduction allowed Jungmann to address this problem anew, at the same time refocusing the energy being spent on disputes over whether this or that Czech author deserved the status of classic. Jungmann does briefly define *klasičnost* for an individual work of literature—it involves the kind of organic fusion of matter and form that was the focus of German Weimar classicism—but the center of attention is rather on the *klasičnost* of a literature, its classical period: "The *classical period* of a literature and language does not arise through one or another excellent writer, nor through the advantageous cultivation of one or another field of *slovesnost,* e.g., poetry, but rather through a remarkable quantity of contemporary, excellent, original minds and the successful cultivation by them of all, or nearly all, of the primary writing forms—poetry, prose, and oratory."[59] The classical period of a literature, then, is simply a synonym for its golden age, and Jungmann goes on to include many of the same characteristics outlined by Dobrovský: all classes read the literature, are educated by it, and create and use it in the daily activities of the nation. An important distinction that Pölitz adds to this discussion is that between living and dead languages. For a dead language, the classical period of its literature can be determined with finality. But "one should remember that *klasičnost* in a living language must be seen from another perspective than for an expired one; one should remember that this *klasičnost* in general only applies to a certain degree; it is relative. For in a living language it is possible that a period will come in which the literature will acquire a greater cultivation and maturity, so that its classics will far surpass the classics of the ancient periods."[60] This was an important corrective to those who were too strident in their insistence on the old language norm, for it opened the door to change and development toward a better future. It also offset the tendency to overemphasize the Greek and Roman classics and the need to imitate them that had manifested itself in discussions of *klasičnost*. Pölitz offered a balanced view on the romantics versus the classics: "Modern classics in languages that have matured to their golden age stand neither beneath the ancient classics nor above them, but beside them in equality; for the difference of ages and the nations to which these exemplary writers belonged, must be preserved."[61] Jungmann thus reminded everyone that the golden age should not be something they were looking back upon, but something they were striving toward. In fact, Jungmann insists that the whole project of Czech culture has no meaning, if not to strive forward: "either we should diligently press forward after the example of other nations or we should leave everything be and join in language the nearest nation, already rich in all types of literature, to which we are already nearly conjoined by our education and thinking as it is."[62] The latter option is the one that opponents of the Czech project continually offered and argued for, but which every convinced patriot had long ago renounced by their decision to be Czech. There was, in fact, no choice.

In his own brief survey of Czech literature in the article, Jungmann challenged both his own prior evaluation of the first period of Czech literature as the golden age and Dobrovský's evaluation of the sixteenth century: "The first age, containing the remains of the oldest poetry, never adequately appreciated, classical in its own way but limited to a few genres, cannot for the lack of other types of poetic, prosaic, and oratorical genres be considered the classical age."[63] As for the sixteenth century, he acknowledged its breadth, "but its poetry remained behind the oldest period in beauty, and the whole literature of that period, for all the other perfections of individual writers, has a primarily one-sided stamp, like a single face: theological."[64] However laudatory some might consider this to be, such one-sidedness ruled out considering it the classical period. These re-evaluations left the field wide open to the future for the embodiment of the Czech classical age.

But if the classical period of Czech literature was yet to come, that meant that, in some sense, the national literature did not yet exist. As Pölitz wrote, and Jungmann translated, "Such a classical period first ordains the national literature, and together [*sic.*] for the future lays a firm foundation for all spiritual and moral learning and a rich language."[65] Jungmann himself draws the conclusions for the contemporary period. Even with all that has been achieved, "If literature is to come to a higher life and its inception, far more remains to be done than has been accomplished."[66] He goes on to outline these tasks:

> What's needed is to take care that a good spirit, pleasing to God and the government, and a true national sense, which has greatly diminished, again be revived and strengthened; what's needed is the unselfish and envy-less influence of *many* experienced, wise writers, and in general a moral higher education and public trust and support obtained in this manner; what's needed are efforts at true *klasičnost* both for individual works and for the entire literature, efforts at superior cultivation of all the learned sciences and arts, from whence in the end all kinds of knowledge and learning would flow into the common literature like blood from the heart into the veins, and so our literature would derive from life and enter into the national life as much as possible; in a word, what we need in all genres poetical, prosaic, and oratorical

are *original* works aplenty, perfect in both content and style, classics similar to those of other nations, which, if the nation makes the effort, will bring in their period for us also.[67]

Some of these tasks had been a part of Jungmann's program for some time. Others were new and reflect the accomplishments of Czech culture since 1806. Jungmann had always pushed for learned discourse to be conducted in Czech, and the journal *Krok* was founded to promote this. But the mark of a patriot continued to be the writing of poetry in Czech, and too little had been accomplished in other fields.[68] This overemphasis on poetry, and especially on the most exclusive sort of poetry, proved to be divisive in the national movement, for it failed to include the common masses into the project in any way, and in particular, it failed to bring them their education in Czech. The *Časopis českého musea*, edited by Palacký, announced in its first issue (which included Jungmann's article) that it aimed to take on this developing problem: "This need presses upon us all the more, the more our literature distances itself from common life, with which it has not proceeded in step for a long period, and now, through the intentional actions of certain people within it (for which there is reason to fear that what is most needed for genuine national education will be kept less in view), even threatens to separate from it entirely."[69] Historically speaking, one might include Jungmann and Palacký among those certain people whose actions, in the past, had helped to distance Czech literature from the common people, for they were among the most outspoken advocates of exclusive poetry. At this point, however, both are clearly with the program. Jungmann writes that, "every classical literature must also have its common side, if it is to enter into national life."[70] And in the fourth volume of the journal, Palacký asks, "What good is that abundance of writings, soaring so high in content and form that few in the nation can use their cunning to catch them, as long as there is no attention to the needs of our common life?"[71] This emphasis is new for Jungmann and Palacký, and it is a position that would find more and more support in the 1830s, with continual calls for greater comprehensibility. Palacký and Jungmann are both responding to a problem that is the product of the new paradigm of national literature: the problem of the unity of the national body in its literature. If the nation was to be conceived on the analogy of an individual, then the national literature should reflect that unity of identity and not be split into high literature and mass literature.[72] Also new for Jungmann is the demand for more original works. Jungmann himself had been far more active as a translator, and Czech journals continued to be filled with a great quantity of translations. Many of these were valuable contributions, but he recognized that for Czech literature to take the next step, it had to begin to produce its own literary models. Calls for originality would also increase in number in the 1830s.

BY CLAIMING THAT the *libozvučnost* of the Czech language had been on the demise since the fourteenth century, Kollár helped precipitate the demise of the term *libozvučnost* in Czech literary discourse in a far shorter amount of time. For Dobrovský, *libozvučnost* had been both a historical principle at work in the development of the Czech language and an aesthetic goal to be achieved by careful accentual verse composition. For Palacký, the historical principle was worthless if it contributed nothing to the goal of the future perfection of Czech verse; and in his judgment, the writers of accentual verse had utterly failed in their pursuit of *libozvučnost*. Palacký and Šafařík articulated an alternate vision of *libozvučnost* that connected it to quantitative verse and a visionary and very romantic ideal of a national literature with classical qualities. They thus promised a new stage in Jungmann's program of building the national literature, one that moved beyond the creation of language to the creation of a new "golden age" of Czech literature in the future, rather than in the sixteenth-century past. Kollár, with at least as much of an eye to the ideal future, combined the historical principle of *libozvučnost* with an aesthetic critique of Czech language development. Instead of a poetic solution, he proposed a radical reversal of certain select historical developments in Czech phonology. The goal of such changes was not a new golden age of poetry, but rather the further integration of the national community envisioned by Jungmann, building from Czech and Slovak unity out into a future ideal of a Slavic nation united by a single literary language. Jungmann had founded his project on linguistic creativity and the revival of a national culture through language, but Kollár's active work on the utopian ideal of the greater Slavic nation and linguistic unity, at a time when the Czech language seemed finally to have developed the necessary resources to begin to compete for cultural laurels on its own, forced Jungmann to rearticulate his goals in a way that marginalized quantitative verse and even, to his likely regret, the Slavic ideal.

Libozvučnost is not a term unique to Czech literary criticism, but the uses to which it was put in the second and third decades of the nineteenth century in the budding Czech national literary program and the minor controversy it generated are exceptional. In Russia, in the later eighteenth century, Aleksandr Radishchev and Semen Bobrov employed similar terms, *blagoglasie* and *dobroglasie,* in advocating unrhymed verse, with classical and folkloric antecedents. Radishchev analyzed the hexameter verse of Vasily Trediakovsky in terms of its *blagoglasie,* and for Bobrov, *dobroglasie* consisted in "the artful and correct selection of vowels and consonants, used appropriately."[73] But in the second decade of the nineteenth century, when Sergei Uvarov began to advocate for the imitation of Greek metrical forms, and the hexameter in particular, as a means to the creation of a more national literature, he did not suggest that any improved sound qualities were to result—because Radishchev had in fact argued only that the hexameter form did not prevent *blagoglasie,* not that it led to it. Kapnist's suggestion that the use of folkloric verse forms would lead to a greater *blagozvuchnost'* did not resonate with anyone. Nor were the terms tied to the active Russian debates over the literary language in the first decades of the nineteenth century. There were no competing dialects of Russian to be considered, for the language of the urban imperial centers clearly dominated. As already noted, the integration of the language of folklore and the simple folk and of literary Russian Church Slavonic was debated as a question of style rather than of dialect, and opponents appealed to either taste or directly to national loyalty, rather than to euphony.

In German literature, *Wohlklang* was a prominent term, and Czech writers adapted the discourse of German language defenses, in which it was most prominently employed, to their own ends. Such German language defenses also considered, under the rubric of *Wohlklang,* the question of the relationship of German to Greek. But as literary High German was becoming established in the mid-eighteenth century, *Wohlklang* seems not to have played an important role in the defense of competing literary dialects, though sound was a consideration in some attacks on Johann Christoph Gottsched's codification of High German.[74] The defense of the rights of the dialects was instead conducted as a question of style, with the Swiss critic Johann Jakob Bodmer defending the expressiveness of certain dialectal phrases and words, even as he submitted to Gottsched's orthographic and grammatical norms.[75] The German literary norm was established before the ideology that tied national identity to language was fully developed, so the emotional investment in the dialects lacked this ideological justification. The German dialects surrendered relatively quickly. In fact, euphony was used as an argument *for* the High German standard, along with the comparison to Greek.[76] Ignaz Weitenauer defended Gottsched's norm in 1764 against the proponents of other dialects by noting that German is like Greek in having a variety of dialects, but unlike Greek, it should not allow the literary development of multiple dialects and instead agree on a common norm. Friedrich Gedike repeated the argument in 1779 and compared particular dialects of Greek to German dialects. He associated High German with the Attic dialect as the most euphonic, which eventually displaced the Doric and Ionic in literary usage.[77]

In the Czech language realm, the analogy with Greek and *libozvučnost,* particularly in Kollár's treatment, both favored the multiple dialects of the "Slavic language." Though Kollár argued for the eventual synthetic integration of the Slavic literary languages, his defense of the values carried by the dialects and his publication of Slovak folk songs in fact contributed to the consolidation of different Slavic literary languages, including a separate Slovak norm. The Slavic version of the Greek dialects theme was first articulated by the Slovene Jernej Kopitar, who was introduced in chapter 4. In a number of works published around 1810, Kopitar argued that the Slavic dialects should be allowed to develop like the Greek dialects, that they should develop as literary languages and that eventually they would evolve toward one another and consolidate, like the Greek language under Alexander the Great.[78] One such article appeared anonymously in 1813 in Josef Jungmann's Czech translation. Whether directly or through the mediation of one of the many Czech writers with whom Kopitar corresponded, including Šafařík beginning in 1819, this article likely helped to inspire Kollár's vision of Slavic synthetic integration.[79] Certainly the comparison of the Slavic and Greek dialects became a commonplace in Czech revival discourse, particularly in the wake of Kollár's defense of the contribution Slovak could make to the *libozvučnost* of Czech.[80] But the Greek dialects theme was a double-edged sword, for the ideal of future integration had to contend with the reality of growing separation in the present. In his well-known and influential program for Slavic reciprocity, which he formulated in the 1830s and which moderated somewhat his utopian vision of the Slavic future, Kollár himself made explicit comparison between the Greek and Slavic dialects.[81] But Ľudovít Štúr made the comparison as well the following decade in arguing for his codification of a separate Slovak literary language, anathema to Kollár. He granted the Czechs their comparison of Czech to the Attic dialect but contended that Slovak carried the essential values of the Ionian dialect: ancient strength and antiquity.[82]

The unique fate of the Czech literary-critical term *libozvučnost* suggests a number of important points about the relationship between literary values and national movements. The crisis in literary values of the eighteenth century and the subsequent paradigm shift that made the collective subject of the nation a central locus of literary values gave tremendous impetus to national movements, as literary figures began to formulate conceptions of national identity upon which to ground new literary values. It has been a commonplace to note of the second period of the Czech national awakening (1806–1830) that political issues were often debated indirectly, by means of philological and literary issues. But the fate of *libozvučnost* shows that, in fact, with the advent of the national literature paradigm, *all* literary values that are connected to the national literary project take on political weight. Literary criticism becomes unavoidably politicized. This is not a case of the instrumentalization of literary discourse for covert political activity, but a natural result of the transformation of literary discourse, its modernization and nationalization. When literature and the nation come together in a new constellation of values, debates over literary values become directly, not indirectly, political.

The Czech discourse on *libozvučnost* also illustrates the mixing, characteristic for the period, of romantic and neo-classical (with the classics reinterpreted along national lines) literary discourse. These discourses and their privileged terms were worked out in other literary and cultural centers, as were modern conceptions of the nation. But as the Czechs respond in turn to the crisis in literary values that is one aspect of modernity, the borrowed terms and discourses are inevitably recreated to respond to the particular situation of Czech literature and the Czech-speaking people. On the one hand, one should note the central role that literary values play in the articulation of the national movement's ideology (the perceived lack in the existing Czech literary tradition of works corresponding to the highest aesthetic values drives the comparison to and imitation of Greek language and literature to the center of the national movement). On the other hand, one can observe how the political context shapes the debate on literary values and alters the terms of discussion (the *libozvučnost* of Czech is initially linked to the classical qualities that would also result from quantitative verse, but when that value is questioned from the perspective of speakers of another dialect/language within the Czech-language cultural sphere, the term is effectively dropped and a new constellation of values has to be articulated). In the accepted periodization of the Czech revival, the adjustment of the national ideology to the actual needs and values of the people is seen as characteristic of the third period (1830–1848), when the national movement began to win a larger number of adherents.[83] The articulation of the national ideology in the second period is characterized as abstracted and idealized.[84] Even in this period, however, the ideology is not constructed in a vacuum but responds to on-the-ground conditions—

even the early, seemingly abstract concept of a Slav nationality, which moves to the background as intellectuals respond to the more concrete and immediate needs of the Czech national population, is a product of the Czech awareness of kinship with other Slavic peoples that are a part of the same political entity. One might suggest that there is a constant adjustment of ideology to perceived "reality" throughout the Czech revival and that the "borrowed" discourses of romanticism, neo-classicism, and nationalism are created anew, from the start, to respond to the modern Czech situation.

Dissent over *Narodnost'* and Romanticism

Viazemsky had made *narodnost'* the quality that linked romantic and classical poetry in an argument for the literary practices of his allies, with Pushkin in the first place. Wilhelm Küchelbecker would soon employ the connection of *narodnost'* to true romanticism and true classicism to argue for the literary practices of the opposing camp and to try to sway Pushkin to undertake work in more weighty genres. One of the particularly incisive aspects of Küchelbecker's critique of the "elegiac school" was his suggestion that it failed to address an audience larger than its own intimate circle. Pushkin himself responded to the debates over *narodnost'* and romanticism in a characteristic way, with a pair of drafts of short definitional articles.[1] Notably, his definitions of *narodnost'* and romanticism are entirely separate, without referring either term to the other, and thus they mark a radical departure from the intimate connection between them that had characterized the use of the term *narodnost'* to that point. Pushkin also responded to some of the specifics of Küchelbecker's article, reacting explicitly to the understanding of inspiration and rapture (*vostorg*) found in the piece and engaging in a fundamental way with the question of the relative value and weight of different genres.[2] But he also seems to have been haunted by the problem of audience raised by Küchelbecker and the question of how to go from addressing an intimate audience of high society familiars to addressing the broader, anonymous audience of the national public.

Küchelbecker's 1824 article in the almanac *Mnemozina*, entitled "O napravlenii nashei poezii, osobenno liricheskoi, v poslednee desiatiletie" ("On the Trend in Our Poetry, Especially Lyrical, in the Last Decade"), responds also to Somov and to the European discourse on romanticism in which Somov sought to include Russia. Like Somov, Küchelbecker begins with first principles. Instead of imagination, though, he proposes that "strength, freedom, and inspiration: those are the three conditions of any poetry."[3] On that basis, he argues that the ode is the primary lyric form, as it best embodies those principles. He then derides the elegy and epistle, which had become the leading genres in Russia, and questions the direction set by Zhukovsky and Batiushkov. Because these two are the leaders of the "new school" for Viazemsky, Bestuzhev, and others, this raises the issue of romanticism: "Zhukovsky and Batiushkov have become, *for a time,* the leading lights of our poets and especially of that school that is now passed off to us as romantic. But what is romantic poetry? It was born in Provence and fostered Dante, who gave it life, strength and boldness, bravely threw off of himself the yoke of slavish imitation of the Romans, who themselves were only imitators of the Greeks, and decided to struggle with them. As a result, in Europe any free, national [*narodnaia*] poetry came to be called romantic."[4] Küchelbecker is concerned to distinguish between the Russian school that was being promoted as romantic and true romanticism. Like Somov, he follows Sismondi's narrative of the birth of romanticism, but where Somov raised doubts concerning Provençal poetry, Küchelbecker instead ties this narrative to a harsh critique of imitation and a new interpretation of the ancient literary heritage. Somov had limited his explicit critique of imitation primarily to the unimaginative imitation of leading writers like Pushkin and Zhukovsky, but the European discourse on romanticism had done much more to critique this pillar of classicist literary method. As already noted, a new reading of Roman literature viewed as different in spirit from Greek literature had emerged, and combined with the romantic critique of imitation, this led to a new reading of Roman literature as derivative of the Greek original. Küchelbecker makes use of this critique and even extends it, in the next paragraph, to address German literature, where he allows that Goethe alone has on occasion been sufficiently original to be worthy of the name romantic, whereas German literature as a whole has been derivative of French, Roman, Greek, and English literature. Somov, too, had implied that

Portrait of W. K. Küchelbecker. An engraving by I. I. Matiushin (1880s), based on the drawing by an unknown artist from 1845. Courtesy of The State Literary Museum, Moscow, Russia.

the imitation of the Germans would do the Russians no better than imitation of the French, but he did not dare to question the romantic credentials of the Germans, for his primary source on romanticism was de Staël's book on the Germans. For him, the Germans were exemplary of the kind of originality and *narodnost'* that marked romanticism.

Küchelbecker had different examples in mind: "By studying nature, by their strength, by their excess and variety of feelings, images, language and thoughts, by the *narodnost'* of their works, the great poets of *Greece, the East, and Britain* have carved their names indelibly into the annals of immortality. Can we really hope that we will compare to them by following the path we are on now? No one translates a translator, except our work-a-day translators. An imitator does not know inspiration: he speaks not from the depths of his own soul, but forces himself to retell others' ideas and feelings."[5] Küchelbecker agrees with Viazemsky here that *narodnost'* is a quality that guarantees the immortality of certain literatures. But he puts it alongside other poetic qualities as well, so it is not the sole guarantor.[6] The content of the term is left undefined here, though it clearly connects to the "free, national poetry" that defines romanticism.[7] Also clear is the fact that methods of imitation and translation are not the means to achieve it. The attack on translators is another aspect of Küchelbecker's assault upon the literary leadership of Zhukovsky, who had become known for his translations.[8] One sees here the beginning of a far stronger resistance to translation that accompanies the ever rising demand for original, national works, so that the fertile cross-breeding and introduction of new forms that translation offers is coming to be perceived as a threat to the emergence of pure native forms.

Like Viazemsky, Küchelbecker connected *narodnost'* and the critique of imitation not only to romanticism, but also to classicism: "Freedom, invention and novelty are the primary advantages of romantic poetry over the so-called classical poetry of later Europeans. The progenitors of this pseudo-classical poetry were more the Romans than the Greeks."[9] He connects true romanticism and true classical poetry to freedom and *narodnost'* and opposes this to the current "romantic" school in Russia, which Viazemsky was promoting, and the latter-day classicism of Europe. Thus, he too exposes "romantic" and "classical" as problematic terms. He agrees with Viazemsky on the centrality of the term *narodnost'*, if not on romanticism, but the content he gives it puts him into direct conflict with Viazemsky.[10]

Toward the end of his essay, Küchelbecker qualifies somewhat his attack upon imitation:

It is best of all to have a national [*narodnaia*] poetry. But is France not partly indebted to Euripides and Sophocles for Racine? A person of talent, pursuing the path of his great predecessors, sometimes uncovers regions of new beauties and inspiration that remained hidden from the gaze of those giants, his teachers. Therefore, if one must imitate, it's not a bad idea to know which of the foreign writers is straightaway worthy of imitation. Meanwhile, our living catalogues, whose 'Surveys,' 'Analyses,' and 'Discourses' one constantly meets with in [the leading journals], usually place on the same level: Greek literature and Latin, English and German; the great Goethe and the immature Schiller; that giant among giants Homer and his student Virgil; the opulent, thunderous Pindar and the prosaic versifier Horace; the worthy inheritor of the ancient tragedians Racine and Voltaire, who was a stranger to true poetry; the vast Shakespeare and the monotonous Byron![11]

Unlike others who took up the question of whom to imitate, Küchelbecker here does not propose an entire country with its literature. Rather, he proposes a careful selection from among the best of all the European and ancient literatures. This is similar to the canonization bestowed by classicist poetics on particular authors for particular genres. While Küchelbecker has not entirely abandoned the classicist genre hierarchy (in his preference for the ode), his emphasis here is rather on originality and general poetic worth. His independence in forming this canon is striking, for he not only rewrites the classicist canon, he also ignores the newest romantic canons by devaluing Schiller and Byron.

He is similarly independent in evaluating the Russian literary scene, and opens the essay with a canon of Russian authors that is striking for some of its inclusions and omissions: "From Lomonosov to the most recent transformation of our literature by Zhukovsky and his followers we had a series of lyricists almost without a pause whose names remain a treasure of posterity and in whose works Russia ought to take pride. Lomonosov, Petrov, Derzhavin, Dmitriev, Derzhavin's friend and companion Kapnist, Bobrov in a certain way, Vostokov, and, at the end of the previous decade, a poet who deserves to occupy one of the prime spots on the Russian Parnassus, Prince Shikhmatov. These are the leaders of this mighty tribe; they have had almost no successors in our time."[12] To a certain degree this canon is formed on the basis of the ode, which he is about to champion, but the exclusion of Karamzin and Zhukovsky from a canon of Russian lyricists at this point was heretical, as was the inclusion of Bobrov and Shikhmatov. It was heretical, that is, to the members of the leading school of poets and critics, brought up in the Karamzinian line. But this line had always had its polemical opposite in the school associated with Shishkov. Now Küchelbecker, who was quite close personally to members of the Karamzinian-Zhukovskian school, was canonizing the opponents' poets!

Küchelbecker's turn toward the Slavic camp in the early 1820s raised many eyebrows among his associates, but Pushkin too, in the early 1820s, was making gestures of accommodation toward the Shishkovian line. Neither author accepted Shishkov's chauvinism or his linguistic fictions, but as the debate on the national literature gained momentum, some of Shishkov's pronouncements started to sound less outlandish. Küchelbecker, for example, followed Shishkov quite closely in suggesting sources for the Russian national literature: "Let a truly Russian poetry be created to the glory of Russia [*Rossiia*]; let holy Russia [*Rus'*] be the first power in the universe not only in the political world, but also in the moral! The faith of our ancestors, the morals of our fatherland, the national [*narodnye*] chronicles, songs and sayings: these are the best, purest and truest sources for our literature [*slovesnost'*]."[13] Such suggestions and canons were completely unacceptable to Viazemsky, who always remained true to the literary line of his brother-in-law and guardian, Karamzin. The one other time Küchelbecker used the term *narodnost'* in this article, he used it in a way that was specifically rejected by Viazemsky: "Some eighty lines in 'Svetlana' and in the 'Epistle to Voeikov' of Zhukovsky, a few smaller poems of Katenin, and two or three places in Pushkin's *Ruslan and Liudmila* are marked by the stamp of *narodnost'*."[14] What the poems mentioned have in common is the use of folkloric language and motifs. As already noted, Viazemsky rejected this method, which he referred to as *prostonarodie* instead, and questioned its value.

Küchelbecker linked the question of *narodnost'* also to his critique of the elegiac school. Somov had lamented the reduction of all poetry to the monotonous genre of the elegy in the third part of his essay, but saw it as a failure of imagination or a failure to attend to the imagination's desire for novelty. Küchelbecker begins with a critique of the imitativeness and monotonous vocabulary of the elegy, which shares much with Somov's critique, but proceeds to expose the social role of this trend: "From the Russian word, rich and mighty, they strain to extract a small, decorous, cloying, artificially lean language suitable for the few, un petit jargon de coterie. They mercilessly banish from it all Slavic words and phrases and enrich it with . . . Germanicisms, Gallicisms, and barbarisms. . . . As for ideas, it's better not to discuss it."[15] This is followed by the remark on the extent of *narodnost'* cited above. The poetic language of Zhukovsky's school is, for Küchelbecker, oriented toward exclusivity, represented by Zhukovsky's poetry collection entitled "Für Wenige" ("For the Few"). This is explicitly opposed to the *narodnost'* of a few Russian verses and implicitly to the *narodnost'* that is characteristic of the national literatures that are exemplary to Küchelbecker, those of Greece, Britain, and the East. Küchelbecker thus suggests that since "it is best of all to have a national poetry," poetry must address a national audience and make use of an appropriate poetic language, appropriate sources, and appropriate genres in order to do so. The aesthetics and criticism of salon and small literary circles that had produced and dominated the leading trends in Russian poetry is thus exposed as inimical to the new project of creating a national literature.

THE DEVELOPING DEBATES ON *narodnost'* and romanticism attracted the attention of Aleksandr Pushkin (1799–1837) while he was still in internal exile on his family's estate in Mikhailovskoe. The various uses to which the two terms were being put bothered his sense of order (he was concerned by the lack of clear and precise writing in Russian prose, the lack of a "metaphysical language"),[16] and he responded with drafts of two definitional articles, "O poezii klassicheskoi i romanticheskoi" ("On Poetry Classical and Romantic," taking his title from a chapter of de Staël's *De l'Allemagne*), and the other without a title, usually published as "O narodnosti v literature" ("On *Narodnost'* in Literature"). Some date both articles to 1825; some date the second to 1826. While certain writers had reduced romanticism and *narodnost'* to near synonyms and others had used *narodnost'* to trouble the distinction between the romantic and classical, making those terms far less useful than *narodnost'* itself, Pushkin defines his terms separately. Moreover, he seems to be at some pains to separate the terms: not once in the article on *narodnost'* does he mention romanticism, and not once in the article on romanticism does he use *any* form of a word related to the noun *narod*. The terms are clearly not equivalent for him, though neither are they entirely unrelated.

In attempting to clarify the term *narodnost'*, Pushkin does not go along with M. Dmitriev in his critique of Viazemsky, using Ancillon to insist on the distinction between the *national* and the *populaire*. Rather, both of these senses play a role in Pushkin's definition.[17] Pushkin begins instead by critiquing the usage of others:

Some time ago it became customary for us to speak of *narodnost'*, demand *narodnost'*, to complain of the lack of *narodnost'* in literary works, but no one has thought to define what he understands by the word *narodnost'*.

One of our critics, it seems, considers that *narodnost'* consists in choosing subjects from the history of our country.

But it is difficult to deny Shakespeare in his *Othello, Hamlet, Measure for Measure,* etc., the merit of great *narodnost'*; Vega and Calderón are constantly moving to all parts of the world and take the subjects of their tragedies from Italian novellas and French lays. Ariosto sings praises to Charlemagne, French knights, and the Chinese princess. Racine took his tragedies from ancient history.

It is difficult, nonetheless, to contest for all of these writers the merit of great *narodnost'*. On the other hand, as Prince Viazemsky has rightly observed, *what is there of a national nature in the "Petriada" and "Rossiada" besides names?* What is there of a national nature in Xenia, who discusses parental authority with her confidante in iambic hexameter in the middle of Dmitrii's encampment?

Others see *narodnost'* in words, that is, they take joy in the fact that they use Russian expressions when expressing themselves in Russian.[18]

Annotators of Pushkin's critical prose have suggested a variety of candidates for the first critic, from Bulgarin[19] to Küchelbecker[20] to Ryleev and even Somov and Viazemsky.[21] Pushkin may not, in fact, have had any single critic in mind. Attempts to make use of national subjects in the theater in Russia date to the later eighteenth century, which also produced the concept of "*sklonenie na nashi nravy*" (adaptation to our ways) for the Russianizing of borrowed themes and characters. This tradition was readily incorporated into the new thinking being done around the term *narodnost'*, but sometimes with additions or reservations (like Pushkin's here) that reflected dissatisfaction with the results of multiple attempts along these lines (recall Turgenev's complaints of Frenchmen with Russian names on the stage and Somov's use of the example of Schiller). The theater is central to Pushkin's thinking on the subject: most of his examples come from drama, though a few refer to epic.

The second objection that Pushkin raises to this method (taking it first in the analysis here) is that national historical themes are insufficient to produce *narodnost'*. He quotes Viazemsky on two Russian epic poems where the themes are insufficient, and follows this up with his own example from the theater, from Ozerov's *Dimitry Donskoi* (1807). In quoting Viazemsky here, though, he is making an argument against him: Viazemsky had written a praise-filled introduction to Ozerov's works in 1817, in which he had indicated that Ozerov's tragedies "already belong somewhat to the new dramatic genre, the so-called *romantic*."[22] Pushkin had protested this characterization to Viazemsky vehemently. Given the close relationship *narodnost'* and romanticism had taken in Viazemsky's thought, it is as if Pushkin now felt obliged to add, "and he hasn't any *narodnost'* either," in spite of the national historical theme of the play.

Pushkin's first, and more lengthy, objection is that writers who undoubtedly have the "merit of great *narodnost'*" do not by any means limit themselves to national themes, nor is that merit absent from their works set in or involving characters from other nations. Pushkin is warning that narrow nationalism will not produce *narodnost'* in a manner that is suggestively parallel to Somov's example of Goethe. Pushkin's first example is Shakespeare, but rather than emphasizing Shakespeare's ability to embody the national characteristics of other nations as Somov did with Goethe, Pushkin suggests that Shakespeare remains palpably an Englishman, a part of English literature, in his works with foreign settings.[23] In a later draft article on Pogodin's drama *Marfa Posadnitsa* from 1830, Pushkin gives some specific examples of what he here relates to *narodnost'*, in connection with a discussion of verisimilitude: "If we will suppose verisimilitude lies in the strict observation of costume, colors, time and place, we shall see here as well that the greatest dramatic writers did not submit to this rule. Shakespeare's Roman lictors retain the customs of London aldermen. Calderón's brave Coriolanus challenges the consul to a duel and throws him his glove. Racine's half-Scythian Hippolyte speaks the language of a young, polite marquis. . . . And in spite of all this, Calderón, Shakespeare and Racine stand on unattainable heights, and their works for the constant object of our study and delight."[24] The *narodnost'* that Pushkin refers to, then, is not as much involved in incorporating foreign material as was Somov's use of the term in relation to Goethe, perhaps because his argument here had the narrow rhetorical goal of refuting the method of national themes.[25] Rather, it points to how Shakespeare remains recognizably an Englishman.

Pushkin refutes the other idea of *narodnost'*—the idea that it resides in language—not with argument, but with the heavy irony of his formulation of the idea. Here too, many suggestions have been made as to the identity of the "others" among the critics who held to this opinion—the more plausible possibilities seem to be Bestuzhev and Katenin. But again, a whole cultural tradition stands behind this idea, and assigning it to any individual would be an over-simplification. Pushkin's irony and impatience seem to be directed toward the endless arguments on style that began with Admiral Shishkov's treatise in 1803 and that still manifested themselves in the newer debates over *narodnost'*. As already noted, Shishkov emphasized the national and patriotic qualities of a particular style, and in the last few years leading up to the 1820s, with the debate over the ballad, his opponents began to argue that it was their style instead that best embodied the national character. In the 1820s, Pushkin began to move from his orthodox Karamzinian youth toward a kind of reconciliation with some of the ideas and methods of the Shishkovite camp.[26] His own language program was moving quickly toward a rapprochement between the two styles. Neither side in the earlier language arguments, then, proved entirely convincing, and recent polemics had introduced so many new aspects into the debate over *narodnost'* that Pushkin saw little need to reduce the problem, once again, to one of language.

After refuting the ways in which other critics had used the terms *narodnost'*, Pushkin turned to a few positive statements, with which the brief draft ends:

> *Narodnost'* in a writer is a merit that can only be fully appreciated by his compatriots—for others it either does not exist or might even seem to be a defect. A learned German is indignant over the courtesy of Racine's heroes; a Frenchman laughs at seeing Calderón's Coriolanus challenging his opponent to a duel. All of these, however, bear the stamp of *narodnost'*.
>
> Climate, form of government, and religious faith give to each nation [*narod*] its particular physiognomy, which to a greater or lesser degree is reflected in the mirror of poetry. There is a way of thinking and feeling, there is a multitude of customs, superstitions, and habits that belong exclusively to a given nation [*narod*].[27]

Pushkin describes *narodnost'* as a merit (*dostoinstvo*), using the same word as Viazemsky and Somov (in relation to Schiller). There appears to be some hesitation as to whether this merit belongs to the writer, as he states here, or to the work, as he implies with the example of Shakespeare, though one might suggest that "in a writer" here is to be understood as "in the works of a writer." The metaphor of the stamp (*pechat'*, the same term as Küchelbecker used, also related to Viazemsky's "*otpechatok*," imprint), of a readable trace in the work, reinforces this. *Narodnost'* is an objective quality, the trace or reflection of the particular cultural and moral physiognomy of a nation in its literature. That this reflection can exist "to a greater or lesser degree" is exactly the problem for Russian writers at this time, for most clearly felt that in Russian literature, the reflection existed in a lesser degree, and they wished it to be greater.

And their judgment is key evidence in determining the presence of *narodnost'*, for Pushkin states that only the compatriots of a writer can fully appreciate this presence. Such judgments might seem to introduce an element of subjectivity into Pushkin's definition. Pushkin refers, however, not to actual judgments, but only to the capacity to judge or appreciate. He is pointing to a kind of cultural limit in the appreciation of works of literature, insofar as only members of a given *narod* can fully appreciate the *narodnost'* of a work of its literature. But this is only a limit. Pushkin himself has demonstrated an appreciation for the *narodnost'* of Shakespeare and Lope de Vega, among others. He also provides examples of foreigners failing to appreciate certain aspects of particular works that he himself (though he too is a foreign reader) has recognized as bearing the stamp of *narodnost'*. The learned German is none less than August Schlegel in his *Über dramatische Kunst und Literatur,* and the Frenchman none other than Sismondi in his *De la littérature du midi de l'Europe,* both key sources for the formulation of Russian ideas of romanticism and *narodnost'*.[28] There is also a third hidden European in Pushkin's discussion, first revealed by Boris Tomashevskii as being influential on Pushkin's definition of *narodnost'*: Ancillon. Ancillon may have been influential in the initial formulation by Viazemsky of *narodnost'* as a kind of imprint: in discussing what makes a nation, Ancillon wrote, "The nation is really a nation in the highest sense of the word only when it contains the greatest number of unifying elements, chief among them being a common government and a common language. Only then may members of the nation possess a truly national imprint (*empreinte*), a national individuality."[29] This imprint was already a part of the Russian discourse when Pushkin took up the subject of *narodnost'*, so he may have had the idea from there, rather than from Ancillon directly. But another aspect of Pushkin's definition that was not so prominent a part of the Russian discussion may have also had its inspiration in Ancillon, who wrote, in discussing national character: "the ideas, habits, and inclinations prevailing in a people form its character, and works of art will be beautiful in its eyes only to the extent in which it corresponds to the national character."[30] The limit that Pushkin outlines in the appreciation of *narodnost'* seems to be derived from this idea; both the German and the Frenchman failed to see the beauty of a particular moment in a work, but the beauty of it was visible to the author's countrymen because it corresponded to some aspect of the national character.

Pushkin may have been led to Ancillon by a flattering review of his novel in verse, *Evgenii Onegin,* by Nikolai Polevoi, published in the *Moscow Telegraph* in 1825. Polevoi quotes Ancillon to introduce the term *narodnost'* as he is applying it to Pushkin:

> "The main symptom of the elegant is simplicity," wrote one German philosopher—and what could be simpler, more good-natured than this laugh at the expense of the talk of fashionable followers of [Adam] Smith? The same philosopher wrote that "*narodnaia* (*nationale*) literature takes from the imagination that which speaks most powerfully to the mind and character of the nation"—and this *narodnost'*, this accuracy of description of contemporary mores, Pushkin expressed in a masterful way. Onegin is not copied from the French or the English; we see what's ours, hear our own native proverbs, look upon our caprices, which we all were not strangers to at some time in the past.[31]

The possibility of speaking "powerfully to the mind and character of the nation" is something that Pushkin was becoming more and more concerned with at the time, especially in connection with work on his drama, *Boris Godunov.* One of the attractions of Ancillon for Pushkin, and probably for other writers on *narodnost'*, is an implicit connection between the national qualities of a work and the work's popularity. Ancillon seems to promise that if a work reflects the national character, it will be found beautiful by the members of the nation, it will speak to them powerfully. He thus ties together the multiple meanings of the Russian terminology in a way that is very promising for the development of Russian literature, assuming that the writers find a way to embody the national character.[32] If one glances again at Pushkin's definition of *narodnost'*, one can see some latent suggestion that popularity, and specifically popularity among the people for whom the work was written, is a sign of or aspect of *narodnost'*. In an article reviewing the French translation of Krylov's fables,

also published in the *Moscow Telegraph* in 1825, Pushkin makes the connection explicit:

> In conclusion I will say that we all should thank Count Orlov for choosing a truly national [*narodnyi*] poet for introducing to Europe the literature of the North. Of course, not a single Frenchman would dare to place anyone, no matter who he be, above La Fontaine, but we, I think, may be allowed to prefer Krylov to him. *Both of them will eternally remain favorites among their countrymen.* Someone has rightly observed that simple-heartedness (naiveté, bonhomie) is

an inborn feature of the French nation [*narod*]; in contrast, the distinctive trait in our mores is a kind of gay craftiness, a mocking tone, and a picturesque way of expressing ourselves: La Fontaine and Krylov are representatives of the spirits of both nations.[33]

Of the authors Pushkin mentions in the article on *narodnost'*, all were included by Somov in his examples of the popularity of other national literatures, with the notable exception of Racine, whom Somov cites as a negative example. That Pushkin includes Racine alongside Shakespeare here is important, for the opposition between them was critical to his thoughts on the drama. It indicates, among other things, that *narodnost'* is not strictly tied to popularity in all cases.

With the exception of Racine again, all of these authors also appear in Pushkin's draft essay on romanticism as examples of romantic writers. At issue for Pushkin in this essay, however, is not the question of some kind of reflection of national culture. He defines romanticism and classicism in terms of form (understood as genre) and argues against any definition that relies on theme or the spirit in which the work was written. This essay, too, is a definitional essay that begins with the complaint that "our critics have not yet agreed on a clear difference between the classical and romantic types. We owe our confused understanding on this subject to French journalists, who usually assign to romanticism everything that seems to them to be marked by the stamp of dreaminess and German ideology or based on folk [*prostonarodnye*] superstitions and legends: this is the most inexact definition."[34] He goes on to insist that form is central to the difference. The forms of classical poetry are those that were known to the Greeks and Romans: "epics, didactic poems, tragedy, comedy, odes, satires, epistles, *heroides*, eclogues, elegies, epigrams, and fables. And what genres of poetry should be assigned to romantic poetry? Those that were not known to the ancients and those whose earlier forms changed or have been replaced by others."[35] He later notes some of the new forms, with the new feature of rhyme, invented by the troubadours: "the virelai, the ballad, the rondeau, the sonnet, etc."[36]

Pushkin transitions very quickly from his definition into an outline of the history of romantic poetry in Europe (in which the troubadours receive mention). This outline is already familiar, as it is taken from the same European sources, Sismondi, Schlegel, and de Staël (from whom Pushkin took his title for this essay), though Pushkin also makes use of Boileau on French literary history and classical forms.[37] What attracted other Russian writers to the romantic theorists, though, was their focus on the nation and national originality in their historical narratives of romanticism. Pushkin, too, is concerned with native forms and new inventions, and he notes what different nations contributed, but his essay is free of the pathos of arguing for the European forms and the value of the European inventions versus the classical forms. *Narodnost'* is neither a term nor a value in his discussion. In fact, he begins his narrative with the fall of the Roman Empire and the period of the Dark Ages that followed, describing the almost total loss of learning, a point of view very far from the medievalism cultivated by romantics like Schlegel. He is also conscious of the contribution of classical forms to the creation of European forms: note that he includes genres "whose earlier forms changed or have been replaced by others." On the origin of European drama, he observes, "a dim conception of ancient tragedy along with church festivals gave impetus to the composition of mystery plays (*mystères*)."[38] He does not, in this essay, delve into the later development of romantic tragedy, such as that of Shakespeare, but it is clear that it primarily interested him for its innovation upon classical forms.[39]

Pushkin's essays on *narodnost'* and romantic poetry, then, are strictly separated in their concerns. *Narodnost'* is a merit, a stamp in a work that reflects national culture and thus promises a certain popularity to the work. Romantic poetry is poetry in European genres or European forms of classical genres. The terminology of the two essays does not interact. Many of the same writers, however, offer examples of both the romantic type of poetry and of *narodnost'*. This raises questions of their relation. For example, does the form of Shakespeare's tragedies also lend those works a degree of *narodnost'*? Or can a work be romantic in form and still lack the merit of *narodnost'*? Within the terms of these two essays, such questions cannot be answered. However, in the period 1828–1830 Pushkin returned to many of the ideas outlined in these essays for new drafts of an introduction to his drama *Boris Godunov* and an essay on Pogodin's drama, *Marfa Posadnitsa*. This is natural, for he was writing *Boris Godunov* in 1825, at the same time as he was working on these earlier draft essays, and his thoughts on romanticism and *narodnost'* were clearly important to his ideas of what he intended for that drama. Preparing now to publish that drama, he wanted to provide it with some kind of introduction, to provide a context for its reception, an explanation of what was behind its innovative form.

In these later discussions, both *narodnost'* and, eventually, romanticism disappear as terms. But the popularity implied in the term *narodnost'* was still of central significance to Pushkin, and the question of whether the romantic form of his drama would, in the Russian context, allow for it to become an important and popular drama caused him no small amount of anxiety. In 1828 in a draft of a letter to the *Moscow Herald,* where an excerpt of the play had been published, Pushkin indicated some obstacles to the publication of the full text of the play. He observed that he had been exiled from Moscow and Petersburg society when working on the play, but had been convinced by the furor in the journals that the time was ripe for a romantic tragedy: "Firmly convinced that the obsolete forms of our theater required reform, I arranged my tragedy according to the system of Our Father Shakespeare."[40] When he studied the journals more closely, however, and saw what was meant by romanticism, he began to doubt the wisdom of his actions. "All of this deeply shook my assurance as an author. I began to suspect that my tragedy was an anachronism."[41] While his private readings of the play in his intimate literary circles in 1826 had met with overwhelming enthusiasm, the initial reception of the published excerpt was far less promising. He was reluctant to publish it, then, because he had concluded that, "brought up under the influence of French literature, the Russians have grown used to rules, confirmed by its criticism, and look unwillingly on anything that does not come under the jurisdiction of these laws."[42]

Nonetheless, in a few years preparations for publication were begun, and in 1830 Pushkin returned to the topic of his trepidation in a draft introduction: "For a long time I could not make up my mind to publish my drama. Up until now my self-esteem was little disturbed by the good or ill success of my poems, or by the favorable or stern judgment of the journals on some verse tale . . . But I sincerely admit that the ill success of my drama would grieve me, for I am firmly convinced that the popular [*narodnye*] rules of Shakespearian drama are proper to our theater, and not the courtly custom of Racine's tragedies, and that any unsuccessful experiment could slow down the reformation of our stage."[43] The focus on romanticism of the earlier letter has been replaced here by a distinction between the popular [*narodnaia*] drama of Shakespeare and the courtly drama of Racine. This opposition is developed in a draft review, from the same year, of Pogodin's *Marfa Posadnitsa,* and this latter essay gives some hints as to why the earlier terminology, which bothered him so much that he wrote two essays in 1825, has been dropped. Here Pushkin elaborates on his earlier ideas concerning the origin of drama:

> Drama was born on the public square and was popular [*narodnoe*] entertainment. The people [*narod*], like children, demand something that will engage their attention [*zanimatel'nost'*], action. Drama presents to them extraordinary and strange events. The people [*narod*] demand strong

sensations; for them even executions are spectacles. Laughter, pity, and fear are the three chords of our imagination, set aquiver by the magic of drama. But laughter soon weakens, and one cannot base a full drama on this alone. The ancient tragedians paid little heed to this mainspring. Popular [*narodnaia*] satire mastered it exclusively and took on dramatic form closer to parody. In this way comedy, which became so perfected with time, was born.[44]

He does not distinguish between ancient or classical drama and European or romantic drama in this account. Instead, he points to the commonality of their origin, the commonality of the public square, of popular entertainment. This was not, however, the end of drama's development: "Drama left the square and, at the demand of an educated and select society, transferred to the palace halls. The poet moved to the court. But in fact, drama remained true to its initial purpose: to affect the crowd, the masses, and engage its curiosity. But here drama abandoned the commonly understood language and took on a fashionable, elite, refined dialect. Hence the important difference between Shakespearian popular [*narodnaia*] tragedy and Racine's court drama."[45] The opposition of romantic versus classical has been left behind for one more relevant to the Russian stage. Racine's drama has proved to be not classical, but the product of the demands of French society, and neo-classical drama in general is the product of European elite society.

In turning to the Russian stage, Pushkin notes that "among us, drama was never a popular [*narodnaia*] need." Russian drama began in the courts and had no influence on popular taste. "Ozerov felt this. He tried to give us a popular [*narodnaia*] tragedy and imagined it would suffice to choose his subject from national [*narodnaia*] history, having forgotten that France's poet [Racine] took all his subjects from Roman, Greek, and Hebrew history and that the most popular [*narodnye*] tragedies of Shakespeare are borrowed from Italian novellas."[46] One sees here the return of some of his ideas on *narodnost'*, and now it is possible to explain the inclusion of Racine in the earlier article: his *narodnost'* is simply of a different type than Shakespeare's, having to do with the different nature of French society, the different audience for which it was intended. Where Ozerov failed to create a national/popular tragedy, Pushkin hoped to succeed, and the means he chose was to follow the example of the form of the popular drama of Shakespeare. This meant that Russian drama had to take the reverse course of the development of European drama, and the question of whether this was possible heightened Pushkin's anxiety: "Could our tragedy, modeled on the example of Racine's tragedies, throw off its aristocratic habits? How could it go from its measured, weighty, and decorous dialogue to the rude openness of the people's [*narodnye*] passions, to the free judgments of the square? How could it shed its servility, get along without the rules to which it had become accustomed, without the forced accommodation of everything Russian to everything European? Where, from whom [can one] learn a dialect comprehensible to the people [*narod*]? What are the passions of this people [*narod*], of what fiber the chords of its heart? Where would it find an echo? In short, where are the spectators, where is the public?"[47] Pushkin wanted more than a little popular success with his *Boris Godunov*. He wanted to transform the institution of the Russian theater, to make it relevant to the broader public and to engage that public as its audience; to make it, in other words, a part of the national literature. And the question was: how to do so? This question, again, seems to have been planted by Küchelbecker's critique of the elitism of the elegiac school and its failure to meet the needs of a national literary audience. Pushkin's draft essays of 1825 on romanticism and *narodnost'* developed key ideas related to dramatic form and the imprint of the character of the people or nation (*narod*) in dramatic works, but in those essays, they were strictly separate. The question that cannot be formed on the basis of those two essays, of the relationship between form and popularity, turned out to be the one that most concerned Pushkin, and was directly linked to his hopes for *Boris Godunov*. In Europe, Greece, and England, popular drama developed in response to its audience and form followed function, but for the Russian dramatist was there any guarantee that function would follow form, that a popular audience would appear for a tragedy along Shakespearean lines? The reversal of the question, the turning of the discourse from one of description to one of prescription, put in doubt the link. Perhaps this is why the two terms, *narodnost'* and romanticism, are so strictly separated in 1825. The question of their linkage was to be answered by *Boris Godunov*.

Later, Pushkin put aside the terminology of romanticism and *narodnost'*, because the discourse in which they were implicated did not answer his most pressing questions. The European narratives of the development of romanticism proved unsatisfactory in their description of the development of drama: there was commonality between ancient and European drama, and the denigrated neo-classical drama turned out to have its own social foundations. Other Russian writers had found similar problems in the romantic/classic dichotomy and had focused instead on *narodnost'*. But the European discourse on national form was largely descriptive, while Russian literature, everyone agreed, needed a prescription, a way to increase its reflection of the national characteristics. Pushkin's own experience with *Boris*

Godunov, his atttempt to use a European national/popular form to engage the Russian context, put very much into doubt for him such a prescription. If Russian society was not ready to accept such forms, then they could become just more forms imposed from above and their whole meaning would be distorted (the reaction against the German spirit introduced by Zhukovsky's ballads is an example of this). How could Russian literature and the broader Russian society, so long separate, become conjoined?

Pushkin thus takes very seriously the role of the national poet, which is to address a national audience. This is a new authorial role, introduced by the paradigm of "national literature," that involves a relationship to a newly imagined national audience. In a recent article on Pushkin as a critic, Caryl Emerson observes that "writers of the Golden Age participated in a complicated paradigm shift," which she associates with the professionalization of criticism and the rise of the journal and book market. Criticism went from the salon, with its semiprivate genres and intimate circles, to the role of mediator of public opinion and the relationship between writer and audience.[48] Even more recently, Melissa Frazier has argued, eloquently and convincingly, that the frequently cited rise of the literary marketplace in the 1820s and 1830s and the emergence of literary professionalism may have less to do with actual changes in literary commerce—which, when examined closely, are rather elusive in the period in question—and more to do with romantic theory about a literary marketplace. "Romanticism," she suggests instead, "simulates not just writers but also readers and the relationship between the two," and romantic aesthetics simulates a literary marketplace so that the writer-critic can attain to "critical omnipotence."[49] Frazier finds the origin of this romantic theory of the literary market in the Jena journal *Athenaeum.* One might add that the advance of the broadly romantic paradigm of "national literature" contributes to and reinforces this reimagination of authorial roles and literary audience.

As seen throughout this study, in Russian and Czech letters in the first third of the nineteenth century, new conceptions of literary language and genre founded themselves on the nation. In order to introduce new literary values, writers appealed to the imagined community of the nation. Writers acted as if the nation existed in order to introduce innovations in genre and literary language that "responded" to that national community. What is seen here, in Pushkin and Küchelbecker's concerns with addressing a larger, national audience, and in the Czech concerns in the late 1820s with the problem of an elite literature that does not address the needs of common life, is a transformation of the imagined relationship between author and audience conditioned by the new, national basis of literary value. The classicist understanding of literary value did not consider the mass market and its needs and so the separate markets and audiences for mass literature and high literature were not a problem. But the nation is always imagined on the model of an individual human, with an identity that is projected as unitary. A national literature, then, projects a unified literary marketplace and presumes that works can address that national collective en masse. Any rift between mass literature and high literature is a wound in the national body that must be healed.

This problem became the basis for the conflict in German letters between Bürger and Schiller in the 1790s.[50] Bürger had developed an ideal conception of national popularity (*Volkstümlichkeit*) that would join the nation as a whole audience for the right literary work. *Volkstümlichkeit* entered the German critical vocabulary in the *Sturm und Drang* period and particularly in the work of Bürger. The term is similar to the Russian term *narodnost'* in its conjoining of the national and the popular/folksy. Both aspects are evident in the definition in *Grimms Deutsches Wörterbuch*, where the term *Volkstümlichkeit* is defined as "whatever makes up the unique essence of the people, that is, its national character. Harmony with the essence, the conception, the feelings of the uncultivated, naïve people, its lower strata."[51] Schiller's harsh review of Bürger's second edition of poems (1791) is in large part a critique of what he saw as Bürger's naive concept. Schiller observes, "A popular poet in the sense in which Homer was for his age, or the troubadours for theirs, might be sought in vain in our time. . . . Now a great disparity is evident between the *elite* of a nation, and its *masses*. . . . It would therefore be futile to cast together arbitrarily in a single concept what has long since ceased to be one."[52] But Schiller does not give up on the unifying ideal of poetry. Far from it, for "it is poetry almost alone that reunites the separated powers of the soul, that occupies head and heart, acumen and wit, reason and imagination in a harmonious cooperation that, as it were, restores in us *human wholeness*."[53] The ideas Schiller would develop later in *On the Aesthetic Education of Man* (1795) are already here in embryo. But poetry does not only reunite the faculties of the individual. The split between the elite and the masses can also be healed: "A popular poet for our times would therefore merely have the choice between the *easiest thing in the world,* and the *hardest:* either to accommodate himself exclusively to the powers of comprehension of the great mass, and to renounce the applause of the cultivated class, or to compensate for the enormous distance between the two by the greatness of his art, and to pursue both ends together."[54] In

Schiller's view, Bürger in attempting the latter had too often given in to the former. Perfect art, rather than popular art, was Schiller's means to the creation of a unified national public and a proper *Volkstümlichkeit*.

Intimations of a similar problem emerge, as already noted, in Russian criticism of the mid-1820s in debates in which *narodnost'* plays a prominent role, and the term would continue to play a key role in Slavophile discourse in the 1830s and 1840s, in which the rift between the elite and the masses was taken as a fundamental problem. Thus far, discussion of the corresponding Czech term, *národnost*, has been avoided. That is not because the term did not occur in Czech literary discourse. But it occurred with less frequency than in Russian discourse and was in general a far less problematic term, though it was still prominent in the discourse on the national literature. It did not initially seem to require special definition and treatment. Unlike Russian, Czech had a separate term, *lid,* to refer to the people, and so, by the nineteenth century, "*národ*" and words derived from it were used much more frequently in the modern sense of nation and only occasionally in reference to the common people. *Národnost,* then, unambiguously meant "nationality." The signs of a particular nationality can still be multiple, from form of government to dress, to habit and language. As already noted, however, in the Czech situation and in Jungmann's program the almost exclusive sign of Czech nationality was taken to be the Czech language. In the early 1820s, then, the term was narrow to a peculiar degree.

One can see an example of a slight broadening of this narrow usage in Kollár's discussion of folk songs (chapter 9): "The songs of the common people are precious and useful not only linguistically, but also in regard to aesthetics and ethnology. They are images in which each nation paints and presents its character most faithfully; they are the history of its internal world and life, the keys to the sanctuary of *národnost*; and whoever is unable or unwilling to open it with them will never know even what humanity, which is manifested in pastoral songs no less than in the Egyptian pyramids, is like."[55] The folk songs are artifacts of language, and as such, they are the keys to the sanctuary of *národnost.* Language remains the primary sign of nationality. But the folk songs are more than just language, they are an aesthetic use of language and so are artifacts that reflect especially on the aesthetic particularity of the Slavic nation. They are a special kind of sign, relating to a particular aspect of the nationality, and in that sense, Kollár moves beyond the general use of language to stand in for all other signs. Kollár reads these songs as reflecting the synthesizing and balanced nature of the nation in its aesthetic and intellectual undertakings.

Jungmann ended his article on *klasičnost* with two paragraphs on the topic of *národnost*. These were not, however, included in the published version, edited by Palacký. Jungmann's remarks on *národnost* are aimed at a certain broadening of the concept as well: "There are two infallible signs of *národnost*: history [*dějiny*] and language, or written history [*historie*] and literature, the fruits of national life."[56] His remarks on the history of the nation, however, are quite short and commonplace. Aside from the most general positive characteristics, he credits the nation with twice saving Europe from "a cruel yoke—that of the Avars and the Tatars" and with defending its language and religion against all of Europe.[57] His remarks on language and literature are somewhat longer, for this sign is "even more important than the first."[58] As in his 1806 dialogues, he here equates the loss of a language with the loss of a nationality, and a literature remains the primary means to preserving one. There is little in these remarks that could have displeased the censor, so Palacký's removal of them for publication may represent some dissatisfaction with them. He himself had already authored two articles on Czech literary history in which the Czech defense of its nationality is conceived primarily as the defense of its language.[59] But as a budding historian, he may have considered Jungmann's general remarks on Czech history to be insufficient.

Moreover, he may have had his own ideas about the expansion of the term *národnost*. Though he cut Jungmann's discussion of the term, he also edited the term into the body of Jungmann's text, replacing Jungmann's "*národovost*." This had been Jungmann's translation for the term *Volkstümlichkeit* in Pölitz's text, and it can be opposed to his use of the term *národnost* for *Nationalität*. Jungmann's use of two distinct terms in the article was thus eliminated by Palacký.[60] In his own articles on Czech literary history, written in German, Palacký had made use of the term *Volkstümlichkeit* alongside the term *Nationalität*.[61] If Palacký had the original as well as Jungmann's translation in editing the article, his usage of the term appears as a distinct attempt to broaden the term, allowing it to encompass both German terms. Even if he did not, the context in which the term appears gives it a meaning that is counter to Jungmann's usual conception: it is included in a list of things that are given to the language by the poets who cultivate the language. That language should have to be cultivated with *národnost* implies that *národnost* is not simply automatically reflected in language and that language itself may not be the only or best sign of *národnost*. It opens the possibility that *národnost* might as well be embodied in customs, traditions, or other cultural realia that in a given use of language, such as in certain genres of poetry, may not be reflected very well or at all. As the Czech national movement grew, such ideas gained more relevance and the initial language focus of Jungmann's program gave way to broader cultural work and activities that kept conceptions of the Czech national identity growing and expanding. A literary program that began by projecting an imaginary nation in order to create the simulacrum of a literature founded in a national community then attempted to address that nation, to try to actually constitute that nation as a real social phenomenon, and thus grew into a full-blooded national movement.

Toward the Reform of Institutions
Education and Narodnost'

The classical literary canon was never only a literary canon. It was, from the moment of its earliest formation in the work of the Hellenistic critics, always a canon defined for the purposes of education. The epics of Homer, which were foundational school reading throughout late Greek antiquity, were a model not only for literary education, but also for moral, intellectual, and civic education.[1] When this educational model and its literary canon were adopted in the European Renaissance, an idealized picture of a culturally and historically undifferentiated antiquity was both their product and their essential support. That is, classical literary works derived their educational value from their modeling of idealized, timeless cultural values, and the reading and interpretation of these works within that frame reinforced the abstract image of classical antiquity. It would be strange criticism today to cite among Homer's failures the barbarous ethics of his characters or the failures in his scientific understanding of the natural world, but for the French Moderns, such criticisms went to the heart of the values that had been attributed to Homer's works. The rethinking of the classical educational model that they initiated went hand-in-hand with the reconception of the classical literary model that led eventually, as already noted, to a new system of literary value in which the modern nation played a foundational role. Education would be transformed as well by this new relationship to classical antiquity.

Classical literature was not immediately replaced, however, by the national literatures in educational institutions, and its staying power is not entirely ascribable to the inertia of such tradition-bound institutions. Rather, a perspective that differentiates between Greek and Roman literature could still ascribe a fundamental value to one of those model national cultures, as in the German approach to *Bildung,* in which Greek culture played a central role (chapters 4 and 5). The modern Russian term for education is *obrazovanie,* which is a good equivalent to the German *Bildung* in that its etymology points to formation, shaping into an image; but unlike the German term, it was not used as a general term for culture. The Czech term for education, *vzdělání,* is equivalent to the Latin *cultura* and reflects, again, the essential agricultural metaphor of cultivation; it was used as a general term for culture. In both the Czech and Russian cases, the new conception of culture as a *product* of national cultivation focused renewed attention on the educational *process* of cultivation and on the place of Greek and Roman literatures, as well as the national literature and other modern literatures, in that process.

For the Czechs in the early nineteenth century, the fate of their national literature and culture was understood to be intimately connected to the place of Czech language and literature in the schools. Dobrovský's 1792 history of the cultivation of the Czech language (see chapter 3) was also a history of Czech learning, of Czech culture, and of the Czech nation. He concludes on a rather pessimistic note, observing that with the new decree (1780), which made knowledge of German an entrance requirement for the Latin secondary schools, the prospects for the renewed development of the Czech language as a cultivated language were highly diminished.[2] Jungmann also emphasized the educational barriers presented to Czechs by the institutionalization of education in German, with the result that few Czechs were able to occupy positions in the Austrian bureaucracy.[3] Slavomil's closing wishes in Jungmann's second dialogue indicate that Jungmann understood very well the effect of institutional structures on the language culture, so cogently delineated by Dobrovský in his history. But he held out hope for change: "Before we leave for home, let me yet pronounce a few pious wishes, since these are good for your dreams: for our dear tongue to be reintroduced to the schools and town halls, for youth to be required to learn Czech, because unfortunately, they only learn what they must!–for a large society of Slavic scholars to appear that would have a patron and workers in every province, and for the Slavic book trade to be improved, because there is nothing more useful than it in the world. . . ."[4] Jungmann also knows that several of those things are circumstances beyond his control, but he suggests that if the Czechs were of one voice in asking the emperor for changes, they would not be denied.[5] When, in 1816, a decree by the Imperial Study Commission allowed Czech-speaking pupils in Latin gymnasia to receive instruction in Czech language as a subject, but only in Czech-speaking and mixed Czech-German areas, Jungmann responded by writing a textbook for that instruction, his *Slovesnost.*[6] Moreover, he worked as a gymnasium professor from 1799 to 1815 in Litoměřice, where he offered Czech language as an elective subject beginning in 1800.[7] It was during this period that he elaborated the program for the Czech literary and national revival that made him the intellectual father to all the Czech patriots to come. Demands for instruction in Czech became a constant platform of Czech national political expression in the nineteenth century.

In Russia, by 1800, the problem of education was usually framed as a problem of the education of the upper classes and the obstacle that their excessive Francophilia posed for national identity. Denis Fonvizin had satirized Russian Gallomania in his comedy *Brigadir* (*The Brigadier*, 1768–1769) and had examined problems of education and moral upbringing in his comic masterpiece, *Nedorosl'* (*The Minor*, 1782). As the national perspective on literature developed in the early nineteenth century, writers began to connect the problem of the education of the upper classes by French tutors to the lack of a national character in Russian literature. Already as a young Moscow University student and a member of the Friendly Literary Society, Merzliakov had linked the problem of the national spirit in literature to the Russian forms of education in a speech entitled "O trudnostiakh ucheniia" ("On the Difficulties of Education," see chapter 1). Admiral Shishkov, in the opening of his tract *Rassuzhdenie o starom i novom sloge rossiiskogo iazyka* (see chapter 2), named education as the source of the Francophilia he felt was ruining Russian letters: "The origin of this is in the form of education: for what knowledge can we have in our natural language when the children of our highest-ranking boyars and courtiers, from their first moments, find themselves in the hands of Frenchmen, adhere to their mores, learn to disdain their own customs, impalpably take on their entire way of thought and understanding, speak their language more fluently than their own, and become so infected by bias for them that not only do they never do exercises in their own language and are not embarrassed not to know it, many of them boast and glory in that most shameful ignorance as if it were some kind of embellishment of their merit."[8] Following Napoleon's burning of Moscow, Murav'ev-Apostol railed against the education of Russian nobles by French tutors, based on French educational models, and also connected that to the lack of progress in Russian literature. He proposed, instead, that a return to the ancient classics would allow Russia to develop its national taste and a national literature. And while Count Sergei Uvarov did not broadly attack the education of nobles or Russian Francophilia, he did argue for the greater value of Greek literary models over French in the development of an independent national literature (see chapter 7). In this chapter, one more program will be examined, the philosophical program of Dmitry Venevitinov (1805–1827), which connected the problem of education to the lack of a proper national literature and proposed an educational solution to remedy that lack. Then, there will follow a consideration of the direction in which actual educational institutions went in subsequent years in both the Bohemian lands and in Russia, and in particular to the place of the classical literatures and the national literature in the curriculum.

PUSHKIN WAS NOT THE ONLY one who was less than satisfied with the prescriptions for Russian literature that were emerging in the dialogue around romanticism and *narodnost'*. Another who came to similar thoughts concerning the appropriation of European literary forms was the poet Dmitry Venevitinov, who wrote in 1826, "we, as if we were predestined to contradict the history of literature, received the forms of literature before its essence."[9] What led him to such a conclusion, however, was not, as it was for Pushkin, doubts about the applicability to the Russian context of European narratives of romanticism and national literature raised by the concrete problem of the reception of a literary work, but rather a more abstract historical-philosophical argument on education. Venevitinov was secretary of the Moscow Obshchestvo liubomudriia (Society of Philosophy— *liubomudrie* being a Slavonic calque of the Greek word "philosophy"), a group of Moscow University graduates who studied and discussed German philosophy, and were especially enamored of Schelling. The group met in secret from 1823 to 1825, when in the aftermath of the Decembrist uprising, they burnt their protocols and halted their meetings. Many were involved in the founding, in 1827, of the *Moscow Herald,* including Venevitinov, and in 1826 he drafted an essay outlining the envisioned role of that journal. The essay did not appear in the journal, but was published posthumously in 1831 with Venevitinov's collected works under the title, "Neskol'ko myslei v plan zhurnala" ("A Few Thoughts on the Plan for a Journal"). In his manuscripts, though, the title was "O sostoianii prosveshcheniia v Rossii" ("On the State of Enlightenment in Russia").

For Venevitinov, the literary forms Russia had taken from Europe were just a subset of the various forms of cultivated and enlightened life that had been borrowed by Russia, to its own detriment: "The source and cause of the slowness of our successes in enlightenment was the very rapidity with which Russia assumed the outward forms of learning and raised a sham edifice of literature without any basis, without any exertion of its inner strength."[10] Venevitinov's language here marks the essay as a reply to a question that had been posed by Bestuzhev-Marlinsky in his series of survey articles for the almanac *Polar Star*. Some development of Bestuzhev-Marlinsky's position is necessary to contextualize Venevitinov's reply. After reviewing the history of the Russian language in the first survey, Bestuzhev-Marlinsky proposed "running through the political obstacles that have slowed the pace of enlightenment and success in literature in Russia."[11] In the second survey, he opened with laments that the love of literature and the patriotism shown during the years of the Napoleonic Wars had faded and that the Francophilia of the prewar years had returned and become even stronger. The result was the grinding halt that Russian literature had come to in 1823 (the year he was surveying as it came to a close). He further promised that "of the other causes that have slowed the pace of literature, we will speak at the proper time."[12] That time turned out to be in his third survey, written in early 1825. That survey begins with a crude conception of what the development of a literature ought to look like: opening with an age of genius, of great creativity, followed by an age of mediocrity, where songs and comedy replace lyrics and tragedy, and leading ultimately to a period of histories, criticism and satires. "That's how it was everywhere, except in Russia, for here the age of analysis precedes the age of creativity; we have criticism, and literature does not exist; we have become sated without eating, we have become grumbling old men in our youth! Let us attempt to solve the riddle of the causes of such a strange phenomenon."[13] The idea of literature's slow development had now become the assertion that Russia had no literature in the proper sense. The causes he cites, however, are further developments of the same causes he had listed earlier: "The first is contained in the fact that we are raised by foreigners. With our mother's milk we sucked a-nationality [*beznarodnost'*] and awe for foreign things only."[14] As others had before him, Bestuzhev here connects the earlier discussion of Francophilia and education and joins it to the problem of the national literature. In general, Russian education is the cause of the lack of *narodnost'* in Russian literature and culture, which cannot measure up to its models, so Russian literature resorts to criticism. In fact, Russians cannot even understand the true value of its models: "We are too impassive, too lazy and insufficiently enlightened to see all that is sublime, appreciate all that is great, in foreign authors."[15] The second and main cause is related to the first: "Now we are beginning to feel and to think, but gropingly. Life absolutely requires movement and a developing intellect, activity; it wants at least to stir when it cannot fly, but, since it is unoccupied by politics, it is quite natural that its activity grabs at anything that comes along, and since the sources of our intellect are quite trivial for serious undertakings, is it any wonder that it has thrown itself into nepotism and gossip?!"[16] The political obstacles of the earlier essay have been transformed into the lack of the possibility of political activity in the current situation. The Russian intellect is spoiled by its education and its lack of meaningful activity.

However crude Bestuzhev's conception of the proper development of a literature (Pushkin would critique it mercilessly in another draft article), the idea that Russian literature had developed improperly or in reverse order was becoming a common one (Pushkin himself had come to such a conclusion concerning the popular drama). Venevitinov agrees with this and with Bestuzhev's negation of Russian literature, calling the edifice of Russian literature false and the status of Russia in the literary world "entirely negative"; he did not even entirely agree that criticism did exist.[17] He also agreed that the state of Russian learning was bad, that education, in some sense, was to blame. But he was not concerned with Francophilia in the narrow sense. He was troubled by the historical development of Russia's enlightenment in comparison to that of model European nations. Somov had tried to keep open the European historical narratives of romanticism for the inclusion of Russia, drawing parallels in Russia to European phenomena whenever possible. But if one were to take seriously these historical narratives, including the similar narratives of the development of European civilization and learning by writers like François Guizot or Hegel, and if the process of this slow, organic development was at all important to the end results, then Russia's historical separation from Europe and its late appropriation of European forms of learning would continue to be a serious problem. This is the issue Venevitinov proposes to confront.

Like Küchelbecker and Somov, Venevitinov begins with first principles, but his first principles make a philosophical argument, rather than a literary one. He starts off with Socratic self-knowledge (*samopoznanie*), which is the goal of all our actions and the goal of humanity, driving our search for enlightenment. "From this perspective, we must look upon each nation [*narod*] as on a separate person that directs all its mental [*nravstvennye*] efforts, marked by the stamp of a particular character, toward self-knowledge."[18] Venevitinov here makes explicit one of the principles central to the discourse on national character: treating nations as if they were individual humans. The "stamp of a particular character" that marks all the efforts of a nation in the intellectual realm, including literature, is exactly what was meant by *narodnost'* for many Russian writers. But Venevitinov does not use that term here, nor anywhere at all in this essay. He does use the term elsewhere, however, and its sense is at least related to this stamp (see below). This individual character of a nation is the result of a long development: "Among all the independent nations, enlightenment developed from a native [*otechestvennoe*], so to speak, origin: their works, having reached a certain degree of perfection and becoming, as a result, a part of worldwide achievements of the intellect, did not lose their differentiating character."[19] Russia, on the other hand borrowed everything from outside itself.

If this had not been the case, "if [the Russian intellect] had followed a natural process, then the character of the nation would have developed by its own strength and would have taken on an independent [*samobytnyi*] direction, appropriate to it."[20] Such an independent development, based on the nation's own intellectual resources, was essential in Venevitinov's conception. In this sense, even the recent advance of romanticism and the break with classicist rules represented no progress: "Such a liberation of Russia from the fetters of convention and from the ignorant self-assurance of the French would have been her triumph, if it had been a matter of independent reasoning; but unfortunately, it did not produce significant benefit; for the cause of our weakness where literature is concerned consists not so much in our manner of thought, but in our inactivity of thought. We cast off the French rules not because we were able to refute them with some kind of positive system, but only because we could not apply them to some works of modern writers in which we took pleasure in spite of ourselves. Thus false rules have been replaced by the absence of any rules at all."[21] Venevitinov believed that the fine arts had to have a founding in philosophy, had to be based on an aesthetic system, and in his criticism, he was principled and grounded, and demanded the same of other critics, so that there could be a principled discussion when disagreement arose. He diagnoses here a problem with the paradigm shift in literary values in Russian letters. The old classicist values had been discarded because they did not respond to the new trends in literature, but they had not been replaced by a new system of values. He senses the need for such a new system and connects the lack of this new system to the lack of an independent national system of thought.

Venevitinov proposes what appears to be a rather radical solution to Russia's problem, to its lack of intellectual independence and activity: "Given Russia's intellectual state, only one means presents itself to anyone who takes her welfare as the goal of his activity. It would be necessary to put a full stop to the current of her literature and force her to think more and produce less. . . . For the sake of this goal it would be necessary to remove Russia somewhat from the current progress of other nations, hide from her view all the unimportant events in the literary world that uselessly distract her attention and, relying on the firm bases of philosophy, present her a full picture of the development of the human intellect, a picture in which she could see her own destiny."[22] By no means should this be read as an early Slavophile document, though it certainly shares a similar concern that Russia develop her own resources. What Venevitinov means by this, however, is not Russia's distinct traditions and customs, but her intellect, and in order to develop it he would certainly not give up the European philosophical tradition. In fact, that tradition is precisely what he proposes that Russia needs to learn. Like Uvarov, he also points to the special value of the classics for Russia's literary and philosophical education: "It would not be without benefit to turn Russia's particular attention to the ancient world and its works."[23] For Venevitinov, this meant Plato and Aristotle more than Homer and Sophocles, but he confirmed the assertions of Uvarov and Murav'ev-Apostol that Russia needed a classical education in order to develop its own distinct national culture.

Venevitinov proposes that a sufficient means for this re-education of Russia would be a journal dedicated to philosophy and the application of philosophy to the arts and sciences. Given the large goals and radical means for achieving them that he has outlined, the proposal of a philosophical journal as the solution is almost anti-climactic. It had the advantage, however, of being realizable, at least to a degree. Over the long term, it might even bring about the desired benefits: "And so, philosophy and its application to all epochs of the arts and sciences—these are the subjects that deserve our special attention, subjects all the more essential to Russia because she still needs a solid basis in the aesthetic sciences [*iziashchnye nauki*] and will find this basis, this token of her independence [*samobytnost'*] and thus her intellectual freedom in literature, only in philosophy, which will force her to develop her own strengths and formulate a system of thought."[24] The essential new aesthetic grounding that Venevitinov sought was thus to be found in a distinct national tradition of thought—for him, as for so many others, the new system of aesthetic values would put the nation and its unique identity at its center.

The *Moscow Herald* was begun in 1827 by Venevitinov and his colleagues from the Society of Philosophy. It closed in 1830. If the journal did not live up to his expectations and the goals he had envisioned for it, he and his colleagues did contribute greatly to the development of philosophical thought in Russia. One member of the group, Ivan Kireevsky, by the late 1820s began to develop ideas that made him a leader among the Slavophiles. Questions of Russia's historical development, its national character, and its relation to Europe or "the West" and its cultural forms and development were to become central to Russian philosophical debate, to the competition between westernizing tendencies and Slavophile alternatives. Both sides struggled with the problem outlined here by Venevitinov, which had already been developed to a degree by the debates over romanticism and *narodnost'* in the early to mid-1820s.

Venevitinov's denial of Russian culture and enlightenment because of its inorganic development fits into a larger tradition in Russian critical thought in the early nineteenth century: a cultural tradition of denying the cultural tradition. Andrei Turgenev may have been the first to deny the existence of Russian literature based on its lack of a national character, but he was eventually followed by numerous others. Viazemsky revived the judgment in the 1820s, and Belinsky would state it most famously in 1834. The lack of an organic national development was felt by Somov, too, who tried to compensate for that lack in his discussion of Russian literature. Venevitinov sees no way around the lack other than its correction by forcing Russia to undergo an independent development. His own discourse broadens the question, so that not only literature, but learning and culture in general in Russia can be said not to exist in a proper form. This line of thought was developed most radically by Petr Chaadaev in his *Philosophical Letters*, undertaken in 1829. Chaadaev considered that Russia was entirely outside of the development of Christian civilization in the West, which was the only true line of historical development, and left little hope of Russia joining or contributing to this development. In spite of the fact that verdicts were handed down by critic after critic in the early nineteenth century that Russia had no literature, this was only rarely an actual denial of the entire literary tradition (Chaadaev and perhaps Venevitinov being exceptions). Rather, it was usually a polemical move to project an alternative ideal for the literary tradition that had not yet been embodied.

Czech critics never sided with such a verdict on their own tradition. The judgment that there is no Czech literature worthy of the name was continually offered by those outside patriotic circles, and Czech critics repeatedly had to defend their own tradition and their decision to work in it against such a charge, even as they offered alternative ideals for the future of their literature. For example, Šafařík asked, "Is it proper, because *** is not a poet, because **, or * is not, to straightaway pronounce the conclusion that there is no Czech poesy?"[25] On the other hand, he offers a withering critique not only of the current poetic school, but of the entire history of Czech literature, finding no classics among its exaggerated "thousands and thousands" of poets.[26] Jungmann, too, in his article on *klasičnost* flirts with the idea that there is no Czech literature yet, and suggests that if Czech literature is not determined to move forward, the whole project should be given up and the Czechs should join in the stream of German literature.[27] The latter suggestion is more of a warning than a real suggestion, though, for the idea was truly unthinkable for Czech patriots, all of whom had made the conscious decision to be Czech and not German. This difference in Czech and Russian criticism reflects the different degree and nature of the hegemony exercised by French culture over the Russians in comparison with that of German culture over the Czechs. Russian critics could deny their literature within their critical discourse because it was not threatened from the outside with absorption into the French cultural realm. Czech critics could only whisper of the danger and hint at the lacks within their literary realm.

In Russia the negative assessment continually brought forth its counterpart. Chaadaev's pessimism about Russia's place in European culture is countered by Ivan Kireevsky's optimism, expressed first in his article entitled "XIX [Deviatnadtsatyi] vek" ("The Nineteenth Century"), also from 1829.[28] For Kireevsky, Russia's status as a latecomer to enlightenment indicated, much as it did for Kollár concerning the Slavs and Uvarov for the Russians, that Russia was soon to take a leading role and bring Europe to its true goals and ends. This was to become a prominent point of view among the Russian Slavophiles.[29] Kollár was not the only one to have considered the historical role to be played by his nation in relation to European enlightenment and education. Most other conceptions, though, focused on the Czech nation, rather than the Slavic nation. Even the journal *Krok,* which was programmatically Slavic-oriented, in the announcement of its goals in the first issue focused on the role of the Czech nation within the Slavic family:

"Our place of situation among other nations, the stories of our tribe, and the learning we have thus far achieved prove to us that our mission is to serve the transmittal of European learning to the educated others of our kin."[30] This mission was also one to which the journal itself, by promoting learned discourse in Czech, could contribute.

LIKE ALL THE OTHER RUSSIAN WRITERS discussed in this section, Venevitinov too addressed the specific issue of the term *narodnost'*. This occurred in a polemical exchange with Polevoi over his review of the first chapter of Pushkin's *Evgenii Onegin*. Venevitinov was dissatisfied with the lack of a proper aesthetic system behind Polevoi's judgments and with his general loose thinking, including his application of the term *narodnost'*: "A few words about *narodnost'*, which the publisher of the *Telegraph* finds in the first chapter of *Onegin*: 'We see,' he says, 'and hear our own native proverbs, look upon our caprices, to which we all were not strangers at some time in the past.' I do not know what is national here [*chto tut narodnogo*], except the names of Petersburg streets and restaurants. In France and England corks also shoot off the ceiling and devotees attend the theater and balls. No, Mr. *Telegraph* publisher! To ascribe excessive things to Pushkin means to detract from the things that truly belong to him. In *Ruslan and Liudmila* he proved to us that he can be a national [*natsional'nyi*] poet."[31] Strikingly, Venevitinov uses the same rhetorical formula as Turgenev, made standard by Viazemsky: What's national about it?! It is clear that Venevitinov does not see *narodnost'* in the aspects of *Onegin* listed by Polevoi, the native proverbs and the caprices of Petersburg society. The example, once again, of *Ruslan and Liudmila* points to a conception of the nation more inclusive of other classes, their language and verbal art. By using the word *natsional'nyi* as a synonym to *narodnyi*, Venevitinov also makes clear the fact that he, like our other writers, uses the term *narodnost'* not only in relation to the folk, the *narod*, as opposed to the upper classes, but in relation to the nation as a whole.

But what exactly Venevitinov meant by the term remains unclear. Like so many of the writers examined here, he found it easier to critique others' use of the term and to give his own examples than to say positively what he meant by the term. But such examples are always ambiguous and require careful interpretation. Polevoi, in his reply, joked that Venevitinov saw *narodnost'* in some unique objects related to peasant life. In response, Venevitinov did manage to say rather more specifically what he meant by the term, though even here, he could not do so without an example:

> It remains for me to say something about *narodnost'* and what I understand
> by that expression. I put *narodnost'* not in *chereviki* [high-heeled women's
> leather boots, worn in Ukraine] or in beards and such (as Mr. Polevoi
> wittily considers), but also not where the publisher of the *Telegraph* seeks it.
> *Narodnost'* is reflected not in images belonging to any particular region, but in
> the very feelings of a poet permeated with the spirit of a single nation [*narod*]
> and living, so to speak, in the development, successes, and differentiation
> of its character. One should not confuse the concept of *narodnost'* with the
> expression of national [*narodnye*] customs: such images only truly please
> us when they are warranted by the proud participation of the poet. Thus,
> for example, Schiller in *William Tell* takes us not only into a new world of
> national life, but also into a new realm of ideas: he captivates because with his
> enflamed rapture he himself belongs to Switzerland.[32]

Narodnost' lies not in any conventional signs or customs belonging to a
nation, then, but in the feelings of a poet who is a central participant in the
enlightenment of the nation, whose works contribute to its development
and differentiation among nations. It reflects an independent national
development and thought. The advance in ideas is critical to *narodnost'*, more
critical than any element of local color. Venevitinov's example here should
be placed alongside Somov's use of Goethe and, in a more limited way,
Pushkin's argument against the sufficiency of national-historical themes:
all emphasize a certain transcendence of national borders and narrow
conceptions of national specificity. Schiller, who was not Swiss, belongs to
Switzerland not because he accurately portrayed its national life through
one of its legends, but because in doing so, he advanced art and contributed
something of Switzerland to the human intellect. Venevitinov's conception
of *narodnost'*, then, has everything to do with the organic development of a
nation's own progress in education and enlightenment and the contribution
that makes to the development of European civilization.

VENEVITINOV HIMSELF WOULD NEVER be in a position to
put his ideas into practice in Russian educational institutions, but Uvarov,
whose ideas were similar, was. In 1810 he married Catherine Razumovsky,
the daughter of the head of the Ministry of National Enlightenment (as the
ministry concerned with public education was called), and was quickly
appointed to the post of superintendant of the St. Petersburg educational
district.[33] That was the same year he had published his *Projet d'une académie*

asiatique, and he began to implement some of his ideas in the reform of the secondary school curriculum in his district beginning in 1811. The new curriculum for the gymnasia was based on the classical languages and designed as a fundamental preparation for university study. Uvarov put into the curriculum Greek and additional Latin, cut the French and German literature hours in half, and added Russian grammar, history, literature, and a few hours of study of Orthodox theology.[34] Uvarov's interest in the development of a distinctly Russian national culture thus led him to augment instruction in the classical languages and literatures as well as in the national literature.

In 1820 Uvarov left the ministry, which had been in Prince Aleksandr Golitsyn's hands since 1816 and had gutted educational institutions and subordinated the ministry to the Holy Synod of the Orthodox Church. But he returned to Tsar Nicholas I's School Committee in 1826 and eventually was appointed minister of national enlightenment in 1833. The 1828 statutes of the School Committee represented the expansion and statewide implementation of Uvarov's 1811 reforms, including the classical gymnasium curriculum and a new emphasis on Russian studies at all school levels.[35] At the gymnasia, the classical languages and literatures made up 16–29 percent of the curriculum (the larger percentage where Greek was taught, the smaller where only Latin was taught) and modern languages and literatures (French and German) 11–19 percent (the smaller number where Greek was taught). Meanwhile, the Russian part of the curriculum—including Orthodox religion, Russian language and literature, Russian history, and geography and statistics—made up 36 percent of the total hours. In the Prussian curriculum, upon which the School Committee modeled its reform, the classical languages made up 46 percent and modern languages only 4 percent of the curriculum.[36] The new Russian curriculum thus gave a comparatively greater emphasis to the modern languages and literatures even as it brought Russia's secondary schools much closer to the Latin school model that had dominated in Europe for centuries.

The new statute for the universities of 1835 under Minister Uvarov required students at all three faculties to take core courses, particularly in Russian history and literature. In addition, it created three new academic departments: Russian history, Russian language and literature, and comparative Slavic studies. The minister justified the addition of the third field as a means to "fathoming *Russian narodnost*," and sent his new Slavic scholars to study with the most prominent European Slavists, including the Czechs Šafařík and Hanka.[37] Uvarov's educational reforms at all levels responded to his conception of how to cultivate an independent national culture and to his ideas of what the particular form of Russia's nationality could be, immortalized in his slogan of "official nationality": Orthodoxy, Autocracy, *Narodnost*.

But if the problematic group for the forging of a Russian national identity had traditionally been the nobility, then Uvarov's reforms of the public school system missed this key constituency. The nobles, in an effort to protect their special status, largely refused to attend the public schools and instead continued to use private tutors or to attend special private educational institutions that were limited to the nobility, such as the lyceum at Tsarskoe selo that Pushkin and Küchelbecker had attended or the *pansion* at the university in Moscow that had produced the Friendly Literary Society of Zhukovsky's youth. Uvarov's predecessors Count Aleksei Razumovsky and Shishkov (minister, 1824–1828) had passed regulations requiring that the Russian language be taught in private schools. As superintendant of the St. Petersburg educational district, Uvarov tried to entice nobles into the public schools with special incentives and he opened a state-run *pansion* for nobles at the St. Petersburg Pedagogical Institute.[38] As minister he would do more, including setting up a system of government certification of tutors, asserting more control over the private schools through a system of inspections, requiring lecturing in Russian, as opposed to French, and putting a greater emphasis on national subjects like geography, history, and literature.[39] He thus addressed the problem of the national education of the noble class as well.

Nicholas I grew ever more suspicious of the access of the lower and serf classes to secondary and higher education and in particular to the danger that the classics could foster in these classes political ideas inimical to autocracy. Thus, in the European revolutionary year of 1848, Uvarov's educational institutions came under increasing scrutiny. All across Europe the classical curriculum was under attack both for its fostering of revolution and its failure to meet the needs of an increasingly industrializing society. In 1849, Uvarov was forced to gut the classical curriculum at the gymnasia before he finally resigned his post.[40] But the Russian intelligentsia had already been formed in his educational institutions and the ground had been prepared for the later period of reforms that changed Russian society forever.

ALTHOUGH MARIA THERESA had introduced instruction in Czech at her elite officer's academy (the Kadettenhaus) in 1752, somewhat earlier at her elite gymnasium, the Theresianum, and in 1775 at the university in Vienna, the subject was offered to equip bureaucrats and officers with the necessary tools to further the enlightened administration of her realm, not out of any inherent value in the subject itself.[41] In fact, the same rationalizing logic led to reforms that eliminated Czech as a language of instruction in secondary and higher educational institutions in 1775 (fully implemented by 1780), while allowing German to gradually replace Latin as the language of instruction and permitting instruction in Czech as a modern language only in certain select institutions—Germanization was to be the primary linguistic means to a better administration. Czech was not a part of the new curriculum for the Latin gymnasia, although after 1777 German was, and the university at Prague did not begin to offer Czech until 1793, after the death of Joseph II.[42] Czech was not to return as a language of instruction for almost 70 years and as a subject for nearly 40—the optional instruction offered by Jungmann at the gymnasium in Litoměřice from 1800 and on was semi-legal at best. Only in 1816 did the Imperial Study Commission issue a decree that allowed Czech-speaking pupils to have instruction in Czech language as a subject, and then only in gymnasia in Czech or mixed Czech-German areas.[43] As an elective subject, it was taught only at the personal initiative of the teachers, but this introduced instruction in Czech as a subject to seven of the 22 gymnasia in the Bohemian lands.[44]

The multiple petitions and campaigns by Czech patriots to get Czech reinstated as a language of instruction for the middle schools (*hlavní škola/Hauptschule*) and gymnasia produced no results until the revolution of 1848 finally forced imperial concessions. The Study Commission was disbanded and a Ministry of Education was formed. Already in April of 1848, Czech was given equal rights with German in the elementary and secondary schools, and in September, the ministry made Czech a required subject in ten gymnasia and made Czech the language of instruction for some additional subjects in those gymnasia. In 1850, Czech became the exclusive language of instruction at the gymnasium in Prague, and several other gymnasia were allowed Czech as a language of instruction for a few subjects.[45] But in the early 1850s, a retrenching government was able to mitigate some of these concessions: a new entrance requirement for the gymnasia in 1853 mandated that incoming students had to have had instruction in all subjects in German and instruction in Latin on the basis of German. The Czech middle schools were thus forced to use both Czech and German for instruction, and at the Czech gymnasia, instruction in the lower levels was in both languages, but only in German in the final classes.[46] When oversight of education was made part of the competence of the representative bodies of the Habsburg crown lands in 1860, the battle for the equal rights of Czech resumed. In 1866 the Bohemian diet granted equal rights for Czech and German in the schools, but mandated that the schools had to choose only one as the language of instruction while the other remained as a subject for study; this eliminated the possibility of bilingual instruction even in mixed Czech-German areas.[47] Thirteen of twenty-five gymnasia in the Bohemian crown lands became Czech gymnasia and the place of Czech in the schools was secured. The logic of dividing schools into Czech or German institutions, mandated by the provincial law for the schools, eventually altered the universities as well. In 1869 the Prague technical university split into Czech and German institutions, and in 1882, Prague university split as well.[48] The Czechs had won separate educational institutions, but in many ways these were not yet equal institutions, especially as facility in German remained essential to many elite career paths.

In the schools, 1848 was a revolutionary year, not only for the reintroduction of the Czech language as a language of instruction but also for the end of the dominance of the gymnasium curriculum by Latin. During the time of Maria Theresa, the 52 gymnasia in the Bohemian crown lands, including 21 belonging to the Jesuit order and 19 belonging to the Piarists, had been put under state control and the curriculum revised (in 1775). In Prussia and Bavaria, the "new humanism" looked to ancient culture broadly (beyond literature and art) and to Greek culture, in particular, for values. As it began to find its way into revised gymnasia curricula, it met with resistance among Catholics because it was seen as a kind of pagan revival, and thus in Austria the reform was based on a Piarist proposal instead.[49] The classical languages, and Latin in particular, dominated the curriculum. In 1805, after a small reform that further emphasized Latin and religion, students were required to take nine hours of Latin in each year (of a five-to-six-year course of study), two hours of Greek in the final three years, and only two to three hours each in other subjects, which included religion, history, geography, natural science, and mathematics, but not modern languages. Additional Greek instruction was added in 1819, increasing it to three hours per week over four years.[50]

This curriculum remained fundamentally unchanged until 1848, when it was altered, not as in Russia out of autocratic fears of the dangerous influx of democratic ideas it fostered, but in response to the pressure of the revolutionary forces for reform, which saw Latin as the instrument of the Catholic church, a privilege of the higher classes, and as an obstacle to scientific progress.[51] The result was not at all a revolution in which the rule of Latin was replaced by the modern languages, but Latin did lose its privileged place at the center of the curriculum. The gymnasia curriculum was expanded to eight years, during which students received 47 hours of instruction in Latin and 28 in Greek over the final six years, out of 187 total hours: the classical languages thus accounted for only 40 percent of the total curriculum. Of the modern languages, students studied only Czech or German, whichever was not the language of instruction in their school.[52] Like Uvarov's earlier reforms of the Russian school system, this reform was based on the Prussian reforms of Wilhelm von Humboldt, which emphasized classical general education over practical professional preparation, but the Austrian reform made less accommodation to the modern languages.[53] Karel Havlíček-Borovský, the prominent Czech journalist, compared the Austrian reform to the Russian one unfavorably on precisely that account.[54]

Modern languages—usually French—could be studied, however, at the *reálky* (*Realschule*), the new vocational schools that were recognized as full secondary educational institutions in 1848. In the second half of the nineteenth century the real challenge to the classical curriculum came not in the gymnasium, which remained largely unchanged into the twentieth century, but from the rise of the *reálky*. The expansion of secondary education saw a much larger increase in the number of these vocational schools than gymnasia.[55] While the general public was largely against the classical curriculum, the experts continued to debate the issue throughout the later nineteenth century. In those debates, one hears constant echoes of the themes and issues of the Quarrel between the Ancients and Moderns in suggestions of the superiority of the modern sciences and thus the central place they should occupy in the curriculum, in the defense of Christian learning against pagan culture, and so on.[56] The suggestion was often made that mathematics or the modern languages offered equivalent material for the development of abstract thinking as the study of the grammar of the classical languages, but only rarely did anyone suggest that the native literature could fully replace the classics in the curriculum. Even Jaroslav Durdík, writing in 1880, when he suggested that "the Greeks and Romans will be surpassed; for us only our national literature [jen národní literatura] has an absolute value," saw that cultural equivalence only as a future possibility: "let us hope that we too will have our Sophocles."[57] A new gymnasium curriculum emphasizing the national language and literature over the classics would wait until after the formation of the Czechoslovak state.

The long and stable tradition of classical secondary education in the Bohemian lands proved to be a resource to the Russian schools. When Dmitri Tolstoy, who was minister of education from 1866 to 1880, revived the classical gymnasium curriculum in Russia in 1871, requiring 49 hours of

Latin and 37 of Greek over eight years, he had a great need for new teachers to provide instruction. Rather than turning to Germans, as had been done in the past, he turned to the Czechs, whose interest in Russia was as great as Russia's need for teachers. Soon there were over a hundred Czech instructors of classical philology in Russia, alongside instructors in modern languages, the sciences, physical education, and singing. They joined the many Czech musicians, technicians, and tradesmen also working in Russia at that time.[58]

EDUCATION WAS A CENTRAL TOPIC in the discussions that articulated a new system of literary values, with the nation at the center, but the new literary programs that sought the development of a recognizably national literature did not pose an immediate challenge to the place of the ancient classics in the educational curriculum. In fact, insofar as it was allied with the new humanism, which put a greater value on Greek culture as an original national culture, the national perspective helped temporarily to give Greek a more prominent place in the gymnasia. The reforms undertaken by Uvarov, which created an entirely new classical curriculum for Russian secondary schools, demonstrate that proponents of the national literature, when given control over educational institutions, continued to place a very high value on the ancient classics both as literature and as educational material. While none of the Czech awakeners was ever in the position of Uvarov, Kollár was asked by the Viennese government for a school reform proposal in 1848. His proposal, which was not adopted, maintained a central place for Latin instruction and somewhat surprisingly reduced the hours of Greek, even as he promoted the Greek ideal of exercising body and spirit by suggesting the introduction of physical education to all levels of education.[59] Still, the educational question that was posed by the Quarrel between the Ancients and Moderns, and that had echoed throughout the early nineteenth-century Czech and Russian debates about their national literatures, continued to reverberate in debates over the forms of secondary education in the later nineteenth century. The educational value ascribed to the national literature would continue to grow, while the value of the classics continued to deteriorate, challenged not only, or even primarily, by the national literatures, but by the rise of modern technological civilization and its new educational needs. While the national literatures would eventually displace the classics from educational curricula, they never took the original place of the classics at the absolute and dominant center of the curriculum.

Conclusion

By the turn of the nineteenth century, classicist aesthetics and its model for assigning literary value were being challenged fundamentally by a new historical consciousness, by literary works in new genres outside the classicist canon, and by new ideas about creativity and authorship. One who perceived the incommensurability of the classicist rules with the new writing was Venevitinov, who complained at the lack of a new system of valuation: "We cast off the French rules not because we were able to refute them with some kind of positive system, but only because we could not apply them to some works of modern writers in which we took pleasure in spite of ourselves. Thus false rules have been replaced by the absence of any rules at all."[1] In fact, however, by 1826 much had been done in Russian literary-critical and literary-historical discourse to develop new ways of understanding literary value. The modern concept of the nation took a central place in this new discourse.

Again we need to ask, why the nation? Why did literature need the nation in order to develop a modern notion of literary value? In the classicist system, Greek and Roman antiquity had been the locus of literary value. Conceived of as a timeless and universal model, the literature of classical antiquity became the ground upon which aesthetic worth was founded. With the advance of technology and scientific and philological knowledge, however, the model status of antiquity came to be questioned. Antiquity came to be seen as distant and distinct, a place with different mores, customs, and values. Literature thus needed a new ground, a new site upon which to found concepts of literary value. The developing modern concept of the nation presented itself as an ideal site: conceived of as self-identical, historically continuous and developing, and of sufficient importance to lay claim to independent values, the nation was a locus that overcame the deficiencies of the classicist system. In his 1727 "Essay on Epick Poetry," Voltaire became one of the first to make the nation a discrete unit of differentiation—poetic values, manners, and taste vary from nation to nation in his discourse.[2] Many others would follow. In many ways, the nation had no competition for this role. While some continued to explore universal human values embodied in literature (like the Jena romantics with their "universal, progressive poetry"), when it came to accounting for historical and cultural *difference*, writers found in the nation an ideally-sized unit of measure. Anything larger (say, Europe) was questionable in terms of its unitary identity. Anything smaller was of questionable significance. František Ladislav Čelakovský in 1824 warned Czech writers against the dangers of provincialism in a satirical article entitled "Literatura Krkonošská" ("Krkonoše Literature"— referring to the mountainous region in northeast Bohemia).[3] While his wit is directed against self-congratulatory criticism and the low quality of original Czech literary productions and translations, his title indicates that the threat to Czech literature that such practices constitute is the threat of insignificance, of becoming a literature locked into tiny regional concerns that would be of no interest to the outside world. It could also be read as a warning against any separatist ideas among Moravian and Slovak writers. Kollár, who opposed the Slovak movement toward literary independence, also saw such separatism as a threat to the significance of the literature: "A national literature is the more successful the wider its compass and the more freely it can fly on its wings far and wide, from shore to shore and mountain to mountain. It certainly finds more support and more stimuli in this way, and it develops a character that is not one-sided, but great, sublime, and purely human, that reflects not the rays of villages, towns, schools, guilds, and parties, but regions, nations, and humanity."[4] The nation is ideally situated to address humanity while synthesizing the specificities of a variety of regions and cities.

Kollár and Čelakovský here take the model of a "national literature" as their basic frame of reference, a model that it had been the work of the preceding two decades to establish. Translation played a significant role in putting that model into place. Czech and Russian writers sought to establish the identity of their own national literature and its language through translations and appropriations from the literature of model nations, including Germany and England as well as classical Greece. Translations also helped to establish new literary values of particular significance for the new paradigm: in both Czech and Russian letters, the rich native folklore traditions gain entry to high literature only after translations of foreign ballads and folk songs establish the value of folkloric discourse for the national literature. Translation was a critical site for the transfer of cultural values and for the exploration of national identity in the encounter with national Others.

By the third decade of the nineteenth century in both Russian and Czech letters, the nation had become the norm against which, not only new, but any, literary productions were judged. Šafařík and Palacký gave the Czech "poetic palm of victory" to Polák in 1818, in spite of the fact that he did not employ the quantitative prosody for which they had so ardently advocated, because "up until now no one has given us so much genuine originality, sublimity, and individual beauties"—attributes that made his work "a national work; a work that the nation should boast of and will boast of in the future."[5] And in 1825, in his monumental history of Czech literature, Jungmann wrote, on the basis of the Rukopis královédvorský, that "the oldest Czech poetry was purely national [čistě národní], lyrico-epic with definite rhythm but without rhyme, containing events memorable to the nation: wars, battles, changes in leadership, the founding of law, but also expressions of the finest emotions, games, love songs, in short, masculine and feminine song just as we find among other Slavs, the Serbs in particular. It was the golden age, a beautiful blossom of national poetry, not grafted in from elsewhere, but home-grown [samorostlý], full of living colors, head and shoulders above everything composed in later times until the renewal of the literature."[6] The national qualities of the forged manuscript made it the carrier of the highest literary values, embodying the golden age of Czech literature and the Czech nation. In Russia, Somov made the value of *narodnost'* observable in the literary practices of Bürger, Schiller, and Goethe a model for Russian literary practice—in his use of the term, *narodnost'* carried all of its multivalent ambiguity, referring at various times to popularity, folksiness, or nationality, or all of them simultaneously. In both places, then, national qualities had become fundamental to literary value. In many ways, in fact, literary value became inextricable from its relationship to national identity. *Libozvučnost* (melodiousness) had been a quality assigned by Czech and German patriots to their languages in the discourse of language defenses for many years before Šafařík and Palacký connected it to quantitative verse and to the national qualities they wanted to promote in Czech poetry. Once it became a part of a system of national literary values, however, melodiousness became a potential point of political contestation—Kollár promoted greater Czech and Slovak linguistic integration in his use of the term, threatening the only recently established modern identity of the Czech literary language in a way that made Czech writers like Jungmann look for other values to promote. The fact that *melodiousness* became a contested term in the nascent Czech and Slovak national politics shows how fundamentally literary values had come to be linked to national identity.

When literature and the nation come together in a new constellation of values, both are transformed, a conclusion that has important implications for the field of nationalism studies. The prominent place of literature and literary figures in the early stages of many national movements has been frequently noted, but not sufficiently analyzed. In the literature on nations and nationalism, literary intellectuals are treated along with other intellectuals and the motivation for their involvement in national movements is found in the broader social, cultural, and political transformations of the period. The impetus for the nationalization of culture is conceived as coming from outside the cultural spheres. But there is sufficient motivation for forming a national identity within the institution of literature itself. As I have shown, a modern crisis in the constitution of literary values motivated a transformation of the institution of literature through which the modern concept of the nation came to serve as the ground for new conceptions of literary value. Literary figures are centrally involved in the early phase of many national movements because literature needed the nation to found its new aesthetic values.

Nathaniel Knight, in an insightful article on Russian national modernity, offers a valuable formulation of the role and motivation of Russian writers in the creation of the Russian nation:

> The ideas expressed in the works of Ancillon, de Staël and other romantic nationalists raised fundamental questions for young educated Russians about the place of their nation in the modern world. Russia had shown its military prowess in the struggle against Napoleon. In the Igor Tale, Russia had found its epic tradition. Karamzin was busily engaged in crafting his *History of the Russian State*. But these achievements were still not enough to establish Russia's modernity. Russia needed to be not only a modern state, but also a

nation that manifested its unique and inimitable character through a national literature, created by men of genius imbued with the spirit of the nation. Romantic nationalism imposed upon Russian writers the task of creating the nation. . . . What is striking about Viazemskii and his contemporaries is the deliberateness with which they sought to create a Russian national literature.[7]

We certainly have witnessed the deliberateness of these efforts. We should also note the seeming paradox in the fact that, in order to be recognized as a modern nation, Russia needed a national literature, but in order to create a national literature the writers also had to create the nation. Before I concur that "[r]omantic nationalism imposed upon Russian writers the task of creating the nation," I would further specify what we mean by romantic nationalism and include in that notion the institution of literature: what imposed that task upon Russian writers was not just something outside of literature, the social fact of developing national consciousness that had its causes elsewhere, but the need within the institution of literature for a new locus upon which to ground a new conception of literary value that we would not be wrong to call "romantic."

But is the task really given to writers to create the nation? Or is their need sufficiently fulfilled by the articulation of a national identity, whether there is any real national community that embodies that identity or not? Whether one measures by mass national consciousness or merely a developed discourse of national identity, neither the Czech nor the Russian nation can be said to have existed in the first decades of the nineteenth century. And yet, Russian and Czech writers needed "a nation" to serve as the ground of a new system of literary values, the basis for new works of literary art that would constitute the national literature. Both Karamzin and Jungmann envision a potential nation and suggest a program of creating a language and literature that respond to that absent social reality. In terms I have borrowed from Vladimír Macura, we might suggest that the national literature is initially an explicit simulacrum. The problem with Macura's terminology is that it presupposes a normative model of national culture formation that Czech culture differs from in being more artificial, a product of intellectual cultivation rather than a natural and organic emanation from an existing national culture. He suggests that Czech culture is different because "the striving for a quick and immediate transformation of Czech culture as a complex and fully developed whole, occurred under circumstances in which a differentiated, developed and self-confident Czech society, sure of its national identity, did not yet exist."[8] But this is true of any national movement that begins as a cultural movement. Rather than opposing a model of a whole, organic national culture to the Czech model, it would be better to generalize the Czech model and see how all national culture is a simulation, an artificial construct whose "organic whole" is always a projected ideal. The transformation of culture into a national form produces this artificiality everywhere—though the particular manifestations in each case are individual. The extreme forms that Macura cites in the Czech case may be suggestive of a general cultural rule, rather than of an exception; the comparison to Russian culture helps to confirm this.[9] On the other hand, there is no escaping the imperative of the organic whole for the creators of national culture—while we can recognize the absence of the social reality they project, proponents of national culture consistently conceive of their culture-creating activities in terms of the reawakening, rebirth, or revival of an eternal national body. The articulation of national identity is always in the service of an envisioned reconstitution of that national body, the reawakening of national consciousness among their fellows.[10] That is why Czech and Russian writers become pioneers not only in the articulation of national identity but also in their respective national movements. The task of creating the nation is inseparable from the task of articulating the national identity.

In many histories of the Czech national revival, the activity of writers and the role of literature has been seen as fundamentally driven by the need to develop the national language as a marker of a distinct national identity. This mirrors the value system articulated by Jungmann, drawing upon Dobrovský's history, where cultural progress in general is seen as primarily benefiting the language. But it misses, once again, the literary motivation for writers' activity. Similarly, Russian writers are not driven to articulate conceptions of Russian national identity only out of a need for an alternative to the official court discourse on national identity, but also out of a fundamental literary need. Again, the symbiotic relationship of literature and nation in a new constellation of values has important consequences for both sides of the relationship. Cultural concerns may not be so easily separable from political concerns. To return again to Miroslav Hroch's periodization of national movements, the transition from phase *A* of antiquarian and scholarly interest to phase *B* when the national ideology is articulated and political agitation begins has sometimes been seen as a transition from mere cultural to real political concerns. But what if that very transition is driven by the nationalization of literary culture? What if the "real" political concerns are created in response to a cultural need? The problem of the simulacrum raises its head again and threatens to implode our distinction between cultural and political phases. Joep Leerssen has argued that cultural concerns pervade all three phases of national movements.[11] In another context, he has also put his finger on a key moment for understanding how antiquarian literary interests are converted into national interests: the reconstruction by James Macpherson of Ossian's epic poems. In publishing his first Ossianic fragments, Macpherson responded to antiquarian interests in ancient poetry, but in combining and reworking those fragments just a couple of years later into epic poems, Macpherson helped to generate and crystallize new ideas about the nature of European national literary traditions and the epic's particular place in those traditions. Macpherson thus helped to give birth to national literary historicism out of literary antiquarianism.[12] The nationalization of literary culture helps to transform antiquarian and scholarly interests into national literary interests that also have a potential political aspect. I will suggest here once again, then, that the modern crisis in literary values motivated the development of modern national identities as much as any other social, political, or religious crisis that has been examined in the field of nationalism studies. In fact, the aesthetic crisis might even be among the most important factors that drives the Czech and Russian national movements at this point.

Literary studies have largely remained on the periphery of nationalism studies, because literature and high culture have mostly been conceived of as responding to, rather than motivating, the development of nations and nationalism. And in spite of a healthy tradition in the later nineteenth and mid-twentieth centuries—and a real potential for revival in the post-socialist era—comparative Slavic literary studies have failed to thrive. I hope to have shown that comparative Slavic literary studies can open up productive new perspectives on the literatures it surveys, and that literary studies can address the central concerns of nationalism studies without abandoning issues of literary aesthetics and form.

Notes

Introduction

1. Ernest Gellner, *Nations and Nationalism: New Perspectives on the Past* (Ithaca, NY: Cornell University Press, 1983), 97; Peter Bugge, "Czech Nation-Building, National Self-Perception, and Politics, 1780–1914" (Ph.D. diss., University of Aarhus, 1994), 5.

2. Anthony D. Smith, *National Identity, Ethnonationalism in Comparative Perspective* (Reno: University of Nevada Press, 1991), 91.

3. Ibid., 94.

4. Ibid., 93.

5. Ibid., 96.

6. Jonathan Culler, "Anderson and the Novel," *Diacritics* 29, no. 4 (1999): 37.

7. Culler argues that the novel itself is a condition of possibility for imagining something like a national community, and thus, it seems to me, only misreads Anderson in a more subtle way. His assertion that as a result "we have considerable warrant for maintaining [the novel's] importance in the face of the historian's insistence on socioeconomic and political factors, from markets to wars," is another dubious claim of literature's importance to nationalism studies. Ibid.

8. Benedict Anderson, *Imagined Communities: Reflections on the Origin and Spread of Nationalism,* rev. and extended ed. (London: Verso, 1991), 36.

9. Ibid.

10. See his programmatic website, "Philology and National Culture," at http://cf.hum.uva.nl/natlearn/.

11. Joep Leerssen, *National Thought in Europe: A Cultural History* (Amsterdam: Amsterdam University Press, 2006), 59, 55–59. Emphasis in the original.

12. Ibid., 52, 106.

13. Smith also cited the importance of "medievalist literary historicism" in "providing the concepts, symbols, and language for the vernacular mobilization of demotic *ethnies* and a mirror in which members could group their own aspirations." Smith, *National Identity,* 90.

14. Some recent examples with attention to Czech developments include Chad Carl Bryant, *Prague in Black: Nazi Rule and Czech Nationalism* (Cambridge: Harvard University Press, 2007); Eagle Glassheim, *Noble Nationalists: The Transformation of the Bohemian Aristocracy* (Cambridge: Harvard University Press, 2005); Pieter M. Judson, *Guardians of the Nation: Activists on the Language Frontiers of Imperial Austria* (Cambridge: Harvard University Press, 2006); Jeremy King, *Budweisers into Czechs and Germans: A Local History of Bohemian Politics, 1848–1948* (Princeton: Princeton University Press, 2002).

15. This direction has been pursued explicitly in the editorial programs of the journals *Kritika* and *Ab Imperio*. Representative studies include Chris Chulos and Johannes Remy, eds., *Imperial and National Identities in Pre-Revolutionary, Soviet, and Post-Soviet Russia* (Helsinki: Suomalaisen Kirjallisuuden Seura, 1999); Mark Bassin, *Imperial Visions: Nationalist Imagination and Geographic Expansion in the Russian Far East, 1840–1865* (Cambridge: Cambridge University Press, 2000); Ronald Gregor Suny and Terry Martin, eds., *A State of Nations: Empire and Nation-Making in the Age of Lenin and Stalin* (New York: Oxford University Press, 2001); David Brandenberger, *National Bolshevism: Stalinist Mass Culture and the Formation of Modern Russian National Identity, 1931–1956* (Cambridge, Mass.: Harvard University Press, 2002); Francine Hirsch, *Empire of Nations: Ethnographic Knowledge and the Making of the Soviet Union* (Ithaca: Cornell University Press, 2005); Aleksei Miller, *The Romanov Empire and Nationalism: Essays in the Methodology of Historical Research*, trans. Serguei Dobrynin (Budapest: Central European University Press, 2008). Primordialist theories have been examined closely and found wanting in Serhii Plokhy, *The Origins of the Slavic Nations: Premodern Identities in Russia, Ukraine, and Belarus* (Cambridge: Cambridge University Press, 2006).

16. Thomas Wallnig, "Language and Power in the Habsburg Empire: The Historical Context," in *Diglossia and Power: Language Policies and Practice in the 19th Century Habsburg Empire*, ed. Rosita Rindler Schjerve (Berlin: Mouton de Gruyter, 2003), 15.

1—A New Paradigm Emerges

1. N. M. Karamzin, *Izbrannye sochineniia v dvukh tomakh*, 2 vols. (Moscow: Izdatel'stvo Khudozhestvennaia literatura, 1964), 2:162, 169.

2. A. P. Sumarokov, *Izbrannye proizvedeniia*, Biblioteka poeta, bol'shaia seriia (Leningrad: Sovetskii pisatel', 1957), 125.

3. Boileau's treatise was also translated by Vasily Trediakovsky in 1752—the competition over Boileau was a part of the general competition between Trediakovsky, Sumarokov, and Lomonosov to be recognized as the founder of the new Russian poetry. See V. M. Zhivov, "Tserkovnoslavianskaia literaturnaia traditsiia v russkoi literature XVIII v. i retseptsiia spora 'drevnikh' i 'novykh,'" in *Istoriia kul'tury i poetika*, ed. L. A. Sofronova (Moscow: Nauka, 1994), 63; and A. M. Peskov, *Bualo v russkoi literature XVIII–XIX veka* (Moscow: Izdatel'stvo Moskovskogo universiteta, 1989), 22–23. See also the discussion below.

4. Ladislav Varcl et al., *Antika a česká kultura* (Praha: Academia, 1978), 6.

5. Jean Paul Friedrich Richter, "From *School for Aesthetics*," in *German Romantic Criticism*, ed. A. Leslie Wilson, The German Library (New York: Continuum, 2002), 46.

6. Josef Jakub Jungmann, *Boj o obrození národa: Výbor z díla*, ed. Felix Vodička (Prague: F. Kosek, 1948), 102.

7. As late as 1820, however, in one of the last defenses of the classicizing method of the Puchmajer school, Šebestián Hněvkovský had called Antonín Jaroslav Puchmajer alternatively the Czech Horace and the Czech Virgil. Felix Vodička, ed., *Dějiny české literatury,* vol. 2, *Literatura národního obrození* (Prague: Nakladatelství Československé akademie věd, 1960), 2:57.

8. N. I. Gnedich, "A. S. Pushkinu po prochtenii Skazki ego o tsare Saltane i proch," in *Stikhotvoreniia, Biblioteka poeta* (Leningrad: Sovetstkii pisatel', 1956).

9. See Joseph M. Levine, "Ancients and Moderns Reconsidered," *Eighteenth-Century Studies* 15, no. 1 (1981): 79–80; and Joseph M. Levine, *Humanism and History: Origins of Modern English Historiography* (Ithaca: Cornell University Press, 1987), 155–77.

10. Douglas Lane Patey, "Ancients and Moderns," in *The Eighteenth Century,* ed. H. B. Nisbet and Claude Rawson, *The Cambridge History of Literary Criticism* (Cambridge: Cambridge University Press, 1997), 34. Anthony D. Smith has also noted the importance of the Quarrel to the emergence of historicism, with all of its implications for nationalism. Smith, *National Identity,* 86.

11. Patey, "Ancients and Moderns," 35–39. Levine ascribes the initial insight to William Wotton rather than Fontenelle. Levine, "Ancients and Moderns Reconsidered," 85.

12. See the literature cited in Patey, "Ancients and Moderns," 40n.17.

13. Jochen Schulte-Sasse, "1735: Aesthetic Orientation in a Decentered World," in *A New History of German Literature,* ed. David E. Wellbery and Judith Ryan (Cambridge: The Belknap Press of Harvard University Press, 2004), 351.

14. Patey, "Ancients and Moderns," 45–46.

15. Ibid., 48. On the precedents, see p. 36n.8, and Levine, "Ancients and Moderns Reconsidered," 85.

16. Levine, "Ancients and Moderns Reconsidered," 86–87. This, too, is a part of the narrowing of the field of literature.

17. On the importance of philology to national thought, see Leerssen, "Philology and National Culture."

18. Levine, "Ancients and Moderns Reconsidered," 84.

19. Ibid., 83.

20. Patey, "Ancients and Moderns," 46–52. Also Levine, "Ancients and Moderns Reconsidered," 82–87.

21. Patey, "Ancients and Moderns," 54. Perrault had suggested that modern French prose was a more exact medium than verse (58). On her treatment of "taste" see Kirsti Simonsuuri, *Homer's Original Genius: Eighteenth-Century Notions of the Early Greek Epic (1688–1798)* (Cambridge: Cambridge University Press, 1979), 53–56.

22. Patey, "Ancients and Moderns," 54.

23. Simonsuuri, *Homer's Original Genius,* 50–52.

24. See Simonsuuri's survey as well as that of Donald M. Foerster, *Homer in English Criticism: The Historical Approach in the Eighteenth Century* (n.p.: Archon Books, 1969).

25. Simonsuuri, *Homer's Original Genius,* 57–58. Regarding Homer's central role, see also Joseph M. Levine, "Giambattista Vico and the Quarrel between the Ancients and the Moderns," *Journal of the History of Ideas* 52, no. 1 (1991): 69n.55.

26. For her formulation of the translator's difficulties, see Simonsuuri, *Homer's Original Genius,* 49–50.

27. See examples in Patey, "Ancients and Moderns," 57–58.

28. Levine, "Giambattista Vico," 77 and passim.

29. Peter Hans Reill, *The German Enlightenment and the Rise of Historicism* (Berkeley: University of California Press, 1975), 112–18. See also René Wellek, *The Rise of English Literary History* (Chapel Hill: The University of North Carolina Press, 1941), 47–94, esp. 53–54.

30. For an analysis of Russian developments along these lines in particular, which further highlights the role of translation in stimulating this conception of the universal poet, see David L. Cooper, "Vasilii Zhukovskii as a Translator and the Protean Russian Nation," *The Russian Review* 66, no. 2 (2007).

31. Simonsuuri, *Homer's Original Genius*, 33–34, 45. Patey, "Ancients and Moderns," 64.

32. Varcl et al., *Antika a česká kultura*, 310, 319. The collective authors of this volume suggest that the roots of this fundamental revaluating of values lie in the dispersion of Greek scholars after the fall of Byzantium in 1453.

33. Levine, "Ancients and Moderns Reconsidered," 86.

34. Levine, "Giambattista Vico," 75–76. Patey cites similar conclusions from Richard Hurd, Voltaire, and Herder. Patey, "Ancients and Moderns," 69.

35. Patey makes this observation in relation to Herder. Patey, "Ancients and Moderns," 68. Levine notes Vico's movement in this direction. Levine, "Giambattista Vico," 75.

36. Patey, "Ancients and Moderns," 65.

37. Ibid., 67. Simonsuuri, *Homer's Original Genius*, 108. We should recall that Charles Perrault did his share to expand interest in European folk traditions with his early publications of folktales, though he could not yet argue for them with the force lent by this new conception of history. See Simonsuuri, *Homer's Original Genius*, 28–30.

38. Simonsuuri, *Homer's Original Genius*, 111.

39. Patey, "Ancients and Moderns," 43.

40. Simonsuuri, *Homer's Original Genius*, 68. Voltaire makes the nation the discrete unit of differentiation—poetic values, manners, and taste vary from nation to nation. See the multiple examples from the essay in Florence Donnell White, *Voltaire's Essay on Epic Poetry: A Study and an Edition* (Albany, NY: Brandow Printing Co., 1915), 64–65.

41. Patey, "Ancients and Moderns," 43–44, 66.

42. For an overview of some of the history of the term, see Liah Greenfeld, *Nationalism: Five Roads to Modernity* (Cambridge: Harvard University Press, 1992), 8–9; and Eric Hobsbawm, *Nations and Nationalism Since 1780: Programme, Myth, Reality* (Cambridge: Cambridge University Press, 1990), 14–23. For a broad discussion of Czech concepts of nation in the Czech revival, see Vladimír Macura, *Znamení zrodu: české národní obrození jako kulturní typ* (Jinočany: H&H, 1995), 153–69.

43. See the history of the term in A. L. Kroeber and Clyde Kluckhohn, *Culture: A Critical Review of Concepts and Definitions* (New York: Vintage Books, 1963), part I.

44. René Wellek, *A History of Modern Criticism: 1750–1950*, 2 vols. (New Haven: Yale University Press, 1955), 1:181–82. See also Maike Oergel, *The Return of King Arthur and the Niebelungen: National Myth in Nineteenth-Century English and German Literature* (New York: Walter de Gruyter, 1998), 26.

45. Klaus Weimar, *Geschichte der deutschen Literaturwissenschaft bis zum Ende des 19. Jahrhunderts* (Munich: Wilhelm Fink Verlag, 1989), 202. The creation of such a term helps to reify the phenomenon—we have seen that Voltaire already operated with a concept of national literatures in 1727.

46. Hermann Bausinger, *Formen der "Volkspoesie,"* 2, verb. und verm. Aufl. ed., Grundlagen der Germanistik. 6 (Berlin: E. Schmidt, 1980), 14. In this case, this meant

in some sense also the invention of the phenomenon of *Volkspoesie,* for the term pulled together a variety of practices and forms that had not been associated and that we would no longer associate today, even under the term folk poetry. See Bausinger, *Formen der "Volkspoesie,"* 11–19, and chap. 5 here.

47. See Patey, "Ancients and Moderns," 70.

48. Varcl et al., *Antika a česká kultura,* 107–56, 207–50, 328.

49. Nonetheless, traditions did develop, including using 8-syllable lines in rhyming couplets to translate hexameter. See Anežka Vidmanová, "Staročcské pokusy o hexametr a pentametr," *Slovo a smysl: Časopis pro mezioborová studia* 1, no. 1 (2004).

50. Varcl et al., *Antika a česká kultura,* 214–18, 383–85.

51. Ibid., 317, 221–22, 328.

52. Weimar, *Geschichte der deutschen Literaturwissenschaft,* 47; and Josef Vintr, "Josef Valentin Zlobický—zapomenutý český vlastenec z ocvícenské Vídně," in *Vídeňský podíl na počátcích českého národního obrození: J. V. Zlobický (1743–1810) a současníci: Život, dílo, korespondence,* ed. Josef Vintr and Jana Pleskalová (Prague: Akademia, 2004), 14–15.

53. Weimar, *Geschichte der deutschen Literaturwissenschaft,* 91. Instruction in Czech language and literature in Prague, however, would wait until 1793 with the appointment of František Martin Pelcl. Hugh LeCaine Agnew, *Origins of the Czech National Renascence* (Pittsburgh: University of Pittsburgh Press, 1993), 61.

54. See Zdeněk V. David, "Národní obrození jako převtělení Zlatého věku," *Český časopis historický* 99, no. 3 (2001).

55. Varcl et al., *Antika a česká kultura,* 314–24, 328–29.

56. Ibid., 385–86, 337. See chaps. 4 and 6 below.

57. Peskov, *Bualo v russkoi literature,* 6–7.

58. Cf. Zhivov, "Tserkovnoslavianskaia literaturnaia traditsiia," 63.

59. Ibid.

60. Peskov, *Bualo v russkoi literature,* 26.

61. J. Klein, "Russkii Bualo? (Epistola Sumarokova 'O stikhotvorstve' v vospriiatii sovremennikov)," *XVIII vek* 18 (1993): 57. Karamzin, in his *Panteon,* notes that Sumarokov's "contemporaries called him our Racine, Molière, La Fontaine, Boileau. Their descendents do not agree." Karamzin, *Izbrannye sochineniia,* 2:170. Klein suggests that there is little evidence that his contemporaries ever honored him with the desired comparison to Boileau.

62. Zhivov, "Tserkovnoslavianskaia literaturnaia traditsiia," 63–65, 75. See also Karen Rosenberg, "Between Ancients and Moderns: V. K. Trediakovskij on the Theory of Language and Literature" (Ph.D. diss., Yale University, 1980).

63. Zhivov, "Tserkovnoslavianskaia literaturnaia traditsiia," 66–74. For an in depth examination of the development of the Russian odic tradition and its deployment of the sublime, see Harsha Ram, *The Imperial Sublime: A Russian Poetics of Empire,* Publications of the Wisconsin Center for Pushkin Studies (Madison: University of Wisconsin Press, 2003). Ram also notes the irony of Trediakovsky and Lomonosov's choice of an odic model (43–44).

64. See also Peskov, *Bualo v russkoi literature,* 35–40, for an analysis of M. N. Muravev's sentimentalist translation of Boileau's *Art poétique* and its minor shifts in emphasis.

65. Ibid., 57–59. See chap. 3 below for a discussion of Shishkov and the divided Russian literary sphere. We can remark here that the quarrels between the Russian "archaists" and "innovators" in certain ways reprise aspects of the Quarrel between

the Ancients and Moderns, but each side reflects varied aspects of the ancient and modern positions.

66. Ibid., 94. See chap. 8 for an analysis of Somov's article on romantic poetry, from which this characterization is taken.

67. Miroslav Hroch, "From National Movement to the Fully-formed Nation: The Nation-building Process in Europe," in *Mapping the Nation*, ed. Gopal Balakrishnan (London: Verso, 1996), 81. Hroch's widely known analysis, which divides national movements into three phases, is explicated most fully in Miroslav Hroch, *Social Preconditions of National Revival in Europe: A Comparative Analysis of the Social Composition of Patriotic Groups Among the Smaller European Nations* (Cambridge: Cambridge University Press, 1985). Naturally, this analysis works best for the Czech case, as it is formed on a long-standing periodization of the Czech national revival. Adjustments are necessary in analyzing other national movements. See Maria Todorova, "The Trap of Backwardness: Modernity, Temporality, and the Study of Eastern European Nationalism," *Slavic Review* 64, no. 1 (2005): 158–60.

68. Hroch, "From National Movement to the Fully-formed Nation," 85.

69. See Todorova, "The Trap of Backwardness."

2—Is There a Russian Literature? No . . .

1. Andrei L. Zorin, "U istokov russkogo germanofil'stva (Andrei Turgenev i Druzheskoe literaturnoe obshchestvo)," in *Novye bezdelki: Sbornik statei k 60-letiiu V. E. Vatsuro*, ed. S. I. Panov (Moscow: Novoe literaturnoe obozrenie, 1995–1996). On German criticism of the *Sturm und Drang*, see Klaus L. Berghahn, "From Classicist to Classical Literary Criticism," in *A History of German Literary Criticism, 1730–1980*, ed. Peter Uwe Hohendahl (Lincoln: University of Nebraska Press, 1988), 70–78.

2. N. A. Marchenko, "Andrei Ivanovich Turgenev," in *Russkie pisateli: Biobibliograficheskii slovar'*, ed. P. A. Nikolaev (Moscow: Prosveshchenie, 1996), 2:321.

3. Zorin, "U istokov russkogo germanofil'stva," 9.

4. V. M. Istrin, "Druzheskoe literaturnoe obshchestvo 1801 g. (Po materialam Arkhiva brat'ev Turgenevykh)," *Zhurnal Ministerstva narodnago prosveshcheniia*, no. 8 (1910): 284–85.

5. Zorin, "U istokov russkogo germanofil'stva," 10.

6. Aleksandr Nikolaevich Veselovskii, *V. A. Zhukovskii: Poeziia chuvstva i "serdechnogo voobrazheniia"* (Moscow: Intrada, 1999).

7. Zorin, "U istokov russkogo germanofil'stva"; Il'ia Vinitskii, *Utekhi melankholii* (Moscow: Izdatel'svto Moskovskogo kul'turologicheskogo litseia, 1997); Marc Raeff, "Russian Youth on the Eve of Romanticism: Andrei I. Turgenev and His Circle," in *Political Ideas and Institutions in Imperial Russia* (Boulder, CO: Westview Press, 1994); Andrei L. Zorin, "The Perception of Emotional Coldness in Andrei Turgenev's Diaries," *Slavic Review* 68, no. 2 (2009).

8. Iurii M. Lotman, "Andrei Sergeevich Kaisarov i literaturno-obshchestvennaia bor'ba ego vremeni," *Uchenye zapiski tartuskogo gosudarstvennogo universiteta* 63 (1958); Iurii M. Lotman, "Stikhotvorenie Andreia Turgeneva 'K otechestvu' i ego rech' v 'Druzheskom literaturnom obshchestve,'" in *Dekabristy—literatory*, Literaturnoe nasledstvo 60, no. 1 (Moscow: Izdatel'stvo Akademii Nauk SSSR, 1956); Iurii M. Lotman, "Problema narodnosti i puti razvitiia literatury preddekabristskogo perioda," in *O russkom realizme XIX veka i*

voprosakh narodnosti literatury: Sbornik statei, ed. P. P. Gromov (Moscow: GIKhL, 1960).

9. Lotman, "Andrei Sergeevich Kaisarov," 25.

10. Lotman's conclusion in the article on *narodnost'* is similarly vague. There, Andrei Turgenev belongs to a group "in the worldview of whom features of the future noble revolutionary tendency were being formed [namechalis' cherty budushchei dvorianskoi revoliutsionnosti]." Lotman, "Problema narodnosti," 51.

11. Kaisarov's public activity and publications, and particularly his friendship with future Decembrists such as Nikolai Ivanovich Turgenev, Andrei's younger brother, obviate the need to make an explicit argument for influence.

12. Lotman, "Stikhotvorenie Andreia Turgeneva," 338n.33. Turgenev published only two poems before his untimely death. Zorin, "The Perception of Emotional Coldness in Andrei Turgenev's Diaries," 248.

13. Raeff, "Russian Youth on the Eve of Romanticism," 50–51.

14. Lotman, "Problema narodnosti," 44.

15. Yuri Tynianov's micro-history of the critical discussions of the 1820s in "Arkhaisty i Pushkin" maps out a far more complex picture of literary affiliation and inheritance for the "younger arkhaists," many of whom were political radicals and Decembrists, and their relationship to Shishkov. Tynianov has little to say, however, about Merzliakov and, because of his focus on the 1820s, nothing about Andrei Turgenev. Iurii N. Tynianov, "Arkhaisty i Pushkin," in *Pushkin i ego sovremenniki* (Moscow: Nauka, 1969).

16. V. M. Istrin, "Iz dokumentov Arkhiva brat'ev Turgenevykh: I. Druzheskoe Literaturnoe Obshchestvo 1801 g.," *Zhurnal Ministerstva narodnago prosveshcheniia,* no. 3 (1913): 9.

17. A. A. Fomin, "Andrei Ivanovich Turgenev i Andrei Sergeevich Kaisarov: Novye dannyia o nikh po dokumentam arkhiva P. N. Turgeneva," *Russkii bibliofil,* no. 1 (1912): 25. I would emphasize that any demand for *narodnost'* that one might read in Turgenev's speech is a *narodnost' avant la lettre.* See the discussion below. Any conception of "realism" is clearly out of place in 1801.

18. Lotman, "Andrei Sergeevich Kaisarov," 54.

19. Lotman, citing N. Mordovchenko's doctoral thesis, dates the romantic "revaluing of values" to Küchelbecker's 1824 article. See, Lotman, "Andrei Sergeevich Kaisarov," 53. A. M. Peskov dates the decline of the reputation of Boileau in Russia, the "revaluing of values," to the 1820s and 1830s. Peskov, *Bualo v russkoi literature,* 7, 89–102.

20. Hybridization is emphasized by Boris M. Gasparov, *Poeticheskii iazyk Pushkina kak fakt istorii russkogo literaturnogo iazyka* (Vienna: Wiener Slavistischer Almanach, 1992), 19. Syncretism is the term of the great student of the Czech national revival, Vladimír Macura, in Macura, *Znamení zrodu,* 13–30. Tynianov's ideas on the complexity of literary evolution were worked out in part in his history of the critical discussions of the 1820s, in which he saw a similar mixing of different historical layers of critical ideas. Tynianov, "Arkhaisty i Pushkin," 52–53. In speaking of a certain clarification in the 1820s, then, I do not mean to imply the end of all hybridization.

21. See Part III, esp. chap. 8, on the entry of the term into critical discussions. In examining literary developments in the pre-Decembrist period, Lotman consistently organizes certain ideas and trends around the future critical term *narodnost',* a problematic anachronism that inclines him to draw clear lines of distinction between ideas and figures that are, in fact, not easy to separate within that context.

22. Fomin, "Andrei Ivanovich Turgenev i Andrei Sergeevich Kaisarov," 26.

23. Ibid. Lotman corrects Fomin's "стоны" instead of "стопы" at the end. Lotman, "Stikhotvorenie Andreia Turgeneva," 338n.30.

24. Filipp Dziadko notes that one of the rules of the society was to give and accept criticism "without fail and without excuses." Filipp Dziadko, "'Za chto nam drug ot druga otdaliat'sia?' K istorii literaturnykh otnoshenii A. F. Merzliakova i V. A. Zhukovskogo: 'Versiia' Merzliakova," *Pushkinskie chteniia v Tartu* 3 (2004): 115. N. I. Mordovchenko also notes the contrast of Merzliakov's strict criticism of eighteenth-century authors with Shishkov's pietism. N. I. Mordovchenko, *Russkaia kritika pervoi chetverti XIX veka* (Moscow: Izdatel'stvo Akademii Nauk SSSR, 1959), 267.

25. Fomin, "Andrei Ivanovich Turgenev i Andrei Sergeevich Kaisarov," 26.

26. Ibid.

27. See Zorin, "U istokov russkogo germanofil'stva."

28. Fomin, "Andrei Ivanovich Turgenev i Andrei Sergeevich Kaisarov," 26–29. (These are continuous pages, interrupted by an illustration.)

29. M. K. Azadovskii, *Istoriia russkoi fol'kloristiki* (Moscow: Gosudarstvennoe uchebno-pedagogicheskoe izdatel'stvo, 1958), 131–32; Iurii M. Lotman, "A. F. Merzliakov kak poet," in *Stikhotvorenie,* by Aleksei F. Merzliakov, Biblioteka poeta (Leningrad: Sovetskii pisatel', 1958), 28–29; and Lotman, "Problema narodnosti," 47.

30. Fomin, "Andrei Ivanovich Turgenev i Andrei Sergeevich Kaisarov," 29.

31. Ibid.

32. In his later, similar critique of the elegy, Küchelbecker would also have recourse to the hierarchy of genres, but would base his critique on the spirit of true romanticism, which demanded *narodnost'* (see chap. 10). Turgenev does not explicitly connect the ideas in the first part of his speech (which seem to prefigure ideas of *narodnost'*) to the critique of Karamzin.

33. Fomin, "Andrei Ivanovich Turgenev i Andrei Sergeevich Kaisarov," 29, 30.

34. B. Gasparov, *Poeticheskii iazyk Pushkina,* 26–28.

35. V. E. Vatsuro, "V preddverii pushkinskoi epokhi," in *Arzamas: Sbornik v dvukh knigakh,* vol. 1, *Memuarnye svidetel'stva. Nakanune "Arzamasa." Arzamasskie dokumenty* (Moscow: Khudozhestvennaia literatura, 1994), 14.

36. Iurii M. Lotman and M. G. Al'tshuler, eds., *Poety 1790–1820kh godov,* Biblioteka poeta (Leningrad: Sovetskii pisatel', 1971), 825.

37. Fomin, "Andrei Ivanovich Turgenev i Andrei Sergeevich Kaisarov," 29.

38. V. M. Istrin, *Pis'ma i dnevnik Aleksandra Ivanovicha Turgeneva gettingenskago perioda (1802–1804 gg.) i pis'ma ego k A. S. Kaisarovu i brat'iam v Gettingen 1805–1811 gg.* (St. Petersburg: Tipografiia imperatorskoi akademii nauk, 1911), 71 (first pagination series). The young Andrei Ivanovich himself dined at Karamzin's home on August 10, 1800, and recorded with delight an invitation by I. I. Dmitriev to dine again at Karamzin's, an invitation he had to decline. See 72n.97. His enthusiasm in general for contact with Karamzin suggests that further visits, had there been any, would have been noted.

39. Istrin, *Pis'ma i dnevnik Aleksandra Ivanovicha Turgeneva,* 70.

40. Ibid., 73. Following the September 9, 1800, invitation to dine with Karamzin, which he had to turn down, Turgenev had composed a letter to Karamzin that expressed many of the same sentiments, but there is no evidence he ever sent it.

41. Karamzin, *Izbrannye sochineniia,* 2:183–85. He does not consider the possibility that he himself might be to blame.

42. Raeff, "Russian Youth on the Eve of Romanticism," 56.

43. On the correspondence, see Andrei Turgenev's letter to Zhukovskii from

August 19, 1800, in V. E. Vatsuro and M. N. Virolainen, "Pis'ma Andreia Turgeneva k Zhukovskomu," in *Zhukovskii i russkaia kul'tura*, ed. R. V. Iezuitova (Leningrad: Izdatel'stvo "Nauka" 1987), 369–70. On the planned publications and other common work, including a joint translation of Goethe's *Werther*, see the editors' introductory notes (351) and Lotman, "Andrei Sergeevich Kaisarov," 54.

44. Istrin, *Pis'ma i dnevnik Aleksandra Ivanovicha Turgeneva*, 74.

45. Some of the order of the text is rearranged and there are slight revisions to wordings, but there are no major additions aside from those I will note below. I would like to thank Andrei Zorin, who provided me with his transcription of the diary entry for comparison with that published by Istrin.

46. Lotman, "Andrei Sergeevich Kaisarov," 54.

47. Compare Fomin, "Andrei Ivanovich Turgenev i Andrei Sergeevich Kaisarov," 29–30, to Istrin, *Pis'ma i dnevnik Aleksandra Ivanovicha Turgeneva*, 74–75.

48. See Istrin, *Pis'ma i dnevnik Aleksandra Ivanovicha Turgeneva*, 42; and Dziadko, "'Za chto nam drug ot druga otdaliat'sia?'"

49. For examples in his letters and diary, see Vatsuro and Virolainen, "Pis'ma Andreia Turgeneva k Zhukovskomu," 377–78, 402, 406, 411, 417, 419; and M. N. Virolainen, "Iz dnevnika Andreia Ivanovicha Turgeneva," *Vostok-Zapad: Issledovaniia, perevody, publikatsii*, 4 (1989): 101, 105.

50. Virolainen, "Iz dnevnika Andreia Ivanovicha Turgeneva," 130.

51. Vatsuro and Virolainen, "Pis'ma Andreia Turgeneva k Zhukovskomu," 381.

52. Istrin, *Pis'ma i dnevnik Aleksandra Ivanovicha Turgeneva*, 74–75.

53. Lotman, "A. F. Merzliakov kak poet," 28–29.

54. Raeff relates, in relation to Andrei Turgenev's feelings of patriotism, that while in Vienna, "he attended a play about Peter the Great and visited a Czech scholar (whose efforts to promote a national literature he approved with quite a touch of patronizing superiority and condescension)." Who this Czech scholar in Vienna in 1802 was, unfortunately, we do not know, because the name is torn off the archival letter—perhaps Zlobický? He did not express his doubts to the foreigner: "I spoke to him as it behooves a Russian to speak about the Russians, praised to him our epic poems, mentioned Derzhavin and [illegible] poets, did not forget also Karamzin, Dmitriev and mentioned Izmailov, finally I promised to send him Russian tea and took my leave. . . ." Raeff, "Russian Youth on the Eve of Romanticism," 54, 64n.57.

55. Istrin, "Iz dokumentov Arkhiva brat'ev Turgenevykh," 12–13. In relation to Kaisarov's similar ideas on education, elaborated in a preface to a comparative Slavic dictionary that was not completed, Lotman noted their origin in the discussions of the Friendly Literary Society and how they prefigured Decembrist ideas (Lotman, "Andrei Sergeevich Kaisarov," 136.). This is, then, another way in which Merzliakov should be seen along with Kaisarov and Turgenev as a Decembrist precursor.

56. Lotman, "A. F. Merzliakov kak poet," 31–32, 27–28.

57. Ibid., 27.

58. Lotman, "Andrei Sergeevich Kaisarov," 25.

59. In fact, Lotman rescues Merzliakov to a certain degree for his Soviet audience by placing him in the developmental line that led from Radishchev to the later radical critics of non-noble background. But the class distinctions are maintained too rigidly for an analysis of the development of a public discourse like literary criticism, as if the fact that Merzliakov himself was not a noble could prevent his ideas from influencing the literary program of noble

revolutionaries. Lotman also tried to rescue Merzliakov from the classicist label by observing that his poetic rules are not given *a priori*, but are empirically based on subjective collective experience ("Andrei Sergeevich Kaisarov," 38–40.). But as Douglas Lane Patey has observed, this change in how classicist rules were conceived occurred early in the multiple exchanges of the Quarrel between the Ancients and Moderns, and it characterized the views of such model classicists as Boileau and Pope (Patey, "Ancients and Moderns," 40–41.).

60. Mordovchenko, *Russkaia kritika,* 259, 267, 268; Z. A. Kamenskii, "Russkaia estetika pervoi treti XIX veka: Klassitsizm," in *Russkie esteticheskie traktaty pervoi treti XIX veka,* vol. 1, ed. Z. A. Kamenskii (Moscow: Iskusstvo, 1974), 33–34, 38, 41, 389. Kamenskii explicitly defends Merzliakov's contribution to Decembrist criticism (41). But he also suggests that classicist terminology became an obstacle to his critical development (33, 38).

61. Mordovchenko, *Russkaia kritika,* 262; Kamenskii, "Russkaia estetika," 35.

62. Lotman, "Andrei Sergeevich Kaisarov," 36. Lotman does not give the date of the letter, so it is unclear whether it belongs to the 1801–1802 period, before Turgenev's stay in Vienna, or 1803, after his return.

63. Ibid.

64. Dziadko, "'Za chto nam drug ot druga otdaliat'sia?'" 132n.31. Dziadko's article inspired me to reconsider, from a new angle, what impact Turgenev's speech might have had on public critical discourse, and thus to a decidedly new analysis of the role of Merzliakov in relation to that speech and program.

65. See Mordovchenko, *Russkaia kritika,* 269.

66. Istrin, "Iz dokumentov Arkhiva brat'ev Turgenevykh," 12.

67. Mordovchenko, *Russkaia kritika,* 260, 264.

68. Aleksei F. Merzliakov, "Ob iziashchnom, ili o vybore v podrazhanii," in *Russkie esteticheskie traktaty pervoi treti XIX veka,* ed. Z. A. Kamenskii (Moscow: Iskusstvo, 1974), 75. The lecture was printed in *Vestnik Evropy* in 1813.

69. Ibid., 78.

70. Ibid., 78, 77.

71. Quoted in Mordovchenko, *Russkaia kritika,* 268. Dziadko connects the promotion of the ancients as models to Turgenev's speech as well, but there is no evidence that Turgenev ever programmatically suggested following Greek or Roman models. This is another example of how the figure of Turgenev, as the acknowledged leader of the Friendly Literary Society, gets credited with all programmatic formulations. Dziadko, "'Za chto nam drug ot druga otdaliat'sia?'" 132n.32.

72. Merzliakov, "Ob iziashchnom," 92.

73. Mordovchenko, *Russkaia kritika,* 223, 226–27.

74. Lotman, "A. F. Merzliakov kak poet," 53.

75. Vissarion Belinskii, *Polnoe sobranie sochinenii,* 13 vols. (Moscow: Izdatel'stvo Akademii Nauk SSSR, 1953–59), 7:261–62. Quoted in Kamenskii, "Russkaia estetika," 36.

76. Zhukovsky clearly had his own conception of what Russian literature most needed, which might be described, to be brief and anachronistic, as Karamzinism modified somewhat in the direction of certain aspects of *narodnost'*. His groundbreaking poetic work, including, perhaps even especially, his translations, evoked a critical response that continually advanced new ideas. On Zhukovsky's role as a translator in the creation of a Russian critical discourse on the national literature, see Cooper, "Vasilii Zhukovskii as a Translator."

3—The Roots of the Russian Language and Literature

1. For a summary of the polemics, see Vatsuro, "V preddverii pushkinskoi epokhi."

2. See chap. 2 for the circumstantial evidence suggesting that Karamzin's article may have been prompted in turn by Andrei Turgenev's speech in the Friendly Literary Society. Vatsuro and M. N. Virolainen note that Turgenev's critique of Karamzin would no longer have been possible in 1802 after Karamzin's series of programmatic articles, because Karamzin had then addressed the very problem raised by Turgenev. Vatsuro and Virolainen, "Pis'ma Andreia Turgeneva k Zhukovskomu," 356.

3. B. Gasparov, *Poeticheskii iazyk Pushkina*, 38–40.

4. Irina Reyfman, *Vasilii Trediakovsky: The Fool of the New Russian Literature* (Stanford, CA: Stanford University Press, 1990), 132–33.

5. Karamzin, *Izbrannye sochineniia*, 1:186.

6. Ibid., 1:185.

7. Ibid. Berghahn discusses the development of the concept of taste in opposition to classicist aesthetic theories and the difficulties the Germans had in appropriating the category in the eighteenth century, due to a similar lack of social basis. German writers responded by developing a philosophical grounding for judgments of taste. Berghahn, "From Classicist to Classical Literary Criticism," 37–49. Taste is also an essential category of Karamzinian aesthetics. It is characteristic that Russian writers develop linguistic and aesthetic grounds first, before taking up metaphysics. The Czechs also respond to their lack of social basis with a linguistic program, that is, the construction of a language simulacrum (see chap. 4).

8. Karamzin, *Izbrannye sochineniia*, 1:185.

9. Aleksandr S. Shishkov, "Razsuzhdenie o starom i novom slogie rossiiskago iazyka," in *Sobranie sochinenii i perevodov Admirala Shishkova* (St. Petersburg: Imperatorskaia Rossiiskaia Akademiia, 1824), 2:1, 3, 6, 26. This practice continues throughout the work.

10. Ibid., 9–10.

11. Ibid., 49.

12. Ibid., 3. Concerning apocalyptic motifs and models in Russian culture of this period, see chap. 5 of A. Zorin, *Kormia dvuglavogo orla . . . : Literatura i gosudarstvennaia ideologiia v Rossii v poslednei treti XVIII—pervoi treti XIX veka* (Moscow: Novoe Literaturnoe Obozrenie, 2001); and chap. 1 of B. Gasparov, *Poeticheskii iazyk Pushkina*.

13. See Boris A. Uspenskii, "Iazykovaia situatsiia i iazykovoe soznanie v Moskovskoi Rusi: Vospriiatie tserkovnoslavianskogo i russkogo iazyka," in *Izbrannye trudy*, vol. 2 (Moscow: Gnosis, 1994). Uspenskii locates the end of diglossia in the seventeenth century.

14. Shishkov quotes the relevant passage from Lomonosov on p. 3 of his treatise.

15. Oleg Proskurin has noted the important role played by an article on the Church Slavonic language by M. T. Kachenovskii in *Vestnik Evropy* in 1816 in debunking Shishkov's thesis. Oleg Proskurin, "Novyi Arzamas—Novyi ierusalim: Literaturnaia igra v kul'turno-istoricheskom kontekste," *Novoe literaturnoe obozrenie*, no. 19 (1996): 109. Kachenovskii concluded that the Church Slavonic language was an old Serb dialect. The most important source for that conclusion was the work in Slavic philology of the Czech scholar Josef Dobrovský, who was preparing his monumental grammar of the Church Slavonic language. He cites Dobrovský's identical conclusion before examining the evidence. M. T. Kachenovskii, "O slavianskom iazykie voobshche i v osobennosti o tserkovnom," *Viestnik Evropy*, no. 19–20 (1816): 251–52. Kachenovskii was also translating some of Dobrovský's articles for *Vestnik Evropy* starting in 1816. V. A. Frantsev, *Ocherki po istorii cheshskago vozrozhdeniia:*

Russko-cheshskiia uchenyia sviazi kontsa XVIII i pervoi poloviny XIX st. (Warsaw: Varshavskii Uchebnyi Okrug, 1902), 47. This is, then, one example of how the early ties between Czech and Russian scholars played a role, however minor, in central literary arguments.

16. Shishkov, "Razsuzhdenie o starom i novom slogie," 37, 42.

17. See B. Gasparov, *Poeticheskii iazyk Pushkina,* 33.

18. Shishkov, "Razsuzhdenie o starom i novom slogie," 33–35.

19. Ibid., 36.

20. Ibid., 39–41.

21. Ibid., 42.

22. See V. V. Vinogradov, *Ocherki po istorii russkogo literaturnogo iazyka XVII–XIX vv.* (Leiden: E. I. Brill, 1949), 155–56; and B. Gasparov, *Poeticheskii iazyk Pushkina,* 39–40.

23. Shishkov, "Razsuzhdenie o starom i novom slogie," 1–2.

24. Ibid., 133.

25. Ibid., 161–63. [Emphasis mine in the English translation.] It is rather humorous that Shishkov's common sense actually seems to leave him in his argument, when he implies that the inadmissible phrase places the *vkus* in the music. He reads too literally and ignores the logic of the phrase, which is really not so different from those which he admits. And by mentioning the dress of his admissible phrase, he nearly destroys his own argument.

26. Logocentrism, as Jacques Derrida uses the term, is that all-pervasive tendency in western thought to want to found all knowledge and meaning on the originary presence of Logos (which has the senses of word, reason, and spirit). See pt. 1 of Jacques Derrida, *Of Grammatology,* trans. Gayatri Chakravorty Spivak (Baltimore, MD: The Johns Hopkins University Press, 1976). Shishkov clearly prefers a stable meaning, rooted in an originary word whose meaning is not abstract or metaphorical, to the possibility of meaninglessness that semiotic processes present. He wants Russian words to maintain their essential identity and not be polluted by the difference introduced by French models. And even though he makes the ancient books the source of good language, he still manages to privilege speech over writing, for the style that he prefers and continually holds up as a model is, as we will see in a moment, an oral declamatory style. In a telling note on censorship from 1815, Shishkov argues that book printing had a negative effect on morals because anyone could become a teacher by printing a book and students could learn alone with their books, as opposed to the teacher on a public square with all his listeners present who had to be responsible to them. Aleksandr S. Shishkov, "Mnienie moe o razsmatrivanii knig ili tsenzurie," in *Zapiski, mnieniia i perepiska Admirala A. S. Shishkova,* ed. N. Kiselov and Iu. Samarin (Berlin: B. Behr's Buchhandlung, 1870), 44.

27. Boris A. Uspenskii and Iurii M. Lotman, "Spory o iazyke v nachale XIX v. kak fakt russkoi kul'tury ('Proischestvie v tsarstve tenei, ili sud'bina rossiiskogo iazyka'—neizvestnoe sochinenie Semena Bobrova)," in *Izbrannye trudy,* by Boris A. Uspenskii, vol. 2, *Iazyk i kul'tura* (Moscow: Gnosis, 1994), 390–94.

28. Shishkov, "Razsuzhdenie o starom i novom slogie," 3–4.

29. N. M. Karamzin, "O sluchaiakh i kharakterakh v rossiiskoi istorii, kotorye mogut byt' predmetom khudozhestv," in *Izbrannye sochineniia* (Moscow: Izdatel'stvo "Khudozhestvennaia literatura," 1964) 2:188–98.

30. Vinitskii, *Utekhi melankholii,* 178–86. Vinitsky, for lack of better evidence, identified the author of the work (given only as A. O.) as Aleksandr V. Obrezkov. However, Thomas Newlin has shown convincingly that the author in fact was Aleksandr P. Orlov. Newlin, "Rural Ruses: Illusion and Anxiety on the Russian Estate, 1775–1815," *Slavic*

Review 15, no. 2 (1998): 315–17. See, also, Newlin, "Aleksandr Petrovich Orlov," in *Slovar' russkikh pisatelei XVIII veka,* ed. A. M. Panchenko (St. Petersburg: Nauka, 1999), 2:387–88.

31. Mordovchenko, *Russkaia kritika,* 45.

32. Shishkov, "Razsuzhdenie o starom i novom slogie," 5n.3.

33. Their discourse also had the additional features of irony, scandalous parody, and satire, which moved it beyond the salon model. Tynianov, "Arkhaisty i Pushkin," 58–59.

34. Ibid., 33. Iurii N. Tynianov, "Oda kak oratorskii zhanr," in *Arkhaisty i novatory* (Leningrad: Priboi, 1929).

35. Shishkov, "Razsuzhdenie o starom i novom slogie," 8. The words "pleasant" (*priiatnoe*) and "charms" (*prelesti*) are keywords of Karamzinian critical discourse. Shishkov here appeals to their fashion but suggests that they actually arise from a very different source.

36. "*Kosnoiazyche*" is what Moses suffered from in the Slavonic Bible: confused articulation. B. Gasparov, *Poeticheskii iazyk Pushkina,* 46.

37. Ibid., 34–35.

38. Shishkov, "Razsuzhdenie o starom i novom slogie," 48.

39. Uspenskii and Lotman, "Spory o iazyke v nachale XIX v.," 391, and 360–402 passim.

40. Ibid., 367–68.

41. Shishkov, "Razsuzhdenie o starom i novom slogie," 25.

42. Ibid., 12.

43. Ibid., 122.

44. Aleksandr S. Shishkov, "Riech' pri otkrytii Besiedy liubitelei ruskago slova," in *Sobranie sochinenii i perevodov Admirala Shishkova* (St. Petersburg: Imperatorskaia Rossiiskaia Akademiia, 1825), 4:140–41.

45. Aleksandr S. Shishkov, "Primiechaniia na drevnee o polku igorevom sochinenie," in *Sobranie sochinenii i perevodov Admirala Shishkova* (St. Petersburg: Imperatorskaia Rossiiskaia Akademiia, 1826), 7:36.

46. Aleksandr S. Shishkov, "Razgovory o slovesnosti mezhdu dvumia litsami Az i Buki," in *Sobranie sochinenii i perevodov Admirala Shishkova* (St. Petersburg: Imperatorskaia Rossiiskaia Akademiia, 1824), 3:52.

47. Shishkov, "Razsuzhdenie o starom i novom slogie," 11.

48. Ibid., 121.

49. Shishkov, "Riech' pri otkrytii Besiedy liubitelei ruskago slova," 139.

50. Shishkov, "Razsuzhdenie o starom i novom slogie," 10.

51. Tynianov, "Arkhaisty i Pushkin," 23–27.

52. Uspenskii and Lotman, "Spory o iazyke v nachale XIX v.," 337–38.

53. See also Vatsuro, "V preddverii pushkinskoi epokhi," 14–15.

54. Levine, "Ancients and Moderns Reconsidered," 78. Gasparov comments similarly on the old and new in the Russian polemics. B. Gasparov, *Poeticheskii iazyk Pushkina,* 29.

4   The Culture of the Czech Language and Czech-Language Culture

1. Vladimír Macura discusses the nature of Czech "linguocentrism" (lingvocentrismus) in Macura, *Znamení zrodu,* 42–60.

2. Uspenskii and Lotman, "Spory o iazyke v nachale XIX v.," 2:331–37.

3. The democratization and laicization of culture undertaken by the Hussites with their associated emphatic Czech linguistic-ethnic identity have rightfully been noted as an important pre-national formation in discussions of the development of Czech linguistic nationalism. I would emphasize the descriptor *pre-national,* for the movement had as its goal not the emancipation and elevation of the Czech language community as such, but rather the establishment of the true church as the Hussites understood it, emancipation and elevation being corollaries to this central, religious goal. It is also worth noting that the mission of Cyril and Methodius to Moravia marks the first instance of the confrontation between a vernacular (or near vernacular) religious culture and the Latin-centered, German-dominated Roman Catholic Church. There seems to be little continuity, however, between this brief tradition and the Hussite movement, though some would point to the brief and limited revival of the Slavonic tradition under Charles IV. In an unpublished account of the history of the Czech language and literature from 1822, František Palacký, the future historian of the Czech nation, outlined this progression. František Palacký, *Spisy drobné,* ed. Leander Čech, vol. 3, *Spisy aesthetické a literarní* (Prague: Bursík a Kohout, 1900), 492.

4. Vodička, ed., *Dějiny české literatury,* 2:100–102.

5. Josef Dobrovský, *Výbor z díla,* ed. and trans. Benjamin Jedlička (Prague: Státní nákladatelství krásné literatury, knihy a umění, 1953), 62–63.

6. Ibid., 81.

7. On the ambiguity of the adjective in this period, see Macura, *Znamení zrodu,* 153–56.

8. Josef Hanuš, "Josefa Dobrovského Geschichte der Böhmischen Sprache (1791), Geschichte der Böhmischen Sprache und Litteratur (1792), Geschichte der Böhmischen Sprache und ältern Literatur (1818)," *Bratislava* 3, no. 3–4 (1929): 502–5.

9. Walter Schamschula, *Die Anfänge der tschechischen Erneuerung und das deutsche Geistesleben (1740–1800)* (Munich: Wilhelm Fink Verlag, 1973), 253–55. For surveys of Czech literary historiography of the period in English and Czech, see Agnew, *Origins of the Czech National Renascence,* 93–116; and Benjamin Jedlička, *Dobrovského "Geschichte" ve vývoji české literární historie,* Archiv pro badání o životě a díle Josefa Dobrovského (Prague: Nákladem Komise pro vydáváni spisů Josefa Dobrovského při Královské české společnosti nauk, 1934), 15–31, 153–76.

10. Even as it continues to be broader than the developing modern conception of literature in terms of the types of texts it included.

11. Dobrovský uses the word or phrase ten times, as follows (this source also gives the pagination of the first addition, which will be given in parentheses in all citations): Josef Dobrovský, *Dějiny české řeči a literatury, v redakcích z roku 1791, 1792 a 1818,* ed. Benjamin Jedlička, Spisy a projevy Josefa Dobrovského (Prague: Nákl. Komise pro vydávání spisů Josefa Dobrovského, 1936), 86 (53), 102 (85), 109 (99, twice), 110 (101), 126 (130), 129 (135), 148 (171), 153 (180), 160 (193).

12. Eduard Maur, "Pojetí národa v české osvícenské historiografii: Ignác Cornova a František Marin Pelcl," in *Mezi časy . . . Kultura a umění v českých zemích kolem roku 1800,* ed. Zdeněk Hojda and Roman Prahl, *Sborník příspěvků z 19. ročníku sympozií k problematice 19. století, Plzeň, 4.-6. března 1999* (Prague: Koniasch Latin Press, 1999).

13. On the contribution of Dobrovský's philology to critical historical method, see Agnew, *Origins of the Czech National Renascence,* 35–36. On philology's role in the modernization of literary ideas, see chap. 1 here.

14. Jedlička, *Dobrovského "Geschichte,"* 137, 177. Agnew, *Origins of the Czech National Renascence,* 113.

15. See Hanuš, "Josefa Dobrovského Geschichte," 498n5; and Schamschula, *Die Anfänge der tschechischen Erneuerung,* 257–59. Schamschula observes that Dobrovský greatly surpasses Adelung in his deployment of previously undeveloped factual materials and in the definitiveness of his datings and linguistic analyses—that is, in the quality of his philology (259).

16. Schamschula, *Die Anfänge der tschechischen Erneuerung,* 258; Hanuš, "Josefa Dobrovského Geschichte," 498n5.

17. Schamschula, *Die Anfänge der tschechischen Erneuerung,* 254–56.

18. Hanuš, "Josefa Dobrovského Geschichte," 571.

19. Schamschula, *Die Anfänge der tschechischen Erneuerung,* 255.

20. Kroeber and Kluckhohn, *Culture,* 13n.5. By contrast, Grimm's dictionary did not include it in either 1860 or 1873.

21. Ibid., 35.

22. Dobrovský clearly knew this history as well as Adelung's history of the German language (Hanuš, "Josefa Dobrovského Geschichte," 498.). As a mere sketch, it was not his primary model, but because it has the same set of analytical vocabulary as the German language history, it can serve as another point of comparison.

23. Dobrovský, *Dějiny české řeči a literatury,* 65 (6), 84 (47), 86 (51, 52, 53), 100 (80), 102 (85), 107 (96), 126 (130), 146 (168). Johann Christoph Adelung, "Vorrede," in *Karl Thams Deutsch-böhmisches Nationallexikon,* by Karl Ignaz Tham (Prague: Auf Kosten der von Schönfeldschen Handlung, 1788) (unnumbered pages).

24. Kroeber and Kluckhohn, *Culture,* 37.

25. Adelung, "Vorrede," [iv, ix].

26. Dobrovský refers five times to the cultivation of the language. In one such case, he spells the term "Cultur." Other instances involving the genitive include "in der frühesten Kultur ihres Verstandes" (in the earliest cultivation of their minds), "Spuren einer viel frühern, freilich nur anfänglichen Kultur der ganzen Nation" (traces of the very early, certainly only incipient cultivation of the entire nation), and "die Kultur der böhmischen Geister" (the cultivation of the Czech spirits). Dobrovský, *Dějiny české řeči a literatury,* 102 (85), 65 (6), 86 (53), 146 (168).

27. Adelung, "Vorrede," [v, vii]. Dobrovský's phrase "cultivation of the Czech spirits" even uses "spirit" in a more concrete manner than Adelung.

28. Dobrovský, *Výbor z díla,* 22.

29. Dobrovský, *Dějiny české řeči a literatury,* 126 (130).

30. Ibid., 127 28 (133–34), 150 (175), 148 (171), 160–62 (193–97).

31. Ibid., 171 (216–17).

32. Macura, *Znamení zrodu,* 106.

33. The names of Czech nobility were formed, as with German nobility, by indicating the place of the estate: z Veleslavína = von Veleslavín. For Dobrovský's praise of Veleslavín's work as author, translator, and publisher, see Dobrovský, *Dějiny české řeči a literatury,* 157–58 (189–90).

34. Jungmann, *Boj o obrození národa,* 28. The bad Czech rings with puns: "v Prase" = in the swine/ in Prague; "kte nepyl jako toma" = where I drank as at home/ where I was at home, etc.

35. Jungmann did include the word *kultura* in his dictionary (1836), where he noted that it derived from the Latin *cultura.* As Czech and German equivalents he gives

"wzdělánj, wzdělanost, oswjcenost, oswěta, Bildung" but not Kultur. Josef Jakub Jungmann and Jan Petr, *Slovník česko-německý,* 2nd ed., 4 vols. (Prague: Academia, 1990), 2:223.

36. Jungmann, *Boj o obrození národa,* 29.

37. Ibid., 28. In an earlier passage, Veleslavín represents the efforts of his contemporaries as having been directed toward "the perfection of their language."

38. For more on this new axiology see, again, Macura, *Znamení zrodu,* 50 ff.

39. Ibid., 21ff.

40. Jan Nejedlý, "O lásce k vlasti," *Hlasatel český* 1 (1806): 15.

41. Ibid., 16–17.

42. Jungmann, *Boj o obrození národa,* 32–34.

43. Ibid., 36.

44. Josef Hanuš, "Pavel Josef Šafařík," in *Ottův slovník naučný* (Prague: J. Otto, 1888–1909), 24:528; Felix Vodička, "Slovo uvodní," in *Boj o obrození národa: výbor z díla,* by Josef Jakub Jungmann (Prague: F. Kosek, 1948), 11.

45. Jungmann, *Boj o obrození národa,* 46.

46. He refers later to the lack of terms for "filosofické i artistické umění." Ibid., 47.

47. Ibid.

48. Ibid., 49.

49. Cf. chap. 1 of František Kubka, *Dobrovský a Rusko: Počátky vztahů česko-ruských a názory Josefa Dobrovského na Rusko* (Prague: Čin, 1926). In his *Geschichte,* for example, Dobrovský writes of the "slawische Sprache" in the singular, and of the various Slavic languages as dialects (Mundarten). That the Slavs as a whole constitute a nation, then, follows from Jungmann's definition of a nation.

50. Though Anton Bernolák had codified a Slovak literary norm in 1787 that was in some use among Catholics in western Slovakia, numerous Slovaks, especially from among the culturally leading Lutherans, still embraced the Czech of their Bible and were contributing to the Czech revival. See Vodička, ed., *Dějiny české literatury,* 2:46–49.

51. Ibid., 2:238.

52. There is a significant body of work on Jungmann's translations. For the translation of Milton, see Josef Hrabák, *Studie o českém verši* (Prague: Státní pedagogické nakladatelství, 1959), 183–204; and Ladislav Cejp, "Jungmannův překlad Ztraceného ráje," in *Překlady,* by Josef Jakub Jungmann, vol. 1 (Prague: Státní nakladatelství krásné literatury, hudby a umění, 1958). For Chateaubriand and the role of this translation in the context of Czech prose, see Felix Vodička, *Počátky krásné prózy novočeské: Příspěvek k literárním dějinám doby Jungmannovy* (Prague: Melantrich, 1948), 51–122. For articles on his translations from various languages, see Josef Jakub Jungmann, *Překlady,* 2 vols. (Prague: Státní nakladatelství krásné literatury, hudby a umění, 1958), vol. 2. Many of the conclusions of this body of work are summarized in Vodička, ed., *Dějiny české literatury,* 2:241ff. For a discussion of Jungmann's translations of scholarly work and an overview of the roles played by translation in the *obrození,* see Macura, *Znamení zrodu,* 61–78.

53. Vodička, *Počátky krásné prózy novočeské,* 76.

54. Vodička, ed., *Dějiny české literatury,* 2:243–44.

55. Ibid., 2:243. Vodička accounts for the metrical choice, noting that the trochaic line was most common in Czech, just as the iambic is in English, and that with the final stressed syllable and other means, Jungmann tried to give the line more of a rising rhythm.

56. Mojmír Otruba, "Josef Jungmann," in *Lexikon české literatury,* ed. Vladimír Forst (Prague: Akademia, 1993), 2(pt. I):581, Hrabák, *Studie o českém verši,* 205, 215–17.

57. Josef Jakub Jungmann, *Vybrané spisy původní i přeložené,* Česká knihovna zábavy a poučení (Prague: Jan Otto, 1918), 121. "Ty kytkou se zyvděčuješ mně z Enny a Tempe./ Znám to milé kvítí řecké po vůni lahodné;/ Outlíčkou i trháno rukou, i v krásotě svíží./ O kdyby prostolibým je chtěl také vázati poutkem,/ Jak sama v záňadří je nesla krásná Helenka,/ Neb jako výborný svázal je Tevtoně Herder:/ Záviděly Slavěnce by tvé po celém kraji Nymfy."

58. The reference to Herder is somewhat enigmatic, and the poem is most often cited in Czech criticism by eliding that line and ignoring the problem it presents. Herder, so far as I can determine, never translated Anacreon into quantitative German verse. In fact, he only translated a handful of Anacreon's verses at all, though he did translate extensively from the Greek Anthology. Johann Gottfried Herder, *Herders sämmtliche Werke,* 33 vols. (Berlin: Weidmann, 1877–1913), 1–210, esp. 170–73 for Anacreon. Oldřich Králík, in an article on Jungmann's translations from Greek and Latin, has shown that Jungmann himself used Herder's *syllabotonic* translations from the Anthology in making his own translations of some epigrams into quantitative verse. Oldřich Králík, "Překlady z řecké a latinské literatury," in *Překlady,* by Josef Jakub Jungmann, vol. 2 (Prague: Státní nakl. krásné lit-ry hudby a umění, 1958), 619–21. But Králík also quotes the "Slavěnka" poem without the Herder reference (617). Perhaps there is a disguised polemic here with Herder, who failed, in Jungmann's terms, to embody the Greek in the most essential way—in his prosody.

59. Vodička, ed., *Dějiny české literatury,* 2:246.

60. Jungmann outlined a theory of poetic language in his 1820 primer on literary theory, *Slowesnost.* See Vodička, *Počátky krásné prózy novočeské,* 41–43.

61. Josef Dobrovský, "Numa Pompilious, der zweite König von Rom. In französischer Sprache von Florian geschreiben und in böhmischer ausgelegt von Joh. Nejedlý . . ." in *Literární a prozodická bohemika,* ed. Miroslav Heřman, *Spisy a projevy Josefa Dobrovského* (Prague: Academia, 1974), 145.

62. The work was known to Bobrov's contemporaries, though it remained in manuscript and was considered lost. Uspenskii and Lotman, "Spory o iazyke v nachale XIX v.," 347.

63. Ibid., 469.

64. Ibid., 472.

5—Translating Folk Discourse

1. Berman's footnote at this point reads, "*Bild* (image), *Einbildungskraft* (imagination), *Ausbildung* (development), *Bildsamkeit* (flexibility, 'formability'), etc." In the course of his discussion he also notes the relationship to *Urbild* (original, archetype), *Vorbild* (model), and *Nachbild* (reproduction). Antoine Berman, *The Experience of the Foreign: Culture and Translation in Romantic Germany,* trans. S. Heyvaert (Albany: State University of New York Press, 1992).

2. Ibid., 43.

3. Ibid., 43–44.

4. Ibid., 44–45.

5. Ibid., 46, 47.

6. Ibid., 11–12 and passim. See also Michael Eskin, "The 'German' Shakespeare," in *A New History of German Literature,* ed. David E. Wellbery, Judith Ryan, and Hans Ulrich Gumbrecht (Cambridge: Belknap Press of Harvard University Press, 2004), 463.

7. Berman, *The Experience of the Foreign*, 4.

8. Macura has commented on the "translationality" (*překladovost*) of Czech revival culture, noting that translations were a tool of active cultural competition and "translationality" a general principle of Czech cultural formation. Macura, *Znamení zrodu*, 61–78, esp. 77.

9. Berman, *The Experience of the Foreign*, 13.

10. Bausinger, *Formen der "Volkspoesie*," 12, 16.

11. Ibid., 14.

12. Wellek, *A History of Modern Criticism*, 1:192.

13. See Oergel, *The Return of King Arthur*, 35.

14. Bausinger, *Formen der "Volkspoesie*," 15.

15. Gottfried August Bürger, "Outpourings from the Heart on Volkspoesie," in *Eighteenth-Century German Criticism*, ed. Timothy J. Chamberlain, The German Library (New York: Continuum, 1992), 256, 61.

16. Bausinger, *Formen der "Volkspoesie*," 15–16.

17. Bürger, "Outpourings from the Heart," 253.

18. Ibid., 256.

19. Cf. Vodička, ed., *Dějiny české literatury*, 2:178ff; and Karel Dvořák and Felix Vodička, "Včleňování folkloru do obrozenské literatury," *Česká literatura*, no. 3 (1955): 316.

20. See William E. Harkins, *The Russian Folk Epos in Czech Literature 1800–1900* (New York: Kings Crown Press, 1951), 35–36.

21. Vodička, *Počátky krásné prózy novočeské*, 8.

22. Macura, *Znamení zrodu*, 106.

23. Harkins, *The Russian Folk Epos*, 36; and Mojmír Otruba, "Václav Hanka," in *Lexikon české literatury*, ed. Vladimír Forst (Prague: Akademia, 1993), 2(pt. I):58.

24. Otruba, "Václav Hanka," 2(pt. I):58.

25. Vodička, ed., *Dějiny české literatury*, 2:78–79, 181.

26. I. V. Iagich, *Istoriia slavianskoi filologii*, Entsiklopediia slavianskoi filologii (St. Petersburg: Tipografiia Imperatorskoi Adakemii nauk, 1910), 248–49.

27. Thomas Butler, "Jernej Kopitar and South Slavic Folklore," in *Papers in Slavic Philology 2 to Honor Jernej Kopitar, 1780–1980*, ed. Rado L. Lencek and Henry R. Cooper, Jr. (Ann Arbor: University of Michigan, Department of Slavic Languages and Literatures, 1982), 110, 111–12.

28. Ibid., 111.

29. Harkins, *The Russian Folk Epos*, 33; Butler, "Jernej Kopitar," 118n.5.

30. Harkins, *The Russian Folk Epos*, 33–35.

31. Butler, "Jernej Kopitar," 118n.5.

32. Hanuš, "Josefa Dobrovského Geschichte," 530.

33. This is the entire text, except for the translations, as reprinted by Jan Máchal, "Úvod," in *Hankovy písně a prostonárodní srbská muza, do Čech převedená*, ed. Jan Máchal (Prague: Česká Akademie Císaře Františka Josefa pro Vědy, Slovesnost a Umění, 1918), xix–xx. The article was published in *Hromádkovy Prvotiny* 2 (1814): 121ff. The translated songs are the Ukrainian song "Oi! poslala mene maty zelenova zhita zhaty" from Prach's collection (on which, see below) and "Oi devoiko dusho moia" from Karadžić's first collection, the *Mala prostonarodnja slaveno-serbska pjesnarica* [*Small Songbook of the Slavo-Serbian Simple Folk*, 1814].

34. See the online "Hymnorum Thesaurus Bohemicus," http://www.clavmon.cz/htb/.

35. Margarita Mazo, "Introduction," in *A Collection of Russian Folk Songs,* ed. Malcolm Hamrick Brown (Ann Arbor, MI: UMI Research Press, 1987), 27.

36. In his monumental study of Czech verse, Karel Horálek considers the loss to Czech verse culture that derives from the fact that social and economic conditions forced the majority of excellent Czech musicians in the eighteenth century, at a time when Czech musical culture was highly developed, to seek work abroad. Karel Horálek, *Počátky novočeského verše* (Prague: Nákladem Karlovy University, 1956), 45–46. Still, some were already beginning to contribute to a renewing Czech music tradition. One of the earliest practitioners of the Czech art song was Jan Emanuel Doležálek (1780–1858), a close friend of Beethoven (his memoirs have been valuable for students of Beethoven's life). Like Hanka, he had come to Vienna as a student of law, but then dedicated himself fully to music, studying under J. G. Albrechtsberger and working in Vienna as pianist, cellist, and music teacher. In 1812, he published in Vienna *České pjsně w hudbu vwedené* (Czech songs set to music), which set poems by poets from Puchmajer's group. Doležálek thus represents another likely target of Hanka's goading. "Doležálek, Jan Emanuel," in *Československý hudební slovník: Osob a institucí,* ed. Gracian Černušák, Bohumír Štědroň, and Zdenko Nováček (Prague: Státní hudební vydavatelství, 1963), 251.

37. Richard Taruskin, *Defining Russia Musically: Historical and Hermeneutical Essays* (Princeton, NJ: Princeton University Press, 1997), 17.

38. Ibid., 16. Mazo, "Introduction," 14.

39. Taruskin, *Defining Russia Musically,* 4–13. See also John W. Randolph, "The Singing Coachman or, The Road and Russia's Ethnographic Invention in Early Modern Times," *Journal of Early Modern History* 11, no. 1/2 (2007).

40. See appendix C in Nikolai Lvov and Ivan Prach, *A Collection of Russian Folk Songs,* ed. Malcolm Hamrick Brown (Ann Arbor, MI: UMI Research Press, 1987) for a list of songs and the composers who used them.

41. Taruskin, *Defining Russia Musically,* 24. See his discussion of the collection, 16–24.

42. Mazo, "Introduction," 33–35.

43. Máchal, "Úvod," ix. The first volume was published anonymously. A note at the end indicated that all but one of the songs were by V. Hanka and that they had been set to music, which would be published in the fall, by V. Tomášek (xiv–xvii). In fact, Václav Jan Tomášek published the twelve songs in two installments, both entitled *Šestero písní,* in 1813 and 1814 (op. 48 and op. 50). He would publish six more songs by Hanka in 1823 (op. 71) and songs from the Queen's Court Manuscript (the RK, also later shown to be the work of Hanka, see chap. 6) in 1826 (op. 82). Hanka thus collaborated with the leading Czech composer before Smetana. Jaroslav Pohanka, *Dějiny české hudby v příkladech* (Prague: Státní nakladatelství krásné literatury, hudby a umění, 1958), 48–49 (poznámky). Given that Hanka was still awaiting the publication of the songs in 1815, the dates given by J. Teichman of 1816 and 1817 seem more likely for the song collections. Josef Teichman, *Z českých luhů do světa: Průkopníci české hudby* (Prague: Orbis, 1948), 43.

44. Máchal, "Úvod," ix–xi.

45. Ibid., xliv.

46. Ibid.

47. Harkins, *The Russian Folk Epos,* 44. Machal notes in Václav Hanka, *Hankovy písně a prostonárodní srbská muza, do Čech převedená,* ed. Jan Máchal (Prague: Česká Akademie Císaře Františka Josefa pro Vědy, Slovesnost a Umění, 1918), 255–58. Máchal shows Hanka's

translation to be error ridden and suggests Hanka's lack of knowledge of Serbian as the cause (Máchal, "Úvod," xxii.). Indeed, as his notes show, in addition to the phonetic translation of Russian and Serbian words (which Máchal labels as "slavish" or "literal" translations), there are dozens of faulty translations of other varieties as well. There is evidence that Hanka made use of Kopitar's translations of the songs into German (more than half of the songs Hanka translated had already been translated by Kopitar) to supplement his knowledge of the Serbian idiom (Harkins, *The Russian Folk Epos*, 39.). But Harkins also briefly noted the programmatic nature of the "slavish" phonetic translations (44), which I develop below.

48. Macura, *Znamení zrodu*, 76–77. On the translations from Polish and Russian, Macura cites M. Grepl, "K jazyku obrozenských překladů z ruštiny a polštiny," in *Slovanské spisovné jazyky v době obrození: Sborník věnovaný Univerzitou Karlovou k 300. narození Josefa Jungmanna* (Prague: Univerzita Karlova, 1974), 170–71.

49. On Chulkov's collection see Mazo, "Introduction," 14–16. Chulkov published a total of four volumes from 1770 to 1774.

50. Máchal, "Úvod," xxvii.

51. Harkins, *The Russian Folk Epos*, 44ff.

52. Máchal, "Úvod," xxviii–xxxii.

53. Shishkov, "Primiechaniia na drevnee o polku igorevom sochinenie," 7:36.

54. Shishkov, "Razgovory o slovesnosti mezhdu dvumia litsami Az i Buki," 3:52.

55. Ibid., 3:94, 81–82, 103.

56. Ibid., 3:95–103.

57. Quoted in Mordovchenko, *Russkaia kritika*, 147.

58. Letter to Gogol', 6 (18) February 1847, in V. A. Zhukovskii, *Sobranie sochinenii v chetyrekh tomakh*, 4 vols. (Moscow: Gosudarstvennoe izdatel'stvo khudozhestvennoi literatury, 1960), 4:544.

59. A. S. Ianushkevich, "Put' Zhukovskogo k eposu," in *Zhukovskii i russkaia kul'tura: Sbornik nauchnykh trudov*, ed. Dmitrii Sergeevich Likhachev, Raisa Vladimirovna Iezuitova, and Faina Zinov'evna Kanunova (Leningrad: Nauka, 1987).

60. Mordovchenko, *Russkaia kritika*, 147–48.

61. Zhukovskii, *Sobranie sochinenii*, 2:8.

62. P. A. Katenin, *Izbrannye proizvedeniia*, ed. G. V. Ermakova-Bitner, Biblioteka poeta, bol'shaia seriia (Moscow: Sovetskii pisatel', 1965), 91–97.

63. For a summary of the polemics, see Mordovchenko, *Russkaia kritika*, 148–52.

64. Nikolai Gnedich, "O vol'nom perevodie Biurgerovoi ballady: Lenora," *Syn Otechestva*, no. 27 (1816): 4.

65. Ibid., 5.

66. Ibid., 7–8.

67. On Gnedich's uncomfortable position between the two camps, see A. N. Egunov, *Gomer v russkikh perevodakh XVIII–XIX vekov*, 2nd ed. (Moskva: Izdatel'stvo "Indrik," 2001), 148–56.

68. Gnedich, "O vol'nom perevodie," 18.

69. Ibid., 10.

70. Ibid.

71. Ibid., 12.

72. A. S. Griboedov, "O razborie vol'nago perevoda Biurgerovoi ballady: 'Lenora,'" in *Polnoe sobranie sochinenii* (St. Petersburg: Razriad iziashchnoi slovesnosti Akademii Nauk, 1917), 15, 16. "*Turk*" here is opposed to the standard "*Turok.*"

73. Ibid., 15.

74. Ibid., 21, 23, 24, 23, 22.

75. For the repercussions of this polemics in the 1820s and beyond, see Tynianov, "Arkhaisty i Pushkin," 36–45.

6—*Translatio Studii—Translatio Prosodiae* I

1. Douglas Kelley sees translation, adaptation, and allegory as the three primary means of cultural transfer in medieval France. Douglas Kelley, "*Translatio Studii:* Translation, Adaptation, and Allegory in Medieval French Literature" *Philological Quarterly* 57, no. 3 (1978).

2. Tomáš Hlobil, "Introduction," in *An Historical Survey of the Science of Beauty and the Literature on the Subject,* by František Palacký (Olomouc: Palacký University, 2002), xl–xli. This is likely also one of the sources of Sergei Uvarov's conception of historical inheritance. See chap. 7.

3. Berman, *The Experience of the Foreign,* 48–51, 63.

4. Ibid., 49.

5. Prešpurk is one version of the period name Czech and Slovak speakers used for Bratislava, here taken from the volume's title page. On the renaming of the city, see Peter Bugge, "The Making of a Slovak City: The Czechoslovak Renaming of Pressburg/Pozsony/ Prešporok, 1918–19," *Austrian History Yearbook* 35 (2004).

6. In the commonly accepted periodization of the Czech revival, Jungmann dominates the second period (1806–1830), during which greater demands were placed on Czech literature to aspire to the highest artistic levels and the major outlines of national revival ideology were developed. Jungmann's leadership in Czech cultural matters at the time cannot be denied; however, the focus on Jungmann can also be a distorting lens through which to view the period. Miloslav Hýsek, in an article on Jungmann's critical school, often attributes to Jungmann ideas that were first successfully advocated by others and only later incorporated by Jungmann. And Vladimír Macura often refers in shorthand to Jungmannian orthodoxy in the 1820s, though this orthodoxy was shaped in important ways by Hanka's advocacy and practice of the imitation of folk forms, of little interest to Jungmann, and challenged deeply in its linguistic program by Kollár's passionate embrace of Slavic nationalism (see chap. 9). While Hýsek's assertion that *"Počátkové* did not bring anything new to Czech poetry" is true in some sense—none of the postulates was without precedent—it falsely ignores the novelty of Šafařík and Palacký's emphases, the hierarchy of values they constructed, and the new dialogues they initiated. Miloslav Hýsek, "Jungmannova škola kritická," *Listy filologické* 41 (1914): 263. On periodization, see Vodička, ed., *Dějiny české literatury,* 2:9.

7. Pavel Jozef Šafárik and František Palacký, *Počátkové českého básnictví obzvláště prozódie* (Bratislava: Vydavateľstvo Slovenskej akadémie vied, 1961), 45 (11). This edition provides the original pagination, which will be given in parentheses in all further references.

8. Bernard Jenisch was director of the Academy of Oriental Languages at the university in Vienna and a friend of the Slavist and orientalist Václav Fortunát Durych. Václav Petrbok, "Příspěvek vídeňských a vídeňskonovoměstských bohemistů k české literární historii, bibliografii a knihopisu v letech 1770–1810," in *Vídeňský podíl na počátcích českého národního obrození, J. V. Zlobický (1743–1810) a současníci: Život, dílo, korespondence,* ed. Josef Vintr and Jana Pleskalová (Prague: Academia, 2004), 82. We should recall that it was Durych who encouraged Dobrovský's move from oriental to Slavic languages.

9. Šafárik and Palacký, *Počátkové českého básnictví,* 53 (23).

10. Ibid., 131. Miroslav Kačer, in the annotations to the text, cites on this point Andreas Heusler, *Deutsche Versgeschichte: Mit Einschluss des altenglischen und altnordischen Stabreimverses,* vol. 3, Grundriss der germanischen Philologie; bd. 8, teil 3 (Berlin: Gruyter, 1929), 86.

11. Hanuš, "Pavel Josef Šafařík," 530. Kačer notes that it is unknown whether there really was a letter or whether that is Šafařík's mystification, with the cited opinions based on his conversation with Hermann and his knowledge of the latter's works. Šafárik and Palacký, *Počátkové českého básnictví,* 132.

12. Šafárik and Palacký, *Počátkové českého básnictví,* 70–71 (53). Apel was the author of *Metrik* (1814/1816, 2 vols.), and Bothe was a publisher of German editions of ancient classics and the author of *Opuscula critica et poëtica* (1816).

13. Horálek, *Počátky novočeského verše,* 57.

14. Ibid., 29–33.

15. Ibid., 21, 49–57. This included trochaic, iambic, and dactylic forms.

16. Ibid., 37. Anežka Vidmanová has shown that these hexameters waver, like the medieval Latin verse that was their model, between classical quantitative prosody and syllabotonic prosody. The other traditional verse form used for translating hexameters in Czech was syllabic: 8-syllable couplets. Vidmanová, "Staročeské pokusy," 34.

17. Horálek, *Počátky novočeského verše,* 41–42, 59.

18. Ibid., 59–60.

19. Because of the closeness of the syllabic and syllabotonic systems in Czech, this is less of a radical change than it might seem. Miroslav Červenka invokes Mikhail Gasparov's *Ocherk istorii evropeiskogo stikha* to suggest that the change is best seen as a part of larger European developments in which syllabotonic verse established itself across Europe in the modern period. Miroslav Červenka, "Tři poznámky k Dobrovskému *Prozodiím,"* *Slovo a slovesnost* 64 (2003): 270. Mikhail L. Gasparov, *Ocherk istorii evropeiskogo stikha* (Moscow: Nauka, 1989).

20. Josef Dobrovský, "Böhmische prosodie," in *Literární a prozodická bohemika,* ed. Miroslav Heřman, *Spisy a projevy Josefa Dobrovského* (Prague: Academia, 1974), 75. Horálek, *Počátky novočeského verše,* 63.

21. If Dobrovský understood the difference between the quantity of the ancient languages and the accent of the modern languages, he and his contemporaries did not yet understand that the rhythmical variety available to a syllabotonic versification system is entirely different from that of the classicist system. Because classical verse required the strict fulfillment of the metrical scheme, it developed a large arsenal of verse feet and ways of combining different verse feet in verse forms. In syllabotonic verse systems, there is generally a small repertoire of metrical schemes, and most verse forms use only one type of verse foot, but variety is achieved in the tension between the abstract metrical scheme and its (always partial) realization in the stressed and unstressed syllables of the verse. Červenka, "Tři poznámky," 270–71.

22. Dobrovský, "Böhmische prosodie," 90, 91. In the understanding of classical prosody at the time, caesura meant the ending of a word within a metrical foot. In the dactylic-trochaic imitation of classical hexameter in Czech, if a word were to end within the foot, the stress on the first syllable of the following word would occur in an unstressed position, and Dobrovský's system did not allow for stress in unstressed positions. Thus, caesura was not possible.

23. Quoted in Agnew, *Origins of the Czech National Renascence*, 166; Josef Dobrovský, "Homérova Iliada z řeckého jazyka přeložena do českého od Jana Nejedlého, etc.," in *Literární a prozodická bohemika,* ed. Miroslav Heřman, *Spisy a projevy Josefa Dobrovského* (Prague: Academia, 1974), 116. The review was published in 1803.

24. Agnew, *Origins of the Czech National Renascence,* 167; Josef Dobrovský, "Chrám gnidský, d. i. der Tempel von Gnidus, ein Gedicht, aus dem Französischen ins Böhmische übersetzt von Anton Puchmajer," in *Literární a prozodická bohemika,* ed. Miroslav Heřman, *Spisy a projevy Josefa Dobrovského* (Prague: Academia, 1974), 132. This review was published in 1805.

25. Šafárik and Palacký, *Počátkové českého básnictví,* 55–56 (27–28).

26. Ibid., 44 (9).

27. Dobrovský had used similar arguments in propagating his system. Since two-syllable Czech words were naturally trochaic, the use of iambic meters was blind imitation of German verses. Dobrovský, "Böhmische prosodie," 79.

28. Šafárik and Palacký, *Počátkové českého básnictví,* 53 (23–24).

29. Ibid., 66 (45–46).

30. Ibid., 68 (49). This marvelous characterization of Šafárik's was inspired by Hermann's description in his letter of those who would imitate the Germans' accentual prosody: "das heißt, weil der eine lahm ist, auch den andern lahm zu machen" (71 [53]).

31. Ibid., 45 (11–12).

32. Ibid., 72 (56).

33. Ibid., 57 (30).

34. Ibid., 47, 48, 49 (15, 16, 17).

35. Ibid., 64 (42–43).

36. Ibid., 65 (44).

37. Ibid., 67 (46–47).

38. Jungmann, *Boj o obrození národa,* 51–53. As Macura has observed, such arguments were always relative to their particular context and the polemical point to be made. The opposite stance could just as easily be taken in order to emphasize the suitability of Czech for philosophy or for other purposes, as we shall see with Kollár. Macura, *Znamení zrodu,* 33.

39. Šafárik and Palacký, *Počátkové českého básnictví,* 67 (47).

40. Ibid., 63 (41), 90 (85).

41. Hýsek, "Jungmannova škola kritická," 259. The fact that the authors of *Počátkové* were educated in Slovakian Hungary arguably played a significant role in their adoption of a quantitative program for Czech(oslovak) literature. Not only could they observe Hungarian developments, they also would be aware of Slovak experiments with quantitative verse dating from the mid-eighteenth century. The Czech humanist tradition, which first formulated quantitative principles for Czech in the sixteenth century, was a living tradition in Slovakia, especially among Lutherans, and had not been so sharply interrupted by the Counter Reformation. Moreover, Slovak Catholics who followed the school of Anton Bernolák in his codification of literary Slovak made quantitative verse a programmatic part of their poetic school beginning in the 1780s. Finally, the Slovak language itself may have played a role, for word-initial stress is much less dominant in Slovak in relation to phrasal stress than in Czech (resulting in the very different intonational patterns of these closely related languages). See Mikuláš Bakoš, "*Počátkové českého básnictví, obzvláště prozódie* a ich význam vo vývine českej a slovenskej poézie," in *Počátkové českého básnictví obzvláště*

prozódie, by Pavel Jozef Šafárik and František Palacký (Bratislava: Vydavateľstvo Slovenskej akadémie vied, 1961), 34–36; and Jan Mukařovský, "Polákova *Vznešenost přírody* (Pokus o rozbor a vývojové zařadění básnické struktury)," in *Kapitoly z české poetiky* (Prague: Nakladatelství svoboda, 1948), 2:121–22.

42. That Latin, rather than Greek, played the central role for the Hungarian quantitative movement is a result of the continued high status of Latin, its use for educated and public discourse in Hungary well into the nineteenth century. Horálek comments on what the Hungarian practice of quantitative verse has to contribute to discussions of the viability of the quantitative principle in Czech verse, which has been denied by so many commentators. Horálek, *Počátky novočeského verše,* 14–15.

43. Šafárik and Palacký, *Počátkové českého básnictví,* 87–88 (80).

44. Ibid., 70 (53). In Šafaříkʹs translation of Hermannʹs letter we can see how new the notion of national character is in Czech discourse—he renders the phrase "karakter národu." The Greek term, filtered through Latin and German, has not been assimilated fully into Czech.

45. Ibid., 90 (85).

46. This is not to say that the authors imagined that bringing Czech literature to the level of Greek literature would be easy. In fact, the *difficulty* of quantitative verse, as we have seen, was important to them, for it would force poets to work hard on their language, to *cultivate* it, in the terms of fundamental culture-building metaphor of Jungmannʹs program.

47. Šafárik and Palacký, *Počátkové českého básnictví,* 104 (107).

48. Ibid., 105 (108–9).

49. Ibid., 108 (113).

50. Ibid., 57 (30).

51. Ibid., 86 (77).

52. Ibid., 55 (26). For the interesting, but somewhat reductive, argument that the Czech national revival should be seen as a re-embodiment of the tradition of Czech humanism, see David, "Národní obrození jako převtělení Zlatého věku."

53. Šafárik and Palacký, *Počátkové českého básnictví,* 105–6 (109).

54. Ibid., 72 (56).

55. Ibid., 91 (86).

56. Ibid., 91–92 (86–87).

57. Ibid., 92 (88).

58. Dobrovský, "Böhmische prosodie," 92. On the theory and practice of rhyme in the Czech revival, see Květa Sgallová, "Rým v teorii a v praxi národního obrození," *Česká literatura,* no. 6 (2002).

59. Šafárik and Palacký, *Počátkové českého básnictví,* 92–93 (88–89).

60. In Renaissance England, too, the pursuit of quantitative prosody included attacks on "barbaric" rhyme by such writers as Roger Ascham, William Webbe, George Puttenham, Edmund Spenser, and Thomas Campion. As for Palacký (see further), this was partly a Protestant attack on the early church and medieval learning. The development of English dramatic blank verse may owe something to these experiments. Vernon Hall, Jr., Arthur F. Kinney, and O. B. Hardison, Jr., "Renaissance Poetics," in *The New Princeton Encyclopedia of Poetry and Poetics,* ed. Alex Preminger and T. V. F. Brogan (Princeton, NJ: Princeton University Press, 1993), 1026.

61. Šafárik and Palacký, *Počátkové českého básnictví,* 93 (89).

62. Ibid., 135.

63. František Palacký and Simeon Karel Macháček, *Geschichte der schönen Redekünste bei den Böhmen/Dějiny české slovesnosti,* ed. Oldřich Králík and Jiří Skalička (Brno: Profil, 1968), 96–97. The sentence including this judgment was edited out of the final manuscript, which remained unpublished. It does not appear that doubts about this evaluation prompted the cut, but rather the fact that the sentence itself unnecessarily repeats the preceding discussion.

64. See the overview of these defenses in Agnew, *Origins of the Czech National Renascence,* 53ff. This survey is particularly valuable because many of the original texts are not readily available or easily accessible.

65. Quoted in Albert Pražák, *Národ se bránil, obrany národa a jazyka českého od nejstarších dob po přítomnost* (Prague: Sfinx, 1945), 144. The original text is in German; many of the defenses of Czech were written in German. The use of *libozvučnost* in the Czech translation may or may not correspond to *Wohlklang* in the German. My lack of access to the original texts of these defenses made the question of developments in terminology difficult to address. In the 1820s, *libozvučnost* became a focus term in Czech. Whether this is a result of the influence of *Počátkové* or whether the discussion had coalesced around this term earlier is hard to determine. Certainly, as will be seen, Dobrovský used *Wohlklang* repeatedly. It is worth noting that those defending the Czech language mobilized a German discourse. While the Germans had been and still were defending their language against French detractors, the Czechs used the resources of German defenses to defend against German detractors. Klopstock, who is both the hero and villain of Palacký and Šafařík's discussion of German metrics, had defended German against French attacks as recently as in his 1794 *Grammatische Gespräche,* the third dialogue of which, under the title "Der Wohlklang," compared the German and Greek languages and looked for common words. Eric A. Blackall, *The Emergence of German as a Literary Language, 1700–1775* (Cambridge: Cambridge University Press, 1959), 326–27.

66. Dobrovský, "Böhmische prosodie," 77.

67. Ibid., 93.

68. In 1815, Dobrovský published a large article in the second volume of his *Slovanka* journal entitled, "On the *Libozvučnost* of the Slavic Language, with Special Application to the Czech Dialect" ("Über den Wohlklang der Slawischen Sprache, mit besonderer Anwendung auf die Böhmische Mundart"). Palacký refers to this article rather dismissively: "the discussion on this topic located in the second volume of Slovanka, no matter how learned, is still merely grammatical and not aesthetic, so that a young Czech vaulting towards Parnassus will be made not a whit the wiser by the reading of it." Šafařík and Palacký, *Počátkové českého básnictví,* 99 (100). This is also an accurate assessment, for in that article Dobrovský was not at all concerned with the aesthetics of language, but rather with the phonological development of Czech. According to contemporary theories of phonetic change, sound changes occurred according to the principle of euphony. Dobrovský spends much of his time in the article explaining the insertion and removal of vowels in Czech and other Slavic languages, which were later shown to be the result of the "fall of the jers," through aesthetic considerations of sound. Ant. Frinta, "Dobrovský—fonetik," in *Josef Dobrovský, 1753–1829: Sborník statí k stému výročí smrti Josefa Dobrovského,* ed. Jiří Horák, Matyáš Murko, and Miloš Weingart (Prague: Slovanský seminář University Karlovy, 1929), 93.

69. Šafařík and Palacký, *Počátkové českého básnictví,* 66 (46).

70. Ibid., 94 (91).

71. Ibid., 96 (94–95).

72. Ibid., 97 (95–96).

73. Ibid., 98 (97).

74. Ibid., 99 (98–99).

75. Ibid., 48, 56 (16, 28).

76. See the analysis in Mukařovský, "Polákova *Vznešenost přírody*," 130–45.

77. As Horálek has shown, though, experiments to loosen up the strict identity of words and feet began very early among the members of Puchmajer's group and many poets, including Puchmajer himself and Jungmann, were able to achieve flexible verse forms in the syllabotonic system long before Polák. Horálek argues, contra Mukařovský, that Polák's verse does not distinguish itself very much from these earlier experiments but should be seen, along with *Počátkové*, as part of a more general tendency to try to introduce a variety of verse forms and flexible meter into Czech poetry. Horálek, *Počátky novočeského verše*, 65–86.

78. Mukařovský, "Polákova *Vznešenost přírody*," 175.

79. Šafárik and Palacký, *Počátkové českého básnictví*, 101 (102).

80. The Czech adjective *národní*, unlike the corresponding Russian adjective *narodnyi*, did not generally also carry the sense of "popular."

81. Šafárik and Palacký, *Počátkové českého básnictví*, 106–07 (110–11).

82. Mukařovský, "Polákova *Vznešenost přírody*"; Jan Mukařovský, "Dobrovského 'Česká prozodie' a prosodické boje jí podnícené," *Česká literatura* 2, no. 1 (1954).

83. Horálek, *Počátky novočeského verše*, 92–102.

84. Varcl et al., *Antika a česká kultura*, 332–37.

85. Joep Leerssen, "Ossian and the Rise of Literary Historicism," in *The Reception of Ossian in Europe*, ed. Howard Gaskill (New York: Thoemmes Continuum, 2004), 124.

86. Pavel Jozef Šafárik, "Národní písně a zpěvy. Promluvení k Slovanům," *Prvotiny pěkných umění*, no. 1 (1817): 3–4.

87. Šafárik and Palacký, *Počátkové českého básnictví*, 99–100 (100).

88. Ibid., 100 (101).

89. I examine elsewhere the reception of the Russian *Slovo* as inspiration and model for the Czech reception of the forged manuscripts, particularly in relation to the writing of national literary history. David L. Cooper, "The Rukopis Královédvorský and the Formation of Czech National Literary History," in *Between Texts, Languages, and Cultures: A Festschrift for Michael Henry Heim*, ed. Craig Cravens, Masako U. Fidler, and Susan C. Kresin (Bloomington, IN: Slavica, 2008).

90. Here I must briefly address the thesis of Edward Keenan, who argues that Dobrovský forged *Slovo*. Edward L. Keenan, *Josef Dobrovský and the Origins of the Igor' Tale*, Harvard Series in Ukrainian Studies (Cambridge: Harvard Ukrainian Research Institute and the Davis Center for Russian and Eurasian Studies; distributed by Harvard University Press, 2003). The book has already elicited a flood of reviews and responses whose authors agree that the work is not without its merits, though the majority also agree that the merit of having proven its thesis is not among them. The argument is fascinating, but it most resembles the logic of conspiracy theories. On this, see, Norman W. Ingham, "The *Igor' Tale* and the Origins of Conspiracy Theory" (paper presented at the Davis Center for Russian and Eurasian Studies, Harvard University: 2004) and Olga B. Strakhov, "A New Book on the Origin of the *Igor' Tale*: A Backward Step," *Palaeoslavica* 12, no. 1 (2004). While the largest section of Keenan's book is dedicated to the linguistic evidence in the text, the author treats only lexical evidence, ignoring the truly decisive linguistic evidence

of morphology (especially verbal forms and the dual) and orthography: Olga B. Strakhov, "The Linguistic Practice of the Creator of the *Igor' Tale* and the Linguistic Views of Josef Dobrovský," *Palaeoslavica* 11 (2003); A. A. Zalizniak, *"Slovo o polku Igoreve": Vzgliad lingvista* (Moscow: Iazyki slavianskoi kul'tury, 2004). Moreover, Keenan treats the lexical evidence he does examine in a highly tendentious manner (Francis Butler, "Edward Keenan, Vladimir Dal', and the *Slovo o polku Igoreve,"* *Russian History/Histoire Russe* 33, nos. 2–3–4 (2006); Simon Franklin, "The Igor Tale: A Bohemian Rapshody?" *Kritika: Explorations in Russian and Eurasian History* 6 (2005); Strakhov, "A New Book.") and willfully ignores evidence that would challenge his thesis (Ingham, "The *Igor' Tale*"; Strakhov, "A New Book."). When it comes to the relationship of Dobrovský to *Slovo,* Keenan does not adequately examine the evidence in Dobrovský's publications and correspondence (Ingham, "The *Igor' Tale*"; Strakhov, "A New Book."). In short, the articles and reviews stimulated by Keenan's thesis seem likely to put to rest any further doubts among scholars about the authenticity of the document.

91. Mojmír Otruba, ed., *Rukopisy královédvorský a zelenohorský: Dnešní stav poznání* (Prague: Academia, 1969), 25–26; Milan Otáhal, "The Manuscript Controversy in the Czech National Revival," *Cross Currents* 5 (1986): 249; Derek Sayer, *The Coasts of Bohemia: A Czech History* (Princeton, NJ: Princeton University Press, 1998), 144.

92. Cf. Harkins, *The Russian Folk Epos,* 57–63.

93. Ibid., 45–49. Máchal, "Úvod," xxxiii–xxxvii.

94. Vodička, ed., *Dějiny české literatury,* 2:186–87.

95. Horálek, *Počátky novočeského verše,* 87–88, 98–99.

7—*Translatio Studii—Translatio Prosodiae* II

1. Stephen L. Baehr, "From History to National Myth: *Translatio Imperii* in Eighteenth-Century Russia," *The Russian Review* 37, no. 1 (1978): 2, 13.

2. Ibid., 1.

3. M. Gasparov, *Ocherk istorii russkogo stikha,* 30. See also Richard Burgi, *A History of the Russian Hexameter* (Hamden, CT: Shoe String Press, 1954), 27.

4. Boris Gasparov, "Russkaia Gretsiia, russkii Rim," in *Christianity and the Eastern Slavs,* vol. 2, *Russian Culture in Modern Times,* ed. Robert Hughes and Irina Paperno (Berkeley: University of California Press, 1994), 250.

5. Baehr, "From History to National Myth," 3, 5. See Baehr on this renewal more generally as well.

6. Mikhailo V. Lomonosov, *Sochineniia* (Moscow: Gosudarstvennoe izdatel'stvo khudozhestvennoi literatury, 1961), 263–64.

7. Ibid., 271. As B. Gasparov notes, Lomonosov derides not classical Latin, but the vulgar Latin of the Middle Ages. Classical Latin was as much a part of his ideal as classical Greek. Gasparov, "Russkaia Gretsiia, russkii Rim," 252–53.

8. Harsha Ram has noted Trediakovsky's *"unwillingness to link poetics and ideology"* (emphasis in original). Ram, *The Imperial Sublime,* 46.

9. V. K. Trediakovskii, *Izbrannye proizvedeniia,* Biblioteka poeta, bol'shaia seriia, 2 izd. (Leningrad: Sovetskii pisatel', 1963), 426–27. The discovery of *Slovo o polku Igoreve* would later seem to confirm some of Trediakovsky's speculations. As Trediakovsky's discussion of "feet" in connection to "tonic" prosody suggests, he did not distinguish between syllabotonic

and purely tonic prosody, pace Burgi. Burgi, *A History of the Russian Hexameter*, 64–65.

10. Trediakovskii, *Izbrannye proizvedeniia*, 427.

11. Rollin's discussion, which Trediakovsky translates at the end of his article, is a sedate compilation—not nearly as interesting as the speculations that Trediakovsky develops from it. V. K. Trediakovskii, *Sochineniia*, 3 vols. (St. Petersburg: Izd. A. Smirdina, 1849), 1:179–201. As Karen Rosenberg has suggested, though Rollin was not a particularly original author, he offered to Trediakovsky useful summaries of the French debates, which Trediakovsky knew well. Rosenberg, "Between Ancients and Moderns," 10–11. Rollin was Trediakovsky's professor when he studied in Paris from 1728 to 1730. Reyfman, *Vasilii Trediakovsky*, 263n.9.

12. Trediakovskii, *Izbrannye proizvedeniia*, 448–49.

13. For a fuller discussion of Trediakovsky's position, see Rosenberg, "Between Ancients and Moderns." Viktor Zhivov suggests that Trediakovsky often worked in contradictory directions from one project to the next. Zhivov, "Tserkovnoslavianskaia literaturnaia traditsiia," 64–65.

14. Burgi gives a full translation of this section of the treatise. Burgi, *A History of the Russian Hexameter*, 43–45.

15. Trediakovskii, *Sochineniia*, 2:lxxviii.

16. Ibid., 2: xlvi–xlvii. Burgi gives a full translation of this section. Burgi, *A History of the Russian Hexameter*, 49–50.

17. Trediakovskii, *Sochineniia*, 2:xlvii–xlviii.

18. Ibid., 2:xlvii, li.

19. Ibid., 2:lix. Trediakovsky's polemical simile here of the thirsty man in water up to his mouth is a nice equivalent to Šafařík's metaphor of the Czech limping on two good legs.

20. Ibid., 2:lxiii.

21. Ibid., 2:lxii.

22. Trediakovskii, *Izbrannye proizvedeniia*, 425.

23. Trediakovskii, *Sochineniia*, 2:lvi.

24. For Hurd, see Oergel, *The Return of King Arthur*, 102. Goethe's rhapsody to Gothic architecture was published in Herder's *On German Character and Art* (1773). August Schlegel repeated Hurd's example in his *Lectures on Dramatic Art and Literature* (1809–11).

25. Trediakovskii, *Sochineniia*, 2:xvi–xvii. Note that Fénelon gets included in spite of the lack of hexameter form, or perhaps only because Trediakovsky has done him the favor of putting the work into hexameter. Trediakovsky explicitly remarks on Tasso's, Milton's, and others' failure to use hexameter (xxi).

26. See the examples in L. V. Pumpianskii, "Trediakovskii," in *Istoriia russkoi litertatury*, ed. G. A. Gukovskii and V. A. Desnitskii (Moscow: Izdatel'stvo Akademii nauk SSSR, 1941), 249–59.

27. For a list of compound adjectives with Greek antecedents, see A. I. Malein, "Prilozhenie k stat'e A. S. Orlova 'Tilemakhida,'" in *XVIII vek: Sbornik statei i materialov*, ed. A. S. Orlov (Moscow: Izdatel'stvo Akademii nauk SSSR, 1935). Pumpianskii argues the Latin mediation for these. For additional evidence that Trediakovsky followed Latin hexameter as his model, see Mikhail L. Gasparov, "Prodrom, Tsets i natsional'nye formy geksametra," in *Antichnost' i vizantiia*, ed. L. A. Freiberg (Moscow: Nauka, 1975), 375–77.

28. Patey, "Ancients and Moderns," 58; Simonsuuri, *Homer's Original Genius*, 27–28.

29. Patey, "Ancients and Moderns," 36.

30. See Rosenberg, "Between Ancients and Moderns," 14.

31. Ibid., 294–96.

32. I. M. Murav'ev-Apostol, "Pis'mo pervoe iz Moskvy v Nizhnii Novgorod," *Syn Otechestva*, no. 35 (1813): 91.

33. I. M. Murav'ev-Apostol, "Pis'ma iz Moskvy v Nizhnii Novgorod: Pis'mo tretie," *Syn Otechestva*, no. 39 (1813): 12.

34. I. M. Murav'ev-Apostol, "Pis'ma iz Moskvy v Nizhnii Novgorod: Pis'mo chetvertoe," *Syn Otechestva*, no. 44 (1813): 220.

35. Ibid., 221–22.

36. Ibid., 223.

37. Ibid., 233–34.

38. Reyfman, *Vasilii Trediakovsky*, 23–131. The *Tilemakhida* appeared when Trediakovsky's role as a fool had already been well established in the leading literary circles and he had largely withdrawn from public literary quarrels. He died, poor and defeated, just three years later (30). Still, the work was owned and even read widely by educated Russians (41). Not least among them was Nikolai Gnedich. See Egunov, *Gomer v russkikh perevodakh XVIII–XIX vekov*, 151.

39. Uspenskii and Lotman, "Spory o iazyke v nachale XIX v.," 490.

40. Burgi, *A History of the Russian Hexameter*, 72.

41. A. N. Radishchev, *Polnoe sobranie sochinenii*, 3 vols. (Moscow: Izdatel'stvo Akademii nauk SSSR, 1941), 1:352. Burgi translates the entire relevant section of the chapter. Burgi, *A History of the Russian Hexameter*, 77–79.

42. Radishchev, *Polnoe sobranie sochinenii*, 1:352–53. On the semantics of "*diad'ka*" see Reyfman, *Vasilii Trediakovsky*, 19.

43. A. N. Radishchev, *Stikhotvoreniia*, Biblioteka poeta, bol'shaia seriia (Leningrad: Sovetskii pisatel', 1975), 206, 187.

44. Ibid., 202.

45. Ibid., 188.

46. Radishchev, *Polnoe sobranie sochinenii*, 2:397–98.

47. P. N. Berkov, "A. N. Radishchev kak kritik," *Vestnik Leningradskogo universiteta* 9 (1949): 66–67 and passim. The tract was published with his collected works in 1809, but he had begun work on it in 1792. Radishchev, *Polnoe sobranie sochinenii*, 2:370. Berkov translates Radishchev's term into a more modern Russian form as "*blagozvuchie.*"

48. Berkov, "A. N. Radishchev kak kritik," 70.

49. Radishchev, *Stikhotvoreniia*, 204–05.

50. It is used, however, by Kapnist for the opposing argument, as we will see.

51. Mark Al'tshuller, *Predtechi slavianofil'stva v russkoi literature: Obshchestvo 'Beseda liubitelei russkago slova'* (Ann Arbor, MI: Ardis, 1984), 319.

52. See Reyfman, *Vasilii Trediakovsky*, chap. 4. for deployments of Trediakovsky in the archaist-innovator debates.

53. "The discussion surrounding hexameter at that time concerned not so much the technical side of the issue as the urgent question of *narodnost'* in literature." Egunov, *Gomer v russkikh perevodakh*, 160. This is, of course, a question of *narodnost'* avant la lettre. See chap. 8 on the emergence of the term.

54. Al'tshuller writes that Trediakovsky strove "toward the creation of Russian national [*natsional'naia*] culture." (Al'tshuller, *Predtechi slavianofil'stva*, 310). This is true in the broader sense, but the assertion involves a certain anachronism if we understand this as a conscious striving in the sense that it began to take on in the early nineteenth century, which was opposed to universal, normative aesthetic models. On Trediakovsky's normative

aesthetic universalism, see I. D. Vladimirova, "Evoliutsiia literaturnykh vzgliadov V. K. Trediakovskogo," *Uchenye zapiski Tartuskogo universiteta,* no. 604 (1982): 35, 43, 47. I. D. Vladimirova is a pseudonym under which Irina Reyfman published the article.

55. Al'tshuller, *Predtechi slavianofil'stva,* 318. Reyfman, *Vasilii Trediakovsky,* 160.

56. Aleksandr Vostokov, "Opyt o russkom stikhoslozhenii," *Sanktpeterburgskie vedomosti,* no. 4–6 (1812): 40.

57. Ibid., 41.

58. Ibid.

59. Ibid., 43.

60. Ibid., 47–48.

61. Ibid., 274–76, 287–88.

62. Ibid., 51. Vostokov knew of Czech quantity from Jan Nejedlý's 1804 *Böhmische Grammatik.* But Vostokov here and in general fails to distinguish between true quantitative prosody and syllabotonic systems that used stress in place of length to imitate the Greek and Latin meters. Thus the German language and, eventually, the Russian can stand alongside the Czech. In a later section of the work, Vostokov notes that it is a convention in Russian prosody to equate stress with length, but this convention becomes for him an implicit rule in his discussion of other languages as well. For Czech, where it is possible to distinguish between length and stress, he fails to make the distinction (172, 174).

63. For his discussion of the limitations of Czech quantitative prosody, Vostokov instead cites what was a major complaint against the Czech syllabotonic system: a lack of iambs and other feet beginning with short measure, since the first syllable is always stressed. The lack in the quantitative system most often cited by its opponents was of sufficient long syllables. This is symptomatic of his lack of distinction between the two possibilities: true quantitative prosody or its syllabotonic imitation.

64. Vostokov, "Opyt o russkom stikhoslozhenii," 54.

65. Ibid., 55. On this point and several more of the following points, Vostokov clearly follows Radishchev.

66. Ibid., 56.

67. Ibid., 57–58.

68. Ibid., 58–59.

69. In the second edition of the essay, published in 1817, one of Vostokov's revisions included the addition of a ten page "dissertation" on hexameter that reviewed the history of its use by Russian poets, responded briefly to the polemics between Uvarov and Kapnist, and ended with a few "rules" for how the meter ought to be composed in Russian (Vostokov preferred a line primarily made up of trochees). Here, too, Vostokov's discourse is philological in tone, with no programmatic expectation or promise of a more national literature as a result of following his recommendations. Aleksandr Vostokov, *Opyt o russkom stikhoslozhenii,* 2nd ed. (St. Petersburg: Morskaia tipografiia, 1817), 51–60.

70. Egunov, *Gomer v russkikh perevodakh,* 147–49, 133–35.

71. Nikolai I. Gnedich, "Otvet," in *Arzamas: Sbornik v dvukh knigakh,* ed. Vadim Erazmovich Vatsuro and A. L. Ospovat (Moscow: Khudozhestvennaia literatura, 1994), 2:83–84. Uvarov's letter and Gnedich's reply were both first published in *Chtenie v Besede liubitelei russkogo slova* 13 (1813).

72. V. V. Kapnist, *Sobranie sochinenii,* 2 vols. (Leningrad: Izdatel'stvo Akademii nauk SSSR, 1960), 2:187.

73. See Cynthia H. Whittaker, *The Origins of Modern Russian Education: An*

Intellectual Biography of Count Sergei Uvarov, 1786–1855 (DeKalb: Northern Illinois University Press, 1984), 34–56.

74. Ibid., 38.

75. Ibid., 3–4, 48.

76. Ibid., 18–19. On the influence of Friedrich Schlegel's *Über Sprache und Weisheit der Indier* (1808) on Uvarov, see Andrei L. Zorin, "Ideologiia 'Pravoslaviia—samoderzhaviia—narodnosti' i ee nemetskie istochniki," in *V razdum'iakh o Rossii (XIX vek),* ed. E. L. Rudnitskaia (Moscow: Arkheograficheskii tsentr, 1996), 106–12. While Uvarov was close to Madame de Staël in Vienna and had at least met August Schlegel, his acquaintance with Friedrich was not so immediate (107).

77. Whittaker, *Origins of Modern Russian Education,* 19, 22.

78. Sergei S. Uvarov, *Projet d'une académie asiatique* (St. Petersburg: n.p.; 1810), 26–27. Quoted in Whittaker, *Origins of Modern Russian Education,* 25.

79. Ibid., 15. On Uvarov's prior lack of interest in Russian matters, see Zorin, "Ideologiia 'Pravoslaviia—samoderzhaviia—narodnosti,'" 115, 119.

80. On Olenin, see Mary Stuart, *Aristocrat-Librarian in Service to the Tsar: Aleksei Nikolaevich Olenin and the Imperial Public Library* (Boulder, CO: East European Monographs, 1986).

81. Theophilus Christopher Prousis, *Russian Society and the Greek Revolution* (DeKalb: Northern Illinois University Press, 1994), 90; Whittaker, *Origins of Modern Russian Education,* 15.

82. Stuart, *Aristocrat-Librarian,* 47–48; Peter France, "Fingal in Russia," in *The Reception of Ossian in Europe,* ed. Howard Gaskill (London: Thoemmes Continuum, 2004), 266–68.

83. Sergei S. Uvarov, "Pis'mo k Nikolaiu Ivanovichu Gnedichu o grecheskom ekzametre," in *Arzamas: Sbornik v dvukh knigakh,* ed. Vadim Erazmovich Vatsuro and A. L. Ospovat (Moscow: Khudozhestvennaia literatura, 1994), 2:78.

84. Ibid.

85. Ibid., 2:78–79.

86. Ibid., 2:79.

87. Ibid., 2:80.

88. Ibid.

89. On Uvarov's studies, see Zorin, "Ideologiia 'Pravoslaviia—samoderzhaviia—narodnosti,'" 105.

90. Uvarov, "Pis'mo k Gnedichu," 2:80–81.

91. Ibid., 2:82.

92. Ibid. One should recall here Andrei Turgenev's characterization of French drama (see chap. 2).

93. Ibid.

94. Kapnist, *Sobranie sochinenii,* 2:191. The letter was first published in 1815 in *Chtenie v Besede,* no. 17.

95. Ibid., 2:187–88.

96. Ibid., 2:191–92.

97. Ibid., 2:192.

98. Iu. D. Levin, *Ossian v russkoi literature: Konets XVIII–pervaia tret' XIX veka* (Leningrad: Nauka, 1980), 60–61. One of the folk forms he used that was not a part of the Russian syllabotonic repertoire was the 5 + 5 + 5 form (*stroennyi piatislozhnik*). On the complex topic of Russian folk versification, see James O. Bailey, "Folk Versification," in *Handbook of Russian Literature,* ed. Victor Terras (New Haven, CT: Yale University Press, 1985).

99. Kapnist, *Sobranie sochinenii*, 2:563.

100. Ibid., 2:193.

101. Ibid., 2:210. Kapnist cites Lʹvov's influence in his second letter to Uvarov, which remained unpublished.

102. N. A. Lʹvov, *Izbrannye sochineniia*, ed. K. I. U. Lappo-Danilevskii (St. Petersburg: Pushkinskii dom, 1994), 311–12.

103. Kapnist, *Sobranie sochinenii*, 2:176.

104. Ibid., 2:167–77.

105. Ibid., 2:178. Kapnist here promises that the verse forms would bring *blagoglasie* into Russian poetry, in a manner similar to Šafařík and Palacký's promises of *libozvučnost* as a result of quantitative prosody. But Kapnist's idiosyncratic thesis had little influence on his contemporaries and his terms, *blagoglasie* and *blagozvuchnostʹ*, did not become a part of Russian discussions concerning the national qualities of their literature.

106. Ibid., 2:193.

107. Lʹvov, *Izbrannye sochineniia*, 196, 198.

108. Kapnist, *Sobranie sochinenii*, 2:193–94.

109. Sergei S. Uvarov, "Otvet V. V. Kapnistu na pisʹmo ego ob ekzametre," in *Arzamas: Sbornik v dvukh knigakh*, ed. Vadim Erazmovich Vatsuro and A. L. Ospovat (Moscow: Khudozhestvennaia literatura, 1994), 2:88.

110. Ibid., 2:89.

111. Ibid., 2:90.

112. On A. W. Schlegel, see Berman, *The Experience of the Foreign*, 131–34.

113. Uvarov, "Otvet," 92. Fashion was already a traditional and frequent source of tropes for the assertion of Russian cultural independence. See chap. 2, "Manners and Morals," by Hans Rogger, in his *National Consciousness in Eighteenth-Century Russia*, Russian Research Center Studies, 38 (Cambridge: Harvard University Press, 1960).

114. Uvarov, "Otvet," 93.

115. Levin, *Ossian v russkoi literature*, 63.

116. Ibid., 72.

117. Prousis, *Russian Society*, 103.

118. For summaries of the debates, see Egunov, *Gomer v russkikh perevodakh*, 157–69; and Burgi, *A History of the Russian Hexameter*, 107–17.

119. Prousis, *Russian Society*, 98, 206n.51. Prousis cites an unpublished letter from 1814 from the archives.

120. Neizviestnyi [A. F. Merzliakov], "Pisʹmo iz Sibiri," *Trudy Obshchestva liubitelei rossiiskoi slovesnosti pri Imperatorskom moskovskom universitete*, no. 11 (1818): 57. The incident is analyzed in detail by Dziadko, who underlines the connections to Turgenev's speech. Dziadko, "'Za chto nam drug ot druga otdaliatʹsia?'"

121. Dziadko, "'Za chto nam drug ot druga otdaliatʹsia?'" 118–20.

122. Neizviestnyi [Merzliakov], "Pisʹmo iz Sibiri," 68.

123. Ibid.

8—*Narodnostʹ* Invented and Deployed

1. "Natsionalʹnostʹ," in *Slovarʹ russkogo iazyka XVIII veka* (St. Petersburg: Nauka, 2004). I would like to thank Nathanial Knight for directing me to this occurrence of the term.

2. A. N. Radishchev, *Izbrannye sochineniia* (Moscow: Gosudarstvennoe izdatel'stvo khudozhestvennoi literatury, 1952), 568.

3. Uspenskii and Lotman, "Spory o iazyke v nachale XIX v.," 451–52.

4. The first to so credit Viazemsky was M. Azadovskii, "Fol'klorizm Lermontova," *Literaturnoe nasledstvo* 43–44 (1941): 261n.14. This moment of the "invention" of the term has been widely noted and discussed: Lauren G. Leighton, *"Narodnost'* as a Concept of Russian Romanticism," in *Russian Romanticism: Two Essays* (The Hague: Mouton, 1975), 49–51; and Leighton, *Russian Romantic Criticism: An Anthology,* Contributions to the Study of World Literature, no. 18 (New York: Greenwood Press, 1987), 38; Uspenskii and Lotman, "Spory o iazyke v nachale XIX v.," 451; Katya Hokanson, "Literary Imperialism, *Narodnost'* and Pushkin's Invention of the Caucasus," *The Russian Review* 53, no. 3 (1994): 338–39; Nathaniel Knight, "Ethnicity, Nationality, and the Masses: *Narodnost'* and Modernity in Imperial Russia," in *Russian Modernity: Politics, Knowledge, Practices,* ed. David L. Hoffmann and Yanni Kotsonis (New York: St. Martin's Press, 2000), 49–50; Melissa Frazier, *Romantic Encounters: Writers, Readers, and the Library for Reading* (Stanford, CA: Stanford University Press, 2007), 188.

5. V. I. Saitov, ed., *Ostaf'evskii arkhiv kniazei Viazemskikh,* vol. 1, *Perepiska kniazia P. A. Viazemskago s A. I. Turgenevym, 1812–1819* (St. Petersburg: Izdanie grafa S. D. Sheremeteva, 1899), 357–58.

6. For accounts of the origin of this doctrine of "official nationality" see Zorin, *Kormia dvuglavogo orla,* 339–74; and Whittaker, *Origins of Modern Russian Education.*

7. For an overview in English of the term, see Leighton, *"Narodnost'* as a Concept of Russian Romanticism." Leighton accounts for the diversity of views on the term in the 1820s within the different projects of various authors, and his careful notation of the European sources for numerous Russian ideas on the topic is an invaluable contribution. Occasionally, however, he reads too broadly and not closely enough in formulating the sense of the term for a given author. This includes sometimes taking *narodnost'* as a term when the term was still establishing itself (see my reading of Orest Somov's essay below). I, too, hope to account for the diversity in views on the term, reading closely the essays of a number of authors. But at the same time, I would like to account for the centrality of this term, the unity behind the diversity: *narodnost'* as the agreed upon term for discussion of how Russia was to make its literature national.

8. Ibid., 44.

9. One wonders whether Aleksandr Turgenev would not have heard an echo of his brother's speech in Viazemsky's letter. He was now the head of the Turgenev family, after his brother's and father's deaths, and was in possession of the family papers, until he passed them on in 1835 to his brother Nikolai Ivanovich's children. (Nikolai's son Petr made the family papers available to scholars at the end of the nineteenth century, which enabled the rediscovery of the Friendly Literary Society and Andrei Turgenev's speech.) Istrin, *Pis'ma i dnevnik Aleksandra Ivanovicha Turgeneva,* 5–6 (first pagination series). Moreover, he had had recent occasion to be reminded of his brother. In 1814 he received the papers of Andrei Kaisarov, who had died in the war. He wrote to Zhukovsky: "Do you know what I have been doing, shut off from the world, for three days this week? I was rereading the papers of my brother Andrei, which finally got to me, letters and notes to An[drei] Kaisarov [from 17]99 and the following years. Sweet and bitter minutes!" Istrin, *Pis'ma i dnevnik Aleksandra Ivanovicha Turgeneva,* 58. And in 1818 he received Kaisarov's diary. He wrote to Zhukovsky on February 12, "The past has been resurrected for me *und mancher liebe*

Schatten stieg herauf [and many dear shades arose]*!* All of our youth is there! Youth! I have not felt things so animatedly for a long time. Andrei S[ergeevich]'s entire journal is filled with fiery friendship for my brother, and the memory of Kaisarov has since become more sacred." Istrin, *Pis'ma i dnevnik Aleksandra Ivanovicha Turgeneva*, 58. But there is no suggestion in any of the letters that Aleksandr ever connected Viazemsky's concerns with those of his brother. After all, two decades had not passed in vain for Aleksandr Turgenev. For him, the Friendly Literary Society was followed by a circle in Moscow that included Viazemsky before the close of the first decade of the century, and from which came the Arzamas society in the middle of the following decade. Viazemsky was for him therefore a part of the continuity of his literary life. In a letter to Viazemsky on September 25, 1823, Aleksandr Turgenev swore his loyalty in friendship to Viazemsky and alluded to pain he had experienced in the loss of loyal friends: "I . . . have remained a pure Arzamasian, have not betrayed a single one of them. And what have I got in return from each of them? Where is the Zhukovskii *who was once mine?* I won't even recall the others. What have the *Arzamasians of the old testament,* that is, both the friends and comrades of my brother Andrei, done with me?" Saitov, ed., *Ostaf'evskii arkhiv kniazei Viazemskikh,* 2:351. For Aleksandr Turgenev, the echo of his brother's speech in Viazemsky's letter, if he recognized it, would have been the natural product of a continuity of programmatic literary activity over two decades. At the same time, these were new times, distant from the *Old Testament* days of his brother's speech. I doubt very much that he would have encouraged the revival of his brother's rhetoric for Viazemsky's polemical use—such as in the introduction to Pushkin's "Fountain of Bakhchisarai," which as we will see, echoed the rhetoric of Andrei Turgenev's speech quite closely. The genetic links between Viazemskii's introduction and Andrei Turgenev's speech are, I think, undeniable, but they also had to be indirect and diffuse, mediated by two decades of the literary activity of Andrei Turgenev's comrades, including Merzliakov.

10. Uspenskii and Lotman, "Spory o iazyke v nachale XIX v.," 451; "Natsional'nost'," in *Slovar' russkogo iazyka XVIII veka.*

11. Mikhail A. Dmitriev, "Vtoroi razgovor mezhdu Klassikom i Izdatelem Bakhchisaraiskago Fontana," *Vestnik Evropy* 134, no. 5 (1824): 56. On the larger polemics between Dmitriev and Viazemsky, see Mordovchenko, *Russkaia kritika,* 201–7.

12. Petr Viazemskii, "Razbor Vtorago Razgovora, napechatannago v 7 No Viestnika Evropy," *Damskii zhurnal,* no. 8 (1824): 76–77.

13. Mordovchenko, *Russkaia kritika,* 198–200.

14. Aleksandr Bestuzhev-Marlinskii, "Vzgliad na staruiu i novuiu slovesnost' v Rossii," in *Sochineniia v dvukh tomakh* (Moscow: Khudozhestvennaia literatura, 1958), 2:526, 530.

15. Lauren Gray Leighton, in his annotated collection of *Russian Romantic Criticism,* does an admirable job of tracing the deployment of the ideas of these writers in the essays of many Russian romantic critics. The index is a fortunate guide to the fragmentary notes, which include information on Russian translations of these writers. Leighton, *Russian Romantic Criticism.*

16. Leighton, *Russian Romantic Criticism,* 116, 187. Though he was a minor aesthetician, he was an important Prussian statesman. From 1792 he was professor of history at the Berlin Military Academy and in 1814 was made royal historian. He gave up his professorship in 1810 to tutor the crown prince, later Frederick William IV. In 1814 he began to work in the Prussian Ministry of Foreign Affairs and became minister in

1832, working closely with Metternich and Russia to combat liberalism and preserve the Congress of Vienna settlement.

17. Early in his essay, Somov cites Ancillon's "Essai sur la différence de la Poésie ancienne et de la Poésie moderne." Leighton has tracked down Somov's reference: "Somov probably refers to the Russian translation of an excerpt from Ancillon's *Mélanges de literature et de philosophie* (1809), published in *Amphion* in 1815 (October and November, 45–97) under the title 'On the Difference Between Ancient and Modern Poetry.' The treatise was published in Russian translation in 1813 under the title *Aesthetic Discourses of Mr. Ancillon*. As will be seen in many other essays in this anthology, Ancillon exerted a profound and still insufficiently explored influence on Russian Romantic thought." Leighton, *Russian Romantic Criticism*, 36. See also, Leighton, "*Narodnost'* as a Concept of Russian Romanticism," 75–77; and Knight, "Ethnicity, Nationality," 48–49.

18. Orest Somov, "O romanticheskoi poezii," *Sorevnovatel' prosveshcheniia i blagotvoreniia* 23 (1823): 157.

19. Leighton, *Russian Romantic Criticism*, 40–41.

20. Somov, "O romanticheskoi poezii," 48–52. Somov was perhaps influenced in leaning toward an eastern narrative by the orientalizing predilections of his favorite critic, Madame de Staël, who wrote in her memoirs of her visit to Russia in 1812: "The Russians, as I see it, have much more in common with the peoples of the South, or rather the Orient, than with those of the North. Their European traits pertain to the manners of the Court, which are the same in every country. But their nature is Oriental." Madame de Staël, *Madame de Staël on Politics, Literature, and National Character*, ed. and trans. Morroe Berger (Garden City, NY: Doubleday, 1965), 335–36.

21. Somov, "O romanticheskoi poezii," 155–56.

22. Ibid., 137.

23. Leighton, *Russian Romantic Criticism*, 77–78.

24. Dmitriev, "Vtoroi razgovor," 56.

25. In Leighton's abridged English translation of Somov's essay, the word *narodnost'* appears six times, of which only two correspond to actual usages in the text. (Although the first footnote promises to indicate all the editorial cuts in the commentary, this is not done, and there are dozens of silent cuts of sentences, paragraphs, and larger sections of text.) The other four occurrences in the translation correspond to the adjective *narodnyi*, which Leighton also translates in other places as "native." Both in the annotations to this translation and in his separate study of the term *narodnost'*, Leighton attempts to define the contribution of Somov to the definition and promotion of this term. It seems to me, however, that he is not careful enough to distinguish between actual uses of the term and uses of related terms that also, but less directly, color the term. The use of the abstract noun is less concrete and less natural than the use of the adjectival forms—it is marked as terminological. By overusing the term in his translation, Leighton makes it appear as if *narodnost'* already had an established terminological usage. But this elides the work accomplished by Somov's essay, which is to establish the term carefully and to delineate a particular content. This is not to say that the broader meanings and connections adumbrated by Leighton are not also associated with the term by Somov's essay, with its frequent use of the adjective *narodnyi*. The debate on *narodnost'* that followed demonstrates the validity of many of those connections as well. But the later semantic swelling of the term and its consequent ambiguity are contrary to the terminological usage of Somov. Leighton, *Russian Romantic Criticism*, 21–45; Leighton, "*Narodnost'* as a Concept of Russian Romanticism," 52–54.

26. "Les poésies allemandes détachées sont, ce me semble, plus remarquables que les poëmes, et c'est surtout dans ce genre que le cachet de l'originalité est empreint: il est vrai aussi que les auteurs les plus cités à cet égard, Goethe, Schiller, Bürger, etc., sont de l'école moderne, et que celle-là seule porte un caractère vraiment national. Goethe a plus d'imagination, Schiller plus de sensibilité, et Bürger est de tous celui qui possède le talent le plus populaire." Madame de Staël; *De l'Allemagne*, 2nd ed., 2 vols. (Paris: Chez H. Nicolle, a la Librairie Stéréotype, 1814), 1:308.

27. Somov, "O romanticheskoi poezii," 304.

28. "Bürger est de tous les Allemands celui qui a le mieux saisi cette veine de superstition qui conduit si loin dans le fond du coeur." Staël, *De l'Allemagne*, 1:322.

29. Somov, "O romanticheskoi poezii," 294. This is an extreme condensation of the evaluations of Staël, *De l'Allemagne*, 1:314ff.

30. Somov, "O romanticheskoi poezii," 285–86.

31. Staël, *De l'Allemagne*, 2:159–60.

32. On Gogol and Dostoevsky, see Cooper, "Vasilii Zhukovskii as a Translator." The appeal of this synthetic nationality was not immediate. The first efforts were directed in more obvious directions. See also Andrew Wachtel, "Translation, Imperialism, and National Self-Definition in Russia," *Public Culture* 2, no. 1 (1999).

33. Somov does incorporate the evaluation of Goethe and Schiller from the beginning of de Staël's chapter, but does so when discussing Schiller's poetry: "Schiller's small poems are distinguished by sensibility, Goethe's by strength of imagination." Somov, "O romanticheskoi poezii," 301.

34. Ibid., 298.

35. "Walstein est la tragédie la plus nationale qui ait été représentée sur le théâtre allemand," Staël, *De l'Allemagne*, 2:49.

36. Somov, "O romanticheskoi poezii," 125.

37. Ibid., 128–29.

38. Ibid., 146–47.

39. Ibid., 139.

40. Somov, "O romanaticheskoi poezii," 156.

41. Cf. L. Ginzburg, "O probleme narodnosti i lichnosti v poezii dekabristov," in *O russkom realizme XIX veka i voprosakh narodnosti literatury: Sbornik statei*, ed. P. P. Gromov (Moscow: GIKhL, 1960), 59–63.

42. Ram, *The Imperial Sublime*, 149–50.

43. S. V. Mironenko, "Politicheskii portret Pavla Pestelia," in *"Russkaia pravda"—"La legge russa,"* by Pavel Ivanovich Pestel', ed. A. F. Sivak and S. V. Mironenko (Moscow: Izdatel'stvo "Progress-Akademiia," 1993), 71–73.

44. Pavel Ivanovich Pestel', *"Russkaia pravda"—"La legge russa,"* ed. A. F. Sivak and S. V. Mironenko, trans. Maria Grazia Musneci (Moscow: Izdatel'stvo "Progress-Akademiia," 1993), 107–17, 109. The national rights of the Ukrainians and Belarusians are not considered, as they are defined to be a part of the "Indigenous Russian Nation" (*Korennyi Narod Russkii*) (153–55).

45. Ram, *The Imperial Sublime*, 131–32.

46. Pestel', *"Russkaia pravda,"* 181.

47. Somov, "O romanticheskoi poezii," 130–33.

48. Hokanson, "Literary Imperialism," 339. On Batiushkov's relevant work, see Jacob Emery, "Repetition and Exchange in Legitimizing Empire: Konstantin Batiushkov's Scandinavian Corpus," *The Russian Review* 66, no. 4 (2007).

49. Somov, "O romanticheskoi poezii," 139–40.

50. I argue this at length in Cooper, "Vasilii Zhukovskii as a Translator."

51. Wachtel, "Translation, Imperialism," 56, 53.

52. Emery, "Repetition and Exchange," 604.

53. Ibid., 611–12.

54. See the analysis in Ram, *The Imperial Sublime,* 148–49.

55. Edward W. Said, *Orientalism,* 25th anniversary ed. (New York: Vintage, 1994), 17–19.

56. Melissa Frazier seems to make a move similar to Said's in the conclusion to her book. Importantly, she argues that the Russian form of protean nationality is not at all unique, but reflects the nature of romantic nationality everywhere, which always uses imitation and translation to simulate national originality. Russia perhaps offers only an extreme form. "This extreme form might be described as an empty vessel, a nation with no nationality of its own inside. We might also take the opposite tack and understand this Romantic nation not as nowhere but as everywhere, as that apparent paradox, 'the most imperial of nations, comprising more peoples than any other.' If the two are ultimately the same, *still the Russian context of actual empire might tend us toward the latter approach,* as Russian Romanticism in all its belatedness serves finally to make clear one last tendency that existed in Romanticism from the start." Frazier, *Romantic Encounters: Writers, Readers, and the Library for Reading,* 202, emphasis mine. This looks like a choice of interpretation based on sociopolitical context as well. Frazier goes on to suggest, however, that romantic nationalism itself is formed in the context of European empires, from the Holy Roman to the British and French, so that "Romantic nationalism would then seem to derive from a notion of empire while also ever recurring to it" (203). In that sense, there is no point in distinguishing between imperial and non-imperial forms of national cultural appropriation, because all national cultural appropriation is ultimately imperial.

57. Berman, *The Experience of the Foreign,* 4.

58. Berman thus distinguishes between the Jena romantics' approach to *Bildung,* which sought primarily reflections of their own concerns and idealist visions in the "universal progressive poetry" they translated, and Goethe's, Humboldt's, and Hölderlin's more direct confrontation with the radical otherness of the foreign.

59. Petr Viazemskii, "Vmesto predisloviia: Razgovor mezhdu izdatelem i klassikom s vyborgskoi storony ili s vasil'evskogo ostrova," in *Estetika i literaturnaia kritika* (Moscow: Iskusstvo, 1984), 49–50.

60. Recall that when he coined the term, Viazemsky claimed that this imprint was not a question of merit.

61. Mordovchenko, *Russkaia kritika,* 300.

62. Ibid., 301.

63. Ibid., 302.

64. See Ginzburg, "O probleme narodnosti," 59 and passim.

9—The Fate of Quantity, *"Lihozvučnost,"* and *"Klasičnost"*

1. For details of Jungmann's role, see Václav Zelený, *Život Josefa Jungmanna,* 2nd ed. (Prague: Nakladatel Fr. A. Urbánek, 1881), 225–27.

2. Mukařovský, "Polákova *Vznešenost přírody,"* 136–57.

3. Vodička, ed., *Dějiny české literatury,* 2:195.

4. Krok was the name of one of the legendary founding patriarchs of the Czech people.

5. Josef Jungmann, "Posudek: *Vznešenost přírody,*" *Krok* 1, no. 1 (1821): 153.

6. Ibid., 154. For *doba* as "form," see Josef Jungmann, "doba," in *Slovník česko-německý* (Prague: W. Spinky, 1834), 386.

7. Mukařovský, "Polákova *Vznešenost přírody,*" 124. The interest Mukařovský implicitly ascribes to Jungmann is more a product of his own approach to the history of verse. The article on Polák is very much an attempt to analyze the internal principles that structured the development of Czech verse. The argument need not be made that Jungmann was *consciously* working at such an internal development in order to justify the analysis that Mukařovský makes of that internal development. For a critique of Mukařovský's interpretation, see Červenka, "Tři poznámky."

8. This interpretation is confirmed by an insertion Jungmann makes in his 1827 article on *klasičnost* (see below). Where his source, Karl Heinrich Ludwig Pölitz, cites Greek and Latin in first place among the dead languages that have a classical literature, Jungmann adds in parenthesis that they are first "because knowledge of the oldest Indian literature is not yet very widespread in Europe." Jungmann, *Boj o obrození národa,* 106.

9. See Hýsek, "Jungmannova škola kritická," 255–56.

10. Bakoš, "*Počátkové českého básnictví,*" 27–28. See the discussion at the end of chap. 6 above.

11. Palacký, *Spisy drobné,* 504. The article was entitled "An- und Aussichten der böhmischen Sprache und Literatur 50 Jahren," was written in 1822 and first published in 1874.

12. The *Slovesnost* project was begun in 1816 in response to a government decree that seemed to promise mandatory instruction in Czech in the gymnasia. It is the first extensive handbook of literary theory and poetics in Czech, thus a representative work of Jungmann's linguistic project, for it introduces a number of new terms into Czech in order to make the language capable of this abstract discourse. In this case, the term did not entirely take. In contemporary Czech, *skladba* is the term for composition or syntax, while *skladnost* refers to the space-saving or synthetic character of a thing. Even the title of the volume borrows a Russian term for literature, one that was very much involved in Russian debates over the national language and literature (see chap. 3).

13. Josef Jungmann, *Slowesnost aneb Zbjrka přjkladů s krátkým pogednánjm o slohu* (Prague: Wytištěná u Josefy Fetterlowé z Wildenbrunu, 1820), xxv.

14. Given the correspondence, one might wonder whether Jungmann did not massage this section a bit by in translating from his constant source, Pölitz (see below for a further discussion of Jungmann's use of this source). Karel Hikl gives Jungmann's sources in Pölitz for this section and notes that "what Pölitz discusses concerning the 'numeri,' symmetry and *libozvučnost* (Klang) of poetic discourse Jungmann adopts in his usual condensing and shortening way." (Karel Hikl, "Jungmannova *Slovesnost* a její předlohy," *Listy filologické* 38 (1911): 433.) This is, then, a fine example of how Pölitz's writings appealed to the Czechs for the direct manner in which the author addressed their concerns. Still, the choice of the term *libozvučnost* to translate Klang and not *Wohlklang* points to Jungmann's adaptive method, with an eye for making Pölitz fit.

15. Jan Kollár, "Myšlénky o libozwučnosti řečj wůbec, obzwláště českoslowanské," *Krok* 1, no. 3 (1823): 32.

16. Ibid., 33. Macura notes that the Czech revivalists frequently adopted contradictory conceptual stances on the Czech language, to the point that even the same

person could advocate entirely opposite opinions in different circumstances. But not all of these variations developed into actual differences of opinion—far from it. More important was the valence of a particular stance in a given set of circumstances, its value in the economy of Czech emancipatory efforts. Macura, *Znamení zrodu*, 31–41. Here, too, the consequences of Kollár's line of argumentation were more important than his principles. Although Jungmann disagreed with Kollár, Jungmann never questioned the principles from which Kollár argued.

17. Kollár, "Myšlénky o libozwučnosti," 33. Emphasis in the original.

18. Josef Dobrovský, "Über den Wohlklang der Slawischen Sprache, mit besonderer Anwendung auf die Böhmische Mundart," *Slovanka* 2 (1815). See chap. 6, n.68, for more details on this article.

19. Kollár, "Myšlénky o libozwučnosti," 41–43.

20. Ibid., 40.

21. Much like Somov's transformation of Madame de Staël's discourse (see chap. 8).

22. Ibid., 41.

23. Ľubomír Ďurovič, "Slovak," in *The Slavic Literary Languages: Formation and Development*, ed. Alexander M. Schenker and Edward Stankiewicz (New Haven, CT: Yale Concilium on International and Area Studies, 1980), 212, 214.

24. Ibid., 213.

25. Ľubomír Ďurovič, "Ku vzniku pojmu 'reč československá,'" *Slovenská literatúra* 47, no. 6 (2000): 444.

26. Ibid., 454.

27. R. Auty, "The Evolution of Literary Slovak," *Transactions of the Philological Society* (1953): 152.

28. Not that Šafařík and Jungmann had given up on the greater Slavic project. Throughout the 1820s and into the 1830s, Šafařík would encourage other Slavic literary cultures to adopt a quantitative basis for their poetry, as a means of bringing their literary cultures closer together. Bakoš, "*Počátkové českého básnictví*," 20–21. For an overview in English of Šafařík and Kollár's creation of a "myth of Slavness," with emphasis on the mid-1820s and beyond, see Robert Pynsent, *Questions of Identity: Czech and Slovak Ideas of Nationality and Personality* (Budapest: Central European University Press, 1994), 44–99.

29. Visarion Belinsky, in the opening of his first major critical article, "Literary Reveries" (1834), cajoles his readers not to abandon him when he turns to his own such survey, plying them with the hope of hearing something new, something outside of what had already become stale commonplace in the myriad of such surveys. Belinskii, *Polnoe sobranie sochinenii*, 1:25–26. Because the Czechs had Dobrovský's authoritative history of Czech literature, they had little need to constantly rehash and reconceive of their literary history. In fact, Dobrovský's history was a bit of an obstacle to the writing of a new, national literary history. See Cooper, "The Rukopis Královédvorský."

30. Palacký, *Spisy drobné*, 3:108. See also the English and Czech bilingual edition, František Palacký, *An Historical Survey of the Science of Beauty and the Literature on the Subject*, ed. Tomáš Hlobil, trans. Derek Paton and Marzia Paton (Olomouc: Palacký University, 2002), 62–63.

31. Jan Kollár, *Vybrané spisy*, ed. F. R. Tichý, vol. 2, *Prózy* (Prague: Státní nakladatelství krásné literatury, hudby a umění, 1956), 209.

32. Ibid., 214.

33. Ibid.

34. W. Bergner, "O literatuře vesměs, a žádosti," *Krok* 2, no. 2 (1827): 170.

35. Kollár, *Vybrané spisy,* 218.

36. Ibid., 216. Kollár uses in this article the adjective "Czechoslovak" (*československý*) for the language and literature, as opposed to the more common "Czechoslav" (*českoslovanský*), which he used in the title of his *libozvučnost* article.

37. Ibid., 217.

38. Ibid.

39. Ibid., 218–19.

40. Ibid., 219.

41. Ibid., 220. 42. Ibid., 219.

43. See Macura, *Znamení zrodu,* 209–10.

44. Quoted in Bakoš, "*Počátkové českého básnictví,*" 28.

45. Josef Jungmann, "O klasičnosti literatury vůbec a zvláště české," *Časopis českého musea* 1 (1827). Jungmann's title once again echoes Kollár's, which had echoed Dobrovský's. This form of title was enjoying a kind of fashion at the time, but the echo here seems to be deliberate: Palacký changed Jungmann's original title, which was "O klasičnosti literatury a důležitosti její" ("On *Klasičnost* of Literature and its Importance).

46. Jungmann, *Boj o obrození národa,* 102. I will cite from this edition, which reprints Jungmann's original version of the article, before Palacký edited it for publication and to pass the censor. Changes in the published version relevant to my argument will be noted below.

47. Other aestheticians upon whom Jungmann drew for that work included Johann August Eberhard, Georg von Reinbeck, and Christian August Clodius. Tomáš Hlobil calls them "eclectic systematizers" of the work of the leading German aestheticians and reminds us that Jungmann's goal for the work was not so much the writing of a philosophical tract on aesthetics as a secondary-school textbook that would give a precise and unproblematized overview of the subject. Tomáš Hlobil, "Jungmannova charakteristika metafory a německá estetika 18. století," in *Mezi časy . . . Kultura a umění v českých zemích kolem roku 1800,* ed. Zdeněk Hojda and Roman Prahl (Prague: Koniasch Latin Press, 2000), 225, 231.

48. Palacký, *Spisy drobné,* 3:109; Palacký, *Historical Survey,* 64–65.

49. See Hikl, "Jungmannova *Slovesnost,*" 350–52.

50. See Tomáš Hlobil, "Ossianism in the Bohemian Lands," *Modern Language Review* 101, no. 3 (2006): 792n.12.

51. Luc Jean Beaudoin has suggested repeatedly that Ancillon "likely knew [the Russian poet] Baratynskij personally," an intriguing possibility that would go far to explain the interest in Ancillon in the center of the leading Russian literary circles. But Beaudoin never cites a source for this information and I have not found any corroboration elsewhere. Luc Jean Beaudoin, "Baratynskij's Tales in Verse: The Social Implications of Poetic Genre," *Russian Literature* 38, no. 2 (1996): 114. See also Beaudoin, *Resetting the Margins: Russian Romantic Verse Tales and the Idealized Woman,* Berkeley Insights in Linguistics and Semiotics (New York: Peter Lang, 1997), 59n.29.

52. This is Mojmír Otruba's characterization in relation to *Slovesnost.* See, Otruba, "Josef Jungmann," 582. For a general discussion of Jungmann's translations of learned discourse, see Macura, *Znamení zrodu,* 61–78.

53. Namely, pages 13–30, leaving out certain discussions more relevant to the German context. Karel Heinrich Ludwig Pölitz, *Das Gesammtgebiet der teutschen Sprache,*

nach Prosa, Dichtkunst und Beredsamkeit theoretisch und practisch dargestellt, 4 vols. (Leipzig: J. C. Hinrichssche Buchhandlung, 1825), vol. 1.

54. Ibid., 1:24.

55. Jungmann, *Boj o obrození národa,* 106.

56. As we saw earlier, Jungmann, in the *Slovesnost* volume, translated Pölitz's *Klang* as *libozvučnost* in order to *make* a connection to Palacký and Šafařík's discourse.

57. *Blahozvučnost* itself is a neologism, as is *národovost.* Jungmann's use of two distinct terms in the article, *národovost* and *národnost,* was eliminated by Palacký; in the edited version, the only term used is *národnost,* and the final section of the article, in which Jungmann discusses *národnost,* has been cut. See chap. 10 for a further discussion of this Czech term in comparison to its Russian analogue.

58. See Cooper, "The Rukopis Královédvorský."

59. Jungmann, *Boj o obrození národa,* 103–4.

60. Ibid., 107. Jungmann's loose translation here, "ancient" (*dřevných*) instead of "former" (*vorigen*), already points to a change in interpretation of the oldest period of Czech literature that he will make in this article. Pölitz, *Gesammtgebiet der teutschen Sprache,* 28.

61. Jungmann, *Boj o obrození národa,* 107. Pölitz, *Gesammtgebiet der teutschen Sprache,* 27.

62. Jungmann, *Boj o obrození národa,* 110.

63. Ibid., 108.

64. Ibid.

65. Ibid., 104. Jungmann is careless in his translation. The word "together" (*spolu*) makes no sense here. A glance at Pölitz reveals Jungmann has left out Pölitz's reference to "the people," and that "together" refers to the people with their literature: "Ein Volk gewinnt aber nur erst im Zeitalter seiner Classiker eine *Nationalliteratur,* und **mit derselben** fur die Zukunft . . ." Pölitz, *Gesammtgebiet der teutschen Sprache,* 14. Emphasis mine.

66. Jungmann, *Boj o obrození národa,* 111.

67. Ibid.

68. Šafařík complained about this exclusive focus on poetry in *Počátkové* (106 [110–11]), and the complaint would be repeated by Karel Havlíček in the 1840s.

69. František Palacký, "Ohlášení časopisu tohoto," *Časopis českého musea* 1, no. 1 (1827): 4.

70. Jungmann, *Boj o obrození národa,* 109.

71. František Palacký, "Slovo k vlastencům od redaktora," *Časopis českého musea* 1, no. 4 (1827): 148.

72. See the end of chap. 10 for the analogous problem in Russian letters and the terminology in which it is addressed, in comparison to the Czech situation.

73. Lotman, "A. F. Merzliakov kak poet," 42–43.

74. Blackall, *The Emergence of German as a Literary Language, 1700–1775,* 114.

75. Ibid., 97–101, 112–13, 314–50.

76. Ibid., 143–44.

77. Rado L. Lencek, "Kopitar's Slavic Version of the Greek Dialects Theme," in *Zbirnyk na poshanu profesora doktora Iuriia Shevel'ova = Symbolae in honorem Georgii Y. Shevelov,* ed. William E. Harkins, Olexa Horbatsch, and Jakob P. Hursky (Munich: Logos, 1971), 252.

78. Ibid., 246.

79. Jernej Kopitar, "O Slowanských nářečjch, a prostředcých gim se navčiti," *Prvotiny pěkných umění* (1813). The translation is reprinted in *Papers in Slavic Philology 2, to Honor*

Jernej Kopitar, 1780–1980, ed. Rado L. Lencek and Henry R. Cooper, Jr. (Ann Arbor: Department of Slavic Languages and Literatures, University of Michigan, 1982), 229–34. Lencek, "Kopitar's Slavic Version," 253. Lencek, writing in 1971, suggests at the end of the article that the integrational tendency in modern Serbo-Croatian might have been the only real practical implementation of Kopitar's Slavic ideology (255). Today, of course, the opposite tendency reigns.

80. See Macura, *Znamení zrodu,* 133–38.

81. On the development of the reciprocity program, see Pynsent, *Questions of Identity,* 55–57.

82. See Macura, *Znamení zrodu,* 137.

83. Vodička, ed., *Dějiny české literatury,* 9. In Hroch's scheme for the national movements of small nations, this corresponds to the second part of phase *B,* when the national agitators begin to find a receptive audience. Hroch, "From National Movement to the Fully-formed Nation," 81.

84. Macura frequently points out, correctly, how certain projects are in effect the creation of simulacra. But the projected reality of the simulacrum also responds to the particular Czech situation. Macura, *Znamení zrodu,* 102–17.

10—Dissent over *Narodnost'* and Romanticism

1. William Mills Todd, III, "Pushkin and Literary Criticism," in *The Cambridge Companion to Pushkin,* ed. Andrew Kahn (Cambridge: Cambridge University Press, 2006), 151. Todd describes Pushkin's definitions of critical concepts "more remarkable for their conciseness and historical grounding than for their originality and theoretical profundity." Caryl Emerson suggests that as a critic, Pushkin was "slow to condemn, . . . eager to define." Caryl Emerson, "Pushkin as Critic," in *The Pushkin Handbook,* ed. David M. Bethea (Madison: University of Wisconsin Press, 2005), 321.

2. On the question of genre, see the analysis in Tynianov, "Arkhaisty i Pushkin," 103–18.

3. V. K. Kiukhel'beker, *Puteshestvie, dnevnik, stat'i,* ed. N. V. Koroleva and V. D. Rak (Leningrad: Izdatel'stvo "Nauka," 1979), 454.

4. Ibid., 455–56.

5. Ibid., 456. Emphasis mine.

6. Leighton mistranslates this passage and misreads it, so that the qualities listed alongside *narodnost'* are taken as glossing that term. Leighton, *Russian Romantic Criticism,* 57, 65; Leighton, "*Narodnost'* as a Concept of Russian Romanticism," 66.

7. As in Somov's essay, "narodnaia poeziia" for Küchelbecker is far closer to *Nationalliteratur* than to *Volkspoesie.*

8. That same year, in a draft of a reply to the second of Bestuzhev's "Surveys," Pushkin says, "I agree that . . . all the nations [iazyki = languages or nations in an older sense] would have translated Zhukovsky, if he himself had translated less." Aleksandr S. Pushkin, *Polnoe sobranie sochinenii v desiati tomakh* [hereafter PSS], 10 vols. (Moscow: Nauka, 1964), 7:19. It is not clear exactly when in 1824 Pushkin wrote this draft, but this comment in particular seems to respond to the idea in Küchelbecker, whose article came out somewhat later than Bestuzhev's, rather than to any comment of Bestuzhev's.

9. Kiukhel'beker, *Puteshestvie,* 457.

10. In fact, the elegiac trend that Küchelbecker is critiquing is somewhat older than the romantic trend that Viazemsky is promoting—the romantic *poema*—and Küchelbecker agreed that Pushkin's poemas, or narrative poems, offered hope. But Viazemsky also included the earlier elegiac trend in romanticism while Küchelbecker clearly did not.

11. Kiukhel'beker, *Puteshestvie*, 458.

12. Ibid., 453–54.

13. Ibid., 458. Küchelbecker here identifies himself, in spite of his own ethnic background and father's Saxon nobility, with imperial Russia and its Orthodox religious faith (not, presumably, the faith of his ancestors). He thus, like Somov, allies himself with the Decembrist vision of a dominant Russian nationality.

14. Ibid., 457.

15. Ibid.

16. See his letter to Viazemsky, dated July 13, 1825. Pushkin, *PSS*, 10:153.

17. In an article from 1830, Pushkin would insist on both meanings, calling Krylov "in all ways the most *narodnyi* of our poets (le plus national et le plus populaire)." Ibid., 7:184. He thus took Viazemsky's side on the term, even as he took the opposite side on the question of the fable poets (recall that Viazemsky had preferred Dmitriev to Krylov).

18. Ibid., 7:38–39.

19. Tatiana Wolff, ed., *Pushkin on Literature* (London: The Athlone Press, 1986), 169.

20. Pushkin, *PSS*, 7:658.

21. Leighton, *Russian Romantic Criticism*, 95.

22. Mordovchenko, *Russkaia kritika*, 290. Note how Pushkin repeatedly uses Viazemsky's critical vocabulary and rhetorical moves in hidden polemics with Viazemsky.

23. In a note on *Romeo and Juliet* published in 1830, Pushkin *would* remark on Shakespeare's ability to transmit the Italianness of his setting: "The Italy contemporary to the poet is reflected in it, along with its climate, passions, festivals, languor, sonnets, and its sumptuous language, full of flash and *concetti*. To such a degree Shakespeare grasped dramatic *mestnost'*." Pushkin, *PSS*, 7:94. The final term, meaning something like local color, is one associated with *narodnost'* by Viazemsky and Somov. If we read between these two texts by Pushkin, we might suggest that for him the terms had distinct meanings, though they might very well exist side by side (the dramatic *mestnost'* of *Romeo and Juliet* not preventing the merit of *narodnost'* from being attributed to it as well).

24. Ibid., 7:212.

25. However, we should recall here a certain genealogy of romantic genius as it relates to Pushkin. The Germans were the first to focus on Shakespeare's "universal" genius, his ability to project himself into different times and places and give life to characters and actions from them. For their own genius, Goethe, this universalism becomes somewhat more particular again, as this ability is interpreted as a kind of synthesis—as Goethe giving the Germans the ancient Greeks and other nations, incorporating them into the German nation. In his speech at the unveiling of Pushkin's monument in 1881, Dostoevsky makes Pushkin the embodiment of a Russian nation that is capable of synthesizing all the nations, taking the best from each of them, and he denies this ability to the genius of Shakespeare and Goethe.

26. Yuri Tynianov demonstrates this at length and in detail in "Arkhaisty i Pushkin."

27. Pushkin, *PSS*, 7:39–40.

28. Wolff, ed., *Pushkin on Literature*, 169. The specific complaints of Schlegel and Sismondi are recalled by Pushkin in the discussion of verisimilitude from the 1830 article on *Marfa Posadnitsa* quoted above.

29. Leighton, "*Narodnost*' as a Concept of Russian Romanticism," 76. There is a misprint in the French term in this publication, corrected by Leighton in his later volume. Leighton, *Russian Romantic Criticism*, 81.

30. Leighton, "*Narodnost*' as a Concept of Russian Romanticism," 76.

31. N. A. Polevoi and K. A. Polevoi, *Literaturnaia kritika, stat'i, i retsenzii, 1825–1842* (Leningrad: Khudozhestvennaia literatura, 1990), 21. Polevoi is quoting from a translation of a section of Ancillon's *Nouveaux essays de politique et de philosophie* (1824), which was published in the same volume of the *Moscow Telegraph*. Leighton, *Russian Romantic Criticism*, 109.

32. Recall that Ancillon was useful to M. Dmitriev in his *critique* of Viazemsky's conflation of the popular and the national. These contrary uses of Ancillon do not reflect an internal contradiction in Ancillon's discourse on national literature, however, but rather the use of different aspects of his discourse (the distinction between a modern nation and a primitive one versus the implicit popularity of the literature of a modern nation) at cross purposes within the Russian debate over the term *narodnost*'. Leighton also cites Ancillon as a source for Küchelbecker's definition of the ode and the attention to rapture. I do not find the evidence he presents, however, at all convincing. Leighton, "*Narodnost*' as a Concept of Russian Romanticism," 77.

33. Pushkin, *PSS*, 7:32. Emphasis mine. Note that Pushkin uses the same words to describe the national character as Viazemsky, who saw them reflected in I. I. Dmitriev. Pushkin does not use the term *narodnost*' here, but he thus alludes to the debate over the term.

34. Ibid., 7:32–33.

35. Ibid., 7:33.

36. Ibid., 7:34. This distinction based on form is what is realized in the practice of Kollár and other Czechs who wrote classical forms in quantitative meter and romantic forms in syllabotonic.

37. Leighton, *Russian Romantic Criticism*, 93.

38. Pushkin, *PSS*, 7:34.

39. See also Tynianov's discussion of the article and its focus on genre. Tynianov, "Arkhaisty i Pushkin," 62–64.

40. Pushkin, *PSS*, 7:72.

41. Ibid., 7:73. Chester Dunning suggests a political reading of this anachronism, that the revolution that Pushkin hoped to incite in the Russian theater had to do with the radical political content of his play and that the increasing conservatism of Nicholas I's policies following the Decembrist uprising and later in the 1820s made that aspect of the play "anachronistic." Chester Dunning, "The Tragic Fate of Pushkin's Comedy," in *The Uncensored Boris Godunov: The Case for Pushkin's Original Comedy, with Annotated Text and Translation*, ed. Chester Dunning, et al. (Madison: University of Wisconsin Press, 2006), 102, 114. I suggest that we take Pushkin's own discourse, which concerns the generic form of the play, seriously, rather than reading for aesopic meaning here.

42. Pushkin, *PSS*, 7:75.

43. Ibid., 7:165.

44. Ibid., 7:213.

45. Ibid., 7:214.

46. Ibid., 7:215–16.

47. Ibid., 7:216–17.

48. Emerson, "Pushkin as Critic," 322. On Pushkin's struggle to reshape criticism as a literary institution, see also Todd, "Pushkin and Literary Criticism," 147–54.

49. Frazier, *Romantic Encounters: Writers, Readers, and the Library for Reading*, 87.

50. For a more thorough analysis, see Berghahn, "From Classicist to Classical Literary Criticism," 78–82.

51. Quoted in ibid., 76.

52. Friedrich Schiller, "On Bürger's Poems," in *Eighteenth-Century German Criticism*, ed. Timothy J. Chamberlain, The German Library (New York: Continuum, 1992), 265.

53. Ibid., 263.

54. Ibid., 265.

55. Kollár, *Vybrané spisy,* 217.

56. Jungmann, *Boj o obrození národa,* 111.

57. Ibid., 112.

58. Ibid.

59. Palacký, *Spisy drobné,* 490–91; Palacký and Macháček, *Geschichte der schönen Redekünste bei den Böhmen/Dějiny české slovesnosti,* 70–75.

60. In his 1813 translation of excerpts from F. L. Jahn's *Das Deutsche Volkstüm,* Jungmann had used yet another form, *národství,* to translate the title. But later usage confirms Palacký's instincts here. By the time of Jungmann's Czech-German dictionary (vol. 2 was published in 1836), *národnost* was clearly the term in use, and *národovost* is listed only as an alternative, while *národství* is not to be found. Jungmann and Petr, *Slovník česko-německý,* 2:611–12. Jungmann complained to Kollár about Palacký's extensive cuts in his article in a letter written January 4, 1827. Jungmann, *Boj o obrození národa,* 177.

61. František Palacký, *Gedenkblätter: Auswahl von Denkschriften, Aufsätzen und Briefen aus den letzten fünfzig Jahren* (Prague: Verlag von F. Tempsky, 1874), 20–21. In the modern Czech translation of Palacký's articles, both *Volkstümlichkeit* and *Nationalität* are rendered as "*národnost.*"

11—Toward the Reform of Institutions

1. Varcl et al., *Antika a česká kultura,* 6.

2. Dobrovský, *Dějiny české řeči a literatury,* 171 (217).

3. Jungmann, *Boj o obrození národa,* 39.

4. Ibid., 50.

5. Ibid., 49. On the futility of the Czechs' constant loyal appeals to the emperor, which often replaced real political pressure, see Bugge, "Czech Nation-Building," 64–65, 80–81, 92.

6. Stefan Michael Newerkla, "The Seamy Side of the Habsburgs' Liberal Language Policy: Intended and Factual Reality of Language Use in Plzeň's Educational System," in *Diglossia and Power: Language Policies and Practice in the Nineteenth-Century Habsburg Empire,* ed. Rosita Rindler Schjerve (Berlin: Mouton de Gruyter, 2003), 184.

7. Otruba, "Josef Jungmann," 580.

8. Shishkov, "Razsuzhdenie o starom i novom slogie," 5–7.

9. Dmitrii V. Venevitinov, *Stikhotvoreniia, proza* (Moscow: Nauka, 1980), 129.

10. Ibid.

11. Bestuzhev-Marlinskii, *Sochineniia v dvukh tomakh,* 2:376. Bestuzhev's formulation itself is an allusion to the speech of Nikolai Gnedich at the opening of the

Imperial Public Library on January 2, 1814, entitled "Rassuzhdenie o prichinakh, zamedliaiushchikh uspekhi nashei slovesnosti" ("A Consideration of the Causes That are Slowing the Success of Our Literature"). Venevitinov thus joins an ongoing dialogue about the lack of success of Russian literature. See Mordovchenko, *Russkaia kritika*, 133ff.

12. Bestuzhev-Marlinskii, *Sochineniia v dvukh tomakh*, 2:395.

13. Ibid., 2:401. Bestuzhev here suggests that Russia's process of aging is inorganic. The projection of the process of human growth onto national history is characteristic of historical thought following the Quarrel between the Ancients and Moderns.

14. Ibid.

15. Ibid., 2:402.

16. Ibid.

17. Venevitinov, *Stikhotvoreniia, proza*, 130.

18. Ibid., 128. Recall the exhortation that Murav'ev-Apostol puts into the mouth of a personified Moscow addressing the Russian nation in his first letter (cited in chapter 7): "Know yourself, and throw off from your powerful neck the yoke that has enslaved you—giant!—to the imitation of pigmies who have exhausted all their spiritual energy by centuries of vice. Know yourself!" Murav'ev-Apostol, "Pis'mo pervoe iz Moskvy v Nizhnii Novgorod," 91.

19. Venevitinov, *Stikhotvoreniia, proza*, 129. Venevitinov here seems to share with Uvarov and others the notion that the development of world culture proceeds by the successive contributions of various nations.

20. Ibid.

21. Ibid., 130–31.

22. Ibid., 131–32.

23. Ibid., 132.

24. Ibid., 133.

25. Šafárik and Palacký, *Počátkové českého básnictví obzvláště prozódie*, 106 (109).

26. Ibid., 106 (111).

27. Jungmann, *Boj o obrození národa*, 104, 110–11.

28. Chaadaev's first letter was not published until 1834 but circulated widely in manuscript prior to that.

29. The Russian Slavophiles exhibited some interest in the work of Kollár in the 1830s, though primarily in response to his later essay on Slavic mutuality (1836), which, in the face of Czech resistance to his language reform, gave up on the ideal of a common Slavic literary language and proposed instead a more active cultural and literary exchange. But the Russian Slavophiles were resistant to the Slavic programs of the smaller Slavic nations, particularly those that were not of the Orthodox faith. See G. V. Rokina, *Ian Kollar i Rossiia: Istoriia idei slavianskoi vzaimnosti v rossiiskom obshchestve pervoi poloviny XIX v.* (Ioshkar-Ola, Russian Federation: MGPI, 1998), 146–50.

30. "Oznámení," *Krok* 1, no. 1 (1821): 7.

31. Venevitinov, *Stikhotvoreniia, proza*, 149.

32. Ibid., 259.

33. Whittaker, *Origins of Modern Russian Education*, 24.

34. Ibid., 64–65.

35. Ibid., 72, 129, 143.

36. Ibid., 146–47.

37. Ibid., 162–64.

38. Ibid., 64, 66–67.

39. Ibid., 135–36.

40. Ibid., 146, 229.

41. Vintr, "Josef Valentin Zlobický," 14.

42. Jan Šafránek, *Školy české: Obraz jejich vývoje a osudů,* 2 vols. (Prague: Nákladem Matice české, 1913–1918), 1:143–44, 149, 151–52; Newerkla, "The Seamy Side," 183–84; M. N. Kuz'min, *Shkola i obrazovanie v chekhoslovakii (konets XVIII–30-e gody XX v.)* (Moscow: Nauka, 1971), 59, 65. In fact, shortly after Joseph II took the throne, instruction in the modern languages at the university in Vienna was halted, to save resources, with the exception of Czech, which was considered necessary. Walter Reichel, "Josef Valentin Zlobický—první profesor českého jazyka a literatury: Život, působení a zásluhy na pozadí osvícenství," in *Vídeňský podíl na počátcích českého národního obrození: J. V. Zlobický (1743–1810) a současníci: Život, dílo, korespondence,* ed. Josef Vintr and Jana Pleskalová (Prague: Akademia, 2004), 32.

43. Newerkla, "The Seamy Side," 184.

44. Kuz'min, *Shkola i obrazovanie,* 82. See also Šafránek, *Školy české,* 1:271–75.

45. Kuz'min, *Shkola i obrazovanie,* 89, 92; Karel Svoboda, *Antika a česká vzdělanost od obrození do první války světové* (Prague: Nakladatelství československé akademie věd, 1957), 113.

46. Kuz'min, *Shkola i obrazovanie,* 93.

47. Ibid., 94; Newerkla, "The Seamy Side," 185–86.

48. Kuz'min, *Shkola i obrazovanie,* 95, 124.

49. Svoboda, *Antika a česká vzdělanost,* 6–7. Over half of the gymnasia were closed in 1776 in an effort to keep secondary and higher education the reserve of the elite. Kuz'min, *Shkola i obrazovanie,* 62.

50. Svoboda, *Antika a česká vzdělanost,* 8; Kuz'min, *Shkola i obrazovanie,* 71–72.

51. Svoboda, *Antika a česká vzdělanost,* 111.

52. Ibid., 113; Kuz'min, *Shkola i obrazovanie,* 90.

53. Svoboda, *Antika a česká vzdělanost,* 113; Whittaker, *Origins of Modern Russian Education,* 64. In fact, by 1848 the sense of Humboldt's reforms in Prussia had been lost, and while the Prussian state continued to use the language of Humboldt's reform, it asserted state control over the educational system with the practical goal of preparing qualified bureaucrats, a practical orientation that was alien to Humboldt. The Austrian and Russian reforms also demonstrate this accommodation of the ideal of the classical general education to practical purposes. Peter Uwe Hohendahl, *Building a National Literature: The Case of Germany, 1830–1870,* trans. Renate Baron Franciscono (Ithaca: Cornell University Press, 1989), 248–70.

54. Svoboda, *Antika a česká vzdělanost,* 113.

55. Kuz'min, *Shkola i obrazovanie,* 90, 98.

56. For an overview of the debates, see Svoboda, *Antika a česká vzdělanost,* 152–55, 329–31.

57. Ibid., 154–55.

58. Ibid., 218; Whittaker, *Origins of Modern Russian Education,* 146–47.

59. Svoboda, *Antika a česká vzdělanost,* 112.

Conclusion

1. Venevitinov, *Stikhotvoreniia, proza,* 130–31.

2. White, *Voltaire's Essay on Epic Poetry,* 64–65.

3. František Ladislav Čelakovský, "Literatura Krkonošská," *Čechoslaw: Národnj časopis pro Čechy a Morawany*, no. 7 (1824).

4. Kollár, *Vybrané spisy*, 214.

5. Šafárik and Palacký, *Počátkové českého básnictví obzvláště prozódie*, 101 (102).

6. Josef Jakub Jungmann, *Krátká historie národu, osvícení a jazyka: Uvody k Historii literatury české*, K vyd. připravila a doslov napsal Felix Vodička (Prague: Sfinx, 1947), 36–37.

7. Knight, "Ethnicity, Nationality," 49.

8. Vladimír Macura, "Problems and Paradoxes of the National Revival," in *Bohemia in History*, ed. Mikuláš Teich (Cambridge: Cambridge University Press, 1998), 193. This article offers a useful summary of Macura's simulacrum argument in English.

9. Melissa Frazier's recent work provides another example: the emergence of a "literary marketplace" in Russia "took place" in simulation rather than in actual fact—new roles for writers and readers were worked out and debated *as if* in response to real conditions, but the evidence for any such real conditions in the period of those debates is lacking. Frazier, *Romantic Encounters: Writers, Readers, and the Library for Reading*.

10. When Russian national identity is conceived of in imperial, rather than ethnically Russian, form, however, one occasionally gets the sense that certain writers realize that they are not reviving an old nation, but creating a new one, one that never had existed, and perhaps never would. As Frazier has suggested, here is another extreme form—this time on the Russian side—that again suggests the general rule of the nature of romantic nationality across Europe. Ibid., 202.

11. Leerssen, *National Thought in Europe*, 164–65.

12. Leerssen, "Ossian and the Rise of Literary Historicism."

Works Cited

Adelung, Johann Christoph. "Vorrede." In *Karl Thams Deutsch-böhmisches Nationallexikon*, by Karl Ignaz Tham [n.p.]. Prague: Auf Kosten der von Schönfeldschen Handlung, 1788.

Agnew, Hugh LeCaine. *Origins of the Czech National Renascence*. Pittsburgh, PA: University of Pittsburgh Press, 1993.

Al'tshuller, Mark. *Predtechi slavianofil'stva v russkoi literature: Obshchestvo 'Beseda liubitelei russkago slova.'* Ann Arbor, MI: Ardis, 1984.

Anderson, Benedict. *Imagined Communities: Reflections on the Origin and Spread of Nationalism*. Rev. and extended ed. London: Verso, 1991.

Auty, R. "The Evolution of Literary Slovak." *Transactions of the Philological Society* (1953): 143–60.

Azadovskii, M. K. "Fol'klorizm Lermontova." *Literaturnoe nasledstvo* 43–44 (1941): 227–62.

———. *Istoriia russkoi fol'kloristiki*. Moscow: Gosudarstvennoe uchebno-pedagogicheskoe izdatel'stvo, 1958.

Baehr, Stephen L. "From History to National Myth: *Translatio Imperii* in Eighteenth-Century Russia." *The Russian Review* 37, no. 1 (1978): 1–13.

Bailey, James O. "Folk Versification." In *Handbook of Russian Literature*, edited by Victor Terras, 148–51. New Haven, CT: Yale University Press, 1985.

Bakoš, Mikuláš. "*Počátkové českého básnictví, obzvláště prozódie* a ich význam vo vývine českej a slovenskej poézie." In *Počátkové českého básnictví obzvláště prozódie*, by Pavel Jozef Šafárik and František Palacký, 7–38. Bratislava: Vydavateľstvo Slovenskej akadémie vied, 1961.

Bassin, Mark. *Imperial Visions: Nationalist Imagination and Geographic Expansion in the Russian Far East, 1840–1865*. Cambridge: Cambridge University Press, 2000.

Bausinger, Hermann. *Formen der "Volkspoesie."* 2nd verb. und verm. Aufl. ed, Grundlagen der Germanistik, 6. Berlin: E. Schmidt, 1980.

Beaudoin, Luc Jean. "Baratynskij's Tales in Verse: The Social Implications of Poetic Genre." *Russian Literature* 38, no. 2 (1996): 113–28.

————. *Resetting the Margins: Russian Romantic Verse Tales and the Idealized Woman,* Berkeley Insights in Linguistics and Semiotics. New York: Peter Lang, 1997.

Belinskii, Vissarion. *Polnoe sobranie sochinenii.* 13 vols. Moscow: Izdatel'stvo Akademii Nauk SSSR, 1953–1959.

Berghahn, Klaus L. "From Classicist to Classical Literary Criticism." In *A History of German Literary Criticism, 1730–1980,* edited by Peter Uwe Hohendahl, 13–98. Lincoln: University of Nebraska Press, 1988.

Bergner, W. "O literatuře vesměs, a žádosti." *Krok* 2, no. 2 (1827): 161–74.

Berkov, P. N. "A. N. Radishchev kak kritik." *Vestnik Leningradskogo universiteta* 9 (1949): 66–81.

Berman, Antoine. *The Experience of the Foreign: Culture and Translation in Romantic Germany.* Translated by S. Heyvaert. Albany: State University of New York Press, 1992.

Bestuzhev-Marlinskii, Aleksandr. *Sochineniia v dvukh tomakh.* 2 vols. Moscow: Khudozhestvennaia literatura, 1981.

————. "Vzgliad na staruiu i novuiu slovesnost' v Rossii." In *Sochineniia v dvukh tomakh,* 2:521–39. Moscow: Khudozhestvennaia literatura, 1958.

Blackall, Eric A. *The Emergence of German as a Literary Language, 1700–1775.* Cambridge: Cambridge University Press, 1959.

Bojanowska, Edyta M. *Nikolai Gogol: Between Ukrainian and Russian Nationalism.* Cambridge: Harvard University Press, 2007.

Brandenberger, David. *National Bolshevism: Stalinist Mass Culture and the Formation of Modern Russian National Identity, 1931–1956.* Cambridge: Harvard University Press, 2002.

Bryant, Chad Carl. *Prague in Black: Nazi Rule and Czech Nationalism.* Cambridge: Harvard University Press, 2007.

Bugge, Peter. "Czech Nation-Building, National Self-Perception, and Politics, 1780–1914." Ph.D. diss., University of Aarhus, 1994.

————. "The Making of a Slovak City: The Czechoslovak Renaming of Pressburg/Pozsony/Prešporok, 1918–19." *Austrian History Yearbook* 35 (2004): 205–28.

Bürger, Gottfried August. "Outpourings from the Heart on Volkspoesie." In *Eighteenth-Century German Criticism,* edited by Timothy J. Chamberlain, 252–58. New York: Continuum, 1992.

Burgi, Richard. *A History of the Russian Hexameter.* Hamden, CN: Shoe String Press, 1954.

Butler, Francis. "Edward Keenan, Vladimir Dal', and the *Slovo o polku Igoreve.*" *Russian History/Histoire Russe* 33, nos. 2, 3, 4 (2006): 217–33.

Butler, Thomas. "Jernej Kopitar and South Slavic Folklore." In *Papers in Slavic Philology 2, to Honor Jernej Kopitar, 1780–1980,* edited by Rado L. Lencek and Henry R. Cooper, Jr., 109–21. Ann Arbor: University of Michigan, Department of Slavic Languages and Literatures, 1982.

Cejp, Ladislav. "Jungmannův překlad Ztraceného ráje." In *Překlady,* by Josef Jakub Jungmann. Vol. 1, 360–430. Prague: Státní nakladatelství krásné literatury, hudby, a umění, 1958.

Čelakovský, František Ladislav. "Literatura Krkonošská." *Čechoslaw: Národnj časopis pro Čechy a Morawany,* no. 7 (1824): 51–54, 59–60, 73–75, 87–88, 100–103, 105–9.

Červenka, Miroslav. "Tři poznámky k Dobrovskému *Prozodiím.*" *Slovo a slovesnost* 64 (2003): 269–75.

Chulos, Chris, and Johannes Remy, eds. *Imperial and National Identities in Pre-Revolutionary, Soviet, and Post-Soviet Russia*. Helsinki: Suomalaisen Kirjallisuuden Seura, 1999.

Cooper, David L. "The Rukopis Královédvorský and the Formation of Czech National Literary History." In *Between Texts, Languages, and Cultures: A Festschrift for Michael Henry Heim*, edited by Craig Cravens, Masako U. Fidler, and Susan C. Kresin, 157–67. Bloomington, IN: Slavica, 2008.

———. "Vasilii Zhukovskii as a Translator and the Protean Russian Nation." *The Russian Review* 66, no. 2 (2007): 185–203.

Culler, Jonathan. "Anderson and the Novel." *Diacritics* 29, no. 4 (1999): 20–39.

David, Zdeněk V. "Národní obrození jako převtělení Zlatého věku." *Český časopis historický* 99, no. 3 (2001): 486–518.

Derrida, Jacques. *Of Grammatology*. Translated by Gayatri Chakravorty Spivak. Baltimore, MD: The Johns Hopkins University Press, 1976.

Dmitriev, Mikhail A. "Vtoroi razgovor mezhdu Klassikom i Izdatelem Bakhchisaraiskago Fontana." *Vestnik Evropy* 134, no. 5 (1824): 47–62.

Dobrovský, Josef. "Böhmische prosodie." In *Literární a prozodická bohemika*, edited by Miroslav Heřman, 75–111. Prague: Academia, 1974.

———. "Chrám gnidský, d. i. der Tempel von Gnidus, ein Gedicht, aus dem Französischen ins Böhmische übersetzt von Anton Puchmajer." In *Literární a prozodická bohemika*, edited by Miroslav Heřman, 132–35. Prague: Academia, 1974.

———. *Dějiny české řeči a literatury, v redakcích z roku 1791, 1792, a 1818*. Edited by Benjamin Jedlička, Spisy a projevy Josefa Dobrovského. Prague: Nákl. Komise pro vydávání spisů Josefa Dobrovského, 1936.

———. "Homérova Iliada z řeckého jazyka přeložena do českého od Jana Nejedlého, etc." In *Literární a prozodická bohemika*, edited by Miroslav Heřman, 115–21. Prague: Academia, 1974.

———. "Numa Pompilious, der zweite König von Rom. In französischer Sprache von Florian geschreiben und in böhmischer ausgelegt von Joh. Nejedlý . . ." In *Literární a prozodická bohemika*, edited by Miroslav Heřman, 145–46. Prague: Academia, 1974.

———. "Über den Wohlklang der Slawischen Sprache, mit besonderer Anwendung auf die Böhmische Mundart." *Slovanka* 2 (1815): 1–67.

———. *Výbor z díla*. Translated and edited by Benjamin Jedlička. Prague: Státní nakladatelství krásné literatury, knihy, a umění, 1953.

"Doležálek, Jan Emanuel." In *Československý hudební slovník: Osob a institucí*, edited by Gracian Černušák, Bohumír Štědroň, and Zdenko Nováček, 1:251–52. Prague: Státní hudební vydavatelství, 1963.

Dunning, Chester. "The Tragic Fate of Pushkin's *Comedy*." In *The Uncensored Boris Godunov: The Case for Pushkin's Original Comedy, with Annotated Text and Translation*, edited by Chester Dunning, Caryl Emerson, Sergei Fomichev, Lidiia Lotman, and Antony Wood. Madison: University of Wisconsin Press, 2006.

Ďurovič, Ľubomír. "Ku vzniku pojmu 'reč československá.'" *Slovenská literatúra* 47, no. 6 (2000): 443–57.

———. "Slovak." In *The Slavic Literary Languages: Formation and Development*, edited by Alexander M. Schenker and Edward Stankiewicz, 211–28. New Haven, CT: Yale Concilium on International and Area Studies, 1980.

Dvořák, Karel, and Felix Vodička. "Včleňování folkloru do obrozenské literatury." *Česká literatura,* no. 3 (1955): 293–350.

Dziadko, Filipp. "'Za chto nam drug ot druga otdaliat'sia?' K istorii literaturnykh otnoshenii A. F. Merzliakova i V. A. Zhukovskogo: 'Versiia' Merzliakova." *Pushkinskie chteniia v Tartu* 3 (2004): 112–36.

Egunov, A. N. *Gomer v russkikh perevodakh XVIII–XIX vekov.* 2nd ed. Moskva: Izdatel'stvo "Indrik," 2001.

Emerson, Caryl. "Pushkin as Critic." In *The Pushkin Handbook,* edited by David M. Bethea, 321–33. Madison: University of Wisconsin Press, 2005.

Emery, Jacob. "Repetition and Exchange in Legitimizing Empire: Konstantin Batiushkov's Scandinavian Corpus." *The Russian Review* 66, no. 4 (2007): 602–26.

Eskin, Michael. "The 'German' Shakespeare." In *A New History of German Literature,* edited by David E. Wellbery, Judith Ryan, and Hans Ulrich Gumbrecht, 460–65. Cambridge: Belknap Press of Harvard University Press, 2004.

Foerster, Donald M. *Homer in English Criticism: The Historical Approach in the Eighteenth Century.* N.p.: Archon Books, 1969.

Fomin, A. A. "Andrei Ivanovich Turgenev i Andrei Sergeevich Kaisarov: Novye dannyia o nikh po dokumentam arkhiva P. N. Turgeneva." *Russkii bibliofil,* no. 1 (1912): 7–39.

France, Peter. "Fingal in Russia." In *The Reception of Ossian in Europe,* edited by Howard Gaskill, 259–73. London: Thoemmes Continuum, 2004.

Franklin, Simon. "The Igor Tale: A Bohemian Rapshody?" *Kritika: Explorations in Russian and Eurasian History* 6 (2005): 845–55.

Frantsev, V. A. *Ocherki po istorii cheshskago vozrozhdeniia: Russko-cheshskiia uchenyia sviazi kontsa XVIII i pervoi poloviny XIX st.* Warsaw: Varshavskii Uchebnyi Okrug, 1902.

Frazier, Melissa. *Romantic Encounters: Writers, Readers, and the Library for Reading.* Stanford, CA: Stanford University Press, 2007.

Frinta, Ant. "Dobrovský—fonetik." In *Josef Dobrovský, 1753–1829: Sborník statí k stému výročí smrti Josefa Dobrovského,* edited by Jiří Horák, Matyáš Murko, and Miloš Weingart, 89–94. Prague: Slovanský seminář University Karlovy, 1929.

Gasparov, Boris M. *Poeticheskii iazyk Pushkina kak fakt istorii russkogo literaturnogo iazyka.* Vienna: Wiener Slavistischer Almanach, 1992.

———. "Russkaia Gretsiia, russkii Rim." In *Christianity and the Eastern Slavs.* Vol. 2, *Russian Culture in Modern Times,* edited by Robert Hughes and Irina Paperno, 245–85. Berkeley: University of California Press, 1994.

Gasparov, Mikhail L. *Ocherk istorii evropeiskogo stikha.* Moscow: Nauka, 1989.

———. *Ocherk istorii russkogo stikha.* Moscow: Fortuna, 2000.

———. "Prodrom, Tsets, i natsional'nye formy geksametra." In *Antichnost' i vizantiia,* edited by L. A. Freiberg, 362–85. Moscow: Nauka, 1975.

Gellner, Ernest. *Nations and Nationalism: New Perspectives on the Past.* Ithaca, NY: Cornell University Press, 1983.

Ginzburg, L. "O probleme narodnosti i lichnosti v poezii dekabristov." In *O russkom realizme XIX veka i voprosakh narodnosti literatury: Sbornik statei,* edited by P. P. Gromov, 52–93. Moscow: GIKhL, 1960.

Glassheim, Eagle. *Noble Nationalists: The Transformation of the Bohemian Aristocracy.* Cambridge: Harvard University Press, 2005.

Gnedich, Nikolai. I. "A. S. Pushkinu po prochtenii Skazki ego o tsare Saltane i proch." In *Stikhotvoreniia.* Leningrad: Sovetstkii pisatel', 1956.

———. "O vol'nom perevodie Biurgerovoi ballady: Lenora." *Syn Otechestva*, no. 27 (1816): 3–22.

———. "Otvet." In *Arzamas: Sbornik v dvukh knigakh*, edited by Vadim Erazmovich Vatsuro and A. L. Ospovat, 2:83–85. Moscow: Khudozhestvennaia literatura, 1994.

Greenfeld, Liah. *Nationalism: Five Roads to Modernity*. Cambridge: Harvard University Press, 1992.

Grepl, M. "K jazyku obrozenských překladů z ruštiny a polštiny." In *Slovanské spisovné jazyky v době obrození: Sborník věnovaný Univerzitou Karlovou k 300. narození Josefa Jungmanna*, 169–79. Prague: Univerzita Karlova, 1974.

Griboedov, A. S. "O razborie vol'nago perevoda Biurgerovoi ballady: 'Lenora.'" In *Polnoe sobranie sochinenii*, 3:14–25. St. Petersburg: Razriad iziashchnoi slovesnosti Akademii Nauk, 1917.

Hall, Vernon, Jr., Arthur F. Kinney, and O. B. Hardison, Jr. "Renaissance Poetics." In *The New Princeton Encyclopedia of Poetry and Poetics*, edited by Alex Preminger and T. V. F. Brogan, 1024–30. Princeton, NJ: Princeton University Press, 1993.

Hanka, Václav. *Hankovy písně a prostonárodní srbská muza, do Čech převedená*. Edited by Jan Máchal. Prague: Česká Akademie Císaře Františka Josefa pro Vědy, Slovesnost, a Umění, 1918.

Hanuš, Josef. "Josefa Dobrovského Geschichte der Böhmischen Sprache (1791), Geschichte der Böhmischen Sprache und Litteratur (1792), Geschichte der Böhmischen Sprache und ältern Literatur (1818)." *Bratislava* 3, no. 3–4 (1929): 494–574.

———. "Pavel Josef Šafařík." In *Ottův slovník naučný* 24:528–40. Prague: J. Otto, 1888–1909.

Harkins, William E. *The Russian Folk Epos in Czech Literature, 1800–1900*. New York: Kings Crown Press, 1951.

Herder, Johann Gottfried. *Herders sämmtliche Werke*. 33 vols. Berlin: Weidmann, 1877–1913.

Heusler, Andreas. *Deutsche Versgeschichte: Mit Einschluss des altenglischen und altnordischen Stabreimverses*. Vol. 3, *Grundriss der germanischen Philologie*, bd.8, teil 3. Berlin: Gruyter, 1929.

Hikl, Karel. "Jungmannova *Slovesnost* a jcjí předlohy." *Listy filologické* 38 (1911): 207–19, 346–53, 416–48.

Hirsch, Francine. *Empire of Nations: Ethnographic Knowledge and the Making of the Soviet Union*. Ithaca, NY: Cornell University Press, 2005.

Hlobil, Tomáš. "Introduction." In *An Historical Survey of the Science of Beauty and the Literature on the Subject*, by František Palacký, ix–xlix. Olomouc: Palacký University, 2002.

———. "Jungmannova charakteristika metafory a německá estetika 18. století." In *Mezi časy . . . Kultura a umění v českých zemích kolem roku 1800*, edited by Zdeněk Hojda and Roman Prahl, 224–32. Prague: Koniasch Latin Press, 2000.

———. "Ossianism in the Bohemian Lands." *Modern Language Review* 101, no. 3 (2006): 789–97.

Hobsbawm, Eric. *Nations and Nationalism since 1780: Programme, Myth, Reality*. Cambridge: Cambridge University Press, 1990.

Hohendahl, Peter Uwe. *Building a National Literature: The Case of Germany, 1830–1870*. Translated by Renate Baron Franciscono. Ithaca, NY: Cornell University Press, 1989.

Hokanson, Katya. "Literary Imperialism, *Narodnost'*, and Pushkin's Invention of the Caucasus." *The Russian Review* 53, no. 3 (1994): 336–52.

Horálek, Karel. *Počátky novočeského verše.* Prague: Nákladem Karlovy University, 1956.

Hrabák, Josef. *Studie o českém verši.* Prague: Státní pedagogické nakladatelství, 1959.

Hroch, Miroslav. "From National Movement to the Fully-formed Nation: The Nation-building Process in Europe." In *Mapping the Nation,* edited by Gopal Balakrishnan, 78–97. London: Verso, 1996.

———. *Social Preconditions of National Revival in Europe: A Comparative Analysis of the Social Composition of Patriotic Groups among the Smaller European Nations.* Cambridge: Cambridge University Press, 1985.

"Hymnorum Thesaurus Bohemicus." http://www.clavmon.cz/htb/ (accessed October 2, 2009).

Hýsek, Miloslav. "Jungmannova škola kritická." *Listy filologické* 41 (1914): 230–70, 350–72, 442–50 and 46 (1919): 189–222.

Iagich, I. V. *Istoriia slavianskoi filologii. Entsiklopediia slavianskoi filologii.* St. Petersburg: Tipografiia Imperatorskoi Adakemii nauk, 1910.

Ianushkevich, A. S. "Put' Zhukovskogo k eposu." In *Zhukovskii i russkaia kul'tura: Sbornik nauchnykh trudov,* edited by Dmitrii Sergeevich Likhachev, Raisa Vladimirovna Iezuitova, and Faina Zinov'evna Kanunova, 166–79. Leningrad: Nauka, 1987.

Ingham, Norman W. "'The *Igor' Tale* and the Origins of Conspiracy Theory." Paper presented at the Davis Center for Russian and Eurasian Studies, Harvard University, 2004.

Istrin, V. M. "Druzheskoe literaturnoe obshchestvo 1801 g. (po materialam Arkhiva brat'ev Turgenevykh)." *Zhurnal Ministerstva narodnago prosveshcheniia,* no. 8 (1910): 273–307.

———. "Iz dokumentov Arkhiva brat'ev Turgenevykh: I. Druzheskoe Literaturnoe Obshchestvo 1801 g." *Zhurnal Ministerstva narodnago prosveshcheniia,* no. 3 (1913): 1–26.

———. *Pis'ma i dnevnik Aleksandra Ivanovicha Turgeneva gettingenskago perioda (1802–1804 gg.) i pis'ma ego k A. S. Kaisarovu i brat'iam v Gettingen 1805–1811 gg.* St. Petersburg: Tipografiia imperatorskoi akademii nauk, 1911.

Jedlička, Benjamin. *Dobrovského "Geschichte" ve vývoji české literární historie.* Archiv pro badání o životě a díle Josefa Dobrovského. Prague: Nákladem Komise pro vydáváni spisů Josefa Dobrovského při Královské české společnosti nauk, 1934.

Judson, Pieter M. *Guardians of the Nation: Activists on the Language Frontiers of Imperial Austria.* Cambridge: Harvard University Press, 2006.

Jungmann, Josef Jakub. *Boj o obrození národa: Výbor z díla.* Edited by Felix Vodička. Prague: F. Kosek, 1948.

———. "Doba." In *Slovník česko-německý,* 1:386. Prague: W. Spinky, 1834.

———. *Krátká historie národu, osvícení, a jazyka: Uvody k Historii literatury české.* K vyd. připravila a doslov napsal Felix Vodička. Prague: Sfinx, 1947.

———. "O klasičnosti literatury vůbec a zvláště české." *Časopis českého musea* 1 (1827): 29–39.

———. "Posudek: *Vznešenost přírody.*" *Krok* 1, no. 1 (1821): 150–55.

———. *Překlady.* 2 vols. Prague: Státní nakladatelství krásné literatury, hudby, a umění, 1958.

———. *Slowesnost aneb Zbjrka přjkladů s krátkým pogednánjm o slohu.* Prague: Wytištěná u Josefy Fetterlowé z Wildenbrunu, 1820.

———. *Vybrané spisy původní i přeložené,* Česká knihovna zábavy a poučení. Prague: Jan Otto, 1918.

Jungmann, Josef Jakub, and Jan Petr. *Slovník česko-německý.* 2nd ed. 4 vols. Prague: Academia, 1990.

Kachenovskii, M. T. "O slavianskom iazykie voobshche i v osobennosti o tserkovnom." *Viestnik Evropy,* no. 19–20 (1816): 241–58.

Kamenskii, Z. A. "Russkaia estetika pervoi treti XIX veka: Klassitsizm." In *Russkie esteticheskie traktaty pervoi treti XIX veka,* edited by Z. A. Kamenskii, 1:7–70. Moscow: Iskusstvo, 1974.

Kapnist, V. V. *Sobranie sochinenii.* 2 vols. Leningrad: Izdatel'stvo Akademii nauk SSSR, 1960.

Karamzin, N. M. *Izbrannye sochineniia v dvukh tomakh.* 2 vols. Moscow: Izdatel'stvo Khudozhestvennaia literatura, 1964.

———. "O sluchaiakh i kharakterakh v rossiiskoi istorii, kotorye mogut byt' predmetom khudozhestv." In *Izbrannye sochineniia,* 2:188–98. Moscow: Izdatel'stvo "Khudozhestvennaia literatura," 1964.

Katenin, P. A. *Izbrannye proizvedeniia.* Edited by G. V. Ermakova-Bitner. Biblioteka poeta. Bol'shaia seriia. Moscow: Sovetskii pisatel', 1965.

Keenan, Edward L. *Josef Dobrovský and the Origins of the Igor' Tale.* Harvard Series in Ukrainian Studies. Cambridge: Harvard Ukrainian Research Institute and the Davis Center for Russian and Eurasian Studies; distributed by Harvard University Press, 2003.

Kelley, Douglas. "*Translatio Studii:* Translation, Adaptation, and Allegory in Medieval French Literature." *Philological Quarterly* 57, no. 3 (1978): 287–310.

King, Jeremy. *Budweisers into Czechs and Germans: A Local History of Bohemian Politics, 1848–1948.* Princeton, NJ: Princeton University Press, 2002.

Kiukhel'beker, V. K. *Puteshestvie, dnevnik, stat'i.* Edited by N. V. Koroleva and V. D. Rak. Leningrad: Izdatel'stvo "Nauka," 1979.

Klein, J. "Russkii Bualo? (Epistola Sumarokova 'O stikhotvorstve' v vospriiatii sovremennikov)." *XVIII vek* 18 (1993): 40–58.

Knight, Nathaniel. "Ethnicity, Nationality, and the Masses: *Narodnost'* and Modernity in Imperial Russia." In *Russian Modernity: Politics, Knowledge, Practices,* edited by David L. Hoffmann and Yanni Kotsonis, 41–64. New York: St. Martin's Press, 2000.

Kollár, Jan. "Myšlénky o libozwučnosti řečj wůbec, obzwláště českoslowanské." *Krok* 1, no. 3 (1823): 32–47.

———. *Vybrané spisy.* Edited by F. R. Tichý. Vol. 2, *Prózy.* Prague: Státni nakladatelství krásné literatury, hudby, a umění, 1956.

Kopitar, Jernej. "O Slowanských nářečjch, a prostředcých gim se navčiti." *Prvotiny pěkných umění* (1813): List 22: 83–86, List 23: 89–91.

Králík, Oldřich. "Překlady z řecké a latinské literatury." In *Překlady,* by Josef Jakub Jungmann. Vol. 2, 610–21. Prague: Státní nakl. krásné lit-ry hudby a umění, 1958.

Kroeber, A. L., and Clyde Kluckhohn. *Culture: A Critical Review of Concepts and Definitions.* New York: Vintage Books, 1963.

Kuz'min, M. N. *Shkola i obrazovanie v chekhoslovakii (konets XVIII–30-e gody XX v.).* Moscow: Nauka, 1971.

Leerssen, Joep. *National Thought in Europe: A Cultural History.* Amsterdam: Amsterdam University Press, 2006.

———. "Ossian and the Rise of Literary Historicism." In *The Reception of Ossian in Europe,* edited by Howard Gaskill, 109–25. New York: Thoemmes Continuum, 2004.

———. "Philology and National Culture." http://cf.hum.uva.nl/natlearn/ (accessed July 6, 2009).

Leighton, Lauren G. "*Narodnost*' as a Concept of Russian Romanticism." In *Russian Romanticism: Two Essays*, 41–107. The Hague: Mouton, 1975.

———. *Russian Romantic Criticism: An Anthology*, Contributions to the Study of World Literature, no. 18. New York: Greenwood Press, 1987.

Lencek, Rado L. "Kopitar's Slavic Version of the Greek Dialects Theme." In *Zbirnyk na poshanu profesora doktora Iuriia Shevel'ova = Symbolae in honorem Georgii Y. Shevelov*, edited by William E. Harkins, Olexa Horbatsch, and Jakob P. Hursky, 244–56. Munich: Logos, 1971.

Lencek, Rado L., and Henry R. Cooper, Jr., eds. *Papers in Slavic Philology 2, To Honor Jernej Kopitar, 1780–1980*. Ann Arbor: University of Michigan, Department of Slavic Languages and Literatures, 1982.

Levin, Iu. D. *Ossian v russkoi literature: Konets XVIII-pervaia tret' XIX veka*. Leningrad: Nauka, 1980.

Levine, Joseph M. "Ancients and Moderns Reconsidered." *Eighteenth-Century Studies* 15, no. 1 (1981): 72–89.

———. "Giambattista Vico and the Quarrel between the Ancients and the Moderns." *Journal of the History of Ideas* 52, no. 1 (1991): 55–79.

———. *Humanism and History: Origins of Modern English Historiography*. Ithaca, NY: Cornell University Press, 1987.

Lomonosov, Mikhailo V. *Sochineniia*. Moscow: Gosudarstvennoe izdatel'stvo khudozhestvennoi literatury, 1961.

Lotman, Iurii M. "A. F. Merzliakov kak poet." In *Stikhotvorenie*, by Aleksei F. Merzliakov, 5–54. Biblioteka poeta. Leningrad: Sovetskii pisatel', 1958.

———. "Andrei Sergeevich Kaisarov i literaturno-obshchestvennaia bor'ba ego vremeni." *Uchenye zapiski tartuskogo gosudarstvennogo universiteta* 63 (1958): 1–191.

———. "Problema narodnosti i puti razvitiia literatury preddekabristskogo perioda." In *O russkom realizme XIX veka i voprosakh narodnosti literatury: Sbornik statei*, edited by P. P. Gromov, 3–51. Moscow: GIKhL, 1960.

———. "Stikhotvorenie Andreia Turgeneva 'K otechestvu' i ego rech' v 'Druzheskom literaturnom obshchestve.'" In *Dekabristy—literatory*, Literaturnoe nasledstvo 60, no. 1, 323–38. Moscow: Izdatel'stvo Akademii Nauk SSSR, 1956.

Lotman, Iurii M., and M. G. Al'tshuler, eds. *Poety 1790–1820kh godov*. Biblioteka poeta. Leningrad: Sovetskii pisatel', 1971.

Lounsbery, Anne. *Thin Culture, High Art: Gogol, Hawthorne, and Authorship in Nineteenth-Century Russia and America*. Harvard Studies in Comparative Literature. Cambridge: Harvard University Press, 2007.

L'vov, N. A. *Izbrannye sochineniia*. Edited by K. I. U. Lappo-Danilevskii. St. Petersburg: Pushkinskii dom, 1994.

Lvov, Nikolai, and Ivan Prach. *A Collection of Russian Folk Songs*. Edited by Malcolm Hamrick Brown. Ann Arbor, MI: UMI Research Press, 1987.

Máchal, Jan. "Úvod." In *Hankovy písně a prostonárodní srbská muza, do Čech převedená*, edited by Jan Máchal, v–xliv. Prague: Česká Akademie Císaře Františka Josefa pro Vědy, Slovesnost, a Umění, 1918.

Macura, Vladimír. "Problems and Paradoxes of the National Revival." In *Bohemia in History*, edited by Mikuláš Teich, 182–97. Cambridge: Cambridge University Press, 1998.

———. *Znamení zrodu: České národní obrození jako kulturní typ*. New, expanded ed. Jinočany: H&H, 1995.

Malein, A. I. "Prilozhenie k stat'e A. S. Orlova 'Tilemakhida.'" In *XVIII vek: Sbornik statei i materialov*, edited by A. S. Orlov, 57–60. Moscow: Izdatel'stvo Akademii nauk SSSR, 1935.

Marchenko, N. A. "Andrei Ivanovich Turgenev." In *Russkie pisateli: Biobibliograficheskii slovar'*, edited by P. A. Nikolaev, 2:321–23. Moscow: Prosveshchenie, 1996.

Maur, Eduard. "Pojetí národa v české osvícenské historiografii: Ignác Cornova a František Marin Pelcl." In *Mezi časy . . . Kultura a umění v českých zemích kolem roku 1800*, edited by Zdeněk Hojda and Roman Prahl, 134–45. Prague: Koniasch Latin Press, 1999.

Mazo, Margarita. "Introduction." In *A Collection of Russian Folk Songs*, edited by Malcolm Hamrick Brown, 3–76. Ann Arbor, MI: UMI Research Press, 1987.

Merzliakov, Aleksei F. "Ob iziashchnom, ili o vybore v podrazhanii." In *Russkie esteticheskie traktaty pervoi treti XIX veka*, edited by Z. A. Kamenskii, 1:74–93. Moscow: Iskusstvo, 1974.

———. "Rassuzhdenie o rossiiskoi slovesnosti v nyneshnem ee sostoianii." *Trudy Obshchestva liubitelei rossiiskoi slovesnosti*, no. 1 (1812): 53–110.

Miller, Aleksei. *The Romanov Empire and Nationalism: Essays in the Methodology of Historical Research*. Translated by Serguei Dobrynin. Budapest: Central European University Press, 2008.

Mironenko, S. V. "Politicheskii portret Pavla Pestelia." In *"Russkaia pravda"—"La legge russa,"* by Pavel Ivanovich Pestel'. Edited by A. F. Sivak and S. V. Mironenko. Moscow: Izdatel'stvo "Progress-Akademiia," 1993.

Mordovchenko, N. I. *Russkaia kritika pervoi chetverti XIX veka*. Moscow: Izdatel'stvo Akademii Nauk SSSR, 1959.

Mukařovský, Jan. "Dobrovského 'Česká prozodie' a prosodické boje jí podnícené." *Česká literatura* 2, no. 1 (1954): 1–29.

———. "Polákova *Vznešenost přírody* (Pokus o rozbor a vývojové zařadění básnické struktury)." In *Kapitoly z české poetiky*, 2:91–176. Prague: Nakladatelství svoboda, 1948.

Murav'ev-Apostol, I. M. "Pis'ma iz Moskvy v Nizhnii Novgorod: Pis'mo chetvertoe [4th]." *Syn Otechestva*, no. 44 (1813): 211–34.

———. "Pis'ma iz Moskvy v Nizhnii Novgorod: Pis'mo tretie [3rd]." *Syn Otechestva*, no. 39 (1813): 3–13.

———. "Pis'mo pervoe [1st] iz Moskvy v Nizhnii Novgorod." *Syn Otechestva*, no. 35 (1813): 89–97.

"Natsional'nost'." In *Slovar' russkogo iazyka XVIII veka*. St. Petersburg: Nauka, 2004.

Neizviestnyi [A. F. Merzliakov]. "Pis'mo iz Sibiri." *Trudy Obshchestva liubitelei rossiiskoi slovesnosti pri Imperatorskom moskovskom universitete*, no. 11 (1818): 52–70.

Nejedlý, Jan. "O lásce k vlasti." *Hlasatel český* 1 (1806): 5–42.

Newerkla, Stefan Michael. "The Seamy Side of the Habsburgs' Liberal Language Policy: Intended and Factual Reality of Language Use in Plzeň's Educational System." In *Diglossia and Power: Language Policies and Practice in the Nineteenth-Century Habsburg Empire*, edited by Rosita Rindler Schjerve, 167–95. Berlin: Mouton de Gruyter, 2003.

Newlin, Thomas. "Aleksandr Petrovich Orlov." In *Slovar' russkikh pisatelei XVIII veka*, edited by A. M. Panchenko, 2:387–88. St. Petersburg: Nauka, 1999.

———. "Rural Ruses: Illusion and Anxiety on the Russian Estate, 1775–1815." *Slavic Review* 15, no. 2 (1998): 295–319.

Oergel, Maike. *The Return of King Arthur and the Niebelungen: National Myth in Nineteenth-Century English and German Literature*. New York: Walter de Gruyter, 1998.

Otáhal, Milan. "The Manuscript Controversy in the Czech National Revival." *Cross Currents* 5 (1986): 247–77.

Otruba, Mojmír. "Josef Jungmann." In *Lexikon české literatury*, edited by Vladimír Forst, 2(pt. I): 580–86. Prague: Akademia, 1993.

——, ed. *Rukopisy královédvorský a zelenohorský: Dnešní stav poznání.* Prague: Academia, 1969.

——. "Václav Hanka." In *Lexikon české literatury*, edited by Vladimír Forst, 2(pt. I):57–63. Prague: Akademia, 1993.

"Oznámení." *Krok* 1, no. 1 (1821): 7–12.

Palacký, František. *Gedenkblätter: Auswahl von Denkschriften, Aufsätzen, und Briefen aus den letzten fünfzig Jahren.* Prague: Verlag von F. Tempsky, 1874.

——. *An Historical Survey of the Science of Beauty and the Literature on the Subject.* Translated by Derek Paton and Marzia Paton. Edited by Tomáš Hlobil. Olomouc: Palacký University, 2002.

——. "Ohlášení časopisu tohoto." *Časopis českého musea* 1, no. 1 (1827): 3–8.

——. "Slovo k vlastencům od redaktora." *Časopis českého musea* 1, no. 4 (1827): 145–52.

——. *Spisy drobné.* Edited by Leander Čech. Vol. 3, *Spisy aesthetické a literarní.* Prague: Bursík & Kohut, 1900.

Palacký, František, and Simeon Karel Macháček. *Geschichte der schönen Redekünste bei den Böhmen/Dějiny české slovesnosti.* Edited by Oldřich Králík and Jiří Skalička. Brno: Profil, 1968.

Patey, Douglas Lane. "Ancients and Moderns." In *The Eighteenth Century*, edited by H. B. Nisbet and Claude Rawson, *The Cambridge History of Literary Criticism*, 32–71. Cambridge: Cambridge University Press, 1997.

Peskov, A. M. *Bualo v russkoi literature XVIII–XIX veka.* Moscow: Izdatel'stvo Moskovskogo universiteta, 1989.

Pestel', Pavel Ivanovich. *"Russkaia pravda"—"La legge russa."* Edited by A. F. Sivak and S. V. Mironenko. Translated by Maria Grazia Musneci. Moscow: Izdatel'stvo "Progress-Akademiia," 1993.

Petrbok, Václav. "Příspěvek vídeňských a vídeňskonovoměstských bohemistů k české literární historii, bibliografii, a knihopisu v letech 1770–1810." In *Vídeňský podíl na počátcích českého národního obrození, J. V. Zlobický (1743–1810) a současníci: Život, dílo, korespondence*, edited by Josef Vintr and Jana Pleskalová, 80–100. Prague: Academia, 2004.

Plokhy, Serhii. *The Origins of the Slavic Nations: Premodern Identities in Russia, Ukraine, and Belarus.* Cambridge: Cambridge University Press, 2006.

Pohanka, Jaroslav. *Dějiny české hudby v příkladech.* Prague: Státní nakladatelství krásné literatury, hudby, a umění, 1958.

Polevoi, N. A., and K. A. Polevoi. *Literaturnaia kritika, stat'i, i retsenzii, 1825–1842.* Leningrad: Khudozhestvennaia literatura, 1990.

Pölitz, Karel Heinrich Ludwig. *Das Gesammtgebiet der teutschen Sprache, nach Prosa, Dichtkunst, und Beredsamkeit theoretisch und practisch dargestellt.* Vol. 1 of 4. Leipzig: J. C. Hinrichssche Buchhandlung, 1825.

Pražák, Albert. *Národ se bránil, obrany národa a jazyka českého od nejstarších dob po přítomnost.* Prague: Sfinx, 1945.

Proskurin, Oleg. "Novyi Arzamas—Novyi ierusalim: Literaturnaia igra v kul'turno-istoricheskom kontekste." *Novoe literaturnoe obozrenie*, no. 19 (1996): 73–128.

Prousis, Theophilus Christopher. *Russian Society and the Greek Revolution.* DeKalb:

Northern Illinois University Press, 1994.

Pumpianskii, L. V. "Trediakovskii." In *Istoriia russkoi literatury,* edited by G. A. Gukovskii and V. A. Desnitskii, 215–63. Moscow: Izdateľstvo Akademii nauk SSSR, 1941.

Pushkin, Aleksandr S. *Polnoe sobranie sochinenii v desiati tomakh.* 10 vols. Moscow: Nauka, 1964.

Pynsent, Robert. *Questions of Identity: Czech and Slovak Ideas of Nationality and Personality.* Budapest: Central European University Press, 1994.

Radishchev, A. N. *Izbrannye sochineniia.* Moscow: Gosudarstvennoe izdateľstvo khudozhestvennoi literatury, 1952.

———. *Polnoe sobranie sochinenii.* 3 vols. Moscow: Izdateľstvo Akademii nauk SSSR, 1941.

———. *Stikhotvoreniia.* Biblioteka poeta. Boľshaia seriia. Leningrad: Sovetskii pisateľ, 1975.

Raeff, Marc. "Russian Youth on the Eve of Romanticism: Andrei I. Turgenev and His Circle." In *Political Ideas and Institutions in Imperial Russia,* 42–64. Boulder, CO: Westview Press, 1994.

Ram, Harsha. *The Imperial Sublime: A Russian Poetics of Empire.* Publications of the Wisconsin Center for Pushkin Studies. Madison: University of Wisconsin Press, 2003.

Randolph, John W. "The Singing Coachman or, The Road and Russia's Ethnographic Invention in Early Modern Times." *Journal of Early Modern History* 11, no. 1/2 (2007): 33–61.

Reichel, Walter. "Josef Valentin Zlobický—první profesor českého jazyka a literatury: Život, působení, a zásluhy na pozadí osvícenství." In *Vídeňský podíl na počátcích českého národního obrození: J. V. Zlobický (1743–1810) a současníci: Život, dílo, korespondence,* edited by Josef Vintr and Jana Pleskalová, 24–41. Prague: Akademia, 2004.

Reill, Peter Hans. *The German Enlightenment and the Rise of Historicism.* Berkeley: University of California Press, 1975.

Reyfman, Irina. *Vasilii Trediakovsky: The Fool of the New Russian Literature.* Stanford, CA: Stanford University Press, 1990.

Richter, Jean Paul Friedrich. "From *School for Aesthetics.*" In *German Romantic Criticism,* edited by A. Leslie Wilson, 31–61. New York: Continuum, 2002.

Rogger, Hans. *National Consciousness in Eighteenth-Century Russia.* Russian Research Center Studies, 38. Cambridge: Harvard University Press, 1960.

Rokina, G. V. *Ian Kollar i Rossiia: Istoriia idei slavianskoi vzaimnosti v rossiiskom obshchestve pervoi poloviny XIX v.* Ioshkar-Ola, Russian Federation: MGPI, 1998.

Rosenberg, Karen. "Between Ancients and Moderns: V. K. Trediakovskij on the Theory of Language and Literature." Ph.D. diss., Yale University, 1980.

Šafárik, Pavel Jozef. "Národní písně a zpěvy. Promluvení k Slovanům." *Prvotiny pěkných umění,* no. 1 (1817): 3–5.

Šafárik, Pavel Jozef, and František Palacký. *Počátkové českého básnictví obzvláště prozódie.* Bratislava: Vydavateľstvo Slovenskej akadémie vied, 1961.

Šafránek, Jan. *Školy české: Obraz jejich vývoje a osudů.* 2 vols. Prague: Nákladem Matice české, 1913–1918.

Said, Edward W. *Orientalism.* 25th anniversary ed. New York: Vintage, 1994.

Saitov, V. I., ed. *Ostaf'evskii arkhiv kniazei Viazemskikh.* Vol. 1, *Perepiska kniazia P. A. Viazemskago s A. I. Turgenevym, 1812–1819* and Vol. 2, *Perepiska kniazia P. A. Viazemskago s A. I. Turgenevym, 1820–1823.* St. Petersburg: Izdanie grafa S. D. Sheremeteva, 1899.

Sayer, Derek. *The Coasts of Bohemia: A Czech History.* Princeton, NJ: Princeton University Press, 1998.

Schamschula, Walter. *Die Anfänge der tschechischen Erneuerung und das deutsche Geistesleben (1740–1800)*. Munich: Wilhelm Fink Verlag, 1973.

Schiller, Friedrich. "On Bürger's Poems." In *Eighteenth-Century German Criticism*, edited by Timothy J. Chamberlain, 262–73. New York: Continuum, 1992.

Schulte-Sasse, Jochen. "1735: Aesthetic Orientation in a Decentered World." In *A New History of German Literature*, edited by David E. Wellbery and Judith Ryan. Cambridge: The Belknap Press of Harvard University Press, 2004.

Sgallová, Květa. "Rým v teorii a v praxi národního obrození." *Česká literatura*, no. 6 (2002): 606–13.

Shishkov, Aleksandr S. "Mnienie moe o razsmatrivanii knig ili tsenzurie." In *Zapiski, mnieniia, i perepiska Admirala A. S. Shishkova*, edited by N. Kiselov and Iu. Samarin, 43–52. Berlin: B. Behr's Buchhandlung, 1870.

———. "Primiechaniia na drevnee o polku igorevom sochinenie." In *Sobranie sochinenii i perevodov Admirala Shishkova*, 7:35–124. St. Petersburg: Imperatorskaia Rossiiskaia Akademiia, 1826.

———. "Razgovory o slovesnosti mezhdu dvumia litsami Az i Buki." In *Sobranie sochinenii i perevodov Admirala Shishkova*, 3:1–166. St. Petersburg: Imperatorskaia Rossiiskaia Akademiia, 1824.

———. "Razsuzhdenie o starom i novom slogie rossiiskago iazyka." In *Sobranie sochinenii i perevodov Admirala Shishkova*, 2:1–352. St. Petersburg: Imperatorskaia Rossiiskaia Akademiia, 1824.

———. "Riech' pri otkrytii Besiedy liubitelei ruskago slova." In *Sobranie sochinenii i perevodov Admirala Shishkova*, 4:108–46. St. Petersburg: Imperatorskaia Rossiiskaia Akademiia, 1825.

Simonsuuri, Kirsti. *Homer's Original Genius: Eighteenth-Century Notions of the Early Greek Epic (1688–1798)*. Cambridge: Cambridge University Press, 1979.

Smith, Anthony D. *National Identity, Ethnonationalism in Comparative Perspective*. Reno: University of Nevada Press, 1991.

Somov, Orest. "O romanticheskoi poezii." *Sorevnovatel' prosveshcheniia i blagotvoreniia* 23 (1823): 43–59, 151–69, 263–306; 24 (1823): 125–47.

Staël, Madame de. *De l'Allemagne*. 2nd ed. 2 vols. Paris: Chez H. Nicolle, a la Librairie Stéréotype, 1814.

———. *Madame de Staël on Politics, Literature, and National Character*. Translated and edited by Morroe Berger. Garden City, N. Y.: Doubleday, 1965.

Stuart, Mary. *Aristocrat-Librarian in Service to the Tsar: Aleksei Nikolaevich Olenin and the Imperial Public Library*. Boulder, CO: East European Monographs, 1986.

Strakhov, Olga B. "The Linguistic Practice of the Creator of the *Igor' Tale* and the Linguistic Views of Josef Dobrovský." *Palaeoslavica* 11 (2003): 36–67.

———. "A New Book on the Origin of the *Igor' Tale*: A Backward Step." *Palaeoslavica* 12, no. 1 (2004): 204–38.

Sumarokov, A. P. *Izbrannye proizvedeniia*. Biblioteka poeta. Bol'shaia seriia. Leningrad: Sovetskii pisatel', 1957.

Suny, Ronald Gregor, and Terry Martin, eds. *A State of Nations: Empire and Nation-Making in the Age of Lenin and Stalin*. New York: Oxford University Press, 2001.

Svoboda, Karel. *Antika a česká vzdělanost od obrození do první války světové*. Prague: Nakladatelství československé akademie věd, 1957.

Taruskin, Richard. *Defining Russia Musically: Historical and Hermeneutical Essays*. Princeton, NJ: Princeton University Press, 1997.

Teichman, Josef. *Z českých luhů do světa: Průkopníci české hudby.* Prague: Orbis, 1948.

Todd, William Mills, III. "Pushkin and Literary Criticism." In *The Cambridge Companion to Pushkin,* edited by Andrew Kahn, 143–55. Cambridge: Cambridge University Press, 2006.

Todorova, Maria. "The Trap of Backwardness: Modernity, Temporality, and the Study of Eastern European Nationalism." *Slavic Review* 64, no. 1 (2005): 140–64.

Trediakovskii, V. K. *Izbrannye proizvedeniia.* Biblioteka poeta. Bol'shaia seriia. 2 izd. Leningrad: Sovetskii pisatel', 1963.

———. *Sochineniia.* 3 vols. St. Petersburg: Izd. A. Smirdina, 1849.

Tynianov, Iurii N. "Arkhaisty i Pushkin." In *Pushkin i ego sovremenniki,* 23–121. Moscow: Nauka, 1969.

———. "Oda kak oratorskii zhanr." In *Arkhaisty i novatory,* 48–86. Leningrad: Priboi, 1929.

Uspenskii, Boris A. "Iazykovaia situatsiia i iazykovoe soznanie v Moskovskoi Rusi: Vospriiatie tserkovnoslavianskogo i russkogo iazyka." In *Izbrannye trudy,* 2:26–48. Moscow: Gnosis, 1994.

Uspenskii, Boris A., and Iurii M. Lotman. "Spory o iazyke v nachale XIX v. kak fakt russkoi kul'tury ('Proischestvie v tsarstve tenei, ili sud'bina rossiiskogo iazyka'—neizvestnoe sochinenie Semena Bobrova)." In *Izbrannye trudy,* by Boris A. Uspenskii. Vol. 2, *Iazyk i kul'tura,* 331–566. Moscow: Gnosis, 1994.

Uvarov, Sergei S. "Otvet V. V. Kapnistu na pis'mo ego ob ekzametre." In *Arzamas: Sbornik v dvukh knigakh,* edited by Vadim Erazmovich Vatsuro, 2:85–94. Moscow: Khudozhestvennaia literatura, 1994.

———. "Pis'mo k Nikolaiu Ivanovichu Gnedichu o grecheskom ekzametre." In *Arzamas: Sbornik v dvukh knigakh,* edited by Vadim Erazmovich Vatsuro, 2:78–83. Moscow: Khudozhestvennaia literatura, 1994.

———. *Projet d'une académie asiatique.* St. Petersburg: n.p., 1810.

Varcl, Ladislav, et al. *Antika a česká kultura.* Praha: Academia, 1978.

Vatsuro, V. E. "V preddverii pushkinskoi epokhi." In *Arzamas: Sbornik v dvukh knigakh.* Vol. 1. *Memuarnye svidetel'stva. Nakanune "Arzamasa." Arzamasskie dokumenty,* 5–27. Moscow: Khudozhestvennaia literatura, 1994.

Vatsuro, V. E., and M. N. Virolainen. "Pis'ma Andreia Turgeneva k Zhukovskomu." In *Zhukovskii i russkaia kul'tura,* edited by R. V. Iezuitova, 350–431. Leningrad: Izdatel'stvo "Nauka," 1987.

Venevitinov, Dmitrii V. *Stikhotvoreniia, proza.* Moscow: Nauka, 1980.

Veselovskii, Aleksandr Nikolaevich. *V. A. Zhukovskii: Poeziia chuvstva i "serdechnogo voobrazheniia."* Moscow: Intrada, 1999.

Viazemskii, Petr. "Razbor Vtorago Razgovora, napechatannago v 7 No Viestnika Evropy." *Damskii zhurnal,* no. 8 (1824): 63–82.

———. "Vmesto predisloviia: Razgovor mezhdu izdatelem i klassikom s vyborgskoi storony ili s vasil'evskogo ostrova." In *Estetika i literaturnaia kritika,* 48–53. Moscow: Iskusstvo, 1984.

Vidmanová, Anežka. "Staročeské pokusy o hexametr a pentametr." *Slovo a smysl: Časopis pro mezioborová studia* 1, no. 1 (2004): 21–51.

Vinitskii, Il'ia. *Utekhi melankholii.* Moscow: Izdatel'svto Moskovskogo kul'turologicheskogo litseia, 1997.

Vinogradov, V. V. *Ocherki po istorii russkogo literaturnogo iazyka XVII–XIX vv.* Leiden: E. I. Brill, 1949.

Vintr, Josef. "Josef Valentin Zlobický—zapomenutý český vlastenec z ocvícenské Vídně." In

Vídeňský podíl na počátcích českého národního obrození: J. V. Zlobický (1743–1810) a současníci: Život, dílo, korespondence, edited by Josef Vintr and Jana Pleskalová, 13–23. Prague: Akademia, 2004.

Virolainen, M. N. "Iz dnevnika Andreia Ivanovicha Turgeneva." *Vostok-Zapad: Issledovaniia, perevody, publikatsii*, 4 (1989): 100–140.

Vladimirova, I. D. [Irina Reyfman] "Evoliutsiia literaturnykh vzgliadov V. K. Trediakovskogo." *Uchenye zapiski Tartuskogo universiteta*, no. 604 (1982): 32–47.

Vodička, Felix, ed. *Dějiny české literatury*. Vol. 2, *Literatura národního obrození*, ed. Jan Mukařovský. Prague: Nakladatelství Československé akademie věd, 1960.

———. *Počátky krásné prózy novočeské: Příspěvek k literárním dějinám doby Jungmannovy.* Prague: Melantrich, 1948.

———. "Slovo uvodní." In *Boj o obrození národa: Výbor z díla*, by Josef Jakub Jungmann, 9–22. Prague: F. Kosek, 1948.

Vostokov, Aleksandr. "Opyt o russkom stikhoslozhenii." *Sanktpeterburgskie vedomosti*, no. 4–6 (1812): 39–68, 168–206, 271–88.

———. *Opyt o russkom stikhoslozhenii*. 2nd ed. St. Petersburg: Morskaia tipografiia, 1817.

Wachtel, Andrew. "Translation, Imperialism, and National Self-Definition in Russia." *Public Culture* 2, no. 1 (1999): 49–73.

Wallnig, Thomas. "Language and Power in the Habsburg Empire: The Historical Context." In *Diglossia and Power: Language Policies and Practice in the Nineteenth-century Habsburg Empire*, edited by Rosita Rindler Schjerve, 15–32. Berlin: Mouton de Gruyter, 2003.

Weimar, Klaus. *Geschichte der deutschen Literaturwissenschaft bis zum Ende des 19. Jahrhunderts*. Munich: Wilhelm Fink Verlag, 1989.

Wellek, René. *A History of Modern Criticism, 1750–1950*. 2 vols. New Haven, CT: Yale University Press, 1955.

———. *The Rise of English Literary History*. Chapel Hill: University of North Carolina Press, 1941.

White, Florence Donnell. *Voltaire's Essay on Epic Poetry: A Study and an Edition*. Albany, NY: Brandow Printing Co., 1915.

Whittaker, Cynthia H. *The Origins of Modern Russian Education: An Intellectual Biography of Count Sergei Uvarov, 1786–1855*. DeKalb: Northern Illinois University Press, 1984.

Wolff, Tatiana, ed. *Pushkin on Literature*. London: The Athlone Press, 1986.

Zalizniak, A. A. *"Slovo o polku Igoreve": Vzgliad lingvista*. Moscow: Iazyki slavianskoi kul'tury, 2004.

Zelený, Václav. *Život Josefa Jungmanna*. 2nd ed. Prague: Nakladatel Fr. A. Urbánek, 1881.

Zhivov, V. M. "Tserkovnoslavianskaia literaturnaia traditsiia v russkoi literature XVIII v. i retseptsiia spora 'drevnikh' i 'novykh.'" In *Istoriia kul'tury i poetika*, edited by L. A. Sofronova, 62–82. Moscow: Nauka, 1994.

Zhukovskii, V. A. *Sobranie sochinenii v chetyrekh tomakh*. 4 vols. Moscow: Gosudarstvennoe izdatel'stvo khudozhestvennoi literatury, 1960.

Zorin, Andrei L. "Ideologiia 'Pravoslaviia—samoderzhaviia—narodnosti' i ee nemetskie istochniki." In *V razdum'iakh o Rossii (XIX vek)*, edited by E. L. Rudnitskaia, 105–28. Moscow: Arkheograficheskii tsentr, 1996.

———. "The Perception of Emotional Coldness in Andrei Turgenev's Diaries." *Slavic Review* 68, no. 2 (2009): 238–58.

———. "U istokov russkogo germanofil'stva (Andrei Turgenev i Druzheskoe literaturnoe obshchestvo)." In *Novye bezdelki: Sbornik statei k 60-letiiu V. E. Vatsuro*, edited by S. I. Panov, 7–35. Moscow: *Novoe literaturnoe obozrenie*, 1995–96.

Index

Boldface indicates principal treatment of a topic.

Adelung, Johann Christoph, 69–71, 76, 273n15, 273n22, 273n27
Aeneid, 144
Aeschylus, 92, 183
Aesop, 185
aesthetics, 23, 25, 47, 49, 66, 133, 251, 257, 269n7; Baumgarten invents term, 19; and Jungmann, 201, 298n47; and Kollár, 192–93, 197–98; Palacký on, 109, 155, 189, 195; Venevitinov on, 239, 241, 243
Agnew, Hugh LeCaine, 8–9
Alexandrines, 139, 145, 151, 199; criticized, 149, 150, 154, 155, 159
Alfieri, Count Vittorio, 144
allegory, 39, 279n1
alterity, 4, 21, 89, 90, 174, 182
Al'tshuller, Mark, 287n54
Anacreon, 81, 275n58
Anacreontic verse, 26, 95
ancient classics. *See* classical antiquity; classical prosody; Quarrel between Ancients and Moderns
Ancient Greece. *See* Greece; Greek prosody
Ancillon, Jean-Pierre-Frédéric, 170, 184, 201, 217, 254, 292n16, 298n51, 302n32; *Analyse de l'idée de littérature,* 172; "Essai sur la différence de la Poésie ancienne et de la Poésie moderne," 293n17; on nation and national character, 172, 221–22
Anderson, Benedict, 6–7, 259n7
antiquity. *See* classical antiquity; classical prosody
Apel, Johann August, 112, 280n112
Arabian poetry, 170–71
archaisms, 39, 40, 63, 64, 80, 83
archaists, 28, 41, 52, 143, 147, 263n65; combine pre-romanticism with classicism, 39; and Decembrists, 49, 265n15; Tynianov introduces term, 64. *See also* Shishkov's followers
Ariosto, Ludovico, 93, 218
aristocratic culture. *See* nobility
Aristotle, 7, 26, 28, 183, 184, 240
arkhaisty. See archaists; Shishkov's followers
Arzamas, 63, 104, 106, 107, 292n9
Asia, 152, 158, 181, 195, 293n20
Athenaeum, 228
audience, 5, 60, 217; Czechs' desire to create, 82–83, 133; Pushkin's desire to reach, 211–12, 226–29
Azadovsky, Mark, 38, 291n4

ballad, 22, 161, 223, 253; as developed by
    Bürger, 92–93, 174; Russian debates
    over, 63, **102–7**, 160, 228
Baratynsky, Evgeny, 298n51
baroque style, 25, 60
Batiushkov, Konstantin, 169, 180, 181, 212
Battle of the Books, 18, 19–20. *See also*
    Quarrel between Ancients and Moderns
Battle of White Mountain (1620), 25, 194
Baumgarten, Alexander Gottlieb, 19
Bausinger, Hermann, 92, 93
Beaudoin, Luc Jean, 298n51
Beckovský, Jan František, 133
Beethoven, Ludwig van, 98, 99, 277n36
Belinsky, Vissarion, 31, 37, 49, 241;
    "Literary Reveries," 297n29
Benedikti, Jan, 123, 131, 196
Berghahn, Klaus, 269n7
Berman, Antoine, 89–90, 91, 109, 182,
    275n1, 295n58
Bernolák, Anton, 193, 194, 274n50,
    281n41
Berzsenyi, Dániel, 119
Bestuzhev-Marlinsky, Aleksandr, 179, 212,
    300n8; on lack of Russian literature,
    37, 237–38, 303n11, 304n13; and
    narodnost', 168–69, 172–73, 185, 219
Bible, 24–25, 67, 92, 194
Bildung, 109, 181, 182, 234, 295n58;
    defined, 89–90
blagoglasie, 146–47, 157, 207, 290n105. *See
    also dobroglasie*
Blagorodnyi pansion (Moscow University),
    32, 246
blagozvuchnost', 156, 207, 287n47, 290n105
Blahoslav, Jan, 25
blahozvučnost, 202, 299n57
blank verse, 81, 140, 282n60
Bobrov, Semen, 39, 215; on *dobroglasie*,
    206–7; "Proizshestvie v tsarstve tenei"
    ("An Incident in the Kingdom of
    Shades"), 84–85, 145
Bodmer, Johann Jakob, 207
*Böhmische Litteratur (Bohemian
    Literature)*, 67
*Böhmische und Mährische Litteratur
    (Bohemian and Moravian Literature)*, 67

Boian, 17, 84, 85, 157
Boileau-Despréaux, Nicolas, 265n19,
    268n59; *Art poétique*, 16, 260n3;
    importance to Russian literature, 16,
    26–28, 223, 260n3, 263n61; provokes
    Quarrel of Ancients and Moderns, 18
Bojanowska, Edyta, 10
Bothe, Friedrich Heinrich, 112, 280n112
Bouterwek, Friedrich, 109, 154–55
Bugge, Peter, 5, 6, 9
Bulgarin, Faddei, 185, 218
Bürger, Gottfried August, 97;
    "Herzenausguß über Volkspoesie"
    ("Outpourings from the Heart on
    Volkspoesie"), 93; "Lenore," 103, 104–7,
    174; Somov links to *narodnost'*, 173–75,
    176, 253; on *Volkspoesie*, 92–94; on
    Volkstümlichkeit (national popularity),
    229–30
byliny, 102, 158
Byron, Lord George Gordon, 17, 215;
    "Prisoner of Chillon," 103
Byzantium, 135, 136, 262n32

caesura, 114, 115, 127, 280n22
Calderón de la Barca, Pedro, 218, 219, 220
časomíra (quantitative verse), 110, 111,
    120, 127, 190, 194, 200. *See also*
    quantitative versification
*Časopis českého musea (Journal of the
    Czech Museum)*, 200, 205
Catherine II, the Great (Empress of
    Russia), 145
Catholicism, 25, 66, 194, 248, 272n3,
    274n50, 281n41; Lomonosov's
    dismissal of, 136–37
Catullus, 26, 183, 185
Caucasus, 180, 181
Čelakovský, František Ladislav, 252
censorship, 66–67, 270n26
Červenka, Miroslav, 280n19
Chaadaev, Petr, 31, 36, 242; *Philosophical
    Letters*, 241
Charles IV (Holy Roman Emperor; King of
    Bohemia), 24, 272n3
Charles University in Prague, 25, 67, 247,
    248, 263n53

Chateaubriand, François-René, vicomte de, 80–81, 82, 83, 133

Chénier, André, 181

chivalric culture, 171–72, 176, 177

Christianity, 62, 69, 102, 171, 241, 249; associated with rhyme, 123, 130, 141; interrupts pagan verse tradition, 137–38. *See also* Catholicism; Protestantism; Russian Orthodoxy

Chtenie v Besede, 157, 158

Chulkov, Mikhail, 101, 133

church books, 66; as model for Russian language, 53, 60, 61, 62, 63, 102, 137

church reform movement, 24–25, 66

Church Slavonic, 40, 207; defines high style, 57–58, 60–61; and diglossia, 54, 57–58, 65, 67; in relation to Greek, 53, 135, 137, 153; Shishkov on, **52–54, 56–61,** 63, 269n15; Trediakovsky's use of, 137, 142. *See also* Slaviano-Russian

civic realm, 6, 32, 47, 233; and *narodnost',* 168, 177, 184–85

classical antiquity, 37, 53, 101, 133, 209, 223, 282n44, 283n65; Arab poetry as alternate model to, 170–71; and Byzantium, 135–36; folklore as alternate model to, 103, 152, 156–58; and German literature, 93, 109, 174–75, 181, 195, 301n25; India as alternate model to, 189, 296n8; as means to achieve national literature, 110, 128, 129, 136, 144, 152, 155–56, 159, 207, 236; Merzliakov on, 46–47, 48; as model for Jungmann, 81–84, 275n58; as model for *Počátkové,* 110–11, 117–26, 128–30, 195, 282n46; as model for Republican France, 39, 60; as model for Trediakovsky and Lomonosov, 137–42, 146, 285n7, 286n27; as model for Uvarov, 136, 153–56, 158–59, 207; and *narodnost',* 183–84, 195, 212–15, 217; national literature paradigm replaces and undermines, 16–17, 23, 28, 200, 203, 249, 250, 251–52; Quarrel reinterprets and undermines, 18–24, 89, 109, 189, 233–34, 262n32; reception of in Bohemian lands, 24–26; reception of in Russia, 26–28; represents universalist paradigm, 15–16; and Russian battle over hexameters, 136, 145–60; status of in Czech/Russian education, 143, 233–34, 236, 240, 245–46, 247–50. *See also* classical prosody; Greece; Greek prosody; Homer; Latin language and prosody; Roman literature

classical prosody (Greco-Roman): impossibility of successfully imitating, 114–15, 123, 149, 280nn21–22; Indian prosody as alternate model to, 189; Kapnist rejects in favor of Russian folk prosody, 152, 156–58; as means to achieve national literature, 128, 129, 136, 155–56, 159, 207; as model for Dobrovský, 113–14; as model for German prosody, 109–12, 115–16; as model for Jungmann, 81–84, 275n58; as model for *Počátkové,* 110–11, 117–22, 125, 128, 129, 130, 282n46; as model for Trediakovsky and Lomonosov, 137, 138, 139–42, 146; as model for Uvarov, 136, 153–56, 158–59, 207; as originating from Hyperboreans, 157; in relation to Church Slavonic, 135; as used in Middle Ages and Renaissance, 25, 113, 280n16; Vostokov on, 148–49. *See also* Greek prosody; hexameter; Latin language and prosody; quantitative versification

classicism, 25, 33, 37, 143, 153, 189, 239, 261n7; and Boileau, 27–28; challenged by historicism and national specificity, 16–17, 23, 29, 69, 251–52; contrasted to *Volkspoesie,* 93; Dobrovský represents, 69, 71, 72, 115; as golden age, 203–4; Küchelbecker on, 211, 214–15; merges with modernization in Trediakovsky, 138–42; merges with romanticism in Czech literature, 115, 122–24, 133, 195, 199–200, 206, 209, 210; merges with romanticism in Russian literature, 39, 122, 195; Merzliakov represents, 45, 46, 48, 268nn59–60; and *narodnost',* 165, 178; opposed to taste, 269n7; Pushkin on, 223–24, 226, 227; redefined through Tynianov's terminology, 64; Somov on, 170, 171; Viazemsky on, 183–84, 186, 195, 211; Weimar, 26, 122, 203. *See also* classical antiquity; genre norms; imitation; *klasičnost;* normative aesthetics; universalist paradigm

Colloquium of lovers of the Russian word (Beseda liubitelei russkogo slova), 60, 61, 104, 107, 143, 147, 150

colonialism, 182

common people. *See* folk

consonants, 73, 112; and *dobroglasie,* 207; and *libozvučnost,* 125–26, 190, 192

Counter Reformation, 25, 66, 72, 80, 194, 281n41

Croatian songs, 95

Culler, Jonathan, 6, 259n7

cultivation, 131, 192, 255; Dobrovský on, 70–71, 273nn26–27; and education, 25, 234, 246; Jungmann on, 73, 75–76, 78–80, 83, 85, 110, 118, 202, 203, 204, 231; and *Kultur,* 70–71, 76, 90; *Počátkové* on, 119–20, 122, 126, 282n46. *See also* culture; *vzdělání*

culture, 23, 85, 257, 304n19; as artificial construct, 255–56; and *Bildung,* 89–90; defined in terms of language, 70–72, 73–76, 78, 83, 110, 256; Macura on, 73, 95, 255–56, 276n8; in relation to *Kultur,* 70–71, 75–76, 89–90, 273n26, 273n35; in relation to *vzdělání,* 75–76, 78, 234; requires arduous craft, 122, 282n46. *See also* cultivation

curriculum. *See under* education in Bohemian lands; education in Russia

Cyril, Saint, 69, 272n3

Czech folk songs, 94, 113, 131, 189; and Hanka, **95–101,** 130, 132–34. *See also* folk songs; Slovak folk songs

Czech humanism. *See* humanism

Czech instructors, 250

Czech language, **65–85,** 149, 243; aligned with Greek, 117–18, 123–24, 126, 195; consonants and vowels in, 124, 125–26, 192–94, 200, 206; divided by religion, 66; Dobrovský on, 67–73, 119, 123,

124, 194, 206; embodies nation and national identity, 66–67, 71–72, 76–78, 80, 83–84, 95, 117–20, 134, 230–31, 256, 272n3; Hanka on, 95, 100–101, 134; and idea of union with other Slavic languages, 79–80, 85, 91, 100, 192–94, 196–97, 200, 206, 254; Jungmann's concept of, 73–85, 91, 110, 188–89, 190, 193, 203, 205, 230–31, 256; Kollár on, 192–94, 196–97, 199, 200, 206, 230, 254, 296n16, 304n29; and *libozvučnost,* 120, 124–28, 134, 190, 206, 254, 283n65; and linguocentrism, 65–67, 75; *Počátkové* on, 117–20, 123–28, 134, 195; in relation to culture and cultivation, 70–71, 73–76, 78, 273n35; in relation to Slovak, 193–94, 274n50; during Renaissance and Counter-Reformation, 24–25, 66, 193–94, 272n3; replaces territory as defining basis of literature, 68–69; status of in school curriculum, 25, 234–35, 246–49, 263n53, 296n12, 305n42; threatened by German, 66, 77, 82–83, 84–85, 94, 114–15, 247–48. *See also* Czech prosody; Slavic languages; Slavic unity

Czech literature and poetry: and Bouterwek's periodization, 109, 155; and concern with reaching broader audience, 205, 228, 230, 299n68; and danger of provincialism, 252; Dobrovský's history of, 68–69, 71–72, 297n29; focuses on Czech nation rather than Slavic nation, 242–43; and folklore, 23, 94–102; German as threat to and rival of, 79, 81, 91, 111, 115, 116, 123, 130, 242; golden age of, 72, 73, 75, 202–4, 206, 253; history of from Renaissance to 18th century, 24–26; and idea of return to origins, 22–23, 110, 119, 120, 130–31, 134, 153; impact of *Počátkové* on, 129–30, 187–89, 279n6; Jungmann's desire to create through cultivation of language, 75, 78–79, 80, 82, 83–84, 110, 193; Jungmann's periodization of, 202–4, 299n60; Kollár links to Slavic unity,

190, 193–94, 195–200, 206, 208, 242, 252, 254; and linguocentrism, 65–67; merges romanticism with classicism, 115, 122–24, 133, 194–95, 199–200, 203, 206, 209, 210; and music, 277n36; and politicization of terminology and values, 208–9; rejection of rhyme in, 116, 122–24, 130, 141, 195; and RK, 123, 132–34, 253; should be arduous craft, 116, 121–22, 282n46; status of in school curriculum, 234–35, 249, 263n53. *See also* Czech folk songs; Czech language; Czech national revival; Czech prosody; *klasičnost; libozvučnost;* nation; national character; national literature paradigm; *Počátkové českého básnictví;* quantitative versification; Slavic unity

Czech national revival, 19–20, 101, 232, 235; Hroch's analysis of, 28–29, 256, 264n67, 300n83; importance of language to, 76, 256; Macura on, 265n20, 276n8, 296n16; *Počátkové*'s role in, 279n6; and politicization of literary values, 208–10; and problem of non-existent Czech audience, 82, 94–95; Slovaks contribute to, 274n50

Czechoslovak literature, 197, 298n36

Czech prosody, **110–31**; affinity with Greek, 117–18, 119, 120, 149; attempts to loosen identity of feet in, 129, 284n77; closeness of syllabic and syllabotonic systems in, 113, 280n19; as difficult craft, 121–22, 282n46; Dobrovský's reform and conception of, 26, 72, 113–15, 124, 129, 280n22, 281n27; Greek as model for, 83, 110–11, 113–15, 117–20, 142; Hanka's use of, 99–100; history of from Middle Ages to 18th century, 25, 113, 280n16, 281n41; Hungarian and Slovakian prosody as model for, 281n41, 282n42; Jungmann's conception of, 81–82, 83, 110, 187–89, 190, 275n58; Klopstock as model and anti-model for, 111–12; and *libozvučnost,* 111, 120, 124, 125, 127–28, 134, 146, 187, 190, 206, 290n105; as

means to create national literature, 120, 127–28, 130–31, 133–34, 141, 187–88, 206; trochaic dominance and inherent initial stress in, 114, 274n55, 280n22, 281n27; Vostokov on, 149, 288nn62–63. *See also Počátkové českého básnictví;* quantitative versification; stress; syllabic versification; syllabotonic versification

Dacier, Anne Lefèvre, 20, 21, 22

dactylo-spondaic hexameter, 156

dactylo-trochaic hexameter, 148, 149, 158, 280n22; Radishchev's advocacy of, 145–47; Trediakovsky's conception of, 139

Dante Alighieri, 92, 142, 212

Decembrists, 185, 236, 265n11, 302n41; as imperialist, 178–79, 301n13; in relation to archaists, 35, 49, 265n15; Turgenev and Merzliakov as forerunners of, 32–33, 34, 42, 43, 45, 46, 267n55, 268n60

democratic literature, 33, 45

Derrida, Jacques, 270n26

Derzhavin, Gavrila, 36, 99, 161, 215, 267n54

de Staël, Madame. *See* Staël, Germaine de

diglossia, 54, 57–58, 67, 269n13

Dmitriev, Ivan Ivanovich, 161, 185, 215, 266n38, 267n54, 302n33

Dmitriev, Mikhail A., 168, 172, 185, 217, 302n32

dobroglasie, 207. *See also blagoglasie*

Dobrovský, Josef, 19–20, 25, 28, **67–73,** 133, 269n15, 280n21, 297n29; and Adelung, 69–71, 273n15, 273n22, 273n27; codifies Czech grammar, 72, 194; codifies system of syllabotonic versification, 26, 72, 113–14, 129, 281n27; contrasted to Kollár, 192–93, 200; creates first periodization of Czech language, 69–70; on culture and cultivation, 70–71, 75–76, 273n26; defines nation in terms of language, 68–69, 71, 76, 256; educational background of, 67, 279n8; on golden age, 72, 202–4; on importance of Czech-language instruction, 234; on inadequacy of Czech for translating classical prosody,

114, 119, 123, 130, 280n22; influences
Hanka, 95–96; influences idea of Slavic
unity, 80, 274n49; influences national
literature paradigm, 71–72; and
Jungmann, 73, 78, 80, 81, 82–83, 85,
200; on *libozvučnost*, 124, 206, 283n65;
on phonological development of Czech,
283n68; *Počátkové* attacks, 115–16; and
Slovo, 132, 284n90

Dobrovský, Josef, Works of: *Ausführliches
Lehrgebäude der böhmischen Sprache
(Detailed Grammar of the Czech
Language)*, 72; *Böhmische prosodie*,
114, 123; *Geschichte der Böhmischen
Sprache und Litteratur (History of the
Czech Language and Literature)*, **68–72**,
76, 234, 274n49; *Slovanka*, 283n68;
"Über den Wohlklang der Slawischen
Sprache" ("On the *Libozvučnost* of the
Slavic Language"), 192, 283n68

Doležal, Pavel, 194

Doležálek, Jan Emanuel, 277n36

Dostoevsky, Fyodor, 175, 300n25

drama, 17, 129, 139, 144, 149, 153,
282n60; and *narodnost'*, 174, 175, 176,
218–19; Pushkin's theories of, 218–19,
221–27, 238, 301n23, 302n41; satirizes
Zhukovsky, 104, 105; Turgenev's view
of, 31, 37–38, 43, 46, 176

Druzheskoe literaturnoe obshchestvo. *See*
Friendly Literary Society

Dunning, Chester, 302n41

Durdík, Jaroslav, 249

Durych, Václav Fortunát, 67, 279n8

Dziadko, Filipp, 46, 266n24, 268n64,
268n71

"echo" ("ohlas") poems, 101, 130

education: and *Bildung*, 90; in Prussia, 245,
249, 305n53. *See also under* national
literature paradigm

education in Bohemian lands, 204–5,
242–43; linked to "culture" through
term *vzdělání*, 234; and *reálky*, 249;
and status of classical curriculum,
25, 233–34, 250; and status of Czech-
language curriculum, 25, 234–35,

246–49, 263n53, 296n12, 305n42. *See
also* gymnasia; universities

education in Russia, **235–41, 245–50**;
blamed for lack of national spirit in
Russian literature, 44, 159, 237–38,
241; critique of French emphasis in, 44,
143–44, 235–36, 237, 267n55; Fonvizin
satirizes, 235; and *narodnost'*, 152,
168, 238, 244; and new emphasis on
Russian-studies curriculum, 245–46;
philosophical journal as means to
achieve, 240–41; and status of classical
curriculum, 144, 233–34, 240, 245–46,
249–50; Uvarov's ministerial reforms
of, 244–46, 250. *See also* gymnasia

Egunov, A. N., 287n53

Elagin, Ivan P., 58, 59, 60, 64

elegance, 40, 144, 222; Karamzin
advocates, 52; Shishkov critiques,
58–60, 61, 63

elegies, 60, 111, 138, 149, 223; Kollár's,
189, 199; Küchelbecker critiques, 33,
42, 211, 212, 216, 227, 266n32, 301n10;
Turgenev's, 33, 45, 46

elitism, 52, 226, 228, 229, 230;
Küchelbecker critiques elegiac school
for, 211, 217, 227

eloquence, 18, 47, 166; Shishkov on, 58–59,
60

Emerson, Caryl, 228, 300n1

Emery, Jacob, 181–82

English language and literature, 16, 17, 92,
103, 142, 199, 253; and Bouterwek's
periodization, 109, 154; Jungmann
translates, 80–81, 91, 133; Küchelbecker
on, 214, 215, 217; Pushkin on, 218, 219,
221, 223, 224–27, 301n23; quantitative
versification experiments in, 140,
282n60; Quarrel between Ancients and
Moderns in, 18, 19–20, 21, 22, 23, 24, 64;
as rival, 36, 129; stress patterns of, 117;
Turgenev on, 38. *See also* Milton, John;
Shakespeare, William

Enlightenment, 96; classicism of, 26, 39,
71; historiography of, 69, 76

epic, 84, 102, 218, 223, 233; defined in
relation to oral tradition, 130–31;

as model for national literature, 23, 91, 104, 130–31, 144, 254, 257; RK imitates, 132–34; Turgenev on, 39, 43, 46, 267n54; use of folk meter for, 156, 158; use of hexameter for, 139–42, 147, 148–49, 150, 154, 155, 159. *See also* Homer

epistles, 16, 27, 60, 105, 212, 216, 223

Erasmus, Desiderius, of Rotterdam, 24

euphony, 60, 124, 207–8; *libozvučnost* as translation of, 111, 187; and phonological development of Czech, 192, 283n68. *See also libozvučnost*

fables, 95, 96, 185, 223; and *narodnost'*, 169, 301n17

Fénelon, François, 286n25; *Les aventures de Télémaque,* 139–42, 145–46

Filofei of Pskov, 135

Florian, 82

folk: conflated with idea of "nation," 94, 165; in relation to definition of *narodnost'*, 165, 167, 168, 185, 243; as target audience of literature, 205, 225–30. *See also* folklore; folksiness; folk songs; *narod*

folklore, 28, **91–96,** 165, 223, 262n37; Bürger's conception of, 93–94; and Hanka, 94–96, 110, 133–34, 279n6; Herder's conception of, 92–93; as means to modernization, 91–92; as natural, 92–93, 95, 198; in relation to national literature paradigm, 4, 5, 44, 93–94, 99, 102, 107, 130–31, 216, 253; as return to origins, 22, 130–31, 134, 138, 156–57; and Russian ballad debate, **102–7;** Shishkov's view of, 62, 63, 102–3. *See also* folkloric discourse; folk prosody; folk songs

folkloric discourse, 91, 92, 216, 253; in context of ballad debate, 102, 104–7; Shishkov on, 62, 102

folk prosody, 102, 113, 148, 189; Kapnist advocates, 152, 156–58, 160, 207, 290n105; and *stroennyi piatislozhnik,* 289n98; and Trediakovsky, 138–39; Uvarov rejects, 159

folksiness, 166, 172, 185, 229, 253

folk songs, **91–101,** 107, 113, 189; Chulkov's collection of, 101, 133; and Hanka, 95–101, 130, 132–34; Herder's conception of, 92–93, 263n46; Kapnist on, 136, 152, 156–58, 207; Kollár links to Slavic spirit, 196–99, 208, 230; L'vov's collection of, 98–99, 102; and Merzliakov, 44, 45, 47, 48, 102; represent simplicity and naturalness, 92–93, 95, 97–98, 131, 198; translation establishes value of, 253; Trediakovsky likens Greek poetry to, 138–39, 148; and Turgenev, 38, 44. *See also* folklore; folkloric discourse; folk prosody

Fomin, A. A., 35

Fontenelle, Bernard le Bovier de, 18, 20, 261n11

Fonvizin, Denis, 168; *Brigadir (The Brigadier),* 169, 235; *Nedorosl' (The Minor),* 169, 185, 235

France. *See* French language and literature

Frantsusko-Russian, 58, 59, 61, 63, 85

Frazier, Melissa, 228, 295n56, 306nn9–10

freedom, 177, 212, 214

French language and literature, 25, 70, 103, 147, 171, 199, 215, 249, 279n1; Bobrov mocks with Galloruss, 84–85; and Boileau's influence on Russia, 16, 26, 27; Germans reject, 16, 109, 283n65; Greece as alternative to, 47, 53, 109, 136–37, 144, 153, 155, 236; as inadequate for imitating classical prosody, 140–41, 148, 149, 154, 155; Jungmann translates as means to enrich Czech, 80–81, 82, 83, 91; Karamzin advocates as model, 15, 40, 52–53, 59–60, 63, 91; and periodization of literary history, 109, 154, 171, 176; and Quarrel between Ancients and Moderns, 17–22, 261n21, 286n11; republican revival of the heroic in, 39, 60; Russians critique imitation of Alexandrines from, 149, 150, 154, 155, 159; Russians reject after Napoleonic invasion, 53, 63, 91, 142–43, 236, 237; Russians reject for excessive rules, 170, 225, 239; Russians view as rival and threat, 36, 37–38, 41, 43, 44, 46, 52, 62–63, 85, 91, 143, 160, 216, 235–36, 237, 242; Shishkov rejects as model, 19, 41, **53–63,** 85, 91, 270n26; Shishkov's theory on national specificity of, 54–57; status of in Russian education, 44, 235–36, 245–46; as threat to Czech, 83, 94. *See also* education in Russia; Frantsusko-Russian; salon culture

French Revolution, 53, 143

Friendly Literary Society (Druzheskoe literaturnoe obshchestvo), 37, 44, 45, 46, 235, 246, 266n24, 292n9; as forerunner of Decembrism, 32–33, 34, 35, 267n55; as founded and led by Turgenev and Merzliakov, 31–32; Turgenev mistakenly given sole credit for ideas of, 35, 42, 48, 268n71

Gasparov, Boris, 39, 60, 265n20, 271n54, 285n7

Gedike, Friedrich, 208

Gellner, Ernest, 5

genre norms, 48, 52, 215, 266n32; Aristotle's, 26; replaced by national specificity, 15–17, 23; and Shishkov, 60, 61–62; and Turgenev, 39, 41. *See also* classicism

geographic specificity. *See* locality

German language and literature, 23, 26, 36, 68, 103, 192, 199, 236, 278n47; and *Bildung,* 89–90, 109, 181; competing dialects and codification of, 207–8; Czechs view as rival, 79, 81, 111, 114, 116, 123, 129, 130; as differentiated from Czech and Greek, 117–18, 123–24; Greek as model for, 109, 110, 111, 119, 142, 208, 283n65, 301n25; and historicism, 21; and idea of return to origins, 109, 138, 153; as model for and opponent of *Počátkové,* 111–17, 119, 120, 130, 195, 283n65; as model for Dobrovský's history, 69–71; as model for Jungmann's cultivation of Czech, 73, 75–76, 80, 201, 275n58; as model for Turgenev, 31, 32, 38; and periodization

of literary history, 109, 154–55, 171, 176; prosody of, 111–13, 115, 117, 119, 136, 137, 149, 158–59, 281n27, 281n30, 288n62; Russians reject as model, 43, 152, 161, 212, 214, 215, 228; Somov links to *narodnost',* 173–76, 181, 185, 253; status of in Hapsburg school curriculum, 25, 234, 247–49; stress patterns of, 117; and taste, 269n7; as threat to Czech language and identity, 66, 77, 82–83, 85, 91, 94–95, 114–15, 120, 234, 242, 247–48, 272n3, 283n65; as threat to Russian identity, 44, 57, 216; and translation of term "culture," 70–71, 73, 75, 234, 273n35; and *Volkspoesie,* 24, 91–94; and *Volkstümlichkeit,* 229–30, 231. *See also* Goethe, Johann Wolfgang von

Gnedich, Nikolai, 17, 151fig, 153, 161, 287n38, 303n11; defends Zhukovsky's translation of "Lenore," 105–7; *Prostonarodnye pesni nyneshnikh grekov,* 160; translates *Iliad,* 106, 150–51, 156, 158–60, 181

Goethe, Johann Wolfgang von, 16, 26, 109, 122, 131, 212, 215, 295n58; and *Bildung,* 90; embodies Greek culture in the present day, 17, 174–75, 181, 301n25; on Gothic architecture, 142, 286n24; as protean poet, 21, 175, 181; Somov and de Staël on, 173, 174–75, 176, 177, 181, 219, 244, 253, 294n33; as *Volkspoesie,* 92. *See also* imagination

Goethe, Johann Wolfgang von, Works of: *Iphigenie auf Tauris,* 174; *Roman Elegies,* 174; *Sorrows of Young Werther,* 31; translation of "Hasanaginica," 95

Gogol, Nikolai, 10, 30, 169, 175, 181

golden age: Dobrovský defines, 72; as in the future not the past, 203, 206; Jungmann's view of, 73, 75, 202–4, 253

Golitsyn, Prince Alexander, 245

Gothic architecture, 141, 142, 286n24

Gottsched, Johann Christoph, 25, 207

grammar, 69, 95, 106, 135, 245, 249; Dobrovský on, 72, 194, 269n15

Gray, Thomas, 103

Greece (Ancient), 99, 101, 129, 133, 144, 170, 171, 209, 223, 234, 253, 282n44, 283n65, 285n7; as alternative to French, 47, 53, 109, 136–37, 144, 153, 155, 236; in context of Quarrel between Ancients and Moderns, 20–22, 89, 233; dialects of, 80, 207–8; folklore as alternate model to, 93, 152, 156–58; Goethe's ability to express national character of, 174–75, 181, 301n25; as model for national literature paradigm, 110, 120, 130, 144, 152, 155–56, 159, 207, 236; and *narodnost'*, 183–84, 195, 212, 214, 215, 217; *Počátkové* on Czech affinity with, 117–18, 119, 120, 123–24, 126; and popular drama, 227; in relation to Russian Orthodoxy, 135, 153; represents universalist paradigm, 16; and Russian battle over hexameters, 145–60; as source of originality, 22, 119, 120, 152, 212, 214, 215, 250, 262n32; status of in school curriculum, 245, 248–50; and Trediakovsky, 137, 140, 141, 142. *See also* classical antiquity; Greek prosody; Homer
Greece (modern), 160
Greek Anthology, 92, 275n58
Greek prosody, 135; impossibility of successfully imitating, 114–15, 123, 149; Kapnist rejects in favor of folk prosody, 152, 156–58; as means to achieve national literature, 128, 155–56, 159, 207; as model for Dobrovský, 113–14; as model for German prosody, 109–12, 115–16; as model for Jungmann, 81–84, 275n58; as model for *Počátkové*, 110–11, 117–22, 128, 130, 282n46; as model for Trediakovsky and Lomonosov, 137, 138, 139–42; as model for Uvarov, 136, 153–56, 158–59, 207; as originating from Hyperboreans, 157; Russians debate method of translating, **145–60**; Vostokov on, 148–49. *See also* classical prosody; Greece; quantitative versification
Griboedov, Aleksandr, 107

gymnasia, 305n49; status of Czech-language instruction at, 25, 234–35, 246, 247–49, 296n12; Uvarov's curriculum reforms at, 245–46, 249–50. *See also* education in Bohemian lands; education in Russia

Hanka, Václav, **94–102**, 245, 277n36; composes his own songs, 99–100, 101, 132, 277n43; early background of, 95–96; forges RK, 132–34; influenced by L'vov and Chulkov, 99, 101, 133; in relation to Jungmann, 83, 94–95, 100, 110, 279n6; translates Russian and Serbian folk songs, 97–98, 100–101
Hanka, Václav, Works of: article on Czech folk songs (1814), 96–98, 131; *Dvanáctero písní (Twelve Songs)*, 99–101; "Píseň pod Vyšehradem" ("Song under Vyšehrad Castle"), 132–33; *Prostonárodní Srbská Muza (Serbian Folk Muse)*, 100; Rukopis královédvorský (RK), 123–24, 130, 132–34, 190, 253, 277n43; *Šestero písní*, 277n43
Hankenštejna, Jan Alois Hanke z, 124
Hanuš, Josef, 68, 69, 70
Harkins, William, 96, 278n47
Hasanaginica, 95
Havlíček-Borovský, Karel, 249, 299n68
Hegel, Georg Wilhelm Friedrich, 90, 108, 195, 238
Heldenbuch, 92
Herder, Johann Gottfried von, 16, 38, 47, 54, 109, 131, 138, 262nn34–35; articulates concept of *Volkspoesie*, 23–24, 91–94; and *Bildung*, 90; in Jungmann's poem, 81, 275n58; as translated into Czech and Russian, 94, 97, 98; *Volkslieder*, 95, 97, 98
Hermann, Johann Gottfried, 112, 119, 201, 280n11, 281n30, 282n44
heroic aesthetic, 39, 60
heroic age, 20, 22, 142
heroic verse, 20, 137, 139, 141, 142, 146, 159. *See also* hexameter

hexameter, 218; and arguments about
    Trediakovsky's legacy, 145–50;
    Dobrovský on, 114, 280n22; Gnedich
    uses to translate *Iliad,* 150, 160; Kapnist
    rejects, 156, 158; Klopstock develops
    German version of, 111; as means to
    create national literature, 136, 147, 152,
    155–56, 159–60, 207, 287n53; Russian
    debates over, 63, **144–61,** 287n53,
    288n69; Trediakovsky's conception
    of, **138–42,** 144, 286n25; as used in
    Czech poetry, 81, 113, 129, 130, 188,
    189, 199, 263n49, 280n16; Uvarov on,
    150, 152–56, 158–59, 207; Vostokov on,
    147–50, 288n69
Hikl, Karel, 296n14
historicism, 108, 170, 231, 257, 259n13;
    Bouterwek's, 109, 154–55; challenges
    antiquity and timeless universalism,
    16, 18, 20–23, 89, 251; and Dobrovský,
    68, 69, 71, 76; fostered by Quarrel,
    18–24, 261n10, 262n37; influenced
    by philology, 19–20, 21, 22, 69, 109;
    nationalism as, 6; Uvarov's, 152, 154
Hlasatel český (Czech Herald), 73, 76, 80,
    96, 110
Hlobil, Tomáš, 298n47
Hněvkovský, Šebestián, 261n7; *Zlomky o
    českém básnictví (Fragments on Czech
    Poetry),* 189
Hokanson, Katya, 180
Homer, 17, 129, 133, 181, 215, 240; in
    context of Quarrel between Ancients
    and Moderns, 20–22, 89, 233; debate
    over method of translating, 145,
    150–51, 156, 158–60; *Iliad,* 20, 106, 114,
    144, 145, 150, 156, 158–60, 183–84;
    impossibility of translating, 114;
    Odyssey, 160; as romantic, 183–84; and
    Trediakovsky, 140, 141, 142; as ultimate
    model, 109; as *Volkspoesie,* 92, 93; and
    Volkstümlichkeit, 229
Horace, 17, 28, 215, 261n7; *Ars Poetica,*
    16; and Boileau, 16, 26, 27; "Exegi
    monumentum," 158; as model
    for Russians, 3, 15, 26, 138; and
    narodnost', 183

Horálek, Karel, 113, 129–30, 277n36, 282n42
Hroch, Miroslav, 28–29, 256, 264n67,
    300n83
Hromádko, Jan, 96
humanism, 22, 64, 122; history of in
    Bohemian lands, 24–26, 66; and
    introduction of quantitative verse into
    Czech, 25, 113, 120, 121, 281n41; new,
    248, 250
Humboldt, Wilhelm von, 54, 249, 295n58,
    305n53
Hungarian prosody, 118–19, 281n41,
    282n42
Hurd, Richard, 142, 262n34, 286n24
Hus, Jan, 71
Hussite period, 25, 66, 71–72, 113, 272n3
Hussite wars, 24, 66, 132
hybridization, 36, 265n20
Hyperboreans, 157–58
Hýsek, Miloslav, 279n6

iambic meter, 113, 145, 156, 157, 218,
    280n15; as unnatural for Czech,
    274n55, 281n27, 288n63
Ianushkevich, A., 103
imagination, 18; enables Goethe to embody
    distant places, 174–75, 181; Goethe as
    exemplar of, 173, 294n33; and *narodnost',*
    173–75, 176, 178, 222; and novelty, 170,
    216; and romanticism, 177, 226
imitation, 17, 27, 63, 103, 115, 138, 160,
    203, 281n27; Boileau advocates, 26;
    challenged by Quarrel, 20, 22; as means
    to create national literature, 105, 144,
    154, 155, 295n56; Merzliakov on, 46–
    47, 48; Roman literature exemplifies,
    142, 148, 212, 214; Russians reject,
    37–38, 43, 149, 150, 177–78, 212,
    214–15, 216. *See also* classicism
imperialism, 9, 178–83, 295n56
Imperial Study Commission, 235, 247
imprint. *See under narodnost'*
India, 152, 189, 296n8
innovators, 28, 41, 52, 143, 147, 263n65;
    Tynianov introduces term, 64. *See also*
    Karamzin's followers
intelligentsia, 32, 70, 246

Italy, 24, 129, 154, 174, 199, 226, 301n23; as incapable of imitating classical prosody, 125, 148; rejected as model, 109, 122, 140, 148, 171, 176; response to Quarrel in, 21

Jena romanticism, 228, 252, 295n58
Jenisch, Bernard, 112, 115–16, 279n8
Jesuits, 25, 248
Joseph II (Holy Roman Emperor; King of Bohemia), 66, 247, 305n42
Jungmann, Josef, 26, **73–85**, 74fig, 118, **200–206**, 242, 284n77, 298n47; advocates quantitative versification, 81–82, 187–89, 275n58; on ancient Indian prosody, 189, 296nn7–8; contrasted to Hanka, 94–95, 97, 100; on culture and cultivation, 73–76, 78, 126, 273n35, 282n46; on education, 204–6, 234–35; influenced by Pölitz, 202–4, 296n14, 299n65; on *klasičnost* and golden age, 188, 200–204, 299n60; and Kollár, 190–94, 199, 200, 297n16; and *libozvučnost*, 190, 200–202, 206, 254, 296n14, 299n56, 299n57; links language to national identity, 76–78, 80, 83–84, 110, 230, 231, 232, 255, 256; on *národnost*, 231, 303n60; and national literature paradigm, 17, 28–29, 134, 187–88, 200–201, 204–5, 253; and *Počátkové*, 110, 127, 187–90; on poetic discourse, 79–82, 275n60; proposes borrowing from other Slavic languages, 79–80, 85, 91, 193; scholarly overemphasis on, 279n6; on Slavic unity, 79–80, 196–97, 274n49, 297n28; teaches Czech at gymnasium, 235, 247; translations of, 80–82, 91, 133, 208, 274n55, 275n58
Jungmann, Josef, Works of: *Historie literatury české*, 202, 253; "Krok," 189; "Nepředsudné mínění o české prozódii" ("An Unprejudiced Opinion on Czech Prosody"), 81; "O jazyku českém" ("On the Czech Language"), **73–79**, 84–85, 231, 234–35; "O klasičnosti literatury" ("On *Klasičnost* of Literature"), **200–**

205, 231, 242; "Slavěnka Slavínovi," 81–82, 275n58; *Slovesnost*, 188, 190, 201, 202, 235, 275n60, 296n12, 299n56
Juvenal, 15

Kachenovskii, M. T., 269n15
Kadettenhaus (officer's academy), 25, 246
Kaisarov, Andrei, 32, 46, 49, 291n9; and Decembrism, 33, 265n11, 267n55; helps create Turgenev myth, 41–42
Kaisarov, Mikhail, 32
Kaisarov, Paisy, 32
Kamenskii, Z. A., 268n60
Kantemir, Antiokh Dmitrievich, 15, 27, 58
Kapnist, Vasily, 99, 136, 150, 215, 288n69; advocates folk prosody, 151–52, 156–58, 160, 207, 290n105; on Hyperboreans, 157–58
Karadžić, Vuk, 95, 96, 98, 133
Karamzin, Nikolai, 3, 28, 83, 133, 255, 263n61, 271n35; advocates French salon-language as model, 52–53, 59, 60, 63, 90–91; advocates spoken language as model, 41, 57, 61; embodies universalist paradigm, 15, 17, 26; Küchelbecker turns away from, 215, 216; Shishkov critiques, 40, 51, **56–61**; and taste, 57, 269n7; and Turgenev, 36, 37, 39–43, 161, 266n32, 266n38, 266n40, 267n54, 269n2
Karamzin, Nikolai, Works of: *History of the Russian State*, 133, 254; "Ilya Muromets," 36, 156, 160; "Otchego v Rossii malo avtorskikh talantov?" ("Why Are There So Few Talented Authors in Russia?"), 40, 41, 51, 52–53, 56; *Panteon rossiiskikh avtorov (Pantheon of Russian Authors)*, 15, 17, 28, 263n61; *Pis'ma russkogo puteshestvennika (Letters of a Russian Traveler)*, 43
Karamzin's followers, 3, 28, 40, 51–52, 143, 268n76; and ballad debate, 102, 104, 106, 107; discourse of, 60, 271n33; Küchelbecker and Pushkin turn away from, 216, 220; and Turgenev, 42–43, 45. *See also* innovators
Kashin, D. N., 45

Katenin, Pavel, 105, 216, 219; "Oľga"
    (translation of Bürger's "Lenore"), 104,
    106, 107
Keenan, Edward, 284n90
Kelley, Douglas, 279n1
Kheraskov, Mikhail Matveevich, 36, 39,
    43; "Bakhariana," 156–57; *Rossiada,* 46,
    183, 218
Kievan Rus', 171, 216
Kireevsky, Ivan, 37, 175, 241; "XIX vek"
    ("The Nineteenth Century"), 242
Klang, 296n14, 299n56
klasičnost: achieved through quantitative
    versification, 111, 120–21, 122, 127,
    188; contrasted to barbaric rhyme, 195;
    and golden age, 202–4; Jungmann's
    conception of, 187, 188, 189, 200–204;
    as means to achieve national literature,
    127, 128–29, 188; Palacký on, 111, 116,
    120–22, 124, 127, 128–29, 195; requires
    rigorous craft, 122; RK embodies, 124,
    134. *See also* classicism
Klein, J., 263n61
Klopstock, Friedrich Gottlieb, 92, 129, 146;
    as model and anti-model for *Počátkové,*
    111–12, 115; "Der Wohlklang," 283n65
Kluckhohn, Clyde, 70–71
Knight, Nathaniel, 254
Kollár, Jan, 130, 181, **190–200,** 191fig,
    281n38; advocates reform of Czech
    sound structure, 192–94; advocates
    Slavic unity, 190, 193–200, 206, 208,
    242, 252, 254; on education, 250; on
    folk songs, 131, 197–99, 230; and
    Jungmann, 202, 254, 279n6, 297n16;
    on *libozvučnost,* 192–93, 195, 196, 200,
    206, 254; synthesizes classicism with
    romanticism, 195, 199, 200, 302n36
Kollár, Jan, Works of: essay on Slavic
    mutality, 304n29; "Myšlénky o
    libozwučnosti řečj" ("Thoughts on the
    Libozvučnost of Languages"), **190–93;**
    *Písní lidu slovenského v Uhřích (Songs of
    the Slovak People in Hungary),* **196–99,**
    230; *Slavy dcera,* 189, 199
Kopitar, Jernej, 95–96, 208, 278n47,
    300n79

Kostrov, Ermil Ivanovich, 133, 145, 150,
    159
Kralice Bible, 194
Králík, Oldřich, 275n58
krasnorechie (eloquence), 58–60, 61, 62,
    63, 102
Kroeber, A. L., 70–71
Krok, 190, 196, 201, 205, 242–43; founding
    of, 188–89
Krushchov, A. F., 140–41
Krylov, Ivan, 169, 185, 222–23, 301n17
Küchelbecker, Wilhelm K., 49, 160, 213fig,
    218, 238, 246, 300nn7–8, 302n32;
    combines romanticism with classicism,
    122, 195; critiques elegaic school, 33,
    212, 216–17, 227, 266n32, 301n10;
    defines romanticism and *narodnost',*
    211–17; *Evropeiskie pis'ma (European
    Letters),* 182; identifies with Russian
    nationality, 180, 301n13; "O napravlenii
    nashei poezii" ("On the Trend in Our
    Poetry"), 212–17; on revaluing of values,
    265n19; wants literature to reach a
    broader, national audience, 217, 228
Kultur, 70–71, 75–76, 78, 90, 273n26,
    273n35. *See also Bildung;* cultivation;
    culture; *vzdělání*

La Fontaine, Jean de, 222–23, 263n61
La Motte, Antoine Houdar de, 20
language: accentual vs. quantitative,
    118–19, 125; aesthetic vs. logical, 192;
    analytic vs. synthetic, 118, 125; dead
    vs. living, 203; and linguocentrism,
    65–66, 67, 75; modernization
    engenders emphasis on, 23, 65–67;
    and nationalism, 6, 7; national spirit
    embodied in stress patterns of, 117–18;
    Shishkov on national specificity of, 54–
    57; spoken vs. bookish, 52–53, 57–58,
    60–61, 270n26. *See also* consonants;
    Czech language; folkloric discourse;
    French language and literature;
    German language and literature;
    Greece; Latin language and prosody;
    poetic discourse; Russian language;
    stress; style; vowels

Latin gymnasia, 25, 234, 235, 247. *See also* gymnasia

Latin language and prosody, 26, 66, 68, 135, 158, 275n58, 282n42; medieval version of rejected as model, 123, 137, 285n7; as model for Czechs, 81, 113, 114, 117, 118, 121–22, 124, 130, 280n16; as model for Russians, 137, 139–42, 144, 146, 154, 285n7, 286n27; rejected as more derivative than Greek, 119, 148; status of in school curriculum, 245, 247–50; as threat to Czech, 83, 272n3; and translation of term "culture," 70, 75, 90, 273n35. *See also* classical prosody; Roman literature

Leerssen, Joep, 7–8, 130–31, 257

Leighton, Lauren, 167, 291n7, 292n15, 293n17, 293n25, 302n32

Lencek, Rado, 300n79

Levine, Joseph M., 20, 64, 261n11, 262n35

libozvučnost (euphony; melodiousness): achieved through hard work, 126; achieved through quantitative versification, 111, 120, 127, 190, 206; advocated by *Počátkové*, 111, 116–17, 120, 124–28, 131, 206; compared to *blagoglasie*, 146, 206–7, 290n105; Dobrovský on, 124; embodied in RKZ, 134; exemplifies politicization of literary values, 208–9, 253–54; as inherent quality of Czech, 116–17, 124, 206; and Jungmann, 187, 190, 200–202, 206, 296n14; Kollár on, 190, 192–93, 195, 196, 200, 206, 208; as means to achieve common Slavic language, 190, 193, 195–96, 200, 206; as means to achieve national literature, 127, 128, 206; in relation to placement of consonants and vowels, 124, 125–26, 190, 192–93; syllabotonic detracts from, 116–17, 125; as translation of *Klang*, 296n14, 299n56; as translation of *Wohlklang*, 124, 283n65

Linda, Josef, 83, 132, 133

linguocentrism, 65–66, 67, 75

liquidity, 140

literary marketplace, 228, 229, 306n9

literature: becomes focused on national identity, 4–5, 23, 28, 67, 143–44, 208–9, 251–57; becomes politicized, 67, 208–9; as central to creation of national movements, 29, 254, 256–57; crisis in leads to national literature paradigm, 8, 28–29, 208–9; historicism and specificity transform, 16–18, 251; and linguocentrism, 65–67; narrowed definition of, 19, 23, 261n16; Quarrel transforms, 21–24; in relation to scholarship on nationalism, 5–9, 254, 259n7; as relay race, 109, 154–55. *See also* classical antiquity; Czech literature; English language and literature; folklore; folk songs; French language and literature; German language and literature; Greece; *narodnost'*; national literature paradigm; Roman literature; Russian literature; universalist paradigm

Literaturnaia gazeta, 169

Litoměřice gymnasium, 235, 247

locality: and *narodnost'*, 171, 176, 183–84, 185, 301n23; replaces universalist classicism, 16, 23

logocentrism, 57, 270n26

Lomonosov, Mikhailo, 15, 16, 56, 107, 161, 183, 263n63, 285n7; defines high literary style, 58, 60; reforms Russian verse, 37, 102, 136–37; as rival of Trediakovsky, 27, 138, 145, 148, 149–50, 260n3; as Shishkov's model and ideal, 53, 54, 59, 61, 85; Turgenev critiques, 36, 40; uses Alexandrines, 139, 149, 150, 154

Lomonosov, Mikhailo, Works of: "Pis'mo o pravilakh rossiiskogo stikhotvorstva" ("Letter concerning the Rules of Russian Poesy"), 136–37, 149; "Predislovie o pol'ze knig tserkovnykh v rossiiskom iazyke" ("Foreword on the Utility of Ecclesiastical Books in the Russian Language"), 60, 137; translation of Horace's "Exegi monumentum," 158

Longinus, 28, 184

Lotman, Yuri, 38, 58, 61, 64, 84; on
    linguocentrism and diglossia, 65,
    67; on *narodnost'*, 166, 265n10,
    265n21; on Turgenev, Merzliakov, and
    Decembrists, 32–33, 35, 42–43, 44, 45,
    49, 265n19, 267n55, 267n59
Louis XIV (King of France), 16, 17
Lounsbery, Anne, 10
L'vov, Nikolai Aleksandrovich: book
    of Russian folk songs, 98–99, 102;
    Dobrynia, 102, 158; *Iamshchiki na
    podstave (Coachmen at the Relay
    Station)*, 99; influences Kapnist,
    157, 158
lyceum (Tsarskoe selo), 246

Mácha, Karel Hynek, 29
Máchal, Jan, 100, 277n47
Macpherson, James, 257
Macura, Vladimír, 279n6, 281n38, 296n16,
    300n84; on phonetic translation, 100;
    on simulacrum, 255–56; on syncretism,
    265n20; on translationality, 276n8; on
    use of the term "culture," 73, 95, 255–56
Malherbe, François de, 16, 27
Marek, Antonín, 83, 127, 128
Maria Theresa (Holy Roman Empress;
    Queen of Bohemia), 25, 246, 248
masses. *See* folk
mathematics, 18, 249
medieval era. *See* Middle Ages
Meissner, August Gottlieb, 286n11
melancholy, 32, 38
merit. *See under narodnost'*
Merzliakov, Aleksei Fedorovich, 34fig, **42–
    49**, 266n24; classicism of, 268nn59–60;
    as co-founder of Friendly Literary
    Society, 32; critiques ballad genre, 161;
    on education, 44, 235, 267n55; and
    folklore, 44–45, 99, 102; influences
    Turgenev's speech, 42–43; Lotman on,
    33, 35, 42–43, 45, 267n55, 267n59; as
    mediator of Turgenev's speech, 45, 46,
    49, 268n64, 292n9; as misunderstood,
    45, 48–49, 265n15, 267n55; as true
    author of some of Turgenev's ideas,
    35, 42

Merzliakov, Aleksei Fedorovich, Works
    of: "Letter from Siberia," 161;
    "Ob iziaschchnom, ili o vybore v
    podrazhanii" ("On the Beautiful,
    or on Selection in Imitation"), 47;
    "O dukhe, otlichitel'nikh svoistvakh
    poezii pervobytnoi" ("On the Spirit
    and Distinguishing Characteristics of
    Primitive Poetry"), 45; "O trudnostiakh
    ucheniia" ("On the Difficulties of
    Education"), 44, 235; *Songs and
    Romances*, 48
mestnost' (locality), 171, 176, 183, 185,
    301n23. *See also* locality
meter. *See* dactylo-trochaic hexameter;
    iambic meter; spondaic meter; trochaic
    meter
Methodius, 272n3
Middle Ages, 23, 64, 171–72, 224, 259n13,
    279n1; as childhood of European
    culture, 22; Czech prosody during,
    113, 280n16; and folklore, 91, 92, 96,
    199; and linguocentrism, 65–66, 67;
    Lomonosov disdains, 136, 137, 285n7;
    Palacký disdains, 123, 282n60; and
    translatio studii et imperii, 108
Milton, John, 83, 129, 142, 145, 286n25;
    Jungmann's translation of, 80–81, 133
Ministry of Education (Hapsburg Empire),
    247
Ministry of National Enlightenment
    (Russia), 244–45
modernization, 10, 26; centrality of
    language to, 66–68, 76, 83; importance of
    Počátkové to, 130; leads to politicization
    of literary discourse, 209; merges with
    classicism in Trediakovsky, 139, 142;
    paradoxically includes old values, 64;
    of Russian literary language, 58, 85;
    translation's central role in, 4, 89, 92
moderns. *See* Quarrel between Ancients
    and Moderns
Molière (Jean-Baptiste Poquelin), 27,
    263n61
Montaigne, Michel de, 198
Montesquieu, Charles-Louis de Secondat,
    baron de, 114

Moravia, 68, 131, 194, 252, 272n3
Mordovchenko, N. I., 265n19, 266n24
Moscow: Napoleon's invasion of, 91, 143,
    236; as Third Rome, 135
Moscow Herald, 225, 236, 241
Moscow Telegraph, 222, 243, 244
Moscow University, 47, 49, 236;
    Blagorodnyi pansion at, 32, 246
Mukařovský, Jan, 129, 189, 284n77, 296n7
Müller, Johann, 183, 184
Murav'ev-Apostol, I. M., 236, 240; "Letters
    from Moscow to Nizhnii Novgorod,"
    143–44
music, 57, 113, 270n25, 277n36; and folk
    songs, 97, 98, 99, 100, 102, 157. *See also*
    folk songs

Nadezhdin, Nikolai, 37, 48
Napoleonic Wars, 8, 33, 202, 254; lead to
    Russian rejection of French culture, 53,
    63, 91, 142–43, 236, 237
narod: conflates idea of "nation" and
    "folk," 94, 165; as folk, 38, 168, 180,
    185, 225–27, 243; as nation, 36, 220,
    221, 223, 244; in relation to *narodnost',*
    185, 220, 221, 223; as target audience,
    225–27. *See also* folk
národ: conflates "nation" and "folk," 94; as
    nation, 128, 230
narodnaia poeziia, 170, 177; conflates
    Volkspoesie and *Nationalliteratur,* 94; as
    distinct from *natsional'naia,* 168; refers
    to *Nationalliteratur* and not *Volkspoesie,*
    172, 300n7
národní písně, 96, 97
národní poezie, 94
narodnost', **165–86, 211–27,** 241, 268n76,
    287n53, 291n7, 301n23; becomes
    catch-all term for national qualities of
    literature, 186; Bestuzhev on, 168–69,
    237–38; compared to *popularité,
    nationalité,* and *natsional'nost',* 166–68,
    172, 174; compared to *Volkstümlichkeit,*
    229; definition and early usages of,
    165–69; and education, 237–38,
    243–44; and imperialism, 178–81; as
    imprint, 166, 167, 183–85, 220–21,

224, 227, 239, 295n60; Küchelbecker
    on, 211–17, 266n32; Lotman on, 166,
    265n10, 265n21; as merit, 166, 169,
    175, 183–85, 218–21, 224, 301n23;
    national historical themes and customs
    are insufficient to produce, 176, 218–
    19, 226, 243–44; and popularity, 166,
    168, 174, 222–27, 229–30, 253, 301n17,
    302n32; Pushkin on, 211, 217–27,
    302n33; in relation to language, 169,
    216–20; Somov on, 169–78, 180–81,
    194–95, 253, 293n25; as stamp, 175,
    216, 220–21, 224, 239; Turgenev
    and Merzliakov prefigure, 32–33,
    35, 36, 38, 43–45, 49–50, 265n17,
    266n32; Uvarov on, 152, 167, 245–46;
    Venevitinov on, 243–44; Viazemsky
    on, 166–68, 183–86, 195, 211. *See also*
    nation; national character; national
    literature paradigm
národnost, 197, 231, 299n57, 303n60;
    contrasted to *narodnost',* 230
narodnye pesni (folk songs), 98, 156
narodnyi iazyk (folk language), 62, 102,
    105, 107. *See also* folkloric discourse
národovost, 202, 231, 299n57, 303n60
nation, 143, 203, 232, 242, 301n25;
    Ancillon's notion of, 172, 221, 302n32;
    becomes central locus of literary values,
    4, 5, 17, 23, 28–29, 67, 165, 176–77,
    208–9, 228–29, 251–56; and *Bildung,*
    90; conflated with folk, 94, 165; defined
    in terms of language, 66, 68–69, 71, 72,
    76–78, 230, 231, 274n49; embodied in
    folklore, 94, 99, 197, 230; embodied
    in quantitative verse, 120, 128, 130;
    and imperialism, 179–80, 306n10; as
    individual, 152, 205, 229, 239; and
    national specificity of languages, 54;
    in relation to definition of *narodnost',*
    168, 220–24, 243–44; in relation to
    scholarship on nationalism, 5–9;
    Turgenev influences notion of, 32–33,
    36–37, 41, 50; Venevitinov on, 239,
    241, 243–44; Voltaire defines, 23,
    252, 262n40, 262n45. *See also* Czech
    national revival; national character;

nationalism; national literature
  paradigm; Slavic unity
national character/identity, 17, 232, 253,
  302n33, 306n10; Ancillon on, 221–22;
  Aristotle as model for typology of,
  7–8; as artificial construct, 255–56;
  embodied in folklore, 23, 38, 44, 97,
  99, 133–34, 230; embodied in language
  and prosody, 23, 52, 67, 77–78, 83,
  117–20, 152, 207, 230, 231, 256;
  expressed through synthesis of distant
  times and places, 174–75; importance
  of education to, 44, 235, 241, 267n55;
  Jungmann on, 77–78, 83, 256;
  Merzliakov on, 44, 46–47, 161, 267n55;
  Murav'ev-Apostol on, 144; *Počátkové*
  on, 117–20, 129; and politicization of
  terminology, 209; scholarship on, 5,
  8; Somov on, 170, 173–74, 177–78;
  translated as *karakter národu,* 282n44;
  Turgenev on, 31, 36–39, 38, 41, 44;
  Venevitinov on, 239, 241. *See also*
  nation; national literature paradigm
nationalism, 29, 71, 93, 210, 261n10,
  272n3, 279n6; as distinguished from
  narodnost', 185, 219; and romanticism,
  71, 223–24, 254–55, 295n56, 306n10;
  scholarship on, **5–9**, 254, 257, 259n7.
  See also Czech national revival; nation;
  national character; national literature
  paradigm
Nationalität, 231
nationalité, 166–68, 174, 175, 217, 301n17
nationality: and imperialism, 179–80, 181,
  301n13; as one definition of *narodnost',*
  166–68, 172, 174, 175, 217, 253,
  301n17, 302n32; as Uvarov's slogan,
  246. *See also* nation; national character;
  national literature paradigm
Nationalliteratur, 24, 168, 172, 300n7
national literature paradigm: ancient
  Greece as model for, 110, 120, 130, 144,
  152, 155–56, 159, 207, 236; Ancillon
  says only modern nation can create,
  172, 302n32; as artificial construct,
  255–56; centrality of language to, 67,
  71–72, 110, 234; education as means

to create, 44, 204–5, 234, 235–36, 238,
  240–41, 245–46, 249–50; emerges from
  crisis in literary values, 8, 28–30, 208–9,
  251–57; enhanced by Czech/Russian
  conflation of *Volk* and *Nation,* 94;
  enhanced by Slavic unity, 196; folklore
  contributes to, 4, 92–93, 95, 102, 107,
  130–31, 253; fostered by historicism,
  23, 71, 251; France rejected as model
  for, 41, 62, 235–36, 238; Herder invents
  terminology for, 23–24, 94; hexameter
  as means to achieve, 136, 144, 147, 152,
  155–56, 159, 160, 207, 287n53; and
  idea of return to origins, 22, 109–10,
  120, 130–31, 134, 138; Jungmann on,
  17, 83, 110, 187–88, 200–201, 204–5,
  234; Küchelbecker on, 212, 214–17;
  Merzliakov and Turgenev help advance
  idea of, 31, 35, 36–38, 41, 44, 45–46,
  47, 48, 50, 161, 267n54; and newly
  imagined national audience, 29, 227–
  29; *Počátkové* on, 110, 120, 122, 124,
  127, 128–29, 130, 195, 206; quantitative
  versification as means to achieve, 120,
  127, 130–31, 187–88, 206; RKZ plays
  central role in, 133–34; Shishkov on,
  41, 52, 62, 63–64; Somov on, 169–73,
  175–78, 180–81, 185, 194; translation
  as means to create, 4, 9, 89–90, 91,
  107, 133, 144, 253; and Trediakovský,
  141, 147, 150, 287n54; undermines
  dominance of antiquity, 16–17, 23, 28,
  200, 203, 249, 250, 251–52; Uvarov on,
  136, 152, 155–56, 159, 207; Viazemsky
  on, 167–68, 183–84; Voltaire on, 23,
  252, 262n40, 262n45. *See also* Czech
  literature and poetry; *narodnost';*
  nation; national character; Russian
  literature and poetry; Slavic unity
national movements: central role of
  literature to, 29, 254, 256–57; Hroch's
  analysis of, 28–29, 256, 264n67, 300n83;
  and politicization of literary values,
  208–10. *See also* Czech national revival
national spirit. *See* national character
national taste *(narodnyi vkus),* 144
nation-building, 8–9, 255–56

natsional'nost': contrasted to *narodnost'*, 94, 168, 172; as synonym for *narodnost'*, 243
naturalness, 92, 93, 95, 107, 109, 131, 198
Nedožer, Vavřinec Benedikti z, 25
Nejedlý, Jan, 82, 114, 202; archaisms of, 80, 83, 85, 110; *Böhmische Gramatik*, 288n62; "O lásce k vlasti" ("On Love of the Homeland"), 77
neo-classicism. *See* classicism
neologisms, 64, 80, 83, 110, 188, 202
Nicholas I (Tsar of Russia), 152, 167, 245, 246, 302n41
nobility, 29; education of, 235–36, 246; in relation to Lotman and Merzliakov, 33, 44, 45, 265n10, 267n59
normative aesthetics, 16–17, 27–28, 122, 287n54. *See also* classicism; genre norms
north-south debate, 171
novatory. *See* innovators; Karamzin's followers
novels, 103; and nationalism studies, 6–7, 259n7
novelty, 170, 214, 216

obrazovanie, 234
odes, 95, 119, 189, 223, 302n32; as highest lyric genre, 60, 212, 215; Kollár's, 199; Lomonosov's, 15, 16, 40, 60, 107, 263n63; panegyric, 27
Odoevsky, Vladimir Fyodorovich, 48
officer's academy *(Kadettenhaus)*, 25, 246
"ohlas" ("echo") poems, 101, 130
Old Church Slavonic. *See* Church Slavonic
Olenin, Aleksei Nikolaevich, 150, 153
organicism, 39, 203; and culture, 76, 109, 152, 172, 238, 241, 244, 255–56, 304n13; and Shishkov's view of language, 54–56
Orient, 152, 158, 181, 293n20
orientalism, 182, 293n20
originality, 30, 89, 106, 107; Greek culture as model for, 22, 119, 120, 152, 212, 214–15, 250; as means to achieve national literature and express national spirit, 17, 37–38, 120, 173, 175, 176,

177–78, 205–6; and romanticism, 170, 212, 214–15, 223–24, 295n56
Orlov, Aleksandr P., 59
orthodoxy. *See* Russian orthodoxy
Ossian, 22–23, 92, 93, 133, 257; Russian translations of, 157, 160
otpechatok (imprint), 167, 220. *See also under narodnost'*
Ozerov, Vladislav, 153, 226; *Dimitry Donskoi*, 218–19

Palacký, František, **109–13; 119–128,** 137, 189, 272n3, 283n68; attacks Dobrovský's syllabotonic prosody, 115–17, 125, 127; attacks rhyme, 122–24, 130, 141, 195; on common life, 205; on consonants and vowels, 125–26; contrasted to Kollár, 192–94, 200; on folk songs, 131–32; on Greek as model for Czech, 111, 117, 126; and Hermann, 112–13, 119; and Jungmann, 78, 83, 187–88, 190, 299n56; on *klasičnost,* 120–22, 124, 128–29, 195; Klopstock as model and anti-model for, 111–12, 283n65; on language as reflection of national character, 119–20; legacy of, 134, 187–88, 279n6; on *libozvučnost,* 117, 120, 124–28, 131–32, 146, 206, 254, 290n105; on *národnost,* 231, 303n60; on periodization of modern aesthetics, 109, 155; on poetry as difficult craft, 121–22, 126; on Polák, 127–28, 253; on Pölitz, 201; on quantitative verse as means to achieve national literature, 120, 127, 134, 206; on romanticism, 122–24, 195, 282n60. *See also Počátkové českého básnictví*
pansion (St. Petersburg Pedagogical Institute), 246
pansion, Blagorodnyi (Moscow University), 32, 246
Paradise Lost, 80
Patey, Douglas Lane, 18, 20, 262nn34–35, 268n59
patriotism, 59, 96–97, 177, 237, 242, 247; as defense of Czech language, 70, 73, 77, 124, 190, 253; Jungmann's, 77, 204,

205, 235; and *klasičnost,* 128–29; kvass, 175; and RKZ, 133; of Shishkov and followers, 63, 220; Turgenev's, 39–40, 267n54

people. *See* folk

Perrault, Charles, 19, 22, 262n37; *Parallèle des anciens et des modernes,* 18; on prose as more exact than verse, 142, 261n21; in relation to Quarrel, 18, 20

Persian language, 117–18

Peskov, A. M., 27, 28, 265n19

Pesteľ, Pavel Ivanovich, 178–79, 180

Peter I, the Great (Tsar of Russia), 37, 267n54

philology, 189, 250; and Dobrovský, 19–20, 69, 80, 96, 269n15, 273n15; influences development of historicism, 19–20, 21, 22, 69, 109, 252; influences idea of national identity, 7, 209; Trediakovsky's, 137, 138, 147; Wotton introduces into Quarrel, 19

philosophy, 109, 281n38; opposed to poetry, 22, 118; significance of language to, 65, 66–67, 75, 77, 78; Venevitinov sees as means to enlightenment, 239–41; and Vico's new science of history, 21–22

phonetics, 117, 193, 283n68

phonology, 126, 192, 206, 283n68

Pindar, 3, 15, 16, 27, 215

Počátkové českého básnictví, obzvláště prozódie (Principles of Czech Poetry, Prosody in Particular), **110–34,** 201, 284n77, 299n68; advocates quantitative versification, 110–11, 118–23, 125, 127–28, 130, 134, 146, 206, 282n46, 290n105; analyzes role of consonants and vowels, 125–26; attacks Dobrovský and syllabotonic prosody, 113, 115–17, 125, 127; attacks rhyme and romanticism, 122–24, 130, 199; on folk songs, 131–32; on Greek as model for Czech, 111, 117–20, 123–24, 126; and Hermann's letter, 112–13, 119; Hněvkovský's response to, 189; on *klasičnost,* 111, 120–22, 128–29; Klopstock as model and anti-model

for, 111–12, 283n65; on language as reflection of national character, 117–20; legacy of, 129–30, 133, 134, 187–89, 279n6; on *libozvučnost,* 111, 117, 120, 124–28, 131–32, 146, 190, 283n65, 290n105; on poetry as difficult craft, 121–22, 126, 282n46; on Polák, 127–29, 253; Slovakian and Hungarian verse as model for, 281n41

poetic discourse, 79–82, 275n60

poetry: as arduous craft, 116, 121–22, 282n46; and ballad debate, 102–7; contrasted to philosophy, 22, 118; contrasted to prose, 20, 25, 139–41, 142, 261n21; contrasted to science, 18; as echo of folk song, 45, 93, 99, 101, 132–34; as freedom, 177, 212, 214; and golden age, 202, 204; as harmonious imitation of nature, 47; as liquid and flowing, 140, 141; as novelty, 170, 214, 216; overemphasized during national revival, 205, 299n68; and patriotism, 40; and periodization of literary history, 154–55; protean, 21, 181; as return to origins, 22–23, 120, 130–31, 134, 137–38, 141, 156–57; as sublimity, 127–28; as synthesis of distant times and places, 174–75, 181; as union of form and spirit, 159; as union of head and heart, 198–99, 229; and universalist paradigm, 15–17. *See also* Czech literature and poetry; elegies; English language and literature; epic; folk songs; French language and literature; German language and literature; Greece; hexameter; *narodnost';* national literature paradigm; *Počátkové českého básnictví;* rhyme; Roman literature; romanticism; Russian literature and poetry; *Volkspoesie;* vowels

Pogodin, Mikhail Petrovich: *Marfa Posadnitsa,* 219, 224, 225

Polák, Milota Zdirad, 83, 127–29, 187, 253, 284n77; Jungmann promotes and collaborates with, 188–89, 296n7; "Vznešenost přirozenosti" ("The Sublimity of Nature"), 127–28, 188, 189

Poland, 26, 80, 101, 140, 148, 166, 180; and Russian imperialism, 179; syllabic prosody of, 135, 136–37

Polevoi, Nikolai, 37, 222, 243–44

Poliarnaia zvezda (Polar Star), 168, 237

Pölitz, Karl Heinrich Ludwig, **201–4,** 231, 296n8, 296n14, 299n56, 299n65; *Das Gesammtgebiet der deutschen Sprache,* 202

Pope, Alexander, 20, 268n59

popularité, 168, 174, 217, 301n17

popularity, 128, 166; Pushkin's concern with, 217, 222–28, 301n17; in Somov's use of *narodnost',* 173–74, 253; Viazemsky conflates with nationality, 168, 302n32; and *Volkstümlichkeit,* 229–30. *See also* folk

Portugal, 109, 129, 154

Prach, Ivan (Jan Práč/Johann Pratsch), 97, 157

Prague. *See* Charles University in Prague

primitivism, 22, 23, 45, 92, 131

Prokopovich, Feofan, 27

prose, 32; contrasted to poetry, 20, 25, 139–41, 142, 261n21; and nationalism studies, 6–7, 259n7; use of poetic discourse for, 82

Proskurin, Oleg, 269n15

prosody. *See* classical prosody; Czech prosody; folk prosody; Greek prosody; hexameter; Latin language and prosody; quantitative versification; Russian prosody; stress; syllabic versification; syllabotonic versification; *specific meter names*

prostonarodie, 185, 216

prostonarodnye pesni, 94, 107, 138

protean nationality, 181, 295n56

protean poets, 21, 175, 181

Protestantism, 25, 66, 113, 194, 274n50, 281n41, 282n60

protiazhnaia pesnia, 99

Prussia, 245, 248, 249, 292n16, 305n53

Prvotiny pěkných umění (First-fruits of the Fine Arts), 96, 127, 131

psalms, 25, 92, 113

Puchmajer, Antonín Jaroslav, 26, 261n7, 284n77; *Chrám gnidský,* 114

Puchmajer school, 95, 130, 261n7, 277n36

Pumpianskii, L. V., 286n27

Pushkin, Aleksandr, 17, 37, 46, 169, **217–28,** 236, 238, 246, 301n10; Ancillon's influence on, 221–22; compared to Viazemsky, 218–19, 220, 301n17, 301n22, 302n33; defines *narodnost',* 218–21, 244; defines romanticism and classicism, 223–24; Dostoevsky's speech on, 175, 301n25; on drama, 218–19, 224–27, 238, 301n23, 302n41; importance of popularity and national audience to, 222–28; limitations of as critic, 300n1; as protean poet, 181; separates romanticism from *narodnost',* 211, 217, 224; turns toward Shishkov's camp, 216, 220; on Zhukovsky, 300n8

Pushkin, Aleksandr, Works of: "Bakhchisaraiskii fontan" ("Fountain of Bakhchisarai"), 161, 183, 292n9; *Boris Godunov,* 176, 222, 224–25, 227–28; "Captive of the Caucasus," 3–4, 180; essay on *Marfa Posadnitsa,* 219, 224, 225; *Evgenii Onegin,* 222, 243; "O narodnosti v literature" ("On *Narodnost'* in Literature"), **217–21;** "O poezii klassicheskoi i romanticheskoi" ("On Poetry Classical and Romantic"), 217, 223–24; *Ruslan and Liudmila,* 216, 243

quantitative versification, **110–14; 118–125; 127–131,** 198, 209; developed during Czech humanist period, 25, 113, 120, 280n16, 281n41; Dobrovský replaces with syllabotonic, 26, 72, 113–14; in English poetry, 140, 282n60; in Hungarian poetry, 118–19, 282n42; Jungmann advocates and uses, 81–82, 187–89, 190, 275n58; Kollár uses, 199–200, 302n36; linked to Indian meter, 189; as means to achieve *klasičnost,* 120 21, 122, 127–28, 188; as means to achieve *libozvučnost,* 120, 125, 127–28, 134, 146, 187, 190, 206, 290n105; as means to achieve national literature, 120, 127–28, 134,

187–88, 206; as means to Slavic unity, 120, 297n28; Palacký reconsiders necessity of, 124; *Počátkové* advocates, 110–11, 118–23, 125, 127–28, 134, 146, 206, 253, 282n46, 290n105; rarer than syllabotonic in Czech, 129, 189; in relation to Church Slavonic, 135; requires rigorous craft, 121–22, 282n46; as return to ancient Czech origins, 130–31, 134; in Slovakian poetry, 197, 281n41; as superior to rhyme, 123, 130; Vostokov on, 149, 288nn62–63

quarrel between Ancients and Moderns, **17–22,** 174, 268n59; antiquity's authority undermined by, 22, 89, 109, 189, 233; archaist-innovator war as Russian reprisal of, 64, 263n65; battle over Homer as Russian reprisal of, 160; Czech reception of, 24–26; defined, 17–18; echoed in debates over school curriculum, 249, 250; Fénelon's *Télémaque* as compromise in, 142; first phase (Perrault and Fontenelle), 18–19; German reception of, 24; historicism emerges from, 21–23, 109, 261n10, 304n13; Russian reception of, 26–28; second phase (Battle of the Books), 19–20; third phase (Querelle d'Homère), 19, 20, 21, 89; Trediakovsky's response to, 27, 138–39, 144, 201, 286n11

Racine, Jean, 43, 144, 215; Pushkin links to *narodnost'*, 218, 219, 220, 223, 225, 226; and Sumarokov, 27, 263n61

Radishchev, Aleksandr, 38, 154, 267n59, 288n65; "O cheloveke, ego smertnosti i bessmertii" ("On Man, His Mortality and Immortality"), 146; "Pamiatnik daktilokhoreicheskomu vitiaziu" ("Memorial to the Dactylo-trochaic Knight"), 145–47; *Puteshestvie iz Peterburga v Moskvu (Journey from Petersburg to Moscow),* 145, 147; on Trediakovsky and *blagoglasie,* 145–47, 206–7; uses term *narodnost',* 166

Raeff, Marc, 33–34, 41, 42, 267n54

Ram, Harsha, 178, 263n63, 285n8

rapture, 27–28, 211, 302n32

Razumovsky, Catherine, 244

Razumovsky, Count Aleksei, 246

reálky (realschule), 249

Renaissance, 108, 136, 154; and English quantitative verse, 140, 282n60; history of in Bohemian lands, 24–25, 66; in relation to Quarrel between Ancients and Moderns, 16, 19, 22, 109, 233

revaluing of values, 28, 36, 49, 262n32, 265n19

revolution of 1848, 246, 247, 248

rhyme, 104, 105, 199, 207, 223, 253, 263n49, 282n60; Hněvkovský defends, 189; Palacký and Šafařík reject, 116, 122–24, 130, 141, 195; Trediakovsky rejects, 136, 138, 140, 141; Uvarov rejects, 155; Vostokov rejects, 149

Richter, Jean Paul, 16, 17

RK. *See* Rukopis královédvorský

Rollin, Charles, 138, 201, 286n11

Roman literature, 16, 25, 93, 101, 170, 171, 223, 234; as model for Republican France, 39, 60; as model for Russians, 27, 47, 136, 137, 140, 142, 144, 146, 152, 154, 185; rejected as more derivative than Greek, 22, 109, 142, 148, 153, 212, 214, 215; and romanticism, 109, 183–84. *See also* classical antiquity; Latin language and prosody

romanticism, 24, 104, 107, 142, 221, 239, 241; and *Bildung,* 90; Frazier on, 228, 295n56; and idea of return to origins, 109, 138; in Jena, 228, 252, 295n58; Küchelbecker on, 211–15, 265n19, 266n32, 301n10; merges with classicism in Czech literature, 115, 122–24, 133, 194–95, 199–200, 203, 206, 209, 210; merges with classicism in Russian literature, 39, 122, 195; and *narodnost',* 33, 165, 168–69, 177–78, 183–84, 194, 211–15, 219, 266n32; and nationalism, 71, 223–24, 254–55, 295n56, 306n10; and north-south debate, 170–71; Pushkin on, 211, 217, 223–27, 236; and Shishkov, 54, 64; Somov on, 170, 171–72, 177–78, 180–81, 185, 194,

214; syllabotonic verse linked to, 189, 302n36; and Turgenev, 35–36, 45; Tynianov redefines, 64; Viazemsky on, 168, 183–84, 186, 195, 211, 219

Rosenberg, Karen, 286n11

Rousseau, Jean-Jacques, 16, 166

Rožnay, Samuel, 81–82

Rudolf II (Holy Roman Emperor; King of Bohemia), 72, 73

Rukopis královédvorský (RK), 123–24, 130, **132–34,** 190, 253, 277n43

Rukopis zelenohorský (RZ), 132–34, 190

rules, 93, 115, 122, 170, 239, 251; contrasted to romanticism, 183, 184, 225, 227; critiqued during Quarrel, 22; don't apply to national tradition, 23, 28; and Merzliakov, 46, 47, 48, 268n59

Russian folk songs, 94, 107; Chulkov's collection of, 101, 133; Hanka translates, 97, 100; Kapnist on, 136, 152, 156–58, 207; Ľvov's collection of, 98–99, 102; and Merzliakov, 44, 45, 47, 48, 102; Trediakovsky likens Greek poetry to, 138–39, 148; and Turgenev, 38, 44. *See also* folk songs

Russian language: and folkloric discourse, 62, 102, 104–7, 216; French viewed as threat to and rival of, 41, 44, 53–59, 61, 63, 84–85, 143–44, 150, 216–17, 235–36, 270n26; inherits Byzantine Greek, 135; Karamzin's concept of, 52–53, 57, 60, 61, 63, 90–91, 271n35; Küchelbecker on, 216–17; and linguocentrism, 65–67; Lomonosov's doctrine of three styles for, 58, 60; and *narodnost'*, 169, 216–17, 218, 220; national ideology of, 54–57, 62–63, 64, 67; in relation to Church Slavonic, 54, 56–61, 63, 65, 67, 137; Shishkov's concept of, 51–52, **53–64,** 67, 91, 137, 270n26; status of in school curriculum, 41, 44, 143–44, 245–46; Trediakovsky on, 137, 141; as used by Czechs, 80, 100, 101, 133, 134, 188, 278n47. *See also* Frantsusko-Russian; Russian prosody; Slaviano-Russian; Slavic languages; style

Russian literature and poetry: antiquity as model for, 15–16, 26–28, 136–44, 146, 153–56, 158–59, 195, 207, 212–15, 217, 240, 245, 285n7, 286n27; and ballad debate, 102–7; and Boileau, 16, 26–28, 265n19; denial of, 3–4, 31–32, 36–38, 37, 41, 161, 177, 237–41, 303n11; folklore as model for, 102–7, 136, 137–38, 156–58, 290n105; French as model for, 15, 40, 52–53, 59–60, 63, 91; French as threat to, 37–38, 41, 43, 44, 52, 85, 91, 143, 160, 216, 235–36, 237, 242; French rejected as model for, 19, 41, 53–63, 85, 91, 142–44, 149, 150, 154, 155, 159, 160–61, 170, 225, 239, 270n26; Germany as model for, 31, 32, 38, 170–71; Germany rejected as model for, 43, 152, 161, 212, 214, 215, 228; and hexameter debate, 144–61; and idea of return to origins, 137–38, 141, 153, 156–57; and imperialism, 180–83; importance of education to, 235–36, 238, 240; Küchelbecker on, 212–17; likened to human life cycle, 152, 156, 237; and literary marketplace, 228, 229, 306n9; Lomonosov's and Trediakovsky's reforms of and rivalry over, 27, 37, 136–42, 260n3; Somov on, 170–73, 176–78, 180, 194, 253; status of in school curriculum, 245–46. *See also narodnost';* nation; national character; national literature paradigm; romanticism; Russian folk songs; Russian language; Russian prosody; Shishkov, Aleksandr; Turgenev, Andrei Ivanovich

Russianness, 38, 107, 167, 183

Russian Orthodoxy, 136, 137, 301n13, 304n29; centrality of language to, 66; and doctrine of Third Rome, 135; Uvarov's conception of, 152, 153, 166, 245–46

Russian prosody: and hexameter debates, **144–61;** Kapnist advocates folk verse form of, 151–52, 156–58, 207, 290n105; Lomonosov's reform of, 136–37; as

means to create national literature, 136,
147, 152, 155–56, 159, 207, 287n53;
Trediakovsky's analysis and reform
of, 137–42, 285n9; and Trediakovsky's
legacy, 145–51; Uvarov on, 152–56,
158–60, 207; Vostokov on, 147–50,
288n62, 288n69. *See also* dactylo-
trochaic hexameter
Russkaia pravda, 178–79
Ryleev, Kondraty, 179, 185, 218
RZ (Rukopis zelenohorský), 132–34, 190

Šafařík, Pavel Josef, **115–21**, 189, 208,
242, 245, 299n68; attacks syllabotonic
prosody, 115–16, 121; contrasted
to Kollár, 192, 194, 200; on folk
songs, 131; and Hermann, 112,
119, 201, 280n11, 281n30, 282n44;
and Jungmann, 78, 83, 299n56; on
klasičnost, 121, 195; Klopstock as
model and anti-model for, 111–12,
283n65; later career of, 110; legacy of,
134, 187, 279n6; on *libozvučnost*, 125,
146, 206, 254, 290n105; on linguistic
stress as indication of national
character, 117–18; on Polák, 127–29,
253; on quantitative verse as means to
Slavic unity, 120, 130, 297n28. *See also*
Počátkové českého básnictví
Said, Edward, 182, 295n56
salon culture, 39, 63, 271n33; contrasted
with literary marketplace, 228;
Karamzin advocates as model, 40, 52–
53, 60, 91; Shishkov critiques imitation
of, 41. *See also* French language and
literature
Sapphic verse, 111, 138, 199
Sappho, 26, 92
Sayer, Derek, 8
Scandinavia, 180, 181
Schamschula, Walter, 69, 70, 273n15
Schelling, Friedrich, 170, 236
Schiller, Friedrich, 26, 90, 122, 144, 215; on
difference between ancient and modern
poetry, 24, 98, 184, 189; influences
Turgenev, 31, 38; and *narodnost'*, 175,
176, 244, 253; on national popularity

(Volkstümlichkeit), 229–30; and
sensibility, 173, 175, 294n33
Schiller, Friedrich, Works of: *On the
Aesthetic Education of Man*, 229;
Wallenstein, 175; *William Tell*, 244
Schlegel, August, 24, 159, 170, 184, 195,
286n24, 289n76; advocates quantitative
verse, 112; proposes northern origin for
romanticism, 171; and Pushkin, 221,
223, 224; *Über dramatische Kunst und
Literatur*, 221
Schlegel, Friedrich, 24, 170, 289n76
School Committee, 245
schools. *See* education in Bohemian
lands; education in Russia; gymnasia;
universities
Schulte-Sasse, Jochen, 19, 261n13
science, 18–19, 21, 75
Scotland, 22, 92, 160
Scythians, 157–58
secularism, 37, 61, 135, 136, 138, 139
semantics: Shishkov's theory of, 54–57
sensibility, 173, 175, 294n33
sentimentalism, 24, 28, 32, 35, 37, 98
Serbian folk songs, 95, 97, 100, 101, 131,
133, 134
Serbian language, 100, 269n15, 278n47
Serbo-Croatian language, 300n79
Shakespeare, William, 17, 44, 92, 93, 144,
145, 215; contrasted to Goethe, 21,
301n25; Pushkin on, 218–21, 223,
224–27, 301n23
Shakhovskoi, Aleksandr, 105; "Urok
koketkam" ("A Lesson for Coquettes"),
104
Shikhmatov, Prince Sergei Aleksandrovich,
215
Shishkov, Aleksandr, 35, **51–64**, 76, 132,
166, 266n24, 270n25, 271n35; argues
for national specificity of language,
54–57; critiques Karamzin and
followers, 39, 40, 41, 51–52, 56–59,
61; on folk discourse as model for
poetry, 62, 102, 106, 107; introduces
national ideology of language, 63–64,
65, 85, 137, 220; Lomonosov as model
and ideal for, 53, 54, 59, 61, 137; as

minister of education, 246; rejects French as model, 19, 28, 41, 53, 55–57, 58–59, 61, 62–63, 91, 235, 270n26; on relation between Church Slavonic and Russian, 53, 54, 56–60, 67, 137, 269n15; in relation to Küchelbecker and Decembrists, 49, 216, 265n15; on *slovesnost'*, 61–62

Shishkov, Aleksandr, Works of: *Rassuzhdenie o starom i novom sloge rossiiskogo iazyka (Discourse on the Old and New Style in the Russian Language)*, 40, 51, **53–63**, 235; "Razgovory o slovesnosti" ("Dialogues on slovesnost'"), 62, 102

Shishkov's followers, 39, 60, 63, 102, 104, 147; Küchelbecker and Pushkin turn towards, 49, 216, 220; reject French culture, 41, 84, 143. *See also* archaists

Simonsuuri, Kirsti, 21, 22

simplicity, 20, 134, 222; Czech folk songs embody, 97, 98, 131; Russian folkloric discourse embodies, 62, 106, 107

simulacrum, 133, 257; Jungmann's program creates, 83, 232, 269n7; Karamzin's program creates, 53, 58; literary marketplace as, 306n9; Macura on, 255–56, 300n84

Sismondi, Jean Charles Léonard Simonde de, 212, 223; *De la littérature du midi de l'Europe*, 170–71, 221

Slavdom. *See* Slavic languages; Slavic unity

Slaviano-Russian, 58–59, 61, 63, 137

Slavic languages: consolidated as separate, 208; Dobrovský on, 274n49, 283n68; Hanka treats as single language, 100, 101, 102, 133; Jungmann proposes borrowing from, 79–80, 85, 91, 110; Kollár wants to unite, 190, 193–200, 206, 208, 230, 242, 254, 304n29; Kopitar sees as merging over time, 208, 300n79; and stress as sign of national character, 117–18

Slavic unity: contrasted to Czech national concerns, 210, 242; and Hanka, 97, 100, 101, 102, 133; and Jungmann, 79–80, 85, 91, 196–97, 274n49; Kollár aims

to achieve with common language, 190, 193–200, 206, 208, 230, 242, 254, 279n6, 304n29; Kopitar's view of, 208, 300n79; quantitative verse as means to achieve, 120, 297n28; and Russian Slavophiles, 304n29; as ultimate synthesis of humanity, 198

Slavism. *See* Slavic languages; Slavic unity

Slavonic. *See* Church Slavonic

Slavophiles, 38, 230, 240, 241, 242, 304n29

Slovak folk songs and poetry, 113, 131, 196–99, 208, 230, 281n41

Slovakia, 80, 252, 274n50

Slovak language: history and codification of, 192–94, 208; Kollár wants to unite with Czech, 192–94, 196–97, 200, 206, 208, 254

slovesnost', 143, 155, 159, 216; contrasted to *literatura*, 61–62, 63

Slovo o polku Igoreve (Song of Igor's Campaign), 17, 45, 47, 96, 132, 133, 254, 285n9; Shishkov on, 62, 102

Smith, Anthony D., 6, 7, 259n13, 261n10

Smotritsky, Melety, 135

Society of Lovers of Russian Literature (Obshchestvo liubitelei rossiiskoi slovesnosti), 161

Society of Philosophy (Obshchestvo liubomudriia), 236, 241

Somov, Orest, 28, **169–81**, 195, 218, 238, 241, 293n25; contrasted to Küchelbecker, 212–14, 216; contrasted to Pushkin, 219, 220, 223, 301n23; contrasted to Viazemsky, 183–84, 185–86; establishes *narodnost'* as term, 172–73, 194; explores Ukrainian thematics, 179–80; and imperialism, 179–81; and north-south debate, 170–71, 293n20; "O romancheskoi poezii" ("On Romantic Poetry"), **169–78**, 180–81, 293n17, 294n33; rejects chivalric thesis, 171–72, 176, 177; on romanticism as means to achieve national literature, 176–78; uses German literature and de Staël to define *narodnost'*, 173–76, 181, 238, 244, 253, 294n33

sonnets, 122, 189, 199, 223, 301n23
Sophocles, 92, 215, 240, 249
South Slavic folklore, 95–96
Spain, 109, 140, 154, 171, 176, 181, 199
Spenser, Edmund, 92, 93, 282n60
spondaic meter, 149, 156, 158–59
Staël, Germaine de (Madame de), 217, 223,
    254, 289n76; *De l'Allemagne,* 173, 217;
    influences Somov, 170, 171, 173–75,
    177, 181, 214, 294n33; on Russians as
    Oriental, 293n20
St. Petersburg Pedagogical Institute, 246
stress, 75, 156; always initial in Czech,
    81, 114, 288n63; as expression of
    national character, 117, 119; in Slovak
    contrasted to Czech, 281n41; as used in
    syllabotonic verse, 111, 114, 115, 117,
    148, 280nn21–22, 288nn62–63; as used
    in tonic verse, 158
Study Commission (Imperial), 235, 247
Štúr, Ľudovít, 208
Sturm und Drang, 31, 38, 93, 229
style, 15, 39–40, 106, 207; Karamzin on,
    52, 58–59, 60; Lomonsov's system of,
    57–58, 60–61; Shishkov on, 51, 52,
    54–55, 57–64, 85, 143, 220
sublime, 81, 111, 134, 141, 189, 238, 253;
    Boileau/Longinus on, 28; and folk
    songs, 97–98; Palacký advocates, 122,
    123, 127, 128; Slavic unity as, 196, 252
Sumarokov, Aleksandr, 56, 145, 149, 161,
    260n3, 263n61; "O stikhotvorstve" ("On
    Poetry"), 16, 27; Turgenev critiques,
    36, 43
Swift, Jonathan, 18; *Tale of a Tub,* 20
syllabic versification, 134, 135–36, 189,
    280n16; close to syllabotonic in Czech,
    113, 280n19; Dobrovský replaces with
    syllabotonic, 26, 72, 113, 114; Russians
    reject, 137, 148, 150
syllabotonic versification, 100, 189,
    190, 275n58, 281n30; close to Czech
    syllabic verse, 113, 280n19; Dobrovský
    codifies, 26, 72, 81, 113–14, 129, 130,
    206, 280nn21–22; Kapnist theoretically
    rejects but actually uses, 157–58;
    Klopstock uses, 111–12; Kollár uses,

199–200, 302n36; and *libozvučnost,*
    125, 127, 131, 206; during medieval and
    Hussite eras, 113, 280n16; modified
    through experimental loosening
    of feet, 129, 284n77; *Počátkové*
    denounces, 111–12, 115–17, 119, 121,
    125, 127, 131, 134, 201; Polák uses,
    127; Trediakovsky advocates, 136,
    137–39, 285n9; Vostokov on, 148, 150,
    288nn62–63
syncretism, 36, 265n20
Syn Otechestva, 104, 105, 143

Tablic, Bohuslav, 194
Taruskin, Richard, 99
Tasso, Torquato, 142, 144, 286n25
taste, 106, 147, 207, 236; and German
    aesthetic theory, 269n7; Karamzin on,
    52; relativism of, 18, 20, 47, 48, 144;
    Shishkov on, 56–57
Tatars, 171, 180, 231
Temple, Sir William, 18
temporality: and the novel, 6–7; replaces
    universalist classicism, 15–16, 23
Thám, Václav, 26
theater. *See* drama
Theresianum gymnasium, 25, 246
Third Rome, doctrine of, 135
time. *See* temporality
Todd, William Mills, III, 300n1
Tolerance Patent, 66
Tolstoy, Dmitri, 249
Tomášek, Václav Jan, 277n43
Tomashevskii, Boris, 221
tonic verse, 102, 189; Trediakovsky on,
    138, 285n9; Vostokov on, 147, 148,
    150, 158
tragedy. *See* drama
translatio imperii, 108, 135, 136
translation, **89–92, 100–107,** 114, 295n58;
    and ballad debate, 102–7; and *Bildung,*
    89–90; conflates *Volk* and *Nation,* 94,
    97; in context of Quarrel between
    Ancients and Moderns, 20, 21; during
    Czech humanist period, 24–26; as
    departure from and discovery of self,
    90, 100; and folklore, 4, 91–92, 97–98,

100–101, 253, 278n47; and hexameter debate, 150–56, 159; and imperialism, 9, 178, 181, 182–83, 295n56; Jungmann uses to enrich Czech language, 80–82, 83, 91; Katenin's, 104, 106–7; as means to national literature paradigm, 4, 9, 89–90, 91, 107, 133, 144, 253, 276n8; phonetic, 100–101, 278n47; replaced by emphasis on originality, 205–6, 214; resistance to, 63, 64, 91, 100, 101, 105, 106–7, 214; Shishkov's view of, 63, 64, 91; as *translatio studii,* 108, 109, 136, 152, 279n1; Trediakovsky's conception of, 139–41; and Zhukovsky, 30, 103–7, 160, 268n76, 300n8

translationality, 276n8

translatio prosodiae, 111

translatio studii, 109, 111, 135, 136, 152, 158; defined, 108

Trediakovsky, Vasily, 56, 201, 263n63, 285n9, 286n13, 287n54; and Boileau, 27, 260n3; conception of epic, 139–42, 155, 286n25; influenced by Quarrel between Ancients and Moderns, 27, 138–39, 286n11; lack of ideology in, 137, 285n8; legacy and later reputation of, **144–51,** 153, 155, 287n38; likens Russian folk verse to Greek poetry, 137–38, 182; poetic reforms of, 37, 102, **136–42;** Radishchev on, 145–47, 207; Vostokov's critique of, 147–50

Trediakovsky, Vasily, Works of: "Mnenie o nachale poezii i stikhov vobshche" ("Opinion on the Origin of Poetry and Verse in General"), 138; "Novyi i kratkii sposob k slozheniiu rossiiskikh stikhov" ("New and Short Method for Composing Russian Verses"), 139; "O drevnem, srednem, i novom stikhotvorenii rossiiskom" ("On Ancient, Middle, and New Russian Versification"), 137–38; "Pred"iz"iasnenie ob iroicheskoi piime" ("Explanatory Foreword on the Heroic Poem"), 139–41, 144; *Tilemakhida* (translation of Fénelon's *Télémaque*), 139–42, 144, 145–46, 149, 151, 287n38

trochaic meter, 113, 280n15, 288n69; as inherent to Czech, 274n55, 281n27; Jungmann uses to translate blank verse, 81, 274n55; Polák uses, 127, 188; as substitution for spondees, 156, 159. *See also* dactylo-trochaic hexameter

troubadour poetry, 92, 171, 212, 223, 229

Tsarskoe selo lyceum, 246

Turgenev, Aleksandr, 32, 41–42, 49, 166, 291n9

Turgenev, Andrei Ivanovich, **31–50,** 51, 176, 265n15, 267n54, 289n92; canonization and myth of, 41–42, 45; "Elegy," 33, 45; founds Friendly Literary Society, 31–32; influences national literature paradigm, 48, 50; and Karamzin, 38–41, 266n38, 266n40, 269n2; "K otechestvu" ("To the Fatherland"), 40; on lack of national spirit in Russian literature, 36–38, 41, 177, 241, 243; Lotman views as forerunner of Decembrism, 32–35, 42, 45, 265n10, 267n55; "O russkoi literature" ("On Russian Literature"), 32, **35–50,** 265n17, 266n32, 268n64, 268n71, 269n2, 290n120, 291n9; prefigures idea of *narodnost',* 32–33, 35, 50, 265n17, 266n32; prefigures Shishkov, 39–40; in relation to Merzliakov, 42–49, 161, 268n64; untimely death of, 33, 265n12; Viazemsky as echo of, 167, 185, 291n9

Turgenev, Ivan Petrovich, 32

Turgenev, Nikolai Ivanovich, 265n11, 291n9

Tynianov, Yuri, 49, 64, 143, 265n15, 265n20

Ukraine, 135, 169, 179–80, 294n44

unity. *See* Slavic unity

universalist paradigm, 141, 252, 295n58, 301n25; embodied by Karamzin, 15, 17, 26; replaced by historicism and locality, 16, 18, 21, 23; replaced by national literature paradigm, 17, 122, 287n54. *See also* classicism

universities, 32, 47, 49, 67; classical
curriculum at, 245; status of Czech-
language instruction at, 25, 246–48,
263n53, 305n42. *See also* education in
Bohemian lands; education in Russia
University of Vienna (*Universität Wien*),
25, 246–47, 305n42
Uspensky, Boris, 58, 61, 64, 84, 166; on
diglossia and linguocentrism, 65, 67,
269n13
Utraquists, 66
Uvarov, Sergei, 182, 240, 242, 279n2,
288n69, 289n76, 304n19; advocates
hexameter for translation of Homer,
150, **152–56, 158–60**; links prosody
to national literature paradigm,
136, 155–56, 207, 236; "Projet d'une
académie asiatique," 152–53, 244–45;
serves as minister of education and
institutes curriculum reforms, 167,
244–46, 249, 250

values. *See* revaluing of values
Vatsuro, V. E., 269n2
Vega Carpio, Lope Félix de, 218, 221
Veleslavín, Adam Daniel z, 73–75, 80,
274n37
Venevitinov, Dmitry, 38, 48, 251, 304n19;
on lack of Russian literature, 31, 37,
236–41, 304n11; on *narodnost'*, 243–44;
"O sostoianii prosveshcheniia v Rossii"
("On the State of Enlightenment in
Russia"), 237–41
verisimilitude, 219
versification. *See* classical prosody;
Czech prosody; folk prosody; Greek
prosody; hexameter; Latin language
and prosody; quantitative versification;
Russian prosody; stress; syllabic
versification; syllabotonic versification;
specific meter names
Veselovsky, Aleksandr, 32
Vestnik Evropy (Herald of Europe), 40, 45,
51, 52, 104, 269n15
Viazemsky, Prince Petr, 173, 255; compared
to Küchelbecker, 211, 212, 214, 216,
301n10; compared to Pushkin, 218–19,

220, 301n17, 301nn22–23, 302n33;
contrasts romanticism with classicism,
183–84, 195; denies existence of
Russian national literature, 3–4, 37, 241;
Dmitriev's critique of, 168, 172, 217,
302n32; echoes Turgenev, 161, 167, 185,
243, 291n9; on kvass patriotism, 175;
on *narodnost'*, 33, 166–68, 172, 183–86,
195, 220, 221, 291n4, 291n9, 295n60;
"Pervyi sneg" ("The First Snow"),
166; writes introduction to Pushkin's
Bakhchisaraiskii fontan, 161, 183–86,
292n9
Vico, Giambattista, 22, 262n35; *Scienza
nuova*, 21
Vidmanová, Anežka, 280n16
Vienna. *See* University of Vienna
Vigel', Filipp F., 103
Vinitsky, Ilya, 59
Virgil, 144, 183, 215, 261n7; as model for
Trediakovsky, 140, 141, 142, 146
Virolainen, Mariia, 43, 269n2
vkus (taste), 56–57, 270n25
vlast (homeland), 77
vocational schools (*reálky*), 249
Vodička, Felix, 81, 94, 274n55
Voeikov, Aleksandr, 32
Volk, 92, 94. *See also* folk
Volkslied, 95, 96, 132; Herder introduces
term, 24, 92; as translated into Czech,
97; as translated into Russian, 98
Volkspoesie, 38, 47, 95; as conceived of
by Herder, 24, **92–94,** 263n46; as
distinguished from *Nationalliteratur*,
168, 172, 300n7
Volkstümlichkeit, 229–30, 231
Voltaire (François-Marie Arouet), 16, 145,
215, 262n34; "Essay on Epick Poetry,"
23, 252; on national differences, 23,
252, 262n40, 262n45
Voss, Johann Heinrich, 109
Vostokov, Aleksandr, 158, 215; compared
to Uvarov, 153–55; on hexameter and
Trediakovsky, 147–50; "Opyt o russkom
stikhoslozhenii" ("Essay on Russian
Versification"), 147–50; on stress,
288nn62–63

vostorg (rapture), 27–28, 211
vowels, 75, 283n68; demonstrate affinity
 of Czech and Greek, 117–18; and
 dobroglasie, 207; as expression of
 national character, 119; importance to
 libozvučnost, 117, 124, 125–26, 127,
 190, 192; Kollár's analysis of, 192, 197;
 in relation to quantitative verse, 81,
 111, 113, 117, 127, 197; shift in 14th-
 century Czech, 192
Všehrd, Viktorin Kornel z, 25
vzdělání, 75–76, 78, 79, 234. *See also*
 culture
vznešenost (sublimity), 111, 128, 134. *See
 also* sublime

Wachtel, Andrew, 181
Wallnig, Thomas, 9
Weimar, Klaus, 24
Weimar classicism, 26, 122, 203
Weitenauer, Ignaz, 207
Wellek, René, 24, 92
Winckelmann, Johann Joachim, 16, 109, 153
Wohlklang, 207; *blagoglasie* as, 146;
 blahozvučnost as, 202; contrasted with

Klang, 296n14; *libozvučnost* as, 124,
 283n65, 283n68
Wotton, William, 18, 20, 261n11;
 *Reflections upon Ancient and Modern
 Learning,* 19

Zagoskin, Mikhail, 105, 107
Zhikharev, S. P., 166, 168
Zhivov, Viktor M., 27, 286n13
Zhukovsky, Vasily Andreevich, 160,
 175, 181; and ballad debate, **103–7,**
 228; importance of translation to,
 30, 268n76, 300n8; Küchelbecker
 criticizes, 212, 214, 215–17; as leader
 of Karamzinian camp, 51–52, 143,
 161, 169; in relation to Turgenev
 and Friendly Literary Society, 32, 33,
 41–42, 43, 44, 45, 46, 49, 246, 291n9
Zhukovsky, Vasily Andreevich, Works of:
 "Epistle to Voeikov," 216; "Für Wenige"
 ("For the Few"), 217; "Liudmila"
 (translation of Bürger's "Lenore"), 103,
 104–7; "Svetlana," 216
Žižka, Jan, 132
Zlobický, Josef Valentin, 267n54